T0271289

Current Federal Reserve Policy Under the Lens of Economic History

In December 2012, as a kickoff to the Federal Reserve System's centennial, the Federal Reserve Bank of Cleveland asked leading monetary historians and macroeconomic economists to address current and recurring economic concerns that confront central banks from a historical perspective. The resulting papers, published in this volume, cover a wide range of issues, including the meaning of central-bank independence, the role of communications and rules in fostering credibility, the evolution of the lender-of-last-resort function, the mechanism through which banks transmit economic shocks, and prospects for a European monetary union. A retrospective on the Federal Reserve, this book contains essays by some of the world's most prominent financial historians and provides a thorough overview of the evolution of the monetary standard over the past two centuries. Offering historical context as a complement to economic theory and empiricism, these papers also investigate how financial infrastructure shapes economic outcomes through comparisons of Canada and the United States.

Owen F. Humpage is a senior economic advisor in the research department at the Federal Reserve Bank of Cleveland. His research has been published in the *International Journal of Central Banking*; the *International Journal of Finance and Economics*; the *Journal of International Financial Markets, Institutions & Money*; and the *Journal of Money, Credit and Banking*. Dr. Humpage has taught economics at Oberlin College and Case Western Reserve University.

STUDIES IN MACROECONOMIC HISTORY

Series Editor: Michael D. Bordo, *Rutgers University*

Editors
Marc Flandreau, *Institut d'Etudes Politiques de Paris*
Chris Meissner, *University of California, Davis*
François Velde, *Federal Reserve Bank of Chicago*
David C. Wheelock, *Federal Reserve Bank of St. Louis*

The titles in this series investigate themes of interest to economists and economic historians in the rapidly developing field of macroeconomic history. The four areas covered include the application of monetary and finance theory, international economics, and quantitative methods to historical problems; the historical application of growth and development theory and theories of business fluctuations; the history of domestic and international monetary, financial, and other macroeconomic institutions; and the history of international monetary and financial systems. The series amalgamates the former Cambridge University Press series *Studies in Monetary and Financial History* and *Studies in Quantitative Economic History*.

Other Books in the Series

(*continued after index*)

Current Federal Reserve Policy Under the Lens of Economic History

Essays to Commemorate the Federal Reserve System's Centennial

Edited by

OWEN F. HUMPAGE

Federal Reserve Bank of Cleveland

CAMBRIDGE
UNIVERSITY PRESS

CAMBRIDGE
UNIVERSITY PRESS

32 Avenue of the Americas, New York, NY 10013-2473, USA

Cambridge University Press is part of the University of Cambridge.

It furthers the University's mission by disseminating knowledge in the pursuit of
education, learning, and research at the highest international levels of excellence.

www.cambridge.org
Information on this title: www.cambridge.org/9781107099098

First published 2015

A catalog record for this publication is available from the British Library.

Library of Congress Cataloging in Publication Data
Current Federal Reserve policy under the lens of economic history : essays to
commemorate the Federal Reserve System's centennial / [edited by] Owen F. Humpage.
     pages   cm. – (Studies in macroeconomic history)
Includes bibliographical references and index.
ISBN 978-1-107-09909-8 (hardback)
1. United States. Federal Reserve Board.   2. Federal Reserve banks.   3. Monetary
policy – United States.   4. United States – Economic policy.   I. Humpage, Owen F.
HG2563.C87   2015
339.5'30973–dc23   2014043728

ISBN 978-1-107-09909-8 Hardback

In appreciation of Michael D. Bordo's many contributions to monetary history.

Contents

Contributors

Michael D. Bordo is a professor of economics and director of the Center for Monetary and Financial History at Rutgers University as well as a research associate of the National Bureau of Economic Research and a member of the Shadow Open Market Committee. He is the editor of the series, Studies in Macroeconomic History, for Cambridge University Press and has published a wealth of articles and books on monetary economics and monetary history. Previously, Dr. Bordo held many academic positions including at Cambridge, where he was Pitt Professor of American History and Institutions. He has also spent time as a visiting scholar at the International Monetary Fund, the Federal Reserve Banks of St. Louis and Cleveland, and more. Dr. Bordo holds a B.A. from McGill University, and an M.S. in economics from the London School of Economics, and he recieved a Ph.D. from the University of Chicago in 1972.

Forrest Capie is Professor Emeritus of Economic History at the Cass Business School, City University, London. He has taught at the London School of Economics, the University of Warwick, and the University of Leeds. He has been a British Academy Overseas Fellow at the National Bureau, New York; a Visiting Professor at the University of Aix-Marseille and the London School of Economics; and a Visiting Scholar at the International Monetary Fund. He has written widely on money, banking, and trade and commercial policy. He was head of the Department of Banking and Finance at City University from 1989 to 1992 and editor of the *Economic History Review* from 1993 to 1999. He recently completed the commissioned history of the Bank of England (2010). His latest book (with G. E. Wood) is *Money over Two Centuries* (2012).

Mark A. Carlson is a senior economist in the Division of Monetary Affairs at the Federal Reserve Board of Governors. In addition to contributing to staff efforts supporting monetary policy at the Federal Reserve, he has worked on issues related to financial stability and to developments in the commercial banking sector. His research focuses on understanding financial crises, particularly historical episodes such as the banking crises of the 1930s and the panics of the National Banking Era, and on understanding the impact of such crises on financial intermediation. Dr. Carlson's work has been published in the *Journal of Political Economy*; the *Journal of Money, Credit and Banking*; the *Berkeley Economic Journal of Economic Analysis and Policy*; and *Explorations in Economic History*. He received his Ph.D. from the University of California, Berkeley.

Ehsan U. Choudhri is the Chancellor's Professor in the Department of Economics at Carleton University. He has undertaken research on a wide range of topics in international and monetary economics. His work has been published in many journals, including the *Canadian Journal of Economics, International Economic Review*, and *Journal of International Economics*. Dr. Choudhri has held visiting positions at a number of institutions, including the University of California, Los Angeles; Rutgers University; Georgetown University; and the International Monetary Fund. He has served as a chair of the Department of Economics at Carleton University and as an associate editor for the *Journal of International Economics*. He received his M.A. from Punjab University in Pakistan and his Ph.D. from the University of Chicago.

Barry Eichengreen is the George C. Pardee and Helen N. Pardee Professor of Economics and professor of political science at the University of California, Berkeley, where he has taught since 1987. He is also a research associate at the National Bureau of Economic Research and a research Fellow of the Centre for Economic Policy Research (London). Dr. Eichengreen's research and publications focus on the current and historical operation of the international monetary system. Previously, he was senior policy advisor at the International Monetary Fund; he is currently a Fellow of the American Academy of Arts and Sciences. He earned an A.B. from the University of California, Santa Cruz, and holds his M.A. in history, as well as an M.A., M.P., and Ph.D. in economics from Yale University.

Marvin Goodfriend is the Friends of Allan Meltzer Professor of Economics at the Tepper School of Business at Carnegie Mellon University. His research focuses on monetary policy. He was previously director of research and a policy advisor at the Federal Reserve Bank of Richmond. Dr. Goodfriend has been a visiting scholar at the Federal Reserve Board of Governors, the European Central Bank, and elsewhere. He served on external review panels to evaluate research and policy advice at the European Central Bank, Norges Bank, the Swedish Riksbank, and the Swiss National Bank. Coeditor of the *Carnegie-Rochester Conference Series on Public Policy*, Dr. Goodfriend has served on the editorial boards of several prestigious journals. He is an honorary advisor of the Institute for Monetary and Economic Studies at the Bank of Japan and a member of the Shadow Open Market Committee. Dr. Goodfriend received a B.S. in mathematics from Union College and holds a Ph.D. in economics from Brown University.

Owen F. Humpage is a senior economic advisor in the research department at the Federal Reserve Bank of Cleveland, specializing in international finance. His research has been published in the *International Journal of Central Banking*; the *International Journal of Finance and Economics*; the *Journal of International Financial Markets, Institutions & Money*; and the *Journal of Money, Credit and Banking*. Dr. Humpage has taught economics at Oberlin College and Case Western Reserve University.

Harold James holds joint appointments at Princeton University as the Claude and Lore Kelly Professor in European Studies in the History Department and as a professor of international affairs in the Woodrow Wilson School. He joined the faculty at Princeton University in 1986. Dr. James is also Marie Curie Visiting Professor at the European University Institute. Dr. James specializes in European monetary and financial history. He has written numerous articles and books including *International Monetary Cooperation since Bretton Woods* (1996), *Nazi Dictatorship and the Deutsche Bank* (2004), and recently *Krupp: A History of the Legendary German Firm* (2012). In 2004, he was awarded the Helmut Schmidt Prize for Economic History, and in 2005 he received the Ludwig Erhard Prize for writing about economics. Dr. James is also on the editorial board of the *Financial History Review*. After completing his undergraduate degree at Gonville and Caius College, Cambridge University, he received his Ph.D. at Peterhouse, Cambridge University, in 1982.

John Landon-Lane is an associate professor of economics in the Department of Economics of Rutgers University. His primary research interests are in the areas of time series and Bayesian econometrics, macroeconomics, and macroeconomic history. Dr. Landon-Lane's current research includes comparing the recent global financial crisis to past global financial crises. He holds a B.S. in mathematics from the University of Canterbury, New Zealand, and a Ph.D. in economics from the University of Minnesota.

Christopher M. Meissner is an associate professor of economics at the University of California, Davis. His research focuses on the economic history of the international economy, and his articles have appeared in the _American Economic Review_, the _Journal of Development Economics_, the _Journal of Economic History_, the _Journal of International Economics_, and the _Journal of Monetary Economics_. He has held visiting positions at Harvard, INSEAD, the International Monetary Fund, and the Paris School of Economics. In 2006 he was a Houblon-Norman Fellow at the Bank of England. Dr. Meissner is also a research associate at the National Bureau of Economic Research in the Development of the American Economy program. Previously, Dr. Meissner was on the Faculty of Economics at Cambridge University. He received his Ph.D. in economics from the University of California, Berkeley.

Allan H. Meltzer is a Distinguished Visiting Fellow at the Hoover Institution and the Allan H. Meltzer University Professor of Political Economy at the Tepper School of Business at Carnegie Mellon University. His most recent publication is _Why Capitalism?_ and he has authored several other books, including _A History of the Federal Reserve_. His career includes experience as a self-employed businessman, management adviser, and consultant to banks and financial institutions. Among many other distinctions, Dr. Meltzer was named the Distinguished Fellow for 2011 by the American Council for Capital Formation and received the Bradley Award, the Harry Truman Medal for Public Policy, and the Truman Medal for Economic Policy, also in 2011. Dr. Meltzer received his A.B. and M.A. degrees from Duke University and his Ph.D. from the University of California, Los Angeles.

Kris James Mitchener is the Robert and Susan Finocchio Professor of Economics at Santa Clara University, Research Associate at the National Bureau of Economic Research and the Centre for Competitive Advantage and the Global Economy, and Research Fellow at the Centre for Economic and Policy Research. His research focuses on economic history, international economics, macroeconomics, and monetary economics, and he is a leading expert on the history of financial crises. Professor Mitchener is a current recipient of an Institute for New Economic Thinking grant, and from 2009 to 2011 he was the W. Glenn Campbell and Rita-Ricardo Campbell Hoover National Fellow at Stanford University. Prior to his current positions, he was professor of economics at the University of Warwick, and he has held visiting positions at the Bank of Japan, the Federal Reserve Bank of St. Louis, UCLA, and CREi at Universitat Pompeu Fabra. He is coeditor of _Explorations in Economic History_ and presently serves on the editorial boards of the _Financial History Review_, _Cliometrica_, and _Economics_. He received his B.A. and Ph.D. from the University of California, Berkeley.

Jon Moen is chair and associate professor in the Economics Department at the University of Mississippi. Dr. Moen has studied retirement history in the United States, and his research has shown that older men had been able to retire at rates greater than previously believed, particularly in rural areas. More recently, he has studied the Bank Panic of 1907 and its role in the founding of the Federal Reserve System. He currently is examining the role of clearing houses as lenders of last resort during the National Banking Era. Dr. Moen earned his Ph.D. at the University of Chicago, having studied under Robert Fogel.

Angela Redish is a professor of economics and vice-provost at the University of British Columbia. Her research interests include the monetary systems of medieval Europe and the monetary and banking systems of North America in the nineteenth and, twentieth centuries. Her recent articles include "Why Didn't Canada Have a Banking Crisis in 2008 (or in 1930, or 1907, or 1893, or …)?" and, forthcoming in the *Economic History Review*, "Coin Sizes and Payments in Commodity Money Systems." She is also vice president of the Economic History Association and a Research Fellow of the C. D. Howe Institute. Dr. Redish earned a B.A. in from Wilfrid Laurier University and M.A. and Ph.D. degrees from the University of Western Ontario.

Gary Richardson is a professor in the Department of Economics at the University of California, Irvine, and serves as Federal Reserve System Historian. He is also a faculty research associate at the National Bureau of Economic Research. His research focuses on economic history and banking, macroeconomics, property rights, monetary policy, and the Federal Reserve. Previously, Dr. Richardson held positions with George Mason University; the University of California, Irvine; the University of California, Berkeley; and the University of California, San Diego. He holds a B.A. in political science from the University of Chicago and a Ph.D. in economics from the University of California, Berkley.

Hugh Rockoff is a professor at Rutgers University and a research associate of the National Bureau of Economic Research. His research focuses on the history of monetary policy and financial regulation in the United States and on wartime economic controls. He is the author of books on the U.S. Free Banking Era and the history of price controls in the United States, and of numerous papers in professional journals. His latest book is *War and the U.S. Economy in the Twentieth Century*. He is also the author, with Gary Walton, of the textbook *History of the American Economy*. Dr. Rockoff holds an A.B. from Earlham College and a Ph.D. from the University of Chicago.

Peter L. Rousseau is a professor of economics and history at Vanderbilt University, as well as the secretary-treasurer of the American Economic

Association. Dr. Rousseau is a macroeconomist and economic historian who studies the role of financial markets and institutions in growth and development. He is particularly interested in the monetary history of the United States and Europe and in how financial markets assist in spreading transformative technological changes through an economy. Dr. Rousseau received his doctorate from New York University in 1995.

Lawrence L. Schembri was appointed adviser to the governor of the Bank of Canada in September 2010. His responsibilities focus on financial stability and include coordinating the bank's contribution to the Financial Stability Board. His published research has focused on exchange rate and monetary policy in open economies and the international monetary system. Dr. Schembri is also the chair of the editorial board for the *Bank of Canada Review*. Before joining the bank, he was an assistant professor and, later, associate professor of economics at Carleton University. Dr. Schembri received a bachelor of commerce degree from the University of Toronto in 1979, an M.Sc. in economics from the London School of Economics and Political Science in 1980, and a Ph.D. in economics from the Massachusetts Institute of Technology in 1984.

Ellis Tallman is a senior economic advisor in the Research Department of the Federal Reserve Bank of Cleveland and the Danforth-Lewis Professor of Economics at Oberlin College, where he teaches macroeconomics, financial intermediation, and economic and financial history. His current research interests include macroeconomics, economic forecasting, and historical episodes of financial crises. Previously, Dr. Tallman was a vice president and team leader for the macro group in the Research Department at the Federal Reserve Bank of Atlanta and an adjunct professor at Emory University. In 1996, Dr. Tallman began a two-year appointment as a visiting senior research economist at the Reserve Bank of Australia, where he engaged in policy support and economic research for the Australian central bank. He holds a B.A. in economics from Indiana University and an M.A. and Ph.D. in economics from the University of Rochester.

David C. Wheelock is vice president and deputy director of the Economic Research Division of the Federal Reserve Bank of St. Louis, where he has worked since 1993. He serves as an advisor to the Bank president on monetary and financial policy issues, and conducts policy-oriented research. Prior to joining the St. Louis Fed, Dr. Wheelock was a member of the faculty of the Department of Economics at the University of Texas at Austin. He has written numerous articles on banking and monetary policy issues for professional journals and Federal Reserve publications. He is the author of *The Strategy and Consistency of Federal Reserve Monetary Policy, 1924–1933*. Dr. Wheelock received his B.S. from Iowa State University and his M.S. and Ph.D. degrees from the University of Illinois at Urbana-Champaign.

Eugene N. White is a professor of economics at Rutgers University and a research associate at the National Bureau of Economic Research. His current research focuses on the evolution of bank supervision in the United States from the nineteenth century to the present, the housing market boom of the 1920s, stock market booms and crashes, the microstructure of securities markets in Europe and America, and the management of financial crises by the Banque de France in the nineteenth century. Dr. White is currently coediting a book on historical housing and mortgage markets and another on the economics of Occupied Europe in World War II. He is also editor of a series on financial and economic history for Yale University Press. He received an A.B. from Harvard University, a B.A. from Oxford University, and M.A. and Ph.D. degrees from the University of Illinois at Urbana-Champaign.

Geoffrey Wood is Emeritus Professor of Economics at Cass Business School in London and Emeritus Professor of Monetary Economics at the University of Buckingham. A graduate of Aberdeen and Essex Universities, he has worked in the Federal Reserve System and the Bank of England. Overseas he has advised several central banks and national treasuries. He is currently a director of an investment trust and an adviser to several financial institutions, two pension funds, and the Treasury Select Committee of the House of Commons. He was adviser to the Parliamentary Banking Commission until it ceased to exist on the publication of its report. He has authored, coauthored, or edited more than thirty books, and he has published more than 100 academic papers. His fields of interest are monetary economics, monetary history, and financial regulation.

Discussants at the Conference

Christopher Erceg, Board of Governors of the Federal Reserve System
Joseph Haubrich, Federal Reserve Bank of Cleveland
Robert Hetzel, Federal Reserve Bank of Richmond
Jim MacGee, University of Western Ontario
Bennett McCallum, Carnegie Mellon University
Jon Moen, University of Mississippi
Richard Sylla, New York University
James Thomson, University of Akron and Federal Reserve Bank of
    Cleveland
François Velde, Federal Reserve Bank of Chicago

Preface

On December 12–13, 2012, the Federal Reserve Bank of Cleveland held a conference to commemorate the Federal Reserve System's centennial and to honor Michael D. Bordo for his contributions to economic history. We are indebted to Barry Eichengreen, Hugh Rockoff, and Eugene N. White for helping us organize the conference and suggesting paper topics, presenters, and discussants. Although we elected not to publish the discussants' comments, the authors had ample opportunity to address these, as well as comments from the floor, in their final drafts. We thank all of the authors, discussants, and participants for their fine efforts.

I also want to thank Sandra Pianalto, President and Chief Executive Officer of the Federal Reserve Bank of Cleveland, Mark Sniderman, Executive Vice President and Chief Policy Officer, and Mark Schweitzer, Senior Vice President and Director of Research, for enthusiastically supporting a conference that drew on economic history to address current policy issues. Kelly Banks and Jennifer Ransom provided logistical support and unbound enthusiasm for the project.

Everyone who participated in the event offers a special thanks to Sereta Johnson, Kathy Popovich, and Paula Warren who – in the end – made the whole thing happen.

Introduction

Context and Content

Owen F. Humpage

Economic calamities create and shape central banks. The financial crisis of 1907, for example, led to the formation of the Federal Reserve System in 1914. The Great Depression and subsequent crises – along with changes in economic theory and political pressures – have altered the Federal Reserve's structure and responsibilities a number of times over the past century. The Great Recession saw the Federal Reserve and many of the world's other key central banks push several of their traditional policy operations in decidedly nontraditional directions. These actions have brought praise from some quarters and criticisms from others, but they now have precedence. The Great Recession – like the Great Depression – is likely to caste a long shadow over the institutional arrangements and policy operations of the world's central banks for years to come.

To deepen our insights into these developments, the Federal Reserve Bank of Cleveland invited some of the world's leading monetary, financial, and central-bank scholars to analyze them through the lens of economic history. The conference papers in this volume cover a wide range of issues – from the Federal Reserve's expanded lender-of-last-resort function to the prospects for European monetary union – and do what economic history does best: enhance economic theory with historical context. What better way to commemorate the Federal Reserve System's centennial?

In setting up this conference, the Federal Reserve Bank of Cleveland also sought to honor Michael D. Bordo for his considerable contributions to monetary and financial history. The design of this conference epitomizes Mike's work in terms of both the topics covered and the purpose. Michael Bordo often reviews the historical record with an eye toward distilling important lessons that can inform policy today. That is what most of the essays in this volume look to do.

The first chapter in this volume, however, is the exception. In his essay, Barry Eichengreen discusses both the benefits and the pitfalls of conducting such historical analyses. As such, the chapter functions as a user's guide, of sorts, to the conference papers. Human beings instinctively reason by analogy. History provides a "rich laboratory" of material against which to draw instructive comparisons about current economic developments. Such comparisons, as Eichengreen explains, can enrich policymakers' understanding of current events by filling in the context that economic modelers abandon in their search for parsimony. Historical analogy is particularly useful during economic crises, when events evolve quickly and discontinuously. Yet, reasoning from historical analogy presents dangers, and Eichengreen carefully lays out six pitfalls, which he often illustrates by referring to comparisons – so common of late – between the Great Recession and the Great Depression.

The next three chapters in this volume comment on aspects of the Federal Reserve's recent operations. Marvin Goodfriend, in his keynote address to the conference, focuses on the Federal Reserve's efforts to enhance its credibility through clearer communications. In January 2012, the Federal Open Market Committee – the Federal Reserve's main policymaking organ – issued a statement of its principles and goals for monetary policy. The statement, which announced a 2 percent inflation objective, looked to improve the Committee's transparency and accountability for U.S. monetary policy, and, thereby, to enhance the System's credibility with respect to achieving its policy goals. A credible monetary policy anchors inflation expectations. Goodfriend traces the historical origins of the January 2012 announcement. He first focuses on the Federal Reserve's response to five inflation scares during the Volcker and Greenspan chairmanships, showing how anchored inflation expectations can enhance the effectiveness of monetary policy. Goodfriend then recounts the Federal Reserve System's decisions to become more transparent through the release of the committee's transcripts and the eventual announcement of its federal-funds-rate target. He argues that the Federal Reserve could further enhance its transparency and accountability by distinguishing balance-sheet actions that are monetary policy from those that are credit policy. Goodfriend goes on to explain this crucial distinction and why it matters to central banks.

Allan Meltzer also looks to improve the credibility of U.S. monetary policy, and he favors a rules-based approach. Meltzer argues that the Federal Reserve's powers have greatly expanded since its founding, but at the cost of reduced policy independence. He sees rules-based policy as a shield against the greater potential for political influence over central-bank actions. Monetary policymakers will always confront uncertainties intrinsic to the economy, which rules-based policy will never perfectly overcome, but rules lessen uncertainties associated with how central banks themselves are likely to respond. That in itself fosters good economic outcomes. Meltzer contends that the Federal Reserve's greatest policy successes have occurred when the System followed rule-like policies. He notes, for example, that the Federal Reserve followed a Taylor rule between 1985 and 2003, with a sufficiently large weight on the inflation component to attain price stability. Such a Taylor rule, nevertheless, remained consistent with the Federal Reserve's dual mandate. Meltzer also worries that the Federal Reserve is currently conditioning policy too much on near-term developments, over which it has little influence, instead of on medium-term goals, which it can affect. Rules-based policy minimizes this problem. Moreover, if major countries all adopted rules that emphasized price stability, they could minimize exchange-rate uncertainty and, therefore, volatility.

The Federal Reserve's response to the financial meltdown of 2007–2009 was unmatched in its scale and scope, but it had precedence in the System's actions to stem earlier financial crises. Mark Carlson and David Wheelock trace the development of the Federal Reserve's lender-of-last-resort function from the System's founding through the recent financial crisis. Readers, who may conceive Bagehot's rule as the optimal guide for a lender of last resort, are left to understand how complicated these operations can be in a large, dynamic, and diverse financial climate. The chapter describes how the overall regulatory environment for the financial system and especially the banking system affects the likelihood that a central bank will need to act as a lender of last resort, the nature of any response, and the chances of its success. Carlson and Wheelock's review gives context to the Federal Reserve's recent actions, showing that the Federal Reserve's response to the financial crisis of 2007–2009 was not ad hoc. Its roots run long and deep.

Another way to think about the Federal Reserve's lender-of-last-resort function is to consider banking in its absence. Prior to the establishment of the Federal Reserve System, clearing houses undertook actions that many associate with modern central banks, notably they provided temporary liquidity in the form of clearing house loan certificates during banking crises. Monetary historians have suggested that clearing houses failed to stem banking panics during the National Banking Era because they issued insufficient amounts of loan certificates. If loan certificates were to overcome banking panics, banks had to borrow loan certificates in concert, substitute them for clearing balances, and then inject the cash from their clearing balances into the banking system. Relying on a unique set of data from the minutes of the New York Clearing House's loan committee, Jon Moen and Ellis Tallman investigate how the six largest U.S. banks used clearing house loan certificates during the 1873, 1884, 1890, 1893, and 1907 banking crises. Instead of concerted actions, Moen and Tallman find considerable variation in the biggest banks' use of clearing house loan certificates during panics, which suggests that these banks did not always internalize the beneficial externalities of providing liquidity to the broader banking system. They instead acted in their own self-interests.

Many who have criticized the scope of central-bank actions during the Great Recession have done so out of a fear that these actions have undermined central banks' independence. Forrest Capie and Geoffrey Wood explain that the concept of central-bank independence has always been somewhat nebulous. In theory, a central bank is independent if it is free of political influence. In practice, the definition is less clear cut, because governments create central banks that, in turn, provide services to the government. A completely independent central bank does not exist. Capie and Wood, drawing on the history of the Reserve Bank of New Zealand, the Band of England, and the Federal Reserve System, discuss central-bank independence as a set of governmental instructions to a central bank that expresses the government's intentions for that institution and are clear enough to measure its subsequent performance. Over the past twenty-four years, these instructions have focused on price stability and on the lender-of-last-resort function. During financial crises, governments reshape their central banks' mandate in ways that push central banks "into the arms of government" with unintended consequences for the bank's authority and reputation that linger after the crisis has passed. Capie and Wood wonder if the Great Recession has redefined the relationships between the Bank of England, the European Central Bank, and the Federal Reserve System and their respective governments in ways not consistent with the traditional definition of central-bank independence.

A byproduct of the Great Recession has been a sovereign-debt crisis within the euro area. Although a single currency promotes exchange among its members, it limits their ability to respond to country-specific economic shocks. Consequently, the European sovereign-debt crisis has created uncertainty about the longevity of the European Monetary Union. Peter Rousseau's contribution to this volume asks if political union is a necessary condition for successful monetary union. Rousseau points out that the United States achieved complete political and monetary union through lengthy processes, with the former culminating with the Civil War and the latter in the Federal Reserve System. He shows how the waxing and waning of centralist and decentralist views influenced the evolution of monetary practices and institutions in the United States. He argues, for example, that Andrew Jackson's actions against the Second Bank of the United States and the "specie circular," which seem antithetical to the establishment of monetary union, ultimately had positive consequences. Jackson's policies fostered the regional distribution of specie, and promoted a geographic dispersion of banking services that otherwise might not have occurred. The national bank acts – a centralist proposition – fostered a uniform currency, but did not eliminate state banks. With the Federal Reserve as a lender of last resort, the United States achieved equilibrium – one consistent with monetary union – between ever-evolving political and monetary forces. He expects the process to transpire similarly in Europe, though somewhat faster.

Harold James is also concerned with the process of European monetary union, and he notes that Europeans often turn to the United States for precedents on fiscal and financial integration. He focuses on two aspects of the U.S. experience that are particularly important to Europe today: The U.S. federal government's regard for state debts and the structural evolution of the Federal Reserve System between 1914 and 1933. As is well known, Hamilton in 1790 assumed state debts associated with the Revolution because they sprang from actions taken on behalf of the entire nation. James focuses on the less understood consequences of Hamilton's decision. He explains, for example, how the subsequent moral-hazard problem played out in the 1840s and 1870s and how the establishment of a revenue stream to service state debts had divisive distributional effects among the U.S. states. Drawing on U.S. precedents, James also explains that the design of a central bank governing a large geographic area – like the Federal Reserve – is complicated by a need to address local circumstances while ensuring the cohesive operation of the entire system. Adding further complexity, the design of the central bank may not fit evolving policy demands, as was the Federal Reserve's experience in the 1930s. Consequently, a process of institutional redesign is necessary.

In thinking about the European Monetary Union's current problems, Christopher Meissner draws an important parallel from an unlikely historical source. Meissner shows how France's preference for a bimetallic international monetary system could not compete with the growing international preference for a gold-based system. Moreover, he suggests that France's temporary suspension of silver convertibility in 1873, in conjunction with growing network economies, accelerated the international preference for gold. Meissner estimates that France would have lost its gold reserves and ended up on a silver standard by 1875 had it persisted in its quest for bimetallism. Meissner's key broader point is that long-held perceptions about the viability of an institutional status quo can prove false, if those perceptions are not viable in all states of the world. European monetary union may be a case in point. Policymakers claim that those European countries experiencing sovereign-debt crises and undergoing difficult reforms will not have to vacate the European Monetary Union, but is this claim viable in all possible scenarios? Meissner sees close cooperation – which did not coalesce around bimetallism – as necessary for European Monetary Union.

The depth and duration of the Great Recession has naturally encouraged comparisons with the Great Depression. Kris Mitchener and Gary Richardson consider the role of interbank deposits as an avenue of financial contagion during the Great Contraction (1929–1933). Interbank deposits linked country banks, particularly nonmember banks, to financial centers in New York and Chicago. During the 1920s, interbank deposit flows were largely seasonal and not correlated with measures of bank distress. During the 1930s, however, interbank deposit flows became highly correlated with bank distress in the hinterlands and, consequently, transmitted financial shocks from the periphery to the center of the financial system. The increased volatility of interbank flows during the 1930s encouraged reserve-city banks to shift their portfolio out of loans and into government bonds and to accumulate reserves. Consequently, the volatility of these interbank deposit flows may have contributed to the severity of the Great Contraction. Mitchener and Richardson base their estimates on a new comprehensive data set for all banks in the United States aggregated at the Federal Reserve District level.

One important similarity between the Great Recession and the Great Depression is that in both, short-term interest rates approached their zero bound, weakening the conventional channels for monetary policy. During the Great Depression short-term interest rates effectively reached their zero bound in 1934 and remained there until 1940. Banks held substantial amounts of excess reserves, much like today. John Landon-Lane asks if quantitative easing would have worked during the Great Depression. Using a methodology that approximates an event study, he suggests that the Federal Reserve could have had a small effect on long-term government bond yields during the 1930s by purchasing such bonds. Moreover, Landon-Lane believes that changes in yields of long-term Treasuries would have passed through to corporate bond yields with a greater-than-proportionate impact on low-rated corporates. Quantitative easing could have helped during the Great Depression.

Another way to understand current U.S. policies is through comparisons with the Canadian experience. These can be particularly useful because both economies are similar, closely interconnected, and often experience common economic shocks. Economists can often trace differences between the Canadian and U.S. responses to similar economic shocks to variations in these countries' monetary policies and regulatory environments. Ehsan Choudhri and Lawrence Schembri first compare U.S. and Canadian monetary policies in the 1920s and the 2000s. They find that although Canadian monetary policy was somewhat more conservative than U.S. monetary policy in general, the former did not differ substantially from the latter because of Canadian concerns about adverse exchange-rate movements. Choudhri and Schembri then focus on differences between the countries' financial-stability policies. During the boom period of the 1920s, both the United States and Canada lacked effective financial-stability policies to control credit expansion. Both eventually had to use monetary-policy actions – a particularly blunt instrument. Canada and the United States learned from the experience and, during the Great Depression, introduced substantial changes to laws governing their financial systems. Prior to the recent crisis, however, the United States – unlike Canada – seems to have forgotten that lesson. Choudhri and Schembri attribute differences in Canada's and the United States' recent economic performances to differences in their mortgage-market and bank-regulatory policies.

The Great Recession originated from severe problems in the U.S. housing and mortgage markets, which Canada did not share. Angela Redish extends this volume's cross-border comparisons by reviewing the development of the mortgage markets in Canada and the United States. She relates this process to evolutionary differences to the structure of banking in each country. In Canada mortgages typically have a five-year duration. Consequently, banks in Canada do not face large maturity mismatches on their balance sheets and feel little compulsion to take mortgage loans off of their balance sheets through securitization, as do many banks in the United States, where the maturity mismatches can be considerable. In addition, extensive Canadian bank branching – not found in the United States – gave banks access to a nationwide pool of funds without securitization. The resulting stability in Canada, however, comes with costs: Borrowers must often refinance their mortgages, and banks may face a diminished capacity to access mortgage funding in international markets without securitization.

As noted, the papers in this conference generally reflect aspects of Michael Bordo's work in their breadth of topic, historical focus, and policy relevance. Hugh Rockoff and Eugene White pay tribute to Michael Bordo's rich contributions of monetary and central-bank history, but because the latter's contributions are so extensive – 244 published articles, chapters, surveys, and reviews by their count – the Rockoff and White chapter also serves as a quick survey of scholarly debates on leading issues in the field, particularly those issues of ongoing policy relevance. Among the many areas included in this chapter are the Great Depression, Canadian banking exceptionalism, the gold standard, financial crises, the lender-of-last-resort function, and the relevance of asset bubbles to monetary policy. The section entitled, Historical Guidance for Monetary Policy, for example, includes a compact discussion of the lender-of-last-resort function that briefly discusses external factors that can lead to banking crises, explains why private-sector solutions to banking crises are inadequate, and progresses to the role of open-market operations in such cases. A neophyte monetary historian can find no better starting point than this chapter and Michael Bordo's body of work.

After earning his undergraduate degree from McGill University and a master's degree from the London School of Economics, Bordo received his Ph.D. from the University of Chicago under the tutelage of Robert

Fogel, Harry Johnson, Robert Mundell, and Milton Friedman, his thesis advisor. While working on his thesis, Mike spent a summer at the National Bureau of Economic Research, where he met Anna Schwartz, with whom he frequently collaborated over the next forty years. Bordo is a Research Associate of the National Bureau of Economic Research and a Distinguished Visiting Fellow at the Hoover Institution.

Michael Bordo's concluding essay brings the conference full circle. Bordo notes that traditionally central banks have performed two tasks: they have maintained the purchasing power of money and, in the face of temporary liquidity shocks, served as a lender of last resort to banks – those institutions that provide the means of payment. He argues for the maintenance of this traditional model. In the aftermath of the recent financial crisis, many have called for central banks to adopt a broader mandate for financial stability, including the monitoring of asset prices and the wider financial system. Bordo contends that broad financial stability concerns should fall under the purview of a separate authority or, at a minimum, should not involve the traditional tools of monetary policy. To do otherwise, risks making central banks adjuncts to fiscal policies.

1

The Uses and Misuses of Economic History

Barry Eichengreen

There is a long tradition in economics of making use of historical events and episodes in an effort to shed light on current policy concerns. Earl Hamilton's famous work on the sources of Spain's sixteenth-century inflation appeared, not coincidentally, in the wake of the European hyperinflations of the 1920s.[1] Gayer, Rostow, and Schwartz in *Growth and Fluctuations of the British Economy*; Rostow in *Stages of Economic Growth*; and Gerschenkron in *Economic Backwardness in Historical Perspective* turned after World War II to Britain, America, and Continental Europe's historical experience with industrialization and economic development precisely because this was when economists were preoccupied with how industrialization and modern economic growth might be encouraged in the newly independent nations of Asia and Africa.[2] One would be remiss to not also mention Friedman and Schwartz's *Monetary History of the United States*, which looked back not just at the Great Depression but also at earlier U.S. monetary experience and was written as a reaction against the tendency after World War II to downplay the role of monetary policy in economic fluctuations, most visibly in the United Kingdom but also generally.[3]

This kind of policy-oriented or "presentist" history subsequently fell out of fashion. (The term in quotes is from Mariano 2000, who uses it to characterize the work of the American political historian Arthur Schlesinger Jr., who was notorious among his purist colleagues for high-profile attempts to use history to speak to current events.) To be clear, economic history

This chapter draws on my 2011 presidential address to the Economic History Association, since published in the *Journal of Economic History* (June 2012).

[1] See Hamilton (1934).
[2] The references are to Gayer, Rostow, and Schwartz (1953); Rostow (1960); and Gerschenkron (1964).
[3] See Friedman and Schwartz (1963).

never went away.[4] But it is fair to say that research in economic history in this period was not intimately connected to policymaking.[5] Economic historians did not serve on the Board of Governors of the Federal Reserve System, on the President's Council of Economic Advisors, or in other policy positions.[6] Historical scholarship was not widely invoked in policy discussions.

How markedly the current state of affairs differs from that of the late 1960s and early 1970s has been highlighted by the role that research in economic history played in the policy debate over how to respond to the financial crisis and Great Recession of 2008–2009. As I have noted elsewhere, there was a sharp increase in references in the press to the term "Great Depression" following the failure of Lehman Bros. in September 2008.[7] There was also a surge in references to "economic history," first in February of 2008 with growing awareness that this could be the worst recession since the 1930s, and again in October, coincident with fears that the financial system was on the verge of collapse. Journalists, market participants, and policymakers all turned to history for guidance on how to interpret and react to an otherwise unprecedented news flow – unprecedented, that is, if one looked back fewer than eighty years. In March 2009, at the height of fears that we might be slipping into a new depression, the Council on Foreign Relations convened a symposium on the 1930s Depression and New Deal.[8] Today, as attention turns from the danger of financial collapse to disappointingly slow growth and chronic debt problems, comparisons with the aftermath of earlier crises and the extent to which they were also accompanied by slow growth and sovereign debt problems are again rife.[9]

---

[4] To the contrary, it continued to be actively practiced and taught. The 1960s, when Mike began his graduate work, and the 1970s, when the young Professor Bordo rose to prominence, were precisely when the so-called new economic history flourished.

[5] One might wish to qualify this generalization by observing that some influential early contributions to the new economic history did, in fact, have important connections to the policy issues of the day, although the extent to which they influenced contemporary policy debate is another question. Thus Fogel and Engerman's *Time on the Cross* drew inspiration in part from the Civil Rights movement of the 1960s, and McCloskey's *Economic Maturity and Industrial Decline* was inspired in part by the contemporary debate over British economic performance.

[6] As they have recently. Walt Rostow may have been one of the last of his generation (am I missing others?).

[7] This according to Google Trends, as reported in Eichengreen (2012).

[8] Mike was there (I was not).

[9] Reinhart and Rogoff (2009) is the most widely cited and purchased (if not always read) example of the genus, but it is far from alone. Macmillan (2009, p. 9) describes how it seemed during the Cold War that the history of earlier conflicts seemed to have lost much of its power. "The world that came into being after 1945 was divided up between two great alliance systems and two competing ideologies, both of which claimed to represent the future of humanity.... The old conflicts between Serbs and Croats, Germans and French, or Christians and Muslims, were just that and were consigned, in Leon Trotsky's memorable

The reasons for the influence of historical experience and historical analogies in policymaking – and not just economic policymaking – are no mystery. Cognitive scientists have observed that analogical reasoning is an important and distinctive form of human thinking. Human beings instinctively reason by analogy; they learn to do so, apparently spontaneously, at an early age. In contrast, very few other primate species are able to engage in explicit relational matching (that is, to recognize the existence of analogies and draw implications for behavior from them) and generally only with the benefit of extensive training.[10] If analogical reasoning seems like second nature to us humans, that's because it is.[11]

This observation of course predates the development of the discipline of cognitive science, practitioners of which study analogical and other forms of reasoning.[12] Slightly more than 100 years ago, in 1912, J. Franklin Jameson, co-founder and long-time editor of the *American Historical Review*, wrote that "There is a sense in which we know things only by comparison...."[13] Here Jameson was making the case for analogy in general, but not yet for historical analogy. But he then went on: "The student of the political and social sciences – the economist, the philologian in the broader sense of that term, the student of religious and legal ideas – will never find direct observation of present phenomena sufficient for their purposes, but will continue in the future, as they have so largely done during the last fifty years, to seek in the rich laboratory of history the material for sounder conclusions than today's phenomena alone can give."[14]

The past, in other words, is an obvious place to look for analogies with the present. But it is not the only place. That is to say, historical analogizing is not the only kind of analogical reasoning or analysis in which economists might engage. We might draw analogies between economic systems and other systems – between economics and hydraulics, for example. A case in point is Bill Phillips' famous model of the macroeconomy as a

---

phrase, to the dustbin of history." Or so we thought; now that history has acquired a new salience. One can say the same of histories of the Great Depression and earlier economic and financial crises. During the Great Moderation, it was possible to assert that they were mainly of interest to academics (or, at most, specialists on developing countries). The thawing of our financial cold war has taught us to know better.

[10] As described by Ogden, Thompson, and Premack (2001).

[11] As MacMillan (2009, p. 156) puts it, "Human beings may not always get the right analogy, but they are almost certainly bound to try to use one." I return to the problem of selecting the right analogy later.

[12] There have been examples of analogical reasoning for as long as there have been written records, for example, in the 4,000-year-old Mesopotamian epic *Gilgamesh*. Then there is the term "analogy" itself, which derives from the ancient Greek *analogia*.

[13] Reprinted as Jameson (1959), p. 65.

[14] Ibid, p. 66. Writing a century ago, Jameson evidently appreciated the difficulty macroeconomists have in running natural experiments.

hydraulic system, which he designed and built in 1949 before the availability of the transistor and hence the electronic computer, precisely with the goal of giving policy advice.[15] Some economists draw analogies between economic systems and thermodynamic systems; Duncan Foley and Eric Smith have argued that models of economies with well-defined equilibria are essentially isomorphic to models of physical systems with classic thermodynamic equations of state.[16] When seeking to understand economic problems, my wife, a physician, is drawn to the analogy between economic systems and physiological systems.

So why historical analogy in particular? The economist would probably argue that there are circumstances in which comparisons with another episode that occurred earlier in historical time yield especially powerful implications for analysis and policy. This could reflect an especially close correspondence between the "target case" and the "base case" – the terms that cognitive scientists use to describe the situation at hand and its analogical counterpart. In other words, there are situations or problems for which the comparison between yesterday's and today's economies is closer and more informative than the comparison between, say, the economic system and a thermodynamic system. A historian, in contrast, would argue that historical analogy is particularly informative in situations where human agency, contingency, nuance, and context matter, as historians are trained to study and emphasize human agency, contingency, nuance, and context.[17]

Another answer (to which I'm not sure I entirely subscribe, perhaps because I'm too much of an economist) is that historical analogy is most valuable in situations where partial equilibrium does not suffice. Economic theory is the art of the simplifying assumption. To be tractable, economic models must leave things out; they are all partial equilibrium in some sense whether this is admitted or not. And there are circumstances where wielding Occam's razor is a good way for the policy analyst to cut his throat. History is a means of seeing the big picture. It is, as one historian has put it, "an integrative discipline, and stresses the insistence of the historical imagination upon seeing matters as a whole ... Policy error comes often in the form of a surprise from some impinging factor or factors whose bearing upon one's own narrower plans, indeed whose very existence, was often screened out of the analysis ... We [historians] honor our assignment at contextual reconstruction most often in the breach, perhaps, but our discipline is inherently holistic and better nurtures that

---

[15] On Phillips' focus on using his machine to inform economic policymaking see Laidler (2000).

[16] See Smith and Foley (2005). Both fields, they observe, "seek to describe system phenomena in terms of solutions to constrained optimization problems."

[17] As emphasized by MacMillan (2009).

contextual perspective which is so often defeated by the training of the economist or psychology...."[18]

Finally, historical analogy may be especially valuable when time deformation is important: when the evolution of important economic variables seems to speed up, when some variables evolve more rapidly than others, and when variables that normally evolve continuously display discontinuous changes – as a result of which conventional modes of empirical analysis break down. If this discussion of abrupt changes in otherwise smoothly evolving variables and of events speeding up makes you think of crises, then you are not alone. The utility of historical analysis under such circumstances has long emphasized by practitioners. As Graham (1983) puts it, historians think of the present as composed of strands from the past, but strands of unequal vitality. Some strands are very strong, resulting in situations that have jelled or stalemated and are resistant to change, while others are weak, resulting in situations that are open to sudden movement and innovation. The influence of those different strands, moreover, can be very different in different historical contexts.[19]

The role of historical analogy in providing guidance for policy in times of crises deserves further reflection, and not just in light of recent events. Cognitive scientists have observed that reliance on analogical reasoning (as opposed to induction and deduction, the obvious alternatives) is likely to be greatest when the stakes are high, time is short, and diagnosis is difficult – in situations that will make economists think of crises. Students of human cognition have shown that agents are most likely to resort to analogy when there is limited time to reach a decision and those reaching it have limited information and information-processing capacity – when induction is problematic. Agents are most likely to reason by analogy when they disagree on first principles – when deductive reasoning is difficult. They are most likely to resort to analogical reasoning under pressure of time and there is the need for intellectual shortcuts.

This doesn't seem like a bad representation of how it must have felt in the Oval Office or the Fed's boardroom in late 2008 and early 2009. With the banking system on the verge of collapse, there was intense time pressure to reach a decision. Information on the condition of the financial system and the economy was incomplete; recall how there was dispute over the accuracy of the stress tests, how there was uncertainty about who was on the hook for credit default swaps, and how contemporary releases underestimated the depth of the recession. We economists did not agree among ourselves about the causes of the problem; that we disagreed on the appropriate model with which to analyze the crisis and its consequences

---

[18] Graham (1983), pp. 11–12.
[19] Graham (1983), p. 11.

rendered economic theory of limited utility for formulating a response. In these circumstances, the analogy with the Great Depression had obvious appeal as a guide to comprehension and action.[20]

It also came with dangers. There is a rich tradition in foreign policy studies, stretching back to the work of the Harvard political scientist Ernest May (1973), highlighting the dangers of loose and misleading analogical reasoning. There is the Munich analogy, which implies that you should not back down. There is the Vietnam analogy, which says that you should not become bogged down. And, in the foreign policy sphere, where the role of such analogies has been extensively studied, there is evidence of their widespread misuse.

First, analogical reasoning is often used as an intellectual shortcut, and shortcuts can lead to oversimplification. As one critic has put it, rather unsympathetically, "Historical analogy is the glib man's substitute for analysis."[21] Rather than attempting to understand the causes and course of the Great Depression and precisely what they imply for action in current circumstances, ritual invocation of the Great Depression analogy in the midst of a credit crisis may simply substitute for rather than stimulating a search for deeper understanding.

Second, historical analogies can mislead if they differ from the current situation in important ways and if the analyst fails to test them adequately for fitness. The analogy with Munich led President Truman to intervene in Korea, which he had previously dismissed as strategically worthless, but it is doubtful that the motives of Hitler's Germany and Mao's China were at all the same. President Kennedy, in contrast, considered a range of analogies with the Cuban Missile Crisis, not only Munich but also Suez, Pearl Harbor, the German invasion of Czechoslovakia, and the Berlin blockade, carefully assessing their fitness to the circumstances at hand before attempting to draw implications for policy.

Third, reasoning by historical analogy can lead to overreaction insofar as there is a tendency, when picking the analogy on which to focus, to fasten onto "searing" or "molding" events.[22] It is these exceptional events that spring to mind most readily; thus, Munich was the great foreign policy disaster of Truman's generation. Similarly, it is probably not a coincidence that the dominant analogy to the 2008–2009 financial crisis was

---

[20] Larry Summers, who was there, subsequently remarked that he found historical analysis the most useful form of analysis when seeking to cope with the crisis in real time; the preceding observations are one way of understanding this.

[21] Cited in Rapport (2012). The context for the remark was an analogy between Germany's decision in 1914 to press its momentary advantage over Russia and France, with disastrous geopolitical consequences, and the possibility that Israel might press its momentary military advantage to launch a strike against Iran's nuclear program.

[22] As argued by Zelikow (1999).

not the savings and loan crisis or the 1907 financial panic but the Great Depression, the great macroeconomic disaster of the twentieth century. Insofar as searing events occur when the stakes are highest, reasoning by analogy tends to incline the analogizer to the need for forceful action. Some will argue, in this vein, that the analogy with the Great Depression led policymakers to overreact in 2008–2009.

Fourth, historical analogies may simply be providing justification for decisions taken on other grounds. Analysts may cherry pick analogies so as to reinforce their existing beliefs. Those of skeptical inclination will suggest that such behavior was evident in the recent crisis, when the Great Depression was conveniently invoked by those who were predisposed to exceptional action in response to what they therefore sought to portray as an exceptional crisis. Of course, this kind of cherry picking is not peculiar to analogical reasoning; it extends to inductive and deductive reasoning as well. Those predisposed toward a certain course of action, reasoning inductively, may choose to emphasize those facts that most obviously provide a justification for their preferred course. Those relying on deductive reasoning may choose to emphasize a particular class of models. The protection against this tendency is the same in each case: vigorous debate and careful scholarship.

This brings me to a fifth problem with relying on historical analogy, namely that the content and implications of the analogy are contested. If history is the distilled encapsulation of society's understanding of the past, then the history of the Great Depression, to pursue the current analogy, is still being distilled.[23] Although I like to think that there is a conventional, widely accepted narrative of the causes of the Great Depression that contains a set of concrete implications for the conduct of economic policy, not everyone will. And even if there is a widely accepted mainstream narrative, there will inevitably be dissents. Insofar as understandings and characterizations of that earlier historical episode are disputed, the utility of the historical analogy for guiding policy in a crisis will be limited.[24]

This said, the existence of such disputes may not be an entirely bad thing. The fact that history is contested – that there are multiple accounts and interpretations of the "same historical events" – encourages analysts

[23] Or, if as Voltaire put it, "History is a fable agreed upon."

[24] There is an analogy here (as it were) with postmodern, multicultural criticisms of traditional national histories as simply engaging in the business of constructing a national myth of identity: an imagined social construction based on the experience of "a few successful ... white men" (in the words of Wood 2008, p. 261). Economic historians, in this view, are simply constructing the accepted myth of the Great Depression. Personally, I think this is a view that lends itself to being pushed too far.

to acknowledge that events need to be viewed from different angles
and perspectives. Historical analysis is conducive to a mind frame that
acknowledges objections to conventional wisdoms. Foreign policy specialists have emphasized that historical analogies provide the best guidance for policy when a range of analogies is used to construct a portfolio
of policy choices. This is famously how Kennedy used historical analogies during the Cuban Missile crisis. As May describes, he consciously
sought multiple analogies, weighed their applicability, and contrasted
their policy implications. The president was thereby able to move beyond
the most readily available analogy and identify characteristics of several
historical cases that applied to the crisis at hand. This led to the development of a portfolio of policy options that included not just air strike but
also naval blockade and negotiation. Awareness that there exist different
interpretations of the same historical episode may similarly be conducive
to sensitivity and caution in drawing strong policy implications on the
basis of an historical analogy. For example, the mainstream narrative of
the Great Depression emphasizing the failure to use monetary and fiscal policies in stabilizing ways and cautioning strongly against the same
error in future financial crises is not entirely incompatible with interpretations of 1930s experience emphasizing the role of counterproductive
supply-side policies in slowing the subsequent recovery. Awareness of
both interpretations will serve as a better guide to policy than only one
of them so long as the existence of rival interpretations is not taken as
counseling inaction. And avoiding this trap, where awareness of disagreement simply leads to inaction, requires the analogizer, drawing on historical experience, to attach weights to the rival interpretations and to test
them for fitness with current circumstances.

This brings me to a sixth and final objection to relying on historical
analogy to guide economic policy: that the analogy has no useful content
divorced from the relevant economic theory.[25] In interpreting the Great
Depression, it can be argued, economic historians are simply illustrating
the applicability of principles from economic theory that also provide
guidance for policy independent of that historical experience. There is no
economic history of the Great Depression, in other words, independent
of the economic theory used to organize it. Practitioners of the "new
economic history" acknowledge the importance of theory in framing historical analyses. But this is not the same as asserting that there is no

---

[25] When they go too far down this road, economists end up as strange bedfellows with post-
modernists, or practitioners of the "new historicism," who argue that there is a reality in
the past beyond that described by language and theory, effectively making historical reconstruction impossible. See also later.

underlying historical reality separate from the theory used to interpret it. Some economists might be prepared to make this argument. In so doing, they would be embracing the essence of postmodernism, whether they realize it or not.[26]

So what, at the end of the day, does economic history offer the policymaker? Graham (1983) argues that the utility of history for policy lies not in any "lessons" that might be derived from reasoning by analogy but rather from thinking like an historian. Thinking like an historian means engaging in source criticism and regarding the evidence with skepticism. It directs attention to human agency – the fact that outcomes are driven not just by nations, institutions, and markets but also by the actions of individuals, who have the independence to take idiosyncratic decisions (Thelen 2000). It directs attention to nuance and context.

In any case, history's ultimate utility, as Margaret MacMillan has put it, lies not "in its predictive or even its explanatory value, but in its ability to teach humility, to nurture an appreciation on the limits of our capacity to see the past clearly, or to know fully the historical determinants of our own brief passage in time."[27]

Anything with the capacity to teach economists humility has high value, particularly under present circumstances.

REFERENCES

Eichengreen, Barry. (2012). "Economic History and Economic Policy." *Journal of Economic History* 72:289–307.

Gans, Herbert. (2011). "Some Uses of History." *History News Network* (March 16). Retrieved from http://hnn.us/blogs/entries/137636.html.

Gayer, Arthur, Walt Whitman Rostow, and Anna J. Schwartz. (1953). *Growth and Fluctuation of the British Economy 1790–1850: An Historical, Statistical and Theoretical Study of Britain's Economic Development.* Oxford: Oxford University Press.

Fogel, Robert, and Stanley Engerman. (1974). *Time on the Cross.* 2 vols. New York: Little, Brown.

---

[26] In history, the popularity of postmodernism has clearly peaked and is now on the wane. It would be unfortunate if the discipline of economics did not learn from this earlier historical experience.

[27] Another eminent historian, Gordon Wood (2008, p. 71), makes a similar point. "By showing that the best-laid plans of people usually go awry, the study of history tends to dampen youthful enthusiasm and to restrain the can-do, the conquer-the-future spirit that many people have.... Unlike sociology or political science [or economics], history is a conservative discipline – conservative, of course, not in any contemporary political sense but in the larger sense of inculcating skepticism about people's ability to manipulate and control purposefully their own destinies."

Friedman, Milton, and Anna J. Schwartz. (1963). *A Monetary History of the United States, 1867–1960*. Princeton, NJ: Princeton University Press for the National Bureau of Economic Research.

Gerschenkron, Alexander. (1964). *Economic Backwardness in Historical Perspective*. Cambridge, MA: Harvard University Press.

Graham, Otis L., Jr. (1983). "The Uses and Misuses of History: Roles in Policymaking." *The Public Historian* 5:5–19.

Hamilton, Earl. (1934). *American Treasury and the Price Revolution in Spain 1501–1650*. Cambridge, MA: Harvard University Press.

Iggers, Georg. (2000). "The Uses and Misuses of History: The Responsibility of the Historian, Past and Present." Paper presented to the International Congress of Historical Sciences, Oslo, August 9.

Jameson, J. Franklin. (1959). "The Future Uses of History." *American Historical Review* 59:61–71 [reprint of address delivered in 1912].

Laidler, David. (2000). "Phillips in Retrospect." Working Paper no. 20013, Department of Economics, University of Western Ontario.

MacMillan, Margaret. (2009). *Dangerous Games: The Uses and Abuses of History*. New York: Modern Library.

Mariano, Marco. (2000). "Specialism, Presentism and the 'Public Use of History' in the Historical Profession: The Early Writings of Arthur M. Schlesinger Jr." In David Adams and Maurizio Vaudagna (eds), *Transatlantic Encounters: Public Uses and Misuses of History in Europe and the United States*, pp. 144–167. Amsterdam: VU University Press.

May, Ernest. (1973). *'Lessons' of the Past: The Use and Misuse of History in American Foreign Policy*. New York: Oxford University Press.

McCloskey, Donald. (1969). *Economic Maturity and Entrepreneurial Decline: British Iron and Steel, 1870–1913*. Cambridge, MA: Harvard University Press.

Ogden, David, Roger Thompson, and David Premack. (2001). "Can an Ape Reason Analogically? Comprehension and Production of Analogical Problems by Sarah, a Chimpanzee (*Pan troglodytes*)." In Dedre Gentner, Keith Holyoak, and Boicho Nokinov (eds), *The Analogical Mind: Perspectives from Cognitive Science*, pp. 471–498. Cambridge, MA: MIT Press.

Rapport, Aaron. (2012). "Making the Case for History: Using Historical Analogies in Policy Analysis," Miller Center Blog, University of Virginia (February 22). Retrieved from http://millercenter.org/blog/making-the-case.

Reinhart, Carmen, and Kenneth Rogoff. (2009). *This Time Is Different: Eight Centuries of Financial Folly*. Princeton, NJ: Princeton University Press.

Rostow, Walt Whitman. (1960). *The Stages of Economic Growth: A Noncommunist Manifesto*. New York: Cambridge University Press.

Smith, Eric, and Duncan Foley. (2005). "Classical Thermodynamics and Economic General Equilibrium Theory." Unpublished manuscript, Santa Fe Institute.

Thane, Pat. (2009). "History and Policy." *History Workshop Journal* 67:140–145.

Thelen, David. (2000). "Popular Uses of History in the United States: Individuals in History." *Perspectives: A Publication of the American Historical*

Association (May). Retrieved from http://www.historians.org/perspectives /issues/2000/0005/0005spl3.cfm.

Wood, Gordon. (2008). *The Purpose of the Past: Reflections on the Uses of History*. New York: Penguin.

Zelikow, Phillip. (1999). "Thinking about Political History." *Miller Center Report* (Winter): 4–9.

2

Federal Reserve Policy Today in Historical Perspective

Marvin Goodfriend

In January 2012, "[f]ollowing careful deliberations at its recent meetings," the Federal Open Market Committee (FOMC) reported that it had "reached broad agreement on the following principles regarding its longer-run goals and monetary policy strategy."[1] The statement goes on to say that "[t]he Committee intends to reaffirm these principles and to make adjustments as appropriate at its organizational meeting each January." Emphasizing the time and effort put into developing the statement, the broad agreement, and its forward-looking nature, the FOMC signaled that its statement of principles and goals would provide fundamental guidance for monetary policy in the future.

The FOMC's statement of principles and goals for monetary policy begins with the requisite commitment to fulfill the Congressional mandate "to promote maximum employment, stable prices, and low long-term interest rates." The FOMC then pledges "to explain its monetary policy decisions to the public as clearly as possible." To facilitate "well-informed decision-making," "reduce economic and financial uncertainty," and "enhance transparency and accountability, which are essential in a democratic society." Next, the FOMC acknowledges that "the inflation rate over the longer run is primarily determined by monetary policy, and hence the Committee has the ability to specify a longer-run goal for inflation."

These principles are not news, far from it. Transparency in monetary policy is favored by central bankers today. And the FOMC merely acknowledges formally for the first time what monetarists led by Milton Friedman and Allan Meltzer have long argued, and what Fed Chairmen Volcker and Greenspan proved. Nevertheless, that acknowledgment probably required "careful deliberations at its recent meetings" because with it the FOMC

---

[1] The FOMC "Statement on Longer-Run Goals and Monetary Policy Strategy" is found in Minutes of the FOMC Meeting of January 24, 2012, pp. 7–8.

accepted responsibility for determining inflation on average over time. The FOMC's principle of transparency then called for informing the public of the precise long-run inflation objective that the Fed employs internally for analysis and deliberation of short-run policy options.

The FOMC did not shrink from that implicit logic and announced in its January 2012 statement of principles an explicit 2 percent objective for Personal Consumption Expenditure (PCE) inflation over the longer run as "most consistent with its statutory mandate." The FOMC promoted its 2 percent inflation goal by asserting another principle, saying that an explicit inflation goal "helps keep longer-term inflation expectations firmly anchored," which would "enhance the Committee's ability to promote maximum employment in the face of significant economic disturbances." The announced 2 percent inflation goal was stunning, coming as it did after seventeen years of discussion whether to adopt an explicit inflation objective beginning with two full-fledged debates in the FOMC on inflation targeting in 1995 and 1996.[2]

The statement yields internal and external benefits. It provides an agreed on framework within which internal monetary policy deliberations can be conducted more productively. And it serves notice to Congress and the public of the FOMC's intention to discipline its actions to stimulate employment in the short run against a commitment to target 2 percent inflation on average over time.

The FOMC statement of principles is a combination mission statement and strategic plan for monetary policy that resembles documents drawn up routinely in organizations to provide unity of purpose based on plausible principles and desirable long-run objectives. In viewing it as a stand-alone document, however, one might be forgiven for being skeptical about the relevance of the statement in practice. Governor Tarullo abstained from voting for the FOMC statement "because he questioned the ultimate usefulness of the statement in promoting better communication of the Committee's policy strategy."[3]

In fact, the FOMC statement of principles is much more than that because its roots lie in the mistakes and successes of past Fed policy. The full power of the FOMC statement, the degree to which the FOMC ought to commit to its principles, is rooted in historical Fed experience. Monetary history matters because appreciating the historical reasons for the FOMC's principles is the best and perhaps the only way to perpetuate them within the Fed itself with the support of the public, and eventually with Congressional oversight of Fed monetary policy. Only then can the

---

[2] For the two debates on inflation targeting, see FOMC Transcripts, January 31–February 1, 1995 and July 2–3, 1996.
[3] Minutes of the FOMC Meeting of January 24, 2012, p. 8.

FOMC's policy principles gain the status from which they would derive their ultimate effectiveness.

The statement recalls, in turn, experiences that led the Fed to (1) embrace transparency, (2) accept responsibility for inflation, and (3) anchor inflation expectations against inflation scares – all to maximize the effectiveness of monetary policy for the stabilization of both employment and inflation.

The FOMC's statement of principles also serves as an agreed on basis – grounded in an appreciation of the Fed's own history – upon which the conduct of monetary policy can be improved in the future. In this regard the paper concludes by proposing two directions in which current policy should be modified productively according to the FOMC's own principles to improve monetary policy practice. First, the FOMC must credibly incorporate the 2 percent inflation goal into its policy statements. Second, the Fed should distinguish monetary policy (narrowly defined) from credit policy in its balance sheet operations in the interest of transparency and accountability.

TRANSPARENCY

One dimension of Fed transparency involves the disclosure of the deliberative process by which the FOMC arrives at its decisions. The other involves the policy statements released immediately after each FOMC meeting describing the Fed's operational policy actions and intentions.

The Deliberative Process

The FOMC has kept a record of its deliberations ever since it was established in 1936. Initially, the record took the form of "Memoranda of Discussion," edited narratives of points made by named speakers at FOMC meetings. The FOMC did not release the Memoranda until 1970, after Fed monetary policy came to be suspected of increasing the volatility of inflation and unemployment. The Memoranda were all released subsequently, and current Memoranda were to be released with a five-year lag. However, the FOMC discontinued the preparation of the Memoranda in March 1976 in response to a Freedom of Information Act (FOIA) request, and continued to do so after winning the right in federal court to keep its deliberative process closed.

The public demand for Fed transparency grew as the Great Inflation worsened both inflation and unemployment, especially after the Volcker Fed grabbed the headlines in the early 1980s to bring inflation down at the cost of the most severe recession in the United States since the 1930s. Finally, in 1992 during the so-called jobless recovery from the 1990–1991 Gulf War recession, Henry Gonzales, Chairman of the House Banking Committee, led a campaign to force the FOMC to make public its deliberations. After a series of Congressional hearings that featured contentious questioning of Fed officials, Gonzales succeeded in getting the Fed to admit the existence of nearly a complete set of verbatim written transcripts of FOMC meetings since 1976. Increasingly, the Fed appeared in an unfavorable light with regard to its disclosure policy. Without any explicit guarantee from Congress to protect its deliberations from immediate release, the FOMC announced in 1995 that it would restart release of a record of FOMC meetings as lightly edited Transcripts with a five-year lag. The FOMC eventually released Transcripts for all its meetings going back to 1976. An equilibrium was achieved in which the Fed recognized the principle of transparency for its deliberative process and Congress has respected the Fed's right to delay that transparency for five years.

Statement of Policy Actions

Events in early 1994 encouraged the FOMC to become more transparent about its policy actions. The Fed had a long history of hiding its management of short-term interest rates. The Fed had for decades and was still in early 1994 more comfortable speaking of the stance of current policy in terms of "pressure on reserve positions" rather than its intentions for short-term interest rates such as the federal funds rate. The FOMC released its policy stance only after the subsequent FOMC meeting when the announced policy stance was superseded by the subsequent decision. The public was generally unaware of the Fed's management of short-term interest rates.

Traditionally, when the Fed wished to get the public's attention for an aggressive monetary policy action, the Fed would move the discount rate with the funds rate. Such would be needed when the Fed wished to act decisively against rising inflation and inflation expectations or to act forcefully against a depreciating dollar on the foreign exchange market. On the other hand, when the Fed wished to tighten interest rate policy quietly it would raise the federal funds rate without raising the discount rate. Starting in February 1994 the FOMC would take the federal funds rate from 3 percent to 6 percent by early 1995 to preempt rising inflation. The situation in February 1994 called for a quiet policy action because the Fed acted before the fact to preempt rising inflation. "Sounding the gong" with a discount rate action would have been counterproductive by signaling a degree of Fed concern about rising inflation that would frighten markets needlessly.

A quiet federal funds rate action designed not to make headlines gets widespread recognition by the public only gradually, giving an advantage to professional Fed watchers that pick it up immediately. In 1994, such favoritism was no longer tenable. Chairman Greenspan asked that the FOMC break with tradition and for the first time announce its federal funds rate target changes immediately after the February FOMC meeting. From then on the Fed took full responsibility for the level of short-term interest rates through the public management of the federal funds rate. And federal funds rate policy actions have been front page news ever since.

Other factors contributed to the Fed's talking openly about interest rate policy in 1994. Academics had begun to describe Fed monetary policy as "interest rate policy," and an academic literature had developed indicating that communication could enhance the effectiveness of interest rate policy. Moreover, the Fed was inclined to be more open about interest rate policy because the Volcker Fed and the Greenspan Fed had finally put in place a monetary policy strategy based on a priority for price stability within which the Fed could talk systematically and productively about its interest rate policy. Thereafter, interest rates would be increased as in 1994 not to create a recession to contain rising inflation, but to preempt rising inflation to sustain low unemployment.

RESPONSIBILITY FOR INFLATION

There is no better way to appreciate why the Fed has made low inflation a priority than by recalling the arguments voiced in the FOMC by Chairman Volcker in the late 1970s and early 1980s urging the Fed to take responsibility for inflation and bring it down.

At the April 1979 FOMC meeting when he was still president of the Federal Reserve Bank of New York, Volcker expressed his view that inflation had become the Fed's number one problem:

[Inflation] clearly remains our problem. In any longer-range or indeed shorter-range perspective, the inflationary momentum has been increasing. In terms of economic stability in the future that is what is likely to give us the most problems and create the biggest recession. And the difficulty in getting out of a recession, if we succeed, is that it conveys an impression that we are not dealing with inflation.... We talk about gradually decelerating the rate of inflation over a series of years. In fact, it has been accelerating over a series of years and hasn't yet shown any signs of reversing. (FOMC Transcript, April 17, 1979, p. 6)

Volcker laid out his overall thinking on monetary policy at the August 14, 1979 FOMC meeting, shortly after becoming Fed chairman:

When I look at the past year or two I am impressed myself by an intangible: I think that people are acting on that expectations [of continued high inflation] much more firmly than they used to ... [and] it does produce, potentially, and actually, para-doxical reactions to policy ... I think we are in something of a box – a box that says that the ordinary response one expects to easing actions may not work ... They won't work if they're interpreted as inflationary; and much of the stimulus will come out in prices rather than activity. (FOMC Transcript, August 14, 1979, p. 21)

After grabbing the headlines with a high-profile aggressive increase in the federal funds rate following the secret October 6, 1979 FOMC meeting, the FOMC came under pressure to put its interest rate increases on hold in January and February 1980 as evidence accumulated of a looming recession. Even as inflation continued to rise and long-term government bond rates reflected an increase in inflation expectations, Volcker argued at the March 18 FOMC meeting that the Fed had little room to maneuver:

What stands out to me is that we haven't any room to grow here, given the declines in productivity and other pressures on the economy. And if we tried to stimulate growth very much, we really would have no chance of dealing with the inflation psychology; we'd in fact face a blow-off on the inflation side if we don't already have a blow-off. (FOMC Transcripts, March 18, 1980, p. 35)

On the strength of this argument, Volcker led the FOMC to push the federal funds rate up by 3 percentage points to 19 percent by early April. Unfortunately, the credit control program then enacted by Congress and the Carter Administration in March precipitated a sharp contraction to which the Fed responded by cutting the federal funds rate beginning in April to 9 percent in July.

The recession beginning in January 1980 ended according to the National Bureau of Economic Research (NBER) in July with the sharp reduction in interest rates and the lifting of credit controls. Inflation continued to run in the 10 percent range all year as the economy recovered sharply, and the Volcker Fed took the federal funds rate up steadily from 9 percent in July to nearly 19 percent in December, 6 percentage points of that increase coming in November and December after the election of Ronald Reagan.

At the February 1981 FOMC meeting Volcker recognized that the Fed's high interest rate policy likely would renew recession:

There is a general question, which I guess is the most important question, of how serious we are in dealing with inflation. I got a little feeling, as I listened to the conversation, that we're like everybody else in the world on that: Everybody likes to get rid of inflation but when one comes up to actions that might actually do something about inflation, implicitly or explicitly, one says: "Well, inflation isn't that bad compared to the alternatives." We see the risks of the alternative of a sour economy and an outright recession this year. So, maybe there's a little tendency to shrink back on what we want to do on the inflation side. I don't want to shrink back very far; that is my general bias for all the reasons we have stated in our rhetoric but don't always carry through on. (FOMC Transcript, February 2–3, 1981, p. 129)

Volcker was given an opening by the public's having come to regard inflation as "public enemy number one," and the Volcker Fed continued its 19 percent federal funds rate, a 9 percent real funds rate given that inflation was running around 10 percent. At the July FOMC meeting another recession appeared imminent, but Volcker urged the FOMC to stay with tight monetary policy against inflation:

[Our] job is in assessing where the risks lie ... I haven't much doubt in my mind that it's appropriate ... to take the risk of more softness in the economy in the short run than one might ideally like in order to capitalize on the anti-inflationary momentum ... That is much more likely to give a more satisfactory economic as well as inflationary outlook over a period of time as compared to the opposite scenario of heading off ... sluggishness or even a downturn at the expense of rapidly getting back into the kind of situation we were in last fall where we had some retreat on inflation psychology ... Then we would look forward to another prolonged period of high interest rates an strain and face the same dilemmas over and over again. (FOMC Transcripts, July 6–7, 1981, p. 36)

This is the moment when the Volcker Fed determined to proceed with the disinflation that would eventually drive unemployment up to 11 percent before the recession ended in November 1982. Volcker refused to continue the stop–go policy that had characterized Fed monetary policymaking since the 1960s, and was repeated again in 1980. He knew that stop–go not only failed to keep inflation from rising, but also produced rising unemployment with each policy cycle, as the Fed pursued increasingly restrictive interest rate actions to contain inflation. Volcker was vindicated: the disinflation brought both inflation and unemployment down and yielded two long business expansions punctuated by two mild recessions in 1990–1991 and 2001.

ANCHORING INFLATION EXPECTATIONS AGAINST INFLATION SCARES

The FOMC asserted in its January 2012 statement the important principle that an explicit inflation goal "helps keep longer-term inflation expectations firmly anchored," which "enhance[s] the Committee's ability to promote maximum employment in the face of significant economic disturbances." The Fed came to appreciate the importance of this operational imperative when inflation expectations became volatile during the Great Inflation and remained surprisingly so in the 1980s even as the Volcker Fed worked to bring inflation down.

Goodfriend and King (2005), studying FOMC transcripts then recently released to the public, found that:

... [U]nder Volcker, the FOMC recognized that inflationary expectations were imbedded in long-term interest rates; that volatile expectations about future inflation made long rates highly sensitive to macroeconomic events including policy actions; that imperfect credibility about future monetary policy made long-term rates stubborn in the face of policy actions; and that the management of inflation expectations was a crucial, but very difficult, part of the FOMC's job. This is a remarkably modern set of viewpoints, which many contemporary observers of the FOMC, ourselves included, did not suspect at the time. Such an understanding, however, did not make the job of taming inflation any easier or that of consistently pursuing anti-inflation policy in the face of a weakening real economy less difficult for members of the FOMC, or less costly for the economy. (Goodfriend and King 2005, p. 997)

The remainder of this section recalls five "inflation scare" episodes since the early 1980s in which sharply rising long-term inflation expectations were reflected in sharply rising government bond rates. These inflation-scare experiences are the historical basis for the priority that the FOMC accords in its January 2012 statement of principles to anchoring long-term inflation expectations.

December 1979 to February 1980

Having moved the federal funds rate up sharply from 11.5 percent in September to nearly 14 percent in early January, the FOMC paused in its aggressive tightening as it sensed a turn to recession. But with the federal funds rate held steady, the long-term government bond rate rose by 2 percentage points. In his briefing at the February 4–5, 1980 FOMC meeting Peter Sternlight, Manager for Domestic Operations of the System Open Market Account, reported that long bond rates rose by around 1 percentage point in the intermeeting period even as the funds rate fell slightly,

... reflecting ... a weakening confidence that the long-term inflation problem can be handled successfully ... [He added that] there is also a feeling that the System has relaxed its firm resolve of last October to exercise restraint ... the particularly severe adjustment at the long end seems to reflect deep discouragement about prospects for dealing successfully with inflation. (FOMC Transcripts, February 4–5, 1980, pp. 3–4)

The shocking inflation scare left the Fed no "room for maneuver," as Volcker put it in his aforementioned remarks. Attention to the weakening economy produced a counterproductive jump in long-term interest rates. The Fed had lost the flexibility to address economic weakness and instead was forced to tighten interest rates aggressively in March 1980 to contain inflation expectations. The unhinging of inflation expectations was a "nightmare scenario" for monetary policy.

January 1981 to October 1981

Even as the Fed established its highly restrictive 19 percent federal funds rate in the first half of 1981, long-term Treasury rates moved 3 percentage points higher during the year, reflecting rising inflation expectations. Inflation expectations had become an important constraint on policy, as

Volcker recognized. Governor Schultz put it bluntly at the March 1981 FOMC meeting, saying, "if we were to attempt to ease, it's pretty clear that everybody would think we had let the inflationary cat out of the bag. And it seems to me that interest rates would be even higher under those circumstances" (FOMC Transcripts, March 31, 1981, p. 29). The 1981 inflation scare left the Fed with little choice but to follow through with disinflation. As Goodfriend and King put it, "[t]he second great inflation scare was pivotal because it convinced the Fed that the cost of a deliberate disinflation in 1981–1982 was acceptable in light of the recurring recessions that would be needed to deal with inflation scares in the future" (Goodfriend and King 2005, p. 1001).

May 1983 to June 1984

Inflation settled in the 4 percent range in 1983 after the Fed cut the federal funds rate sharply in mid-1982 to bring the disinflation to an end. The Fed held the federal funds rate in the 8 percent to 9 percent range in the first half of 1983 as the long bond rates fell to 10 percent. With the economy expanding at a 6 percent annual rate in 1983, a third inflation scare took the long bond rate from 10.5 percent in May 1983 to 13.5 percent in June 1984. Incredibly, the 1984 peak was only about a percentage point short of its peak in 1981 even though inflation was 5 percentage points lower.

The Volcker Fed reacted aggressively by raising the federal funds rate to 11.5 percent by August 1984 so that the yield curve remained nearly flat. The Fed brought down the federal funds rate after the long bond rate retreated in June 1984, indicating that the inflation scare had been contained. The Volcker Fed slowed real gross domestic product (GDP) growth to 4 percent in 1984 and held the line on inflation at 4 percent. For the first time in its history the FOMC preempted rising inflation without precipitating a recession. The enormous 6 percentage point plunge in long bond rates to 7 percent that followed from summer 1984 to spring 1986 reflected the full acquisition by the Fed of credibility for 4 percent trend inflation.

March 1987 to October 1987

A fourth inflation scare under Volcker's leadership of the Fed elevated the long bond rate by 2 percentage points from around 7.5 percent in March to around 9.5 percent in October of 1987. Parallel increases in German and Japanese bond rates reflected inflation scares overseas resulting from concerns of a potential international easing of monetary policy. The 1987 inflation scare in the United States coincided with news that Volcker would be leaving the Fed, and probably reflected to some degree doubt that Volcker's successor would sustain low inflation. The Bernanke Fed may have had the succession problem in mind when announcing its 2 percent inflation goal in January 2012.

October 1993 to November 1994

The last inflation scare to date lifted long bond rates by about 2.5 percentage points from 5.8 percent in October 1993 to 8.2 percent in November 1994. The Greenspan Fed responded aggressively by raising the federal funds rate during 1994 from 3 percent to 6 percent, holding the line on inflation at 3 percent, again with little increase in unemployment. The 1994 policy actions, like the 1983–1984 actions, showed once more that well-timed, preemptive interest rate policy actions can confront an inflation scare without precipitating a recession. By anchoring inflation expectations and inflation securely in 1994, the Greenspan Fed laid the groundwork for the long boom of the late 1990s, which saw 4 percent real GDP growth and a 4 percent unemployment rate.

When a recession arrived in 2001, the fact that inflation and inflation expectations were well anchored enabled the Fed to cut the federal funds rate aggressively from 6.5 percent to 1.75 percent to cushion the fall in aggregate demand and employment. The recession from March to November 2001 was short and mild, and might not have been designated a recession at all if not for the contraction caused by the September 2001 terrorist attacks. Thus, the Fed came to appreciate the power that firmly anchored inflation and inflation expectations gives monetary policy to act flexibly and aggressively against adverse shocks to unemployment.

To sum up, the 1994 preemptive interest rate action against inflation was important because it confirmed that (1) the Fed could perpetuate low inflation by raising interest rates without creating a recession, (2) anchoring inflation expectations firmly would enable unemployment to fall further than previously realized, and (3) firmly anchored inflation expectations enhanced the effectiveness of monetary policy against unemployment when a recession arrived. The success of the 1994 preemptive actions against inflation paved the way for the Fed to accept operational responsibility for 2 percent inflation in January 2012.

THE FED MUST CREDIBLY INCORPORATE THE 2 PERCENT INFLATION GOAL INTO ITS POLICY STATEMENTS

The January 2012 FOMC statement of principles recognizes that the "maximum level of employment is largely determined by nonmonetary factors ..." which "may change over time and may not be directly measurable." Importantly, when the objectives for employment and inflation are not complementary, the FOMC says that "it follows a balanced approach to promoting them, taking into account the magnitude of the deviations and the potentially different time horizons over which employment and inflation are projected to return to levels judged consistent with its mandate."

This is all well and good. But what have the FOMC's words meant in practice? We found out initially on September 13, 2012 when, in addition to its intention to keep interest rates near zero for three more years, the FOMC announced that it would begin to add $40 billion of reserves to the banking system every month by acquiring agency mortgage-backed securities until the labor market improved substantially. To reinforce its policy accommodation, the FOMC added that "a highly accommodative stance of monetary policy will remain appropriate for a considerable time after the economic recovery strengthens."

Inflation appears as an afterthought in the September 13 policy statement. The Fed appears willing to tolerate higher inflation in an effort to facilitate a reduction in unemployment with monetary policy. The FOMC expected "that inflation over the medium term likely would run at or below its 2 percent objective." But what if inflation failed to follow the Fed's script? All the FOMC said in its September 13 statement was that it intends to continue its highly accommodative policy actions "in a context of price stability." Incredibly, the FOMC appeared to walk away from its explicit 2 percent inflation goal only months after first adopting it in January 2012. Failure to employ the 2 percent longer run inflation goal only months after its announcement undermined its credibility and defeated its professed purpose of anchoring inflation expectations to improve the flexibility of monetary policy to act against unemployment.

The market was left to wonder how much inflation the FOMC would accept and for how long given open-ended reserve creation, an open-ended tolerance range for inflation, and an open-ended horizon over which a departure from 2 percent inflation would be tolerated. Might not that lack of clarity destabilize inflation expectations and facilitate the uncertainty so detrimental for employment?

The FOMC moved to address the problem following its December 12 meeting with a surprise announcement of numerical thresholds for inflation and the unemployment rate in the policy statement. The FOMC indicated that it "anticipates that this exceptionally low range for the federal funds rate will be appropriate *at least as long* (italics added) as the unemployment rate remains above 6.5 percent, inflation between one and two years ahead is projected to be no more than a half percentage point above the Committee's 2 percent longer-run goal, and longer-term inflation expectations continue to be well anchored."

The FOMC took a step in the right direction by incorporating the 2 percent inflation goal in its policy statement together with a ½ percentage point tolerance range beyond which the FOMC would not wish to see inflation rise. Unfortunately, the FOMC took two steps backward by emphasizing thresholds for raising the federal funds rate that make it unlikely to exit the zero bound in time to preempt rising inflation.

The 6.5 percent unemployment rate threshold is below even the 7 percent that the market had been expecting. The FOMC indicated that it might accept an even lower unemployment rate before it would raise the funds rate appreciably. Moreover, changes in the inflation rate have become difficult to forecast since the Volcker disinflation in the 1980s. Changes in the inflation rate could be forecast earlier mainly because the Fed's stop–go policymaking during the Great Inflation pushed inflation around as it first targeted low unemployment until inflation rose, and then pushed unemployment higher until inflation fell.

In principle, the long-term bond rate could signal rising inflation expectations in time for the FOMC to preempt rising inflation. But there is a problem here, too. The FOMC indicated in its December 12 statement that in addition to its intention to continue purchasing $40 billion of long-term mortgage-backed securities per month indefinitely, it will also "purchase longer-term Treasury securities after its program to extend the average maturity of its holdings of Treasury securities is completed at the end of the year, initially at a pace of $45 billion per month." At that rate, the Fed will expand its balance sheet from around $3 to $4 trillion in 2013. The problem is that by holding long bond rates down, the aggressive open-ended $85 billion monthly purchases of long-term Treasuries and mortgage-backed securities likely will blunt or delay the inflation scare in long bond rates that would otherwise help the Fed to preempt rising inflation without a recession as it did in 1984–1985 and again in 1994.

If the Fed inadvertently pursues highly accommodative monetary policy until inflation becomes a public concern, then pricing decisions will already embody rising inflation expectations. And the Fed may need to precipitate a recession with high interest rates to bring inflation and inflation expectations back down, as it had to do repeatedly during the Great Inflation. Rather than risk that fate, the FOMC should discontinue its expansive open market bond purchases to mitigate the inflation risk, and let long bond rates freely reflect inflation concerns.

THE FED SHOULD DISTINGUISH MONETARY POLICY (NARROWLY DEFINED) FROM CREDIT POLICY IN ITS BALANCE SHEET OPERATIONS FOR THE PURPOSE OF TRANSPARENCY AND ACCOUNTABILITY

All Fed balance sheet operations are commonly referred to as monetary policy. Such terminology is misleading. It ignores the fact that monetary policy (narrowly defined) and credit policy work in very different ways, and in particular, with different fiscal policy implications. It is essential to appreciate the different channels through which the two balance sheet initiatives act to stabilize markets for the purposes of transparency and accountability.

Monetary policy (narrowly defined) involves open market operations that expand or contract high-powered money (currency or bank reserves) by buying or selling Treasury securities. Until the credit turmoil of 2007–2009 the Fed satisfied virtually all of its asset acquisition needs in support of monetary policy by confining its purchases to Treasury securities, an acquisition policy known as "Treasuries only," to avoid carrying credit risk on its balance sheet.

In the past, when the Fed could not pay interest on reserves, monetary policy worked by varying the supply of bank reserves via purchases or sales of Treasuries in order to manage short-term interest rates. In the future, monetary policy via Treasuries only could satiate the demand for bank reserves so that short-term market interest could be managed by varying interest paid on reserves. At the zero interest bound, open market operations in short-term Treasuries have little effect, and monetary policy stimulus is delivered by taking interest rate risk onto the Fed balance sheet via the purchase of long-term Treasuries.

From a fiscal policy perspective, monetary policy saves the government interest that it otherwise would pay on outstanding Treasuries. The central bank returns to the Treasury all the interest it receives on the Treasuries that it buys, after expenses including interest on reserves. The fiscal authorities are then free to allocate the interest savings due to monetary policy as they see fit. Any interest rate risk taken onto the Fed balance sheet by acquiring long Treasuries with reserves or the proceeds from the sale of short Treasuries is effectively borne by the fiscal authorities via the substitution of short interest payments on reserves or short Treasuries for interest that would otherwise be paid by the fiscal authorities on long Treasuries.

Fed credit policy is not monetary policy because it does not alter the stock of high-powered money. Credit policy involves Fed lending to particular borrowers, perhaps by acquiring non-Treasury securities through proceeds from the sale of Treasuries. Fed credit policy is really debt-financed fiscal policy. Why? When the Fed sells Treasuries to finance the acquisition of non-Treasury assets such as mortgage-backed securities, the result is just as if the Treasury financed the purchase by borrowing from the public. The fiscal authorities receive interest on the credit assets acquired by the Fed instead of interest on the Treasuries sold by the Fed to finance the credit initiative. In effect, credit policy commits future taxes to back loans or non-Treasury security purchases via the sale of Treasuries. Thus, credit policy involves the fiscal allocation of public funds in a way that monetary policy does not.

The trillion dollars of bank reserves that currently finances mortgage-backed securities on the Fed balance sheet reflects a combination monetary and credit policy. Credit initiatives financed initially by bank reserves must be refinanced eventually with sales of Treasuries from the Fed's portfolio (if available). Otherwise, the Fed eventually will have to pay a market interest rate on the reserves created to finance its credit initiatives.

Fed credit policy works by interposing the government between private borrowers and lenders and exploiting the government's creditworthiness to lower private borrowing costs and facilitate credit flows to favored borrowers. Unlike monetary policy via Treasuries only, which operates on interest rates in general without favoring anyone, credit policy necessarily favors one borrower or one sector of the economy over another. Moreover, all loans and financial securities other than U.S. Treasuries (and those rare securities also granted "full faith and credit" backing by Congress) involve the Fed in controversial and potentially costly decisions regarding credit allocation.

Thus, we see that monetary policy and credit policy work to stabilize markets through very different channels with very different fiscal policy implications. Therefore, for the purposes of transparency and accountability espoused in the January 2012 FOMC statement of principles, the Fed should discuss its balance sheet operations in terms of monetary policy (narrowly defined), or credit policy, or perhaps a combination of monetary policy and credit policy.

REFERENCES

Atkeson, A., and L. E. Ohanian. (2001). "Are Phillips Curves Useful for Forecasting Inflation?" *Federal Reserve Bank of Minneapolis Quarterly Review* (Winter):2–11.
Board of Governors of the Federal Reserve System. (2012). Minutes of the Federal Open Market Committee, Meeting of January 24.
Federal Open Market Committee. (1979–1981). *Transcripts*, Board of Governors of the Federal Reserve System.
Friedman, M. (1964). "Statement and Testimony (March 3, 1964), Statement before the US Congress, House of Representatives, Committee on Banking and Currency." In US Congress House of Representatives, Committee on Banking and Currency (ed), *The Federal Reserve System after Fifty Years*, pp. 1133–1178. Washington, DC: U.S. Government Printing Office.
Goodfriend, M. (1986). "Monetary Mystique: Secrecy and Central Banking." *Journal of Monetary Economics* 17(1):63–92.
    (1991). "Interest Rates and the Conduct of Monetary Policy." In A. Meltzer and C. I. Plosser (eds), *Carnegie Rochester Conference Series on Public Policy*, Vol. 34 (Spring), pp. 7–30.
    (2005). "Inflation Targeting in the United States?" In Ben S. Bernanke and Michael Woodford (eds), *The Inflation Targeting Debate*, pp. 311–37.Cambridge, MA: National Bureau of Economic Research.
    (2010). "Monetary Policy, Credit Policy, and Interest on Reserves Policy in the Economic Recovery." Testimony before the Committee on Financial Services U.S. House of Representatives, March 25.

(2011). "Central Banking in the Credit Turmoil: An Assessment of Federal Reserve Practice." *Journal of Monetary Economics* (58, January):1–12.

(2012). "The Elusive Promise of Independent Central Banking." *Monetary and Economic Studies*, Vol. 30, November, pp. 39–54. Tokyo: Bank of Japan.

Goodfriend, M., and R. G. King. (2005). "The Incredible Volcker Disinflation." *Journal of Monetary Economics* 52(5):981–1015.

(2013). "The Great Inflation Drift." In M. Bordo and A. Orphanides (eds), *The Great Inflation: The Rebirth of Modern Central Banking*, pp. 181–209. Chicago: University of Chicago Press.

Hetzel, R. (2008). *The Monetary Policy of the Federal Reserve: A History.* New York: Cambridge University Press.

Lindsey, D. E. (2003). *A Modern History of FOMC Communication: 1975–2002*, Board of Governors of the Federal Reserve System.

Meltzer, A. H. (2003, 2009). *A History of the Federal Reserve*, Vols. 1, 2a, and 2b. Chicago: University of Chicago Press.

Romer, C., and D. Romer. (1989). "Does Monetary Policy Matter? A New Test in the Spirit of Friedman and Schwartz." In Olivier J. Blanchard and Stanley Fisher (eds), *NBER Macroeconomics Annual*, pp. 121–170. Cambridge, MA: National Bureau of Economic Research.

Schreft, S. L. (1990). "Credit Controls: 1980." *Federal Reserve Bank of Richmond Economic Review* 76(6):25–55.

Stock, J. W., and M. Watson. (2007). "Why Has Inflation Become Harder to Forecast?" *Journal of Money, Credit, and Banking* 29(1 Suppl): 3–33.

(2008). "Phillips Curve Inflation Forecasts." Paper presented at Federal Reserve Bank of Boston Conference, May. NBER Working Paper 14322, September.

Taylor, J. (1979). "Estimation and Control of a Macroeconomic Model with Rational Expectations." *Econometrica* 47(5):1267–1286.

Woodford, M. (2005). "Central Bank Communication and Policy Effectiveness." In Federal Reserve Bank of Kansas City (ed), *The Greenspan Era: Lessons for the Future*, pp. 399–474. Kansas City: Federal Reserve Bank of Kansas City.

3

How and Why the Fed Must Change in Its Second Century

Allan H. Meltzer

EVOLUTION AT THE FEDERAL RESERVE

The 1913 Federal Reserve Act created an institution with very limited powers. President Wilson's compromise resolved the main political obstacle to passing the act. The Reserve banks became semiautonomous, controlled by their managements, with boards of directors empowered to reject portfolio decisions. The Board in Washington had (undefined) supervisory responsibility.

The United States was on the gold standard, limiting Federal Reserve actions to the requirements of that rule. In addition, the new system authorized Reserve banks to discount commercial paper, banker's acceptances, and the like. The discounting operation was always at the initiative of the borrower. Also, the act prohibited any direct purchases of Treasury debt.

All of these restrictions ended long ago. The gold standard limped to an end in the 1930s. Discounting became an unimportant part of the Federal Reserve's activities, and a limited volume of direct loans to the Treasury replaced the prohibition. Far more important, reliance on open market operations circumvented the prohibition on direct purchases of Treasuries. Currently, and for many years, the Federal Reserve has bought or sold unlimited amounts of Treasury securities in the market at the time of the offering or at any subsequent time.

This transformation occurred in steps, many of them in response to major crises especially the Great Depression, the Great Inflation, and the current prolonged recession. The Reserve banks won the initial struggle for control. Under the leadership of Benjamin Strong, Governor of the New York bank, they dominated policy decisions in the 1920s until Strong's retirement in 1928. The Board did not have a vote at meetings of the Federal Open Market Committee (FOMC). Although Board members attended at times, they were not committee members.

Within months of Strong's departure, Board members gained influence. Later, the Banking Acts of 1933 and especially 1935 shifted power toward the Board by giving the Board a majority on the new FOMC and eliminating the power of Reserve bank directors to decide on their bank's participation in open market purchases or sales.

During the Great Inflation, Congress amended the Federal Reserve Act by adding the so-called dual mandate. After the recent housing and financial crisis of 2007–2009, Congress approved the Dodd–Frank bill containing hundreds of regulations on banks. The act further reduced the much diminished role of Reserve bank directors.

Among the many new regulations is the use of Federal Reserve earnings to allocate credit toward consumers. The Fed had previously resisted credit allocation, but it would henceforth finance it out of its earnings without any right to decide on the allocation. The right is reserved to the director of the consumer agency who does not report to the chairman or anyone else. And although the earnings that the director allocates would otherwise return to the Treasury as receipts, Congress does not vote on the allocation.

This change is a startling reduction in the mandated independence of the Federal Reserve. Federal Reserve independence has often been compromised but never by act of Congress. Earlier examples, discussed in my *History of the Federal Reserve* (2003, 2009), include financing wartime deficits, acceding to pressure from Secretary Morgenthau in the 1930s, maintaining pegged interest rates after World War II until the 1951 Accord; financing 1960s and 1970s budget deficits; and recent decisions to purchase mortgage-backed securities (a fiscal operation) and to manage the debt.

Once Congress understood the importance of monetary expansion for employment, it took extraordinary effort and a strong chairman to remain independent. Paul Volcker was an independent chairman. Alan Greenspan also remained relatively independent. Others were willing to compromise. The current Federal Reserve has engaged in such nonmonetary functions as fiscal policy, debt management, and credit allocation.

To sum up the evolution, I conclude that the Federal Reserve evolved under pressure of events and political responses to crises from an independent agency with constrained powers to become the world's major central bank with nearly unrestricted ability to expand. It retains a vestige of its independence, but it pays the price of much reduced independence for its greatly expanded authority. Within the system, power has shifted from the Reserve banks to the Board of Governors, and the Reserve bank directors have a greatly diminished role.

From the start of the system, the popular view saw the Reserve banks as representatives of business and the Board as reflecting political influence. Increased power of the Board shows increased political influence that rose with diminished independence. No one familiar with political Washington should be surprised to find that increasing Board power greatly increased political influence and substantially reduced independence. Looking across the Atlantic, we find that the tightly constrained European Central Bank according to its original charter has become much more responsive to political pressure also.

WHY INDEPENDENCE DECLINED

The principal reason for central bank independence is to separate money creation from the financing of government. It has long been understood that financing government by creating money causes inflation. Enforcing and maintaining independence is often difficult. Wartime is one example. Society's main interest is winning the war, so concern about inflation diminishes. Inflation rose during most wars followed by deflation after peace returned.

After World War II, governments proposed systematic monetary actions to manage unemployment and economic activity. They agreed also to maintain fixed but adjustable exchange rates. When the United States' domestic policy came into conflict with its obligations to reduce balance of payments deficits (or a declining surplus), policy actions supported employment. In the 1960s, as inflation rose, the Kennedy and Johnson administrations adopted controls to manage the payments problem temporarily. The Federal Reserve considered the balance-of-payments to be a Treasury problem. It cooperated with the administration by lending money to the Treasury to finance so-called swap arrangements that financed U.S. borrowing of foreign exchange. These direct loans to the Treasury's Exchange Stabilization Fund were called "warehousing" to hide the violation of direct lending to the Treasury. Bordo, Humpage, and Schwartz (2011) has a full account of the swap operations. (See also Meltzer 2003.)

The fixed exchange rate system ended in 1971 when President Nixon stopped further gold sales. Attempts to revive the system failed; in 1973 these efforts ended. The Federal Reserve continued to intervene in the exchange market at times. The Treasury requested some of the intervention.

One of the major mistakes made by the Federal Reserve in the 1960s became known as policy coordination. The main idea was to keep interest rates from rising during periods of fiscal expansion. Coordinating policy actions meant that the Federal Reserve financed large parts of a fiscal deficit by issuing money. In principle, but not in practice, the Federal Reserve would raise interest rates when the Treasury ran a surplus to slow or stop inflation.

Two major flaws soon appeared. The Treasury did not achieve surpluses and did not coordinate with the Federal Reserve to reduce inflation. The Federal Reserve sacrificed its responsibility for an independent monetary policy. And it could not, or did not, prevent inflation from rising during the 1960s and 1970s. In part, Federal Reserve failures in the 1960s reflected Chairman Martin's belief that because the Federal Reserve was part of government, it should not refuse to finance large parts of a budget deficit that Congress approved and the president signed.

The policy failure ended in 1979–1980 when Paul Volcker, as Federal Reserve chairman, set out to reduce inflation. To succeed, he abandoned policy coordination, dismissed the Phillips Curve relating unemployment and inflation, reduced control of short-term market interest rates, announced the Federal Reserve's intention to control bank reserves and monetary aggregates, and adopted a medium-term strategy to reduce inflation. Like his predecessors, he had one main objective. Theirs was lower unemployment; his was to lower inflation.

Volcker rejected the idea that inflation rose as a trade-off for lower unemployment. He emphasized, correctly, that the two measures both rose in the 1970s and he predicted they would decline together under his policy. He was right. The anti-inflation policy that he managed reduced both inflation and unemployment in the 1980s.

Volcker gave many speeches and much testimony in Congress claiming that the way to lower unemployment was to lower inflation. This is the anti-Phillips curve policy. It worked very well from 1985 to about 2003. The current Federal Reserve restored the Phillips Curve, a repeat of the mistakes of the 1970s.

There is much more that can be said about Federal Reserve errors that are costly to the public. Let me turn instead to the periods of greatest success. In its 100-year history, there are only two periods in which the Federal Reserve achieved both relatively stable growth and low inflation. In both periods, the Federal Reserve followed a rule, not precisely but consistently.

The first period is 1923–1928, when the Fed was on a gold exchange standard and several major countries – Germany, Britain, and in 1928 France – restored a fixed gold price rule. Other countries joined also.

The Federal Reserve's commitment to the rule was not complete. The principal exception was that it would not inflate, so it sterilized most gold inflows. This led to the breakdown of the rule; countries losing gold had to deflate, but the principal countries receiving gold – France and the United States – chose to sterilize the inflow.

Britain was the main country required to deflate. France and the United States were the principal recipients. Nevertheless, when the rule was generally observed, from 1923 to 1928, the United States had growth, a mild recession in 1926, and low inflation.

The second rule-based period is 1985–2003, during which the economy had a long period of relatively stable growth, mild recessions, and low inflation. The dates are not known precisely. The rule is the Taylor (1993) rule or a variant that weights unemployment and the expected inflation rate. The choice of variables is the same as in the dual mandate that Congress adopted. Inflation has a large weight to ensure that inflation raises nominal interest rates.

Discretionary policy never produced comparable results. Its best period is probably 1953–1957 before the recession of the later year. I exclude wartime years from the comparison because the Federal Reserve's actions, like those taken by the other institutions, concentrated on actions that helped to finance the war.

Economic theory, following Kydland and Prescott's (1977) paper, shows that central banks must follow a rule to achieve an optimum outcome. The evidence from Federal Reserve history shows that evidence supports theory. Rules help the country to achieve economic stability; but we live in an uncertain world, so I must add that surprises and disappointments will occur under rules or rule-based policy. Of course, the same is true of discretionary policies.

The Federal Reserve sacrificed independence by engaging in fiscal policy actions, debt management, credit allocation, and by supplying hundreds of billions of dollars of bank reserves. I believe the only way to restore independence would be to adopt a rule that the Congress accepts. Then the Federal Reserve must make rule-based policy credible by following it. If events compel departure from its rule-based policy, the Federal reserve should announce the departure and offer an explanation for the departure.

THE FED'S PRINCIPAL ERRORS

Any organization that must repeatedly make judgments about future events will, at times, make errors. In an uncertain world, we expect errors of forecast and errors in the action based on those forecasts. In my history of the Fed, I compare quarterly forecast errors in real GDP and inflation to the data revisions. For the period I studied, the 1970s and 1980s, forecasting errors are substantially larger than data revisions (Meltzer 2009). For other years, I compared the Fed's forecast errors to forecasts by others. On average, the Fed forecast errors were about the same as those of others (Meltzer 1987).

In my 1987 presidential address to the Western Economic Association, I summarized errors reported by forecasters for quarterly values of real and nominal gross national product (GNP) growth rates and for inflation. Federal Reserve errors are not very different. Table 3.1 shows these data.

To compare these data to a benchmark, I report the mean growth rates of the variables for 1970–1985. Average real GNP growth rate was 2.7 percent, average inflation was 6.7 percent, and the growth rate of nominal GNP was 9.5 percent for 1967–1982 and 9.9 percent for 1970–1983.[1]

---

[1] The percentages are computed from data reported at the time. Subsequent data version may change the growth rates.

Table 3.1. Quarterly Root Mean Square Forecast Errors, United States Percent per Annum

Variable	Time Period	Range	Median or Actual	Source
Real GNP growth	1980/2–1985/1	3.1–4.4	3.8	McNees (1986)
	1970–1973		2.1	Lombra and Moran (1983)
	1970/4–1983/4	2.8–3.6	3.0	Zarnowitz (1986)
	1970/1–1984/4	4.4–5.4	4.7	Webb (1985)
Inflation	1980/2–1985/1	1.4–2.2	1.6	McNees (1986)
	1970/4–1983/4	2.0–2.6	2.2	Zarnowitz (1986)
	1970/1–1984/4	1.8–2.1	1.9	Webb (1985)
Nominal GNP growth	1967–1982	–	5.5	Federal Reserve
	1973–1982		6.2	
	1970/4–1983/4	3.5–4.3	3.8	Zarnowitz (1986)

Comparison of the data in the table to the average growth rates shows that the reported root mean square errors (RMSE) are a sizable fraction of the actual growth rates for real and nominal growth. Using twice the value of the RMSE as the range within which real GNP growth can fall during the quarter covers the range from deep recession to strong boom. As one example, the median RMSE reported by Zarnowitz for 1970 to 1983, 3 percent, exceeds the 2.4 percent average growth for the period. On average, forecasters do not distinguish between booms and recessions beginning in the same quarter.

The Federal Reserve history shows many examples of forecast errors leading to mistaken actions. When Congress in 1967 at last approved the tax surcharge that President Johnson had requested, the Federal Reserve and the administration forecast a recession. The Federal Reserve reduced interest rates. The temporary surcharge did not slow spending growth. Instead of falling as forecast, inflation rose.

From the mid-1970s to the early 1980s, the Federal Reserve inflation forecast was below actual inflation for sixteen consecutive quarters. The staff used a Phillips Curve to forecast inflation. There is considerable research showing that Phillips Curve forecasts of inflation are unreliable.[2]

---

[2] One reason is that the data Phillips used are mainly for the years in which Britain was on the gold standard. The gold standard restricted expected inflation.

When Paul Volcker became chairman of the Board of Governors, he told the staff that their inflation forecasts were inaccurate. He repeated the message publicly and in Congressional testimony. As chairman, Alan Greenspan told the staff that he did not find their inflation forecasts useful. Like Volcker, he explicitly rejected the Phillips Curve. Under chairman Bernanke, Phillips Curve forecasts have been restored.

Paul Volcker not only rejected use of the Phillips Curve, but he also developed and promoted what I call the anti-Phillips Curve. Unlike the staff approach relying on quarterly data, Volcker emphasized longer term responses. His approach, based on empirical observation, was that during the 1970s, inflation and real growth or the unemployment rate rose and fell together. There was no trade-off in the longer period. As early as 1979, shortly after announcing his new policy procedure of targeting reserve growth and allowing interest rates to be set in the market, he was asked in a television program what he would do when unemployment rose and how policy reduced inflation. His reply cited the co-movement for the 1970s when unemployment rates and inflation rates rose together. He predicted that they would fall together under his policy. They did. His prediction was correct.

One result of his successful policy of lowering the inflation and unemployment rates was widespread acceptance of his anti-Phillips Curve analysis: the way to get a low unemployment rate was to follow policies that yielded low inflation rates. Such policies encouraged investment and growth. Reliance on the Taylor rule to guide policy from the late 1980s to the early 2000s reinforced this good result.

Unfortunately, reliance on a policy rule to guide actions ended when officials and market participants incorrectly forecast deflation after 2003. Policy shifted to discretionary action that helped to finance a housing boom. By keeping interest rates low, the Federal Reserve financed much of the housing boom. Federal Reserve policy was not the main cause of the housing boom and collapse. Housing policy by both political parties endorsed mortgages requiring no down payment for buyers with no credit rating. Government agencies bought a large share of the risky mortgages and offered bankers and mortgage brokers large profits for supplying mortgages for the government mortgage companies.

Volcker knew that policy would not lower the inflation rate quickly. He adopted a longer term strategy. He did not ignore current data, but he also continued to act to achieve his longer-term goal.

When reading transcripts of open market meetings through 1986, I was surprised to find little attention or discussion of expectations of medium-term results of the actions decided at the meeting. No statements such as "if we take this action today, I expect growth and inflation to be in the following range next year" are found. Members see Board staff forecasts of future events made before policy action is selected. Most have their own staff forecasts. Rarely do the members explore differences. Members submit quarterly forecasts of future economic conditions, but these also do not appear to be influenced by the action taken at the meeting.

The result is that current events and market and administration or Congressional pressures drive decisions to focus heavily on near-term events over which monetary actions have little effect and too little on achieving medium-term stability with low inflation and relatively stable growth. As I have emphasized here and elsewhere, in the two periods when the Fed more or less followed rules, policy was more successful than under discretion. A main reason, I believe, is that following rules stabilizes policy actions by forcing more attention on achieving medium- and longer term outcomes based on the rule. The very successful Deutsche Bundesbank combined short-term market information and medium-term objectives by choosing a monetary growth rate to indicate that policy actions tightened or eased too much or too little to maintain medium-term price stability or low inflation.

Adopting and following a rule would induce policymakers to give more weight to medium- and longer term objectives. An explicit rule provides information to markets, investors, and consumers that they use to make their plans. In the absence of a rule markets are more volatile. They have less information about the path to be followed, so they interpret statements by the chairman and other members. The excess variability generated is costly and wasteful.

A problem closely related is the excessive attention given to short-term data. Standard economic theory distinguishes between temporary or transitory and permanent or persistent changes. To gain confidence that policy distinguishes between persistent and transitory events, policy actions must of necessity allow enough time to pass to avoid over-response to transitory changes. Many economic variables of interest are noisy. Real GDP growth is one example of particular interest.

The Federal Reserve responds to temporary changes in reported inflation rates by removing volatile changes in the prices of food and fuel. All such changes are not transitory, so this procedure is flawed. A better way to separate temporary price changes would use the procedures developed in Muth (1960).

Some Federal Reserve officials deny my claim that their actions overweight relevance of current and near-term data. It is true that the chairmen and many others talk about medium- or longer term objectives. Statements about future inflation, emphasizing determination to prevent it, are familiar. But statements differ from actions.

Minutes or transcripts during the period of rising inflation in the 1970s contain many statements about the importance of acting to reduce rising inflation. When unemployment rose, anti-inflation policy ended, replaced by actions to lower interest rates in response to higher unemployment. A main result was that both inflation and the unemployment rate rose. Market participants and the public learned that reducing unemployment had priority. Expected inflation did not decline as it had in 1966.

In the summer of 2010, many traders reported slowing growth, warning that the economy faced renewed recession and deflation. The Federal Reserve promptly responded by announcing an additional $600 billion of purchases of long-term securities. Within a few months, it became clear that the country did not face renewed recession and deflation. The forecast error cannot be explained by the additional stimulus. Stimulus had not started or been approved, and when adopted had little if any effect. More than $500 billion of the additional $600 billion of new reserves went to idle excess reserves.

Alarmed by reports of low job growth and a failure of unemployment rates to decline, in the summer of 2012 Chairman Bernanke and other members of the FOMC called for an additional stimulus. Initial reports of job growth for July and August 2012 showed 141,000 new jobs in July and 96,000 in August. These data heavily influenced a decision to begin a large-scale expansion of reserves to lower interest rates, especially mortgage rates.

Shortly after the Federal Reserve announced the stimulus, job growth data changed. The revisions added 86,000 jobs, 40,000 for July and 46,000 for August. No one can be certain that the revised numbers are correct. Muth's (1960) model does not ignore current data. To separate permanent from transitory changes, it applies weights based on the relative variance of permanent and transitory changes.

Higher future inflation is a likely cost of the Fed's overreaction to noisy employment data. Staff and officials dismiss this problem saying that they can raise interest rates sufficiently to stop inflation. This response is extremely misleading for several reasons. One reason is that banks have more than $1.5 billion of excess reserves, so they can ignore small changes in interest rates. Interest rates are lower than at any time in history, so small increases will not be sufficient. And larger changes will put pressure on the Federal Reserve. Members of Congress, the administration, business groups, labor unions, and many of the public will object to such changes, maintaining that that after a long recession and years of slow growth, the Federal Reserve should not permit a new recession.

Further, the U.S. Treasury debt held outside the government sector (including the Federal Reserve) reached more than $9 trillion at the end of June 2012, and it continues to rise rapidly. Average maturity is about five years, but 40 percent has less than two years to maturity. Each 1 percent increase in interest rates increases interest payments. Within two years, the budget deficit increases by at least $36 billion for each percentage point of interest rate increase, so a 3 percentage point rise in bond rates adds more than $100 billion to government spending. Using the average share held by foreigners, about one third, implies that the balance of payments deficit rises by almost $50 billion a year. This is a conservative estimate because it neglects guaranteed debt that adds to both deficits and privately issued debt partly owned by foreigners.

Congress and the administration have not agreed on policies to reduce the deficit. Adding an additional $100 billion per year raises additional doubt about the Obama administration's relatively optimistic projections that the budget deficit will remain between $500 billion and $1 trillion through 2015.

As time passes, as more outstanding debt reaches maturity, more low-interest debt is replaced at higher interest rates. I have assumed that inflation remains low, an assumption I regard as unlikely. Higher inflation adds additional interest cost.

In its 100-year history, the Federal Reserve never agreed on the model of the economy. I do not find much evidence that they try to reconcile differences about how the economy works. The Board staff has a model of the economy, but Reserve banks use different models. When members of the FOMC offer forecasts, the forecasts are based on different models often modified by judgments. I have not found any serious effort to reconcile differences or to explain their source. There is nothing that can properly be called the Federal Reserve forecast. In the past, the Federal Reserve used several different models or paradigms. It has a history of mistakes. At first, the Board relied on the real bills doctrine and the gold standard. Later, free reserves and tone and feel guided actions, then a simple Keynesian model with an unconstrained Phillips Curve that accepted a permanent trade-off of higher inflation for reduced unemployment rate. None of these guided actions to achieve low inflation and relatively stable output growth. Guidance based on the Taylor rule substantially improved performance.

Recently, the Board staff and principal members used a model based on Woodford's (2003) elegant modeling. This, too, is deficient. In the model, money and credit do not matter for monetary policy. And prices of assets are not part of the transmission mechanism. Only short-term interest rates and rational expectations are relevant. How could we have a credit crisis? Could anyone believe that the decline in housing prices was a rationally expected response to policy?

I find it incredible that a central bank ignores changes in money and credit. Simply put, that is a mistake that ignores much that economists have learned about monetary economics from analysis and history. No less surprising is the total neglect of the role of asset prices in the transmission of monetary impulses. Earlier work done in the 1960s and 1970s, summarized in Brunner and Meltzer (1993) and by Tobin (1969), did not neglect asset prices or credit.

A perennial issue in many countries is the choice between domestic price stability and exchange rate stability. No country acting alone can achieve both domestic price stability and stability of its currency. International agreement must supplement domestic policy.

For many years I have proposed an international arrangement that achieves both ends for countries that choose to participate. The arrangement is voluntary and requires no meetings to coordinate policy. Countries that participate achieve low inflation and greater stability of exchange rates.

Major countries agree to follow domestic policies to hold their inflation rates between 0 and 2 percent. The United States, the European Central Bank, and the Bank of Japan have adopted this policy objective. If China removes exchange controls, it could choose to be a fourth member by adopting the common inflation rate. The three or four main currencies would float to adjust to changes in relative productivity and demand.

All other countries that choose to peg to one or more of the major countries would import price stability and maintain a fixed exchange rate. Their decision to peg their exchange rate permits major countries to trade with them at a fixed exchange rate. The world gains a public benefit.

There is no organized coordination arrangement. Like for the gold standard, discipline is enforced by markets. If one of the major countries runs large budget deficits, markets will depreciate the currency. As Bordo and Schwartz (1984) showed, the system will not work without error or deviations.

If major countries adopt and announce a rule for monetary policy, such as the Taylor rule, market monitoring will be more effective and uncertainty about monetary policy will be reduced. Further, of major importance, a monetary rule that limits central bank financing of government deficits requires increased fiscal discipline.

Discretionary policy produced the Great Depression, the Great Inflation, and many periods of inflation and recession. Exchange rates have varied over a wide range. Rule-based policy will not be perfect. The future is uncertain and unanticipated changes occur. But uncertainty about policy will be lessened.

THE FEDERAL RESERVE'S RESPONSE TO CURRENT CRITICISMS

In a speech to the Economic Club of Indiana on October 1 (Bernanke 2012), Chairman Bernanke responded to five recent criticisms of Federal Reserve policy. Many academic and market economists claimed that the decision to expand would have little if any effect on employment and output because the financial system held $1.5 trillion of idle excess reserves and interest rates were extremely low, lower than at any time in U.S. history.

The enormous volume of excess reserves implied that lenders were not constrained. Very low interest rates meant borrowers could borrow at very low cost. The critics concluded that there was no unsatisfied excess demand for money or credit. Monetary policy was not the reason the unemployment rate remained at 8 percent.

Two of the trenchant criticisms of current Federal Reserve policy are that (1) it fails to recognize that the economy has major real problems, not a monetary problem, and (2) further expansion of reserves increases the risk of future inflation. Chairman Bernanke recognized once again that "monetary problem is no panacea." And he again emphasized such companion actions as "putting the federal budget on a sustainable path, reforming the tax code, [and] improving our educational system." He did not mention the uncertainty created by greatly increased regulation of health care, finance, energy, and labor markets that raises costs, reduces investment, and prevents new companies from starting.

The policy announcement after the September FOMC meeting called for purchases of $40 billion in agency mortgage-backed securities, bringing the total purchases of long-term assets to $85 billion per month. These purchases would continue until the outlook for the jobs market improves substantially "in a context of price stability." The commitment presupposes that the FOMC will recognize the right time to change direction and will act promptly and with sufficient force. And it reinforces the Fed's response to short-term changes. Experience in the Great Inflation of the 1970s, when the FOMC failed to prevent inflation, suggests that it was then, and is now, easy to make the commitment but hard to redeem the promise. The chairman's statement gave no reason for assurance.

The September meeting extended the period during which short-term interest rates remain low. Because long-term rates are a weighted average of expected future short-term rates, the announcement works to hold down long-term rates. Critics within and outside the system point out that the policy design would be improved if the termination was conditional on economic events instead of on a date. Using a date, however, gives markets more certainty. I agree with the critics, but I would specify a medium- or long-term objective.

The chairman expressed his confidence that the Federal Reserve will maintain low inflation in the future, as it has in the years since the Great Inflation. He explained "that we have the necessary tools to withdraw policy accommodation when needed," and can do so in an orderly way. There is no doubt that if the Federal Reserve raises interest rates, inflation will slow. But it never happens quickly, and the chairman does not suggest how high the interest rate might rise to stop inflation. I noted earlier in this chapter that every increase in interest rates quickly adds to government outlays and the budget and payments deficits. The chairman recognizes the link between a higher interest rate and the budget deficit, but he does so when dismissing proposals to use higher interest rates to induce policy-makers to reduce spending. He ignores the problem that will arise when anti-inflation action gets underway.

Finally, the chairman responds to proposals to have the Government Accountability Office audit the open market and review monetary policy decisions at the request of Congressmen. He is opposed, and I agree. The Federal Reserve and Congress should agree on steps to make the Federal Reserve more accountable, but that is not likely to achieve better policy actions and outcomes. Economic analysis implies that a rule that permits Congress to monitor outcomes would increase stability, reduce uncertainty, and be more effective.

I have often proposed that the Federal Reserve announce its provisional targets for two or three years ahead. If it fails to achieve its targets, it would offer an explanation and resignations. The political authorities could choose. This proposal reduces the gap between authority for policy decisions and outcomes and responsibility to the public when policy errors occur. The Federal Reserve has authority to act, but elected officials are punished when the economy falters.

Finally, following the recent financial crisis and in its aftermath the Federal Reserve has engaged in fiscal actions and debt management and has tripled the size of its balance sheet. I believe no agency of government should have as much independent authority. We profess to have a limited government. The Federal Reserve has acquired unlimited authority. Congress should not permit that power to continue without oversight and prior agreement.

CONCLUSION

My conclusion is brief. Rule-based monetary policy has a better record of achieving economic stability and low inflation or even price stability. In its second century, the Federal Reserve and Congress should agree on a rule for monetary policy, and also try to get similar rules in other major monetary centers to restore both price stability and greater exchange rate stability. And the Federal Reserve should announce and enforce a rule for lender of last resort.

We live in a world of uncertainty. No rule will be perfect all the time, but good rules enhance stability, reduce uncertainty, and increase efficiency.

REFERENCES

Bernanke, B. (2012). "Speech to Economic Club of Indiana." Retrieved from www
      .federalreserve.gov.
Bordo, Michael. (2009). "Exits from Recessions: The U.S. Experience 1920–2007."
      In V. Reinhart (ed), *No Way Out: Government Responses to the Financial
      Crisis.* Washington, DC: American Enterprise Institute.

Bordo, Michael, Owen Humpage, and Anna Schwartz. (2011). "U.S. Intervention in the Bretton Woods Era." Federal Reserve Bank of Cleveland, Working Paper, April.

Bordo, Michael, and Anna J. Schwartz. (1984). *A Retrospective on the Classical Gold Standard, 1821–1931.* Chicago: University of Chicago Press for the National Bureau of Economic Research.

Brunner, Karl, and Allan H. Meltzer. (1993). *Money and the Economy: Issues in Monetary Analysis.* Cambridge: Cambridge University Press for the Raffaele Mattioli Foundation.

Goodfriend, Marvin. (2010). "Monetary Policy, Credit Policy, and Interest on Reserves in the Economic Recovery." Testimony, House Committee on Financial Service, February 10.

Kydland, Finn, and Edward Prescott. (1977). "Rules Rather than Discretion: The Inconsistency of Optimal Plans." *Journal of Political Economy* 85 (June): 473–492.

Meltzer, Allan H. (1987). "Limits of Short-Run Stabilization Policy." Presidential Address to the Western Economic Association. *Economic Inquiry* 25 (January):1–14.

(2003). *A History of the Federal Reserve, Vol. 1, 1913–50.* Chicago: University of Chicago Press.

Muth, John F. (1960). "Optimal Properties of Exponentially Weighted Forecasts." *Journal of the American Statistical Association* 55 (June): 299–306.

Taylor, John B. (1993). "Discretion versus Policy Rules in Practice." *Carnegie Rochester Conference Series on Public Policy* 39 (December):195–214.

Tobin, James. (1969). "A General Equilibrium Approach to Monetary Theory." *Journal of Money, Credit and Banking* 1 (February):15–29.

Woodford, Michael. (2003). *Interest and Prices: Foundations of a Theory of Monetary Policy.* Princeton, NJ: Princeton University Press.

4

The Lender of Last Resort

Lessons from the Fed's First 100 Years

Mark A. Carlson and David C. Wheelock

> It is the duty of the United States to provide a means by which
> the periodic panics which shake the American Republic and
> do it enormous injury shall be stopped.
> — Robert L. Owen[1]

The founding of the Federal Reserve System in 1914 established the first official U.S. lender of last resort. Recurrent banking crises in the nineteenth and early twentieth centuries were widely viewed as evidence of defects in the U.S. banking system, including the absence of an official lender of last resort. Panics had been met by ad hoc actions by bankers (from Nicholas Biddle to J. P. Morgan), Secretaries of the Treasury (e.g., Leslie Shaw), and private clearinghouses, but these actions did not obviously reduce the frequency or severity of panics. The Fed's founders sought to prevent panics from arising in the first place as well as provide a mechanism for limiting any crises that did occur.

To achieve this objective, the Fed's founders desired to (1) create an "asset-backed" currency whose supply was tied to the level of commercial activity rather than to the stock of government bonds held by banks and (2) establish reserve banks to hold the reserves of the banking system and to provide additional currency and reserves as needed by rediscounting commercial paper. The Fed's founders expected that discount window lending would be the principal means by which the Federal Reserve would serve as lender of last resort to the banking system. However, the founders gave the Fed other tools as well, notably the ability to invest in government securities and banker's acceptances, which subsequently were used to take lender of last resort actions as well as to implement monetary policy.

---

[1] Robert L. Owen was Chairman of the Committee on Banking and Currency, United States Senate, 1913–1919 (Owen 1919).

This chapter reviews the Fed's near-100 year history as lender of last resort. We do so with two objectives in mind. First, we document changes in the Fed's behavior over time. From the beginning, the Fed acted as lender of last resort in the sense of providing currency and reserves to its member banks by rediscounting commercial paper and purchasing bankers acceptances.[2] In doing so, extensions of Federal Reserve credit apparently eliminated the seasonal stringency in money markets that banking reformers had viewed as an important source of instability (Miron 1986).[3] However, the Fed appears to have been hesitant or timid in responding to crises, and its response to the banking panics of the Great Depression does not seem in keeping with the objective of preventing periodic banking panics; we discuss some reasons why this might have been so. In the wake of the banking panics of the early 1930s, the Federal Reserve was given considerably greater power to act as a lender of last resort. Since World War II, the Fed has shown considerably more willingness to respond to threats to financial stability. We examine how and why the Fed's behavior as lender of last resort changed over time, and how well the lender of last resort adapted to underlying changes in the financial system driven by regulation, financial innovation, and the macroeconomic environment. We argue that a number of the actions taken during the financial crisis of 2007–2009 were anticipated by actions taken during the prior 40 years.

Our second objective in reviewing the Fed's history as a lender of last resort is to identify lessons from that history, particularly lessons that can be gleaned from actions taken between 1970 and 2010. Some economists argue that a central bank can perform effectively as lender of last resort solely by engaging in open market operations or otherwise varying the quantity of high-powered money, that is, through "monetary policy" (e.g., Goodfriend and King, 1998; Schwartz, 1992). Others, such as Goodhart (1999), argue that a lender of last resort may need to engage in targeted responses to prevent financial disturbances from spreading.[4] Arguably, the founder's conception of how the Fed would act as lender of last resort blended aspects of "banking," or credit, policy with aspects of "monetary" policy. Since the Great Depression, however, Fed officials generally have drawn a sharp distinction between lender of last resort actions and monetary policy. This distinction is perhaps best illustrated by the Fed's

---

[2] During World War I, the Fed also supplied a large volume of reserves by lending to banks against their holdings of U.S. government securities.

[3] Clark (1986) notes that interest rates exhibited notably less seasonal patterns in other countries after 1914, and suggests that the suspension of the gold standard at the start of World War I, rather than the founding of the Fed, explains the disappearance of interest rate seasonality.

[4] Bordo (1990) discusses alternatives views about the appropriate role of a lender of last resort and reviews the history of banking panics and their resolution.

response to the recent financial crisis, in which, before September 2008, the Fed prevented a large increase in its lending from increasing the total reserves of the banking system. We sidestep broader issues about the history and performance of the Fed in conducting monetary policy, which have been considered in depth by Meltzer (2003, 2009a) and others.

The first section discusses the Fed's performance up to and including the Great Depression and identifies some key reasons for the Fed's failure to act effectively as lender of last resort during the Great Depression. The second section reviews key legislation from the 1930s affecting the Fed as lender of last resort, comprising changes to the Fed's lending authority (generally expanding it), changes to the Fed's structure (concentrating authority), and changes to the financial system. These changes shaped the environment in which the Fed operated after World War II. The third section discusses the financial environment in the postwar era as initial stability unraveled under the strains of the Great Inflation of the 1970s, financial innovation, and deregulation of the 1980s and 1990s. The fourth section reviews responses to episodes in which the Fed acted as lender of last resort between 1970 and 2000. The fifth section reviews actions taken during the crisis of 2007–2009. We argue that the Fed's actions in the earlier period anticipate its responses to the more recent episode. All of these actions illustrate how the Fed's behavior as lender of last resort had changed since the 1930s. The sixth section provides a discussion of observations from these episodes and lessons from the Fed's history for the future. The final briefly concludes the chapter.

THE FED'S FIRST TWENTY YEARS

The Panic of 1907 was a watershed event that led to the establishment of the Federal Reserve System. Banking reform had been debated off and on since the 1870s. However, the Panic of 1907 provided the impetus for Congress to enact the Aldrich–Vreeland Act of 1908, which established the National Monetary Commission, as well as a temporary mechanism for issuing currency during banking crises. The studies of the National Monetary Commission identified defects of the U.S. banking system and drew lessons from the performance of banking systems in other countries. One study in particular argued that the relative stability of European banking systems reflected the presence of central banks operating in deep, liquid money markets (Warburg 1910). The study's author, Paul Warburg, convinced the chairman of the National Monetary Commission, Senator Nelson Aldrich, of the efficacy of the European model, and Aldrich became an important champion of a central banking system for the United States. Aldrich submitted a bill to Congress in 1912 to establish a central bank with key features of the European systems. Aldrich proposed a National Reserve Association that would oversee a system of local and regional reserve associations and set a discount rate at which the local branches would rediscount notes and bills of exchange for member banks (Wicker 2005). Congress rejected the Aldrich bill, but the Federal Reserve Act of 1913 resembled the Aldrich plan in key respects, including the establishment of regional reserve banks with authority to rediscount commercial paper and bills of exchange for member commercial banks.

The Federal Reserve Act did not address financial crises explicitly nor prescribe how the Federal Reserve should respond to banking panics. The act's proponents believed that the Fed's presence would prevent panics from occurring in the first place. The authors sought to "furnish an elastic currency" supplied as needed to accommodate seasonal and other fluctuations in currency demand. The authors intended the Fed's discount window to be the principal mechanism by which the System would add to the stocks of currency and bank reserves, and thereby serve as lender of last resort. Federal Reserve member banks could obtain currency (Federal Reserve notes) or reserve deposits by rediscounting commercial paper with reserve banks, which were required to maintain reserves in the form of gold and commercial paper against their note and deposit liabilities.

The Fed's founders also sought to promote a U.S. market for banker's acceptances. Warburg (1910) argued that the relative stability of European banking systems stemmed from the presence of deep markets for bills of exchange (such as banker's acceptances) and central banks that provided liquidity to back-stop those markets and serve as lender of last resort in times of stringency. The Federal Reserve Act authorized the reserve banks to purchase acceptances in the open market, which gave the Fed a second mechanism to add currency and reserves to the banking system and thereby serve as lender of last resort.[5]

No banking panics occurred during the Fed's first fifteen years, 1914–1929, which suggested that the Fed had accomplished the founders' objectives. The establishment of the Fed did, apparently, eliminate seasonal strains in financial markets, which had been widely recognized as a source of instability. Seasonal swings in money market interest rates dropped sharply after the Fed's founding as Federal Reserve discount window loans and purchases of banker's acceptances rose and fell with seasonal fluctuations in the demands for currency and credit (Friedman and Schwartz 1963, pp. 292–293; Miron 1986). Seasonal accommodation was largely automatic, as the Fed's founders had intended. At relatively fixed discount rates on loans to member banks and on purchases of acceptances in the

---

[5] Broz (1997) argues that the Fed's founders sought the development of a U.S. market for banker's acceptances to promote the use of the dollar in international trade and finance. See Bordo and Wheelock (2013) for additional discussion of the history and intent of the Federal Reserve Act, especially with regard to the Federal Reserve as lender of last resort.

open market, the reserve banks made more discount window loans and purchased more banker's acceptances at times of the year when demands for credit and currency were high.[6] Unfortunately, the Great Depression demonstrated that accommodating seasonal variation in money and credit demand was not sufficient to eliminate the problem of banking panics.[7]

Lender of Last Resort during the Great Depression

The Great Depression witnessed enormous strains in financial markets and stresses on the banking system associated with banking panics and failures. There were efforts within the Federal Reserve System to respond to these pressures. Following the 1929 stock market crash, the New York Fed extended discount window loans liberally to member banks so that they could take on stock exchange loans held by brokers. The New York Fed also purchased more than $100 million of government securities in the open market.

Some reserve banks also maintained easier lending policies to provide extra liquidity to the banking system. According to Richardson and Troost (2009), the Federal Reserve Bank of Atlanta responded to local panics by moving large quantities of cash to affected regions, extending emergency loans to member banks, and helping member banks make loans to non-member banks. Comparing the performance of the Federal Reserve Banks of Atlanta and St. Louis during a 1930 banking panic that straddled both districts, Richardson and Troost (2009) concluded that the Atlanta Fed's more aggressive response to the panic kept bank failure rates lower, and commercial lending and economic activity higher, in the Atlanta district than in the St. Louis district.

Reserve banks also on at least some occasions shipped large amounts of cash to locations exhibiting signs of stress. The Atlanta Fed shipped large amounts of currency to Florida as part of an aggressive response to banking distress, for example. Carlson, Mitchener, and Richardson (2010) conclude that the reserve bank's swift action stopped the panic and held down the number of bank failures. Similar uses of cash reservoirs to respond to distress were made by the Boston Fed in Bangor, Maine in 1933

---

[6] See Miron (1986) and references therein for discussion of the relationship between seasonal money market stringency and banking crises in the nineteenth and early twentieth century. Clark (1986) notes that interest rates exhibited less seasonality after 1914 in many countries, and suggests that the decline in interest rate seasonality was more likely caused by suspension of the international gold standard with the outbreak of World War I than by the founding of the Fed.

[7] Miron (1986) contends that the Fed was less accommodative of seasonal demands during the Depression, which could explain the increased incidence of financial crises. However, Wheelock (1992) finds that any changes in the seasonal patterns of interest rates and Federal Reserve credit after 1929 were not statistically significant.

and New Haven and Hartford, Connecticut in 1932; the Richmond Fed in Charleston, South Carolina in 1932; and San Francisco Fed in Boise and Twin Falls, Idaho in 1932 and Sacramento, California in 1933 (Federal Reserve Board 1934, 1938).[8] These efforts, termed currency depots, provided instant access to cash from an onsite source maintained by a custodian on behalf of the Federal Reserve, but were not strictly lender of last resort actions. Banks were required to obtain financing from another source, such as a New York correspondent, but once they did so, the presence of a currency depot meant that currency was immediately available to be a source of confidence during a bank run. As in Tampa, currency depots elsewhere appear to have contributed positively to stability:

On January 2 [1932], a situation developed in Hartford, Connecticut, when the City Bank and Trust Company, a large non-member bank, following a run, was forced to close its doors, and its failure forced the East Hartford Trust Company and the Unionville Bank and Trust Company, two small institutions closely allied with it, to close the same day. This disturbance naturally was felt by the banks in that locality. The Federal Reserve Bank of Boston opened on January 2 a temporary currency depot to assist in facilitating the delivery of currency, officials of the bank going to Hartford to supervise the establishment and operations. Through active cooperation of the Hartford Clearing House banks, the National Credit Corporation, and the Federal Reserve Bank of Boston, this situation was localized, so that within two or three days the banking situation in Hartford was apparently back in normal conditions. (Curtiss 1933)

The actions by the various reserve banks suggest that the Fed had tools that could be used to respond to banking crises. However, those tools were used idiosyncratically and required leaders who were willing to improvise and, if necessary, test the limits of the Federal Reserve Act. A truly effective response would have required coordination across the System. The Federal Reserve Act did not provide an automatic, foolproof mechanism for dealing with crises as the founders had hoped. Instead, the Fed responded timidly to the banking panics and failures during 1930–1933, as well as to large declines in the price level and output, and clearly failed to serve effectively as lender of last resort.

Reasons for a Lack of Action during the Great Depression

Bordo and Wheelock (2013) review alternative explanations for the Fed's policy failings during the Great Depression, focusing especially on why the discount window and banker's acceptance mechanisms failed to operate as the Fed's founders intended to prevent or alleviate banking panics.

---

[8] The first use of currency depots to respond to local banking stress appears to have been by the San Francisco Fed in response to troubles in 1921 in Boise, Idaho (a location without quick access to cash from the branch of a Federal Reserve Bank).

Bordo and Wheelock (2013) argue that the Fed was hampered as lender of last resort because the Federal Reserve Act failed to re-create key features of major European banking systems. Those features included deep, liquid money markets; nationwide branch banking; and a central bank that lent anonymously to the market against good collateral.

The Fed's founders sought to promote the development of a large U.S. banker's acceptance market, similar to the bill markets in European financial centers. Accordingly, the Federal Reserve Act permitted national banks to issue banker's acceptances and authorized the reserve banks to purchase acceptances in the open market. However, the market did not grow as envisioned and it declined sharply during the Depression.[9]

The Federal Reserve System helped to integrate and make the U.S. payments system more efficient (Gilbert 1998), but was silent on branch banking. Dual banking, that is, the chartering of banks by both the federal government and state governments, was preserved. Federally chartered, that is, national, banks were required to join the Federal Reserve System, but membership was made optional for state-chartered banks. With its system of semiautonomous regional reserve banks, the Federal Reserve System was made to fit the structure of the U.S. banking system rather than to reform it.[10]

The Federal Reserve Act imposed some fairly strict limitations on the Fed's ability to serve as lender of last resort to the banking system, which became apparent during the Great Depression. The act restricted access to the Fed's discount window to member commercial banks. Nonmember banks, trust companies, savings institutions, and other depository and financial institutions had no direct access to Federal Reserve credit.[11] Few state banks chose Fed membership. By December 1929, fewer than 10 percent of all state-chartered commercial banks were Fed members. Including national banks, only 35 percent of the nation's commercial banks were members, though member banks held nearly 75 percent of total U.S. bank deposits. Still, on the eve of the Great Depression, 65 percent of U.S. commercial banks, holding some 25 percent of total U.S. bank deposits, had no

---

[9] Broz (1997) argues that international objectives were particularly important to the Fed's founders, including the establishment of an active banker's acceptance market to increase the share of world trade financed by U.S. banks.

[10] Grossman (2010) reports and discusses evidence that historically banking crises have been less prevalent in systems with larger banks and nationwide branching. A more detailed comparison of the Canadian banking system with the U.S. system by Bordo, Rockoff, and Redish (1994) finds that the Canadian system of large banks with nationwide branches has been more stable, though less efficient, than the U.S. unit banking system.

[11] The act prohibited member banks from acting as agents for nonmember banks in applying for or receiving Federal Reserve credit "except by permission of the Federal Reserve Board." Lending to nonmember banks is discussed in more detail in the next section.

direct access to the lender of last resort. This proved especially problematic during the Great Depression when banking panics and failures occurred predominately among nonmember banks. The annual average suspension rate among nonmembers was 8 percent during 1930–1932, double the rate for member banks. Similarly, on average, 5 percent of the total deposits held by nonmember banks, but only 1 percent of those held by member banks, were in banks that suspended operations during the Depression.[12]

In addition to prohibiting reserve banks from lending directly to nonmember banks, the Federal Reserve Act also prohibited member banks from acting as agents for nonmember banks in applying for or receiving Federal Reserve credit except by permission of the Federal Reserve Board. During World War I, the Board authorized the reserve banks to discount for nonmembers, with the endorsement of a member bank, notes secured by U.S. Government securities if the proceeds were to be used for holding government securities (Hackley 1973, pp. 118–119). Then in 1921, the Board authorized the reserve banks to discount for member banks any eligible paper acquired from nonmember banks, but that authority was rescinded in 1923 (Hackley 1973, p. 119). Thereafter, Federal Reserve credit was extended to nonmember banks only in exceptional circumstances and with Board approval. However, during the Depression, the Fed rarely authorized loans to member banks as agents for nonmember banks.

The Fed's lending was also constrained by restrictions in the Federal Reserve Act on the types and maturities of loans and securities that banks could rediscount or use as collateral for advances from the discount window. The authors of the act were influenced by the real bills doctrine and believed that Federal Reserve credit should be extended only by rediscounting of short-term self-liquidating commercial and agricultural loans. The act permitted rediscounting of "notes, drafts, and bills of exchange arising out of actual commercial transactions," but forbade rediscounting of loans and securities "covering merely investments or issued or drawn for the purpose of carrying or trading in stocks, bonds, or other investment securities, except banks and notes of the Government of the United States." Further, the act specified that only those loans with a term to maturity of 90 days or less (180 days for agricultural loans) were eligible for rediscounting with reserve banks. During the Depression, many banks apparently were unable to obtain Federal Reserve credit because they lacked sufficient amounts of eligible paper (Chandler 1971, pp. 227–233).

---

[12] These rates are calculated as the annual average total number of suspensions (deposits in suspended banks) for 1930–1932 divided by the number of banks (total deposits) on December 1929. Data on number of banks and deposits by class of bank are from Federal Reserve Board (1943, table 1). Data on suspensions are from Federal Reserve Board (1943, table 66).

Although the Federal Reserve Act expressly limited the types and maturities of paper that reserve banks could rediscount for member banks, the act did not specify how reserve banks were to set their discount rates (or acceptance buying rates) or administer their discount windows. However, the Fed's founders expected that reserve banks would set their discount rates sufficiently high to protect their gold reserves, while adjusting their rates as necessary to respond to and support the unique banking and currency needs of their individual districts.[13] Each reserve bank set its own discount rate, subject to review by the Federal Reserve Board, and administered its discount window. Some reserve banks were more liberal than others in determining and valuing acceptable discount window collateral (Chandler 1971, p. 233), and in responding to local banking disturbances.

Friedman and Schwartz (1963) contend that the Fed suffered from a lack of effective leadership, which enabled parochial interests and petty jealousies to hamstring policy. The individual reserve banks acted competitively, rather than cooperatively, at critical points during the Depression. For example, in March 1933, the Federal Reserve Bank of Chicago refused a request from the New York Fed to exchange gold for U.S. government securities when gold outflows threatened to push the New York Bank's reserve ratio below its legal minimum (Meltzer 2003, p. 387). Although the Federal Reserve Board eventually required the Chicago Fed and other reserve banks to lend to New York, the episode illustrates how the System's structure hampered its response to crises.

There also appears to have been reluctance on the part of some within the Federal Reserve during that period to react to systemic stresses. This is apparent in discussions by the Federal Reserve Board in late February 1933 (two weeks after the state of Michigan had declared a bank holiday and other states had begun to follow suit) where there was a decided aversion to engaging in expansionary open market operations despite clear signs that the banking system was under stress. In response to a call by Treasury Secretary Ogden Mills for Federal Reserve purchases of government securities to improve public confidence and to ease stresses on the banking system, Federal Reserve Governor Meyer responded as follows:

Governor Meyer stated that he feels that the recent thinness in the market for Government securities is incident to the necessary readjustment in a market which has been too high under the conditions that have prevailed; that in view of the recent increase in money rates abroad, over which control cannot be exercised in this county, and the increase in money rates in the New York market and in the bill rates at the Federal Reserve Bank of New York, continued purchases of

---

[13] Reserve banks were required to maintain minimum gold reserves equal to 40 percent of their outstanding notes and 35 percent of their deposit liabilities (plus eligible paper equal to 100 percent of their note issues).

Government securities at the present time would be inconsistent from a monetary standpoint; and that the New York market should protect itself against the higher rate abroad by increased rates and not through open market purchases of government by the Federal Reserve Banks ... He also expressed the view that any reasonable amount of open market purchases at this time would prove to be ineffective and appear to be a vain attempt to prevent a readjustment of rates which is inevitable (Minutes of the Federal Reserve Board, February 27, 1933)[14]

What lessons can be drawn from the Great Depression for the effectiveness of a lender of last resort? The Federal Reserve's shortcomings as a lender of last resort during the Depression stemmed from multiple sources, including the following:

1. The narrowness of its mandate – the Fed was authorized to lend only to member banks. However, during the Depression, banking panics and failures were acute among nonmember banks that had no direct access to the Fed's discount window.
2. The Federal Reserve Act restricted acceptable collateral for Federal Reserve loans to short-term commercial and agricultural loans and U.S. government securities. During the Depression, many banks lacked collateral for discount window loans. Some reserve banks apparently were also conservative in valuing collateral pledged for loans.
3. Some reserve banks focused on local conditions and their own reserve positions with inadequate regard to national conditions, as reflected, for example, in the Chicago Fed's refusal to lend to the New York Fed.
4. The geographically fragmented unit banking system of the United States was particularly vulnerable to shocks.

The Fed's founders limited the System's mandate and imposed strict collateral and reserve requirements on the reserve banks to keep the Fed from being a source of inflation or financial speculation. Similarly, the Fed's regional structure was intended to be responsive to conditions throughout the country and not dominated by either New York banks or Washington politics. However, the regional structure hampered coordinated policy action in response to a national crisis. It seems likely that the Fed would have been more aggressive and more effective as lender of last resort if it had greater freedom to lend to nonmember banks and other depository institutions against a wider array of collateral, and if authority had been concentrated in the hands of policymakers with a better understanding of,

---

[14] The minutes can be found in the records of the Federal Reserve System, Record Group 82, Box 745, index number 2158; National Archives and Records Administration, College Park, MD.

and interest in, national banking conditions. Conceivably, the restrictions on the Fed's discount window would not have mattered if the Fed had pursued an aggressive monetary policy response to the Great Depression, as argued most strongly by Friedman and Schwartz (1963). Even so, the structure of the U.S. banking system made it more crisis prone, which would have challenged even an optimally designed lender of last resort. As Warburg (1910) had argued, the stability of a banking system depends on features of the banking system and financial markets as well as the presence of a lender of last resort.

CREATING A NEW REGIME: DEPRESSION ERA REFORMS TO THE BANKING SYSTEM AND LENDER OF LAST RESORT

This section describes reforms put in place during the Depression that broadened the Fed's lending authority and changed the structure of the Federal Reserve System to make it more effective and responsive to crises. Significant reforms were also implemented elsewhere in the financial system to make the banking system less crisis prone, though the federal prohibition on interstate branching remained.

Federal Reserve Credit Programs

During the Depression, Congress sought to improve the flow of credit to the banking system by easing restrictions on both access to the Fed's discount window and the types of securities that could serve as collateral for discount window loans. For example, the Glass–Steagall Act of February 1932 authorized reserve banks to lend to smaller member banks – those with capital not exceeding $5 million – against *any* satisfactory asset (not just assets that ordinarily were eligible for rediscounting or for use as collateral for advances) in "exceptional and exigent circumstances." Loans made under this authority (Section 10(b) of the Federal Reserve Act) required the approval of five or more members of the Federal Reserve Board and bore an interest rate not less than 1 percent above the regular discount rate (Hackley 1973, pp. 101–102).[15] Section 10(b) was initially set to expire in March 1933, but was subsequently extended by the Emergency Banking Act of March 1933. The act also eliminated the requirement that at least five members of the Federal Reserve Board approve all 10(b) loans (Hackley 1973, pp. 106–107). Further, the act authorized reserve banks to make loans to nonmember banks in limited circumstances on the same terms as advances to member banks under Section 10(b). This authority expired after one year and was not renewed (Hackley 1973, pp. 124–125).

---

[15] The Glass–Steagall Act of 1932 also added Section 10(a), which permitted the Reserve Banks to lend to groups of five or more member banks (see Hackley 1973, pp. 103–105).

Besides giving banks enhanced access to Federal Reserve credit, Congress also sought to improve the flow of credit to bank customers. As the Depression worsened, Congress received complaints that even financially secure borrowers with good collateral had difficulty obtaining loans from banks. In a letter to Carter Glass, Chairman of the Senate Banking Committee, Federal Reserve Board member Charles Hamlin wrote, "I firmly believe, but cannot prove, that there are many merchants in the United States today who are unable to obtain credit, although they can give satisfactory collateral. I know that there are large areas where there are no banks left."[16] As the banking problems lingered so did concerns about credit availability. In 1934, the Federal Reserve reported the following:

The need for this character of loans [working capital loans] has become increasingly apparent in recent months. Many small industrial establishments have suffered severe capital losses during the depression and are now short of working capital. A survey made by the Federal Reserve Board through the Reserve banks and the chambers of commerce showed that this condition is widespread and is not being met by existing facilities.[17]

Congress responded to such concerns first by adding Section 13(3) to the Federal Reserve Act as a provision of the Emergency Relief and Construction Act of July 1932. Section 13(3) authorized the Federal Reserve, "in unusual and exigent circumstances ... to discount for any individual, partnership, or corporation, notes, drafts, and bills of exchange of the kinds and maturities made eligible for discount for member banks." The provision stipulated that before extending credit, "the Federal Reserve Bank shall obtain evidence that such individual, partnership, or corporation is unable to secure adequate credit accommodations from other banking institutions."[18] A similar provision, Section 13(13), allowed for borrowing against obligations of the U.S. government and its agencies. Later, in 1934, amid the ongoing concerns about lack of overall credit availability, Congress added Section 13(b) to the Federal Reserve Act which allowed working capital advances for up to five years to established industrial and commercial businesses. The Banking Act of August 1935

---

[16] Letter from Charles Hamlin to Carter Glass, July 9, 1932 (Box 305, Carter Glass papers, University of Virginia Library).

[17] *Federal Reserve Bulletin*, July 1934, p. 429. See Carlson and Rose (2011) for a further discussion of efforts by the Federal Reserve to study credit availability during this period.

[18] See Hackley (1973, pp. 127–30). Subsequently, the Emergency Banking Act of March 1933 added Section 13(13) to the Federal Reserve Act, which authorized Federal Reserve advances to any individual, partnership, or corporation for periods of not more than ninety days on notes secured by direct obligations of the United States or issued or fully guaranteed by U.S. agencies (Hackley 1973, pp. 122–123). And, Section 13(b), which authorized the Fed to make working capital loans to businesses, was added in June 1934. The latter provision was repealed in 1958 (Hackley 1973, pp. 133–145).

made permanent Sections 10(b) and 13(3), and removed the requirement of "exceptional and exigent circumstances" for loans made under 10(b). It also eliminated a provision requiring that loans made under Section 13(3) be secured by both collateral eligible for discount by member banks and the endorsement of the borrower or a third-party surety.

Section 13(3) was not used extensively. In four years the Fed made just 123 loans, totaling $1.5 million, under its Section 13(3) authority, with the largest loan being for $300,000 (Fettig 2002). Similarly, few loans were made under Section 13(13). Between 1933 and 1937, about $5.5 million in loans were extended under this authority. Section 13(b) was used somewhat more extensively, and the introduction of Section 13(b) was a possible reason why Sections 13(3) and 13(13) were little used. By the end of 1937, $151 million in loans had been approved under Section 13(b) authority.[19]

Federal Reserve lending under Sections 13(3) and 13(13) as authorized in the early 1930s ended around 1940. The Fed extended credit under Section 13(3) during the financial crisis of 2007–2009. Section 13(b) lending continued through World War II but dissipated shortly thereafter. Section 13(b) was repealed in 1958 by a provision of the Small Business Investment Company Act.

The Gold Standard

The founders of the Federal Reserve System sought to create a mechanism by which the supplies of currency and bank reserves would adjust "elastically" to accommodate fluctuations in demand. The founders intended the discount window to serve primarily as that mechanism. However, the Federal Reserve Act also imposed constraints that prevented the Federal Reserve from supplying unlimited liquidity, which bounded the Fed's ability to act as lender of last resort. Fundamentally, the Federal Reserve was constrained by the gold standard. The reserve banks were required to maintain minimum gold reserve ratios against their note and deposit liabilities, as well as collateral in the form of eligible commercial paper against their note issues.[20]

Scholars have debated the extent to which the statutory reserve requirements on Federal Reserve note issues and deposits prevented the Fed

---

[19] For comparison, loans outstanding at all commercial banks in 1934 totaled $20 billion. In 1939, the first year for which such data are available, commercial and industrial loans at all commercial banks totaled about $7 billion.

[20] The Federal Reserve Act imposed gold reserve requirements of 40 percent and 35 percent, respectively, against reserve bank note issues and deposit liabilities. In addition, reserve banks were required to hold collateral in the form of commercial paper equal to 100 percent of their note issues. A 1917 amendment lowered the collateral requirement for note issues to 60 percent, in the form of either commercial paper or gold (Friedman and Schwartz 1963, p. 194).

from responding more aggressively to the Great Depression. In particular, Friedman and Schwartz (1963) contend that, despite the subsequent claims of some Fed officials, a lack of "free gold" could not explain why the Fed failed to offset fully the effects on bank reserves of large currency and gold outflows in the fourth quarter of 1931.[21] Regardless of whether the Fed's gold reserve requirements ever prevented action, Fed officials desired to preserve the gold standard and took actions that they believed were consistent with that objective.[22]

The Glass–Steagall Act of February 1932 eased the Fed's reserve requirements by permitting reserve banks to use government securities rather than commercial paper as collateral for their note issues. The Emergency Banking Act of March 1933 further eased the constraint temporarily by authorizing the Fed to issue an unlimited amount of currency backed only by U.S. government securities, that is, with no gold reserve requirement. The Emergency Banking Act also ratified President Roosevelt's declaration of a bank holiday and suspension of the gold standard. Subsequently, the Gold Reserve Act of 1934 fixed the gold value of the dollar at nearly 40 percent below its pre-suspension level, made permanent the prohibition on ownership of monetary gold by the public or banks (including Federal Reserve Banks), and granted the Secretary of the Treasury broad powers to buy and sell gold and foreign exchange at home and abroad through an exchange stabilization fund.

Although the dollar remained linked to gold, the Gold Reserve Act gave the Treasury broad monetary powers. Further, beginning in 1933, gold inflows kept the gold standard from constraining Federal Reserve or Treasury actions, and were the source of a substantial increase in the money stock between 1933 and World War II (Friedman and Schwartz 1963). Under the postwar Bretton Woods System, gold once again became an influence on monetary policy (Calomiris and Wheelock 1998; Meltzer 2009a, pp. 214–224), but not on the Fed's actions as lender of last resort.

Other Significant Legislation

Several pieces of New Deal legislation modified the structure and authority of the Federal Reserve System, and the environment in which it operated.

---

[21] Free gold was the amount of gold held by Reserve Banks in excess of that required as a reserve against their note and deposit liabilities. See Chandler (1971, pp. 182–191) and Meltzer (2003, pp. 355–357) on the extent to which a lack of free gold limited the Fed's response to the Depression.

[22] Eichengreen (1992), Temin (1989), and Wicker (1966) are perhaps the strongest proponents of the view that the Fed's actions during the Depression reflect primarily a desire to preserve the international gold standard. Meltzer (2003, pp. 272–282) reviews alternative explanations for Federal Reserve policy actions during the Depression.

The Banking Acts of 1933 and 1935 gave the Fed new powers to regulate banks and credit flows and consolidated many existing System authorities within the Federal Reserve Board. For example, the acts authorized the Federal Reserve Board to adjust member bank reserve requirements, set maximum limits on interest rates paid by member banks on time deposits, and regulate margin requirements for purchases and holding of registered securities. They also gave the Board greater influence over reserve bank discount rates and, through a reconstituted Federal Open Market Committee (FOMC), the System's open market policy.

The banking acts and various other legislation enacted during the 1930s also significantly changed the banking and financial regulatory environment. For example, the Banking Act of 1933 introduced federal deposit insurance, which the Banking Act of 1935 expanded and made permanent. Deposit insurance had been given a black eye by the poor performance of state-run deposit insurance schemes in the 1920s. However, federal insurance of bank deposits was viewed as necessary to restore confidence in the banking system and was politically popular. Moreover, the Fed's failure to be an effective lender of last resort suggested that a different approach was needed. Federal deposit insurance seemed to solve the problem of banking panics and thus eliminate the need for a lender of last resort. In the words of Friedman and Schwartz (1963, p. 440), "Adopted as a result of the widespread losses imposed by bank failures in the early 1930s, federal deposit insurance, to 1960 at least, has succeeded in achieving what had been the major objective of banking reform for at least a century, namely, the prevention of banking panics." As subsequent events beginning in the 1970s proved, however, deposit insurance did not eliminate banking or financial instability, or the Fed's willingness to take actions that it viewed as necessary as lender of last resort.

Deposit insurance is a two-edged sword. By reducing, or eliminating, any incentive for depositors to run on banks, deposit insurance can effectively prevent banking panics. However, it also reduces market discipline and encourages banks to take on greater risk than they would in the absence of insurance. The moral hazard created by deposit insurance was well understood in 1933, and Congress initially limited insurance coverage to levels that protected small depositors but did not eliminate market discipline altogether (Flood 1992). At the same time, other measures were imposed to contain risk taking. For example, the Banking Act of 1933 prohibited the payment of interest on transactions accounts and instructed the Fed to set limits on rates banks could pay on time deposits (Regulation Q). Regulation of deposit interest rates, continued prohibition of interstate branching (and, in many states, even local branching), and a conservative chartering regime in which new bank charters were granted only when a market was shown to be underserved by existing banks, all limited competition, protected bank charter values, and thereby discouraged excessive risk taking.[23] Further, the Glass–Steagall Act of 1933, that is, that part of the Banking Act of 1933 that separated commercial and investment banking, prohibited the comingling of commercial and investment banking in a single organization. The act's proponents believed that preventing commercial banks from engaging in securities-related activities would make the banking system more stable.

FINANCIAL INSTABILITY RETURNS

For some time after World War II, economic and financial conditions remained quite stable. Stable monetary policy was a characteristic of the environment that contributed to stability of the banking system and helped obviate the need for lender of last resort action. As noted previously, the Glass–Steagall Act of 1932 relaxed the gold standard constraint on the Fed's note issuance. The Emergency Banking Act of 1933 and Gold Reserve Act of 1934 further relaxed the gold standard constraint on monetary policy and gave the Treasury Department authority and resources to intervene in gold and foreign exchange markets. Beginning in 1933, substantial gold inflows increased the U.S. money stock and promoted economic recovery (Friedman and Schwartz 1963; Romer 1992). During World War II, the Federal Reserve pegged yields on short-term U.S. government securities and maintained ceiling yields on long-term government bonds. Price and wage controls and rationing were also in place throughout the war.

At the behest of the Treasury Department, the Federal Reserve continued to maintain a ceiling on long-term government bond yields into the 1950s. However, rising inflation led to an accord between the Fed and Treasury in March 1951 that restored the Fed's freedom to carry out independent monetary policy. Inflation remained low and economic fluctuations were relatively modest over the subsequent 15 years.[24] Few banks failed; from 1946 to 1960 there were only 42 bank failures.

Inflation began to rise in the mid-1960s amid greater political pressure on the Fed to keep interest rates low and the rising influence of Keynesian macroeconomics. Stability of the market for government securities remained a Fed objective after its 1951 accord with the Treasury Department, which frequently delayed or limited changes in monetary policy around the times when the Treasury offered securities to the market (Meltzer 2009a).

---

[23] Keely (1990) shows that the level of risk among U.S. banks increased as increased competition eroded charter values.

[24] See Friedman and Schwartz (1963), Calomiris and Wheelock (1998), Romer and Romer (2002), and Meltzer (2009a) for discussions of Federal Reserve monetary policy during the 1950s and early 1960s.

President Johnson famously browbeat Fed Chairman William McChesney Martin not to raise the Fed's discount rate in 1965, and though he resisted overt pressure, Martin believed that he had a responsibility to maintain good System relations within the government, which caused him to sometimes delay moves toward tighter policy (Meltzer 2009a, p. 474). The rise of Keynesian macroeconomics, common acceptance of an exploitable, perhaps even favorable, trade-off between inflation and unemployment, and of nonmonetary explanations for inflation also softened the Fed's willingness to tighten policy to halt rising inflation. Finally, the post–World War II Bretton Woods System of fixed exchange rates proved less constraining on expansionary monetary policy than the prewar gold standard had been (Bordo 1993; Calomiris and Wheelock 1998).[25]

Inflation and the financial regulatory environment proved to be a bad mix, especially for depository institutions and, most notably, savings and loan associations (S&Ls). Rising inflation and the Fed's efforts to resist it led to rising market interest rates and occasional "credit crunches" when depositors moved funds from depository institutions, which were subject to caps on the interest rates they could pay on deposits, to higher-yielding money market instruments. The Eurodollar market, an offshore dollar funding market, expanded rapidly as institutions sought to avoid interest rate ceilings. S&Ls, which specialized in housing finance, were especially affected by rising interest rates because their assets consisted primarily of long-term, fixed-rate mortgages while their liabilities were mainly shorter term deposits.[26] Regulators gradually increased deposit interest rate ceilings, which slowed the outflow of deposits from banks and S&Ls, but higher ceilings increased bank and S&L funding costs and reduced their profits.

Financial innovation introduced products that were close substitutes for the regulated deposit accounts offered by banks and S&Ls. Notably, credit union share draft accounts and money market mutual funds offered alternatives to the non–interest-bearing demand-deposit accounts offered by banks and the regulated savings and time deposits offered to small savers by both banks and S&Ls. In an effort to level the playing field, the Depository Institutions Deregulation and Monetary Control Act of 1980 (DIDMCA) and Garn–St. Germain Depository Institutions Act of 1982 permitted banks and S&Ls to offer limited forms of interest-bearing

---

[25] See DeLong (1997), Calomiris and Wheelock (1998), Hafer and Wheelock (2003), and Meltzer (2011, pp. 472–479) for perspectives on the Fed's monetary policies in the 1960s and the origins of the Great Inflation.

[26] The thirty-year fixed rate mortgage was another legacy of the Great Depression – specifically of the federal government's actions to stabilize the mortgage market (Green and Wachter 2005).

transactions accounts and automatic transfer services, expanded permissible investment opportunities for savings institutions, and phased out regulated ceilings on time and savings deposit accounts (Spong 2000, pp. 29–30). The DIDMCA also increased federal deposit insurance coverage limits from $40,000 to $100,000 and permitted all depository institutions to access Federal Reserve services and lending facilities, including the discount window.

Increased competition, deregulation, and expanded deposit insurance coverage contributed to the S&L debacle and sharp increase in the number of commercial bank failures in the 1980s (FDIC 1997). The Federal Deposit Insurance Corporation's (FDIC's) rescue of Continental Illinois Bank in 1984 brought the semi-official designation of banks deemed "too big to fail." Allegations that Federal Reserve loans to troubled banks had increased the costs of resolving failed banks borne by the FDIC insurance funds led to enactment of the Federal Deposit Insurance Corporation Improvement Act of 1991 (FDICIA), which subjected the Fed to potential penalties if it exceeded specified limits on extensions of Federal Reserve credit to undercapitalized depository institutions (Gilbert et al. 2012).[27]

Other significant legislation in the 1990s affecting the structure and competitiveness of the banking industry included the Riegle–Neal Interstate Banking and Branching Efficiency Act of 1994 and the Gramm–Leach–Bliley Act of 1999. The Riegle–Neal Act eliminated most federal barriers to interstate banking and branching, whereas the Gramm–Leach–Blilely Act allowed affiliations of banks, securities, firms, and insurance companies within financial service holding companies, and thus repealed the Glass–Steagall Act of 1933. Branching deregulation increased competition in many markets, and both acts likely encouraged consolidation in the banking industry and reduced impediments to growth of individual banking organizations.

The preceding discussion summarizes the regulatory and macroeconomic environment in which the U.S. banking system operated from the mid-1930s until the financial crisis of 2008–2009. The Fed's failure to act effectively as lender of last resort during the Great Depression prompted legislation that expanded the Federal Reserve's capacity to serve as a lender of last resort with the intention that it respond more to perceived

---

[27] FDICIA did increase the Fed's ability to respond to crises by removing the restriction that loans extended under Section 13(3) were secured by collateral "of the kinds and maturities made eligible for discount for member banks under other provisions of the Act" and only required that the advances be secured to the satisfaction of the Reserve Bank, the same test that applied to borrowings by depository institutions. See Todd (1993) for further details.

credit troubles (see, e.g., *Federal Reserve Bulletin*, July 1934, p. 429).[28] The Depression experience also sparked other reforms, such as federal deposit insurance and a new system of banking regulations that reduced the need for a lender of last resort. The financial legislation of the 1930s focused on promoting stability in the banking system, and few bank failures occurred over the ensuing four decades. However, the regulatory system also limited the ability of banks to adapt to rising inflation or to compete with new financial services offered by less regulated financial firms. Deregulation enabled banks to compete better, but did not halt financial innovation or the growth of a large "shadow" banking system. Ultimately, in 2007–2009, the financial system again required a strong lender of last resort.

We discuss the financial crisis of 2007–2009 and the Fed's response to that crisis in the next section. First, however, we review five episodes beginning in 1970 when the Fed acted in its capacity as lender of last resort to alleviate financial disturbances. We show that these episodes (1) demonstrate a fundamental shift since the Great Depression in the System's view of its lender of last resort responsibilities, and (2) presage the Fed's response to the crisis of 2007–2009.

RESPONSE BY THE FEDERAL RESERVE TO FINANCIAL CRISES, 1970–2000

We discuss in chronological order the Fed's response to five episodes that occurred between 1970 and 2000. Our descriptions of the crises and responses are drawn from publicly available sources. For the most part, discussion of Federal Reserve concerns and actions comes from Congressional testimony of Federal Reserve officials and the minutes and transcripts of the FOMC. Reports of market developments are generally drawn from newspaper reports, especially *The Wall Street Journal*, *The New York Times*, and *The Washington Post*.

Penn Central

In 1970, the Penn Central Company (Penn Central) was the largest railroad company in the United States and through various subsidiaries owned a variety of high-profile assets (including Madison Square Garden); the firm had generally been considered a dependable blue-chip company. However, during 1969 and the early part of 1970, its income had fallen notably relative to its expenses due in part to increased operating costs and required outlays for equipment.[29] Further, the company

---

[28] Similar motivations led to an expansion of the mandate of the Reconstruction Finance Corporation.

[29] Calomiris (1994) also provides a discussion of events surrounding the collapse of Penn Central. Murray (1971) details the decline in the solvency of Penn Central.

had taken on significant debt to purchase and develop real estate and to acquire other corporations. Penn Central's troubles worsened notably with the release on May 9, 1970, of a prospectus for a planned bond offering. The prospectus indicated that Penn Central had a considerable amount of short- and long-term debt coming due soon and that it was having difficulty rolling over its commercial paper (Morris, Sansweet, and Williams 1970). The extent of the difficulties reportedly surprised even investors familiar with the company.

As Penn Central's financial troubles neared a critical juncture, market participants became worried that other firms would be affected by its collapse. Penn Central was a significant issuer of commercial paper and there was reportedly some speculation that the holders of this debt might experience liquidity problems if the company proved unable to redeem its paper (Janssen and Stabler 1970). Uncertainty about corporate credit quality and the ability of the market to absorb a large default raised worries about a possible disruption to the functioning of the commercial paper market. Nixon administration officials and some Wall Street analysts became concerned that a collapse in the commercial paper market could cause liquidity problems for other firms (Janssen 1970; Janssen and Stabler 1970). Attempts by the Nixon administration to organize a rescue of Penn Central failed and Penn Central declared bankruptcy on June 21.

Even prior to the events at Penn Central, Federal Reserve officials were worried about conditions in money markets; at the May 26, 1970, FOMC meeting, members expressed concern about the "crisis atmosphere" prevailing in these markets (FOMC minutes, May 26, 1970, p. 25). The anxiety in financial markets was attributed to problems in the corporate sector and to political events related to the conflict in Southeast Asia. The FOMC noted that the stresses in financial markets might have a detrimental effect on the real economy (FOMC minutes, May 26, 1970, p. 26). When Penn Central declared bankruptcy, Federal Reserve officials were concerned that the commercial paper market might decline rapidly, or possibly collapse, and that firms that depended on the market would be unable to obtain financing elsewhere. Thus, "firms that in other circumstances would be regarded as perfectly sound" would be forced to declare bankruptcy (Burns 1971, p. 402). To prevent the Penn Central collapse from spreading, and to calm financial markets, the Federal Reserve acted to bolster the capacity of alternative sources of funding for firms that might be shut out of the commercial paper market.

As part of its response to the Penn Central bankruptcy, the Board suspended interest rate ceilings (Regulation Q) for certificates of deposit of $100,000 or more with a maturity of between thirty and eighty-nine days to ensure that commercial banks could raise funds to make loans to firms pushed out of the commercial paper market (Burns 1971, p. 402).[30] This action was taken in consultation with the FDIC and Federal Home Loan Bank Board. The Federal Reserve also made clear to member banks that the discount window could and should be open for them to obtain funds to make loans for firms unable to issue commercial paper (Burns 1971, p. 402). The Fed released no official statement regarding discount window borrowing, but *The Wall Street Journal* stated that a Federal Reserve official had indicated "that the circumstances imply a liberal stance towards any bank finding if necessary to borrow temporarily from a district Reserve Bank" (Wall Street Journal [WSJ] 1970).

The Fed's actions caught most market participants by surprise but were generally hailed as constructive.[31] Banks took immediate advantage of the suspension of Regulation Q; rates reported in *The Wall Street Journal* on thirty- to fifty-nine-day CDs issued by New York banks jumped by 1.5 percentage points on the day that the regulation was suspended and remained at the higher level. Commercial paper outstanding declined following Penn Central's bankruptcy announcement but commercial and industrial (C&I) lending rose by about the same amount that commercial paper decreased. Banks were able to fund the increase in C&I loans first by borrowing temporarily at the discount window and subsequently, with the suspension of Regulation Q, by attracting depositors to certificates of deposit (see Figure 4.1).[32] The spread between the yields on four- to six-month prime commercial paper and six-month Treasury bills widened following the Penn Central bankruptcy, likely owing to risk aversion in the commercial paper market and safe-haven flows to government debt. However, this increase in the spread was soon reversed as markets stabilized.

The Fed's response to the Penn Central bankruptcy reflected a notable shift in thinking within the Fed regarding how it should respond to financial instability. By 1970, Fed officials had determined that they should act to prevent financial instability from affecting economic activity even

---

[30] Fed officials quickly decided that suspending Regulation Q was an appropriate response, but were concerned that the action could be inflationary. The FOMC ultimately decided that the new CDs would likely attract the money that would otherwise have funded commercial paper, and thus would have little effect on the expansion of credit or inflation (FOMC Minutes, June 23, 1970, p. 61).

[31] There had been some discussion in the Wall Street Journal that the Federal Reserve would act as a lender of last resort (Janssen and Stabler 1970). However, the articles discussing the lender of last resort option focused on the possibility that aid would be focused on rescuing Penn Central rather than on providing liquidity to the market as a whole.

[32] Prior to the relaxation of Regulation Q, rates on thirty- to fifty-nine-day certificates of deposit reported in *The Wall Street Journal* for New York banks were notably below those on comparable maturity commercial paper.

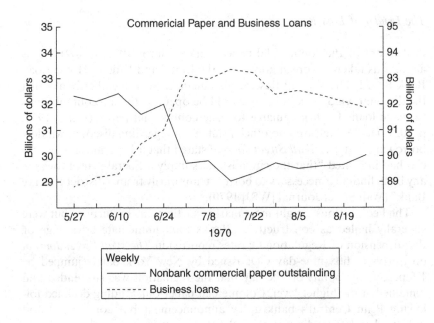

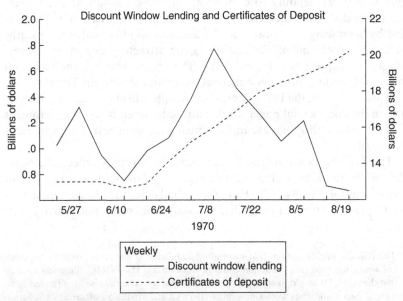

Figure 4.1. Commercial paper, business loans, discount window loans, and certificates of deposit. **(Top)** *Note*: Business loans are commercial and industrial loans and loans to nonbank financial institutions at large, weekly reporting commercial banks. Nonbank commercial paper outstanding is estimated. *Sources*: Banking and Monetary Statistics 1941–1970. Commercial paper: Estimated from Schadrach and Breimyer (1970). **(Bottom)** *Note*: Certificates of deposit are large, negotiable time certificates of deposit at large, weekly reporting commercial banks. Discount window lending includes discounts and advances by Reserve Banks.
Source: Banking and Monetary Statistics 1941–1970.

if that instability originated outside the banking system. Federal Reserve chairman Arthur Burns later summarized the Fed's response to the Penn Central bankruptcy as follows:

Last spring, within a few months after I assumed my present duties, financial markets suffered an erosion of confidence severe enough to cause widespread concern that the country might face a liquidity crisis – a situation in which even creditworthy firms might be unable to borrow the funds they needed to carry on their business.

The sharpest contraction of credit came in the commercial paper market, following the insolvency of the Penn Central Transportation Company, a prominent borrower in that market. Since commercial paper is wholly unsecured, investors backed away from issuers about which there was any question. Concern spread throughout the credit markets, fed by fears that some borrowers might be unable to obtain sufficient credit from alternative sources to refinance maturing commercial paper and thus be forced into bankruptcy. With investors generally becoming more cautious, companies with credit ratings less than Aaa experienced increased difficulty in borrowing through the bond market, as was evidenced by the sharp widening of spreads in the structure of corporate bond yields. In short, there appeared to be a risk of bankruptcies spreading to firms that in other circumstances would be regarded as perfectly sound.

Confronted with an incipient crisis, the Federal Reserve System acted promptly to assure the availability of loanable funds to meet the credit needs of firms that were being squeezed by the contraction of the commercial paper market. First, the System made it clear to member banks that the discount window would be available to assist them in meeting such needs. Second, the Board suspended ceilings on the rates of interest member banks could pay on certificates of deposit of $100,000 or more. In this way banks were placed in a much better position to attract funds to lend to their hard-pressed customers. These two actions helped to restore confidence, and fear of a liquidity crisis abated. We can all take comfort from the fact that the money and credit markets met the tests of mid-1970 successfully. (Burns 1971)

Franklin National

Between the 1950s and 1970s, Franklin National Bank expanded from being a modest-sized regional bank focused in Long Island to the nation's twentieth largest bank. It opened offices internationally in London, England and Nassau, the Bahamas (Brimmer 1976). Franklin worked to expand market share by making loans to riskier borrowers at below market rates. In the year prior to the crisis, Franklin's assets had surged 29 percent to $4.9 billion (Spero 1980).[33] During this period, the bank's capital increased by less than 0.5 percent while its domestic core deposits *decreased* by more than 5 percent. The bank funded its expansion through

---

[33] Adjusted for inflation, the bank would have roughly $20 billion in assets today.

money markets, with about one-sixth of its liabilities consisting of federal funds (Sinkey 1975). Foreign deposits were also an important funding source. Reportedly, Franklin was willing to pay slightly above market rates to fund its expanding balance sheet.

Even before the crisis, both market participants and regulators had grown increasingly concerned about Franklin (Spero 1980). The Office of the Comptroller of the Currency (OCC), Franklin's primary regulator, urged the bank to undertake a sizable retrenchment program. Federal Reserve officials were concerned about weak management, chronic capital deficiencies, excessive reliance on short-term borrowings, and escalating loan losses (Brimmer 1976).

On Tuesday, May 7, Franklin told regulators that "unauthorized" trading had caused the bank to incur severe losses in its foreign exchange department. During this week, the bank started borrowing from the Federal Reserve (Brimmer 1976). On Friday, May 10, the bank announced that it was omitting its second quarter dividend because of poor earnings prospects. Reportedly, this was the first dividend omission by a major bank since the 1930s, which further contributed to investor concerns about the health of the bank.[34]

Over the weekend, the Federal Reserve, Treasury Department, and the FDIC agreed that the Federal Reserve should use the discount window to meet any expected funding difficulties necessary to keep Franklin afloat (Brimmer 1976, pp. 127–128). This decision was made in part out of concern that a failure of Franklin would destabilize money markets and possibly cause the failure of other banks (Burns 1974a). Following its meeting with the Treasury Department and FDIC, the Federal Reserve issued a statement indicating that it was familiar with the troubles at the bank, that it was monitoring the situation, that Franklin had a large amount of acceptable collateral, and that – as with all member banks – the Federal Reserve stood ready to advance funds should the bank experience liquidity problems.

Efforts to support Franklin were also motivated by the bank's foreign exchange positions (Burns 1974b). In June 1974, German authorities closed the Herstatt Bank. The closure rattled foreign exchange markets because at the time of its closure Herstatt had received funds through foreign exchange transactions but had not yet delivered on its legs of the transactions. Franklin was more active in these markets than Herstatt and had large open foreign exchange forward contracts. U.S. regulators were concerned that a failure by Franklin to meet its obligations would

---

[34] The bank subsequently reported a substantial foreign exchange loss, large operating losses, increasing amounts of classified assets, and depreciation in the value of its bond portfolio. Trading in the firm's stock was suspended on May 13.

substantially disrupt market functioning. Newspaper reports indicated that bid-ask spreads in foreign exchange markets had widened considerably amid the troubles at Herstatt and Franklin.[35] Further, the Federal Reserve noted that the value of the German mark had fallen following the Herstatt failure and feared a similar decline in the dollar if the Franklin contracts were dishonored (Spero 1980).

As anticipated, Franklin lost access to private sources of funding – its domestic deposits, federal funds purchased, money market CDs, and foreign deposits all declined. Franklin offset most of these outflows by borrowing heavily at the Fed's discount window (Brimmer 1976).

Even before Franklin's foreign exchange losses and unauthorized trades became public knowledge in May, many banks in foreign exchange markets reportedly had limited, or stopped altogether, their transactions with Franklin. Franklin started to wind down its foreign exchange operations following the public disclosure of its earnings problems. Still, in September, Franklin had more than 300 forward contracts yet to be fulfilled across a range of currencies (Burns 1974b). To prevent Franklin from failing to honor its commitments, the Federal Reserve Bank of New York assumed Franklin's foreign exchange positions after consultations with the Federal Reserve Board, the Treasury, and others. The New York Fed purchased Franklin's foreign exchange balances, amounting to the equivalent of $31.7 million, and acquired Franklin's forward foreign exchange contracts totaling approximately $725 million. These forward positions were gradually wound down. Franklin paid $16 million to the New York Fed to cover the estimated book loss of its positions and potential counterparty risks involved with the foreign exchange book. Franklin's agreement with the New York Fed stated that Franklin would indemnify the New York Fed for any losses in excess of the original estimate, and that any residual balances would be returned to Franklin if realized losses proved less than estimated.[36]

Resolving Franklin's problems posed numerous difficulties. As early as May, efforts were made to find a merger partner for Franklin, but the potential losses from Franklin's loan portfolio and foreign exchange exposures dissuaded potential buyers. It took several months for the FDIC to put together a package that would attract bidders for Franklin. The Comptroller officially closed the bank on October 8,

---

[35] "Bank Foreign Exchange Departments Reducing Their Speculative Positions." *Journal of Commerce*, June 5, 1974.

[36] Part of the payment was to compensate the New York Fed for the risk that some counterparties would not accept the New York Fed's assumption of the contracts. Once the New York Fed was able to confirm with various counterparties that it had assumed the contracts, it returned this portion of the payment to Franklin.

1974. The FDIC, as receiver, auctioned the bank for sale that day and entered into a purchase-and-assumption agreement with the winner, the European-American Bank. Franklin had an outstanding discount window loan of about $1.7 billion when it closed (Sinkey 1975). The FDIC assumed the loan – the first time such an action was taken (Spero 1980).

Continental Illinois National Bank

In 1984, Continental Illinois National Bank (Continental) was the eighth-largest bank in the United States overall and the largest C&I lender.[37] Over the preceding decade, Continental had aggressively expanded its C&I loan portfolio, especially to energy firms. During this period, the bank's business practices were hailed as exemplary, with the manager of bank research at Salomon Brothers reporting that "[i]t's one of the finest managed money-centre banks going" (*Euromoney* 1981, p. 134). Moody's Investors Service rated the long-term debt of Continental's holding company Aaa in 1981 (Moody's Investors Service 1981). Later assessments, however, suggested that the bank's lending standards were lax. Its loans to energy firms proved risky and the bank incurred heavy losses on them.

Continental did not have a large retail banking business; as of December 1983, core deposits comprised less than 20 percent of the bank's liabilities. Continental relied heavily on institutional depositors to meet its funding needs. Over time, domestic institutions became somewhat more hesitant to lend to Continental, and the bank became more dependent on foreign deposits (Moody's Investors Service 1983). By the end of 1983, more than 40 percent of the bank's liabilities consisted of foreign deposits. This reliance on managed liabilities made the firm particularly exposed to deterioration in market sentiment (FDIC 1997).

In early May 1984, concerns about Continental's financial health in the wake of its loan losses resulted in increasing funding difficulties as investors either refused to roll over their Eurodollar deposits or demanded significantly higher rates for renewing them. *The Wall Street Journal* reported that Continental also had difficulty placing large CDs and that investors had tried to dump their Continental CDs in the secondary market (Bailey and Zaslow 1984). Rumors about the bank's funding problems appear to have been partly self-fulfilling in that reports about Continental's funding difficulties led investors to refuse to roll over the bank's other debts as they came due. On May 9, Continental turned to the discount window

---

[37] See also FDIC (1997, 1998) for a detailed history of the events surrounding the troubles at Continental.

(Kilborn 1984; Rowe 1984). By Friday, May 11, its borrowing from the Fed had reached about $3.5 billion (FDIC 1997).

The banking industry rallied to support Continental, and on Monday, May 14, Continental announced that sixteen of the nation's largest commercial banks had agreed to provide it with $4.5 billion in short-term credit (Bailey, Carrington, and Hertzberg 1984). This action reportedly calmed market participants temporarily, but the run on Continental continued as the bank's CDs were not renewed and its Eurodollar funding continued to be withdrawn (FDIC 1997; Sprague 1986, p. 154).

On May 17, the FDIC, Federal Reserve, and OCC announced a temporary assistance plan for Continental in cooperation with a group of commercial banks. The FDIC guaranteed all of the bank's deposits and general creditors. Absent the expanded guarantee, most of Continental's depositors and creditors would not have been insured; the FDIC (1998) reported that at this point Continental had about $3 billion of insured liabilities and $30 billion of uninsured liabilities. The FDIC also injected $1.5 billion into the bank in the form of subordinated notes, with commercial banks adding another $0.5 billion. The Federal Reserve indicated that it would meet any extraordinary liquidity needs of Continental.[38] The short-term credit facility from commercial banks initiated on May 14 was replaced by a $5.3 billion line of credit to Continental from a group of twenty banks.

The initial rescue plan was successful in slowing the run on Continental, and the bank's borrowing at the discount window eased. Newspaper articles reported that the FDIC's guarantee of all deposits was the primary reason that depositors were willing to keep their resources with the bank (WSJ 1984).

Regulators claimed that their extraordinary response to Continental's financial problems was motivated importantly by their concern that the bank's failure would result in a systemic financial crisis that might call into question the condition and liquidity of other large banks.[39] FDIC Director

---

[38] There is some possibility that the liquidity support provided by the Federal Reserve was interpreted more expansively than was intended. The press release issued by the regulatory agencies indicated that "in accordance with customary arrangements, the Federal Reserve is prepared to meet any extraordinary liquidity requirements of the Continental Illinois bank." Thus, the press release affirmed the ability of Continental to borrow from the discount window, provided that it had sufficient collateral. *The New York Times* article describing the assistance package reported that "The Federal Reserve had promised Continental an unrestricted lifeline of loans at the Federal Reserve's otherwise tightly controlled discount window" (Kilborn 1984), which might have been interpreted as suggesting that Continental had special access to the window.

[39] See, for example, the testimony by Comptroller of the Currency Conover and FDIC Chairman Isaac before the House Subcommittee on Financial Institutions Supervision, Regulation, and Insurance on September 19 and October 4, 1984 as well as comments by Federal Reserve Chairman Volcker before the Senate on Banking, Housing and Urban Affairs on July 25, 1984.

Sprague, for example, reported that a collapse of Continental would cause funding difficulties at other large banks and likely bring down two large (unnamed) institutions (Sprague 1986, p. 155).[40] The funding difficulties at Continental did lead to widening risk spreads at other large banks; *The Wall Street Journal* reported:

At the Chicago Mercantile Exchange's International Money Market, the normally tight price spread between Treasury bill futures contracts and those on bank CDs and Eurodollars has been widening all week on rumors that Continental's problems had worsened.

The widening of the spread came even though Continental's CDs aren't among those issued by major banks and traded interchangeably; Continental removed itself from this trading a few years earlier. (Bailey and Zaslow 1984)

Continental also had numerous correspondent banks and the FDIC maintained that some of these banks might fail if their deposits with Continental were not guaranteed.

In July 1984, a permanent assistance plan for Continental was announced (FDIC 1998). Under the plan, the FDIC received loans held by Continental worth $3.5 billion in exchange for assuming an outstanding $3.5 billion discount window loan that Continental had from the Federal Reserve. The FDIC also acquired $1 billion in preferred stock in Continental's holding company (an 80 percent stake), which was down-streamed to the bank in the form of equity. Further, the FDIC received the option to buy stock of the holding company at a rate that depended on the recovery rate on the loans bought by the FDIC. The FDIC also arranged to have the management of the bank and its holding company replaced.

The Federal Reserve agreed to continue to provide liquidity assistance to Continental (and the commercial banks continued to extend a line of credit), and reached a memorandum of understanding with the holding company requiring it to develop a plan to reduce its consolidated assets and preserve the firm's capital (Federal Reserve Board 1984).

The 1987 Stock Market Crash

Stock markets had already experienced a notable decline in the days leading up to the 1987 crash. Stocks declined broadly on October 14, the Wednesday preceding the crash, reportedly because of the introduction of legislation in the U.S. House of Representatives to eliminate tax benefits associated with financing mergers and the announcement of an increase

---

[40] Wall and Peterson (1990) look at abnormal stock returns on the stocks of other large banks and argue that they find little evidence to support the idea that markets were concerned about runs at other banks. They do, however, find negative returns at some banks prior to the guarantee of deposits by the FDIC, which suggests that there may have been some concern about the condition of other banks.

in the U.S. trade deficit, which many expected would lead to a decline in the dollar and a tightening of monetary policy by the Federal Reserve (Securities and Exchange Commission [SEC] Report 1988, pp. 3–10; *WSJ* 1987a). Equity markets continued to decline on Thursday and Friday. The S&P 500 declined more than 9 percent for the week – one of the largest one-week declines in two decades – and helped set the stage for the turmoil during the following week (WSJ 1987b). Investors using a trading strategy referred to as "portfolio insurance" were left with an overhang as their models suggested that they should sell more stocks or futures contracts (SEC Report 1988, pp. 2–10).[41] Mutual funds experienced redemptions and needed to sell shares (Brady Report – The Presidential Task Force on Market Mechanisms – 1988, p. 29). Further, some aggressive institutions anticipated the portfolio insurance sales and mutual fund redemptions and wanted to preempt the sales by selling first (Brady Report 1988, p. 29; SEC Report 1988, pp. 3–12).

Monday, October 19, 1987

Substantial selling pressure on the New York Stock Exchange (NYSE) resumed at the open on Monday with a large imbalance in the number of sell orders relative to buy orders (SEC Report 1988, pp. 2–13). Many specialists did not open for trading during the first hour. The SEC noted that "by 10:00, 95 S&P stocks, representing 30% of the index value, were still not open (1988, pp. 2–13)." As stocks opened notably lower, portfolio insurers' models prompted them to resume sales. These institutions sold in both the cash and futures markets rather than just in the futures market, as was typically the practice (SEC Report 1988, pp. 2–15). The Dow Jones Industrial Average, S&P 500, and Wilshire 5000 declined between 18 and 23 percent on the day amid deteriorating trading conditions (Brady Report 1988, Study III, p. 21). The record trading volume on October 19 overwhelmed many systems. On the NYSE, for example, trade executions were reported more than an hour late, which reportedly caused confusion among traders. Investors did not know whether limit orders had been executed or whether new limits needed to be set (Brady Report 1988, Study III, p. 21).

---

[41] The "portfolio insurance" trading strategy was supposed to limit the losses investors might face from a declining market. Computer models were used to compute optimal stock-to-cash ratios at various market prices. Broadly, the models would suggest that the investor decrease the weight on stocks during falling markets, thereby reducing exposure to the falling market, while during rising markets the models would suggest an increased weight on stocks. Buying portfolio insurance was similar to buying a put option in that it allowed investors to preserve upside gains but limit downside risk. In practice, many portfolio insurers conducted their operations in the futures market rather than in the cash market, as it was less costly (Brady Report 1988, p. 7).

Tuesday, October 20, 1987

Before the opening of financial markets on Tuesday, the Federal Reserve issued a short statement that said: "The Federal Reserve, consistent with its responsibilities as the Nation's central bank, affirmed today its readiness to serve as a source of liquidity to support the economic and financial system." This statement reportedly contributed significantly toward improving market sentiment (Murray 1987), and despite precipitous declines in foreign stock markets overnight, the NYSE rebounded at the open (Brady Report 1988, pp. 36–40). Still, trading remained significantly impaired. Over the course of the day, about 7 percent of stocks, including some of the most active, were closed for trading by the specialists as order imbalances made maintaining orderly markets difficult (Brady Report 1988, p. 45).

Before it opens, the Chicago Mercantile Exchange (CME) clearinghouse collects margin payments from members to cover losses that occurred during the previous day on their open positions. Margin payments are then made to members for open positions in which the value improved the previous day. Typically these payments are completed by noon. On October 20, two CME clearinghouse members had not received margin payments due to them by noon, which precipitated rumors about the solvency of the CME and its ability to make these payments. The rumors proved unfounded but nevertheless reportedly deterred some investors from trading on the CME (Brady Report 1988, p. 40). Bid-ask spreads widened, and trading was characterized as disorderly (Brady Report, Study VI, pp. 64–65).

With the number of trading halts for individual stocks on the NYSE and the possibility that the exchange might close, trading of many stock-index derivative products was suspended on the Chicago Board Options Exchange at 11:45 a.m. and on the CME at 12:15 p.m. (SEC Report 1988, pp. 2–20). These exchanges reopened around 1:00 p.m. Later in the afternoon, there was a sustained rise in equity prices as corporations announced stock buyback programs to support demand for their stocks (Brady Report 1988, p. 41). Corporations had started announcing these programs Monday afternoon but it was apparently not until partway through Tuesday that a critical mass had formed.

Federal Reserve Response

In an effort to restrain the declines in financial markets and to prevent any spillovers to the real economy, the Federal Reserve acted to provide liquidity to the financial system and did so in a high-profile manner that was intended to boost confidence. One of the Fed's most prominent actions was the issuance of the previously noted statement on Tuesday morning. This statement was referred to by one market participant as "the

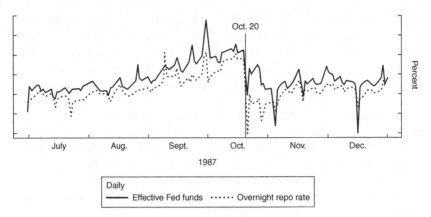

Figure 4.2. Overnight interest rates.
Source: Federal Reserve H.15 statistical release and market data.

most calming thing that was said [Tuesday]" (Murray 1987). The Federal Reserve followed up the statement by carrying out open market operations that pushed the federal funds rate down to near 7 percent on Tuesday from more than 7.5 percent on Monday (see Figure 4.2).

The action was taken to "provide significant liquidity to relieve the turbulence and tension in the wake of the financial market upheaval" (FOMC transcripts, meeting of November 3, 1987, comments by Peter Sternlight, p. 2). Other short-term interest rates followed the federal funds rate lower, thereby reducing costs for borrowers. The Federal Reserve continued to inject reserves over the next several weeks to buoy liquidity in financial markets. Moreover, open market operations were conducted in a high-profile manner, frequently conducted an hour or more before the normally scheduled market intervention period, to underscore to market participants that the Federal Reserve was providing liquidity support (FOMC transcripts, meeting of November 3, 1987, comments by Peter Sternlight, p. 3; Winkler 1987).

The Federal Reserve also worked with banks and securities firms to ensure that credit was extended to support the liquidity and funding needs of brokers and dealers. The sharp price movements on October 19 on futures contracts resulted in record margin calls for members of the CME clearinghouse. The end-of-day margin calls for October 19 needed to be met before the start of business on the morning of October 20. To meet these calls, clearinghouse member firms drew on their credit lines with the four banks that provided settlement services for the CME. These banks were reportedly concerned as the margin calls exceeded lending limits and increased their exposure to the securities industry at a point when financial markets were tumbling. To help make the extensions of credit and transfers of funds proceed smoothly, the Federal Reserve Banks of Chicago and New York reportedly let commercial banks in both districts know that the Federal Reserve would help provide liquidity for the loans and intraday credit to brokers. In part as a result of these efforts, the settlement banks extended the necessary credit and the accounts for CME clearinghouse members were fully funded by market opening. In testimony given in 1994 to the Senate Banking Committee, Chairman Greenspan indicated that "[t]elephone calls placed by officials of the Federal Reserve Bank of New York to senior management of the major New York City banks helped to assure a continuing supply of credit to the clearinghouse members, which enabled those members to make the necessary margin payments" (Greenspan 1994, p. 137).

Government, and in particular U.S. Treasury, securities are often used as collateral in repurchase agreements and other financial contracts (and can also be pledged to satisfy margin calls). Trading and lending these securities is an important source of market liquidity. After the stock market crash, holders of government securities were somewhat reluctant to lend them as freely as normal, possibly owing to concerns about counterparty risk, which led to scarcity of some securities and a rise in fails to deliver (Greenspan 1988, p. 92). To enhance liquidity in the government securities market, the Federal Reserve temporarily liberalized the rules governing lending of securities from its portfolio by suspending the per issue and per dealer limits on the amount of loans (FOMC transcripts, meeting of November 3, 1987, presentation by Peter Sternlight, p. 7).

The Federal Reserve and other agencies also took a variety of supervisory actions to ensure the soundness of the financial system. The Fed placed examiners in major banking institutions and monitored developments, in part to identify potential runs as well as to assess the banking industry's credit exposure to securities firms (Greenspan 1988, pp. 90–92). The Fed's monitoring efforts went beyond the banking industry and included stepped up daily monitoring of the government securities markets and of the health of primary dealer and inter-dealer brokers.

Long-Term Capital Management

Long-Term Capital Management (LTCM) was a hedge fund founded in 1994 by John Meriweather, a former executive at Salomon Brothers. A number of traders from Salomon Brothers' Arbitrage Desk joined LTCM, as did Robert Merton and Myron Scholes, two important figures in finance who won the Nobel Prize in Economics in 1997. Over its first three years, the hedge fund consistently had high profits, with a return on equity of more than 40 percent in 1995 and 1996 and a solid, though lower, 17 percent in 1997 (Siconolfi, Raghavan, and Pacelle 1998). The fund's usual, though not exclusive, investment strategy was to use models to identify deviations from historical relationships in the prices of financial contracts and then enter positions that would pay out as the anomalies disappeared (Edwards 1999). A frequent bet was that the yields on different interest rate contracts would converge. Typically the price discrepancies exploited by LTCM were small and the firm used substantial leverage to profit from these opportunities. With the pedigree of its staff and its high returns, other financial institutions reportedly were convinced that interacting with LTCM involved minimal risk (Lowenstein 2000, pp. 44–48). Institutions also competed to do business with LTCM, partly because they hoped to learn about the highly profitable firm's positions. Thus, the firm was able to get exceptionally low-cost financing and operate with high leverage.

LTCM began to incur losses during the Asian crisis in 1997, which worsened considerably with the Russian default in 1998. Following the Asian crisis and into 1998, risk spreads widened and implied volatility in asset markets increased. LTCM viewed the level of spreads and volatility as out of line with historical experience and took positions that would profit if spreads narrowed and implied volatilities declined (Lowenstein 2000, pp. 124–146, 187–188). Instead, risk spreads widened and implied volatilities surged following the Russian default as investors rushed to Treasury securities, the preferred safe-haven security. Although LTCM reportedly had tested its positions for possible loss, its models were based on historical patterns in the data and did not anticipate the size of the movements in asset prices that followed the Russian default (Dunbar 2000, pp. 202–207). Given the fund's high leverage, these losses quickly eroded its capital (Edwards 1999). As LTCM's losses mounted, its counterparties began to tighten margin and collateral requirements so that the firm's liquidity started to dry up (Lipin, Murray, and Schlesinger 1998).

Meriweather attempted to raise additional capital in an effort to shore up LTCM's capital position. In mid-September, LTCM officials informed the Federal Reserve Bank of New York that its efforts to raise capital had stalled and that the fund's position was continuing to deteriorate. New York Fed President William McDonough testified to the House Committee on Banking and Financial Services that market participants had informed New York Fed staff that the deterioration of LTCM was negatively affecting financial markets (McDonough 1998, p. 18).

Fed officials determined that, given the stress already apparent in financial markets, the failure of LTCM could pose a significant systemic shock and that the Federal Reserve should help facilitate a resolution of the hedge fund's problems. As noted by Chairman Greenspan in testimony before the House Committee on Banking and Financial Services, "[w]ith credit spreads already elevated and the market prices of risky assets under considerable downward pressure, Federal Reserve officials moved more quickly to provide their good offices to help resolve the affairs of LTCM than would have been the case in more normal times" (Greenspan 1998, p. 23). As noted previously, following the Russian default, many markets were already exhibiting high levels of stress. With the already somewhat fragile state of financial markets, officials were concerned about spillover to other financial markets and institutions – both direct counterparties of LTCM and others that may have had similar market positions. Chairman Greenspan noted in his testimony that:

The act of unwinding LTCM's portfolio in a forced liquidation would not only have a significant distorting impact on market prices but also in the process could produce large losses, or worse, for a number of creditors and counterparties, and for other market participants who were not directly involved with LTCM. (Greenspan 1998, p. 24)

A further concern was that the distress in financial markets could have broader negative impact on the U.S. economy. With the elevated risk premiums in bond markets pushing up yields on corporate bonds, especially junk bonds, issuance declined (see Figure 4.3); similarly, *The Wall Street Journal* noted, "[n]ew issuance of junk bonds has almost ground to a halt after a nervous tone gripped the market last week ... Volatility and sharp plunges in the stock market last week cast such a negative tone that many issuers preferred to postpone their deals rather than pay higher interest rates" (Zuckerman 1998). Federal Reserve officials were concerned that liquidating LTCM might further disrupt the ability of firms to raise money in financial markets: "This [liquidation of LTCM] would have caused a vicious cycle: a loss of investor confidence, leading to a rush out of private credits, leading to a further widening of credit spreads, leading to further liquidations of positions, and so on. Most importantly, this would have led to further increases in the cost of capital to American businesses" (McDonough 1998, p. 19).

On September 23, sixteen large financial institutions met at the Federal Reserve Bank of New York where they reviewed the position of LTCM, the possible effects on markets if it were liquidated, and options for resolving the situation (Lowenstein 2000, pp. 201–208). Some banks reportedly expressed surprise when they learned the extent of LTCM's positions (Corrigan and Lewis 1998; Mufson and Dugan 1998). After some discussion, the banks decided to establish a consortium that would recapitalize LTCM and agreed in principle to inject $3.5 billion into the hedge fund (Raghavan and Pacelle 1998). Fourteen banks, all but two of the banks that attended the meeting, agreed to participate in the consortium (Dunbar 2000, pp. 222–223). The largest banks nominated a committee

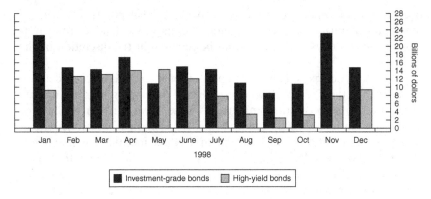

Figure 4.3. Gross bond issuance.
Source: Data are from Securities Data Company.

to oversee LTCM and the unwinding of its positions (Morgenson 1998). LTCM was considered too complex for outsiders to step into managing the positions. Thus, to give management an incentive to stay and liquidate the fund, existing investors, many of whom were LTCM managers, maintained one-tenth of the equity of the fund (Lowenstein 2000, pp. 205–206; Morgenson 1998).

RESPONSE TO THE FINANCIAL CRISIS OF 2007–2009

The recent financial crisis was more severe than any episode since at least the 1930s. The Fed's response to the crisis dwarfed any of its actions in previous crises, but many were anticipated by prior actions. Here we briefly review the Fed's response to the recent crisis and then discuss the parallels with other episodes.

Brief Review of Actions Taken during the Recent Crisis

At the onset of the crisis, the Federal Reserve responded to the rising strains in interbank funding markets with only minor modifications of its traditional tools for providing liquidity to financial markets. Monetary policy was eased swiftly, beginning in September 2007 with a reduction in the target federal funds rate of 50 basis points from 5.25 percent to 4.75 percent.[42] The terms on the main discount window related program, the primary credit facility, were also progressively eased as the crisis deepened. The penalty on discount window loans, normally 100 basis points

---

[42] In October 2008, as the crisis became most intense, the policy rate was reduced to 1 percent. In December 2008, the target rate was reduced further, to a range of 0 to 25 basis points.

over the federal funds target rate, was cut to 25 basis points. Further, the maximum maturity of discount window loans was extended from overnight to ninety days and loans could be renewed at the discretion of the borrower.

As the crisis deepened and the condition of interbank markets deteriorated further, the Federal Reserve established other programs to facilitate access by banks to central bank credit.[43] The Term Auction Facility (or TAF) was the first such program. Under TAF, the Fed auctioned credit to depository institutions for terms of up to three months. The rate banks paid to borrow was determined by the auction process, subject to a floor. The Fed established the TAF in part because the volume of discount window borrowing had remained low despite persistent stress in interbank funding markets, apparently because of a perceived stigma associated with borrowing at the discount window. Possibly because of the auction format and the time between the auction date and the settlement date, the TAF offered a source of term funds without associated stigma. Later in the crisis, the FDIC supported efforts by depository institutions to maintain their liquidity by insuring all transaction deposits; raising the insurance limit for other types of deposits; and, for a fee, providing insurance for bonds issued by depository institutions (the latter being part of the Temporary Liquidity Guarantee Program).

As part of its typical operating framework, the Federal Reserve lends securities to primary dealers from the system open market portfolio; this lending program typically supports market functioning in secured money markets by expanding access to individual securities for which there is exceptional demand. During the crisis, The Fed eased terms on this regular securities lending program by reducing the rate charged for borrowing securities. In addition, the Federal Reserve established an auction facility to lend Treasury securities to dealers for periods of a month against other Treasury securities, agency securities, agency mortgage-backed securities, as well as against highly rated private securities. (The latter part of this program was done under Section 13(3) of the Federal Reserve Act through a program referred to as the Term Secured Lending Facility [TSLF].) The Fed provided additional support to the primary dealers via direct loans through the Primary Dealer Credit Facility (PDCF, another program established under Section 13(3) of the Federal Reserve Act).

Given the global nature of interbank markets, and the importance of the dollar in these markets, the Federal Reserve entered into bilateral currency swap agreements with foreign central banks. The number and size of these

---

[43] Summaries of the credit and liquidity programs introduced by the Federal Reserve during the crisis are available from the Board of Governors of the Federal Reserve System (www.federalreserve.gov/monetarypolicy/bst.htm).

swap agreements increased as the crisis worsened. These facilities enabled the foreign central banks to acquire dollars from the Federal Reserve that they could then lend to banks in their jurisdictions. These swap agreements helped to ease conditions in dollar funding markets globally.

Commercial paper markets are critical sources of short-term funding for many financial and nonfinancial institutions. These markets came under severe pressure during the financial crisis, especially after a money market mutual fund (Reserve Primary Fund) that had been an important supplier of funds in the markets "broke the buck" following the collapse of Lehman Brothers. The Federal Reserve established a variety of programs to address strains in commercial paper markets and the liquidity pressures faced by money market mutual funds that faced heavy investor withdrawals. For example, the Asset-Backed Commercial Paper Money Market Mutual Fund Liquidity Facility (AMLF) assisted money funds by providing loans to depository institutions and bank holding companies to fund purchases of high-quality asset-backed commercial paper from money market mutual funds. Another program, the Commercial Paper Funding Facility (CPFF), provided a more direct liquidity backstop to the commercial paper market by providing funding to a specially created limited liability company that could purchase three-month unsecured and asset-backed commercial paper directly from eligible issuers. Support to the money market mutual fund industry also came from the Treasury Department, which guaranteed investments in money funds.

The Term Asset-Backed Securities Loan Facility (TALF) was yet another program designed to address strains in key financial markets and in particular the market for asset-backed securities. The TALF issued loans to finance purchases of eligible asset-backed securities (ABS) for terms up to five years. ABS had been an important source of funding for the makers of automobile loans and credit card loans that largely collapsed during the crisis. The TALF was intended to assist the financial markets in accommodating the credit needs of consumers and businesses of all sizes by facilitating the issuance of ABS collateralized by a variety of consumer and business loans.

The Federal Reserve also provided support directly to specific non-depository financial institutions. The Fed facilitated the acquisition of Bear Stearns by JPMorgan Chase & Co. by extending a loan to a limited liability company established to acquire certain assets of Bear Stearns. The Fed also extended a loan to American International Group, Inc. (AIG) after the officials determined that, given the circumstances in financial markets at the time, "a disorderly failure of AIG could add to the already significant levels of financial market fragility and lead to substantially higher borrowing costs, reduced household wealth, and materially weaker economic performance" (Federal Reserve Board 2008).

The extraordinary liquidity provision by the Federal Reserve helped reduce systemic risk by assuring market participants that, should short-term investors begin to lose confidence, financial institutions would be able to meet demands for cash without resorting to potentially destabilizing fire sales of assets. As the functioning in financial markets normalized and the liquidity troubles of financial institutions waned, these extraordinary facilities were gradually wound down and terms on standing facilities normalized.

Given the topic of this chapter, in this section we have focused just on programs that are tied to lender of last resort actions, especially those conducted by the Federal Reserve. A number of other programs were introduced by different government agencies during the financial crisis. For instance, the Treasury Department injected equity capital directly into financial institutions through the purchase of preferred stock and the FDIC provided a number of temporary expansions to its usual deposit insurance program.

Relation to Federal Reserve Responses to Preceding Crises

Since the Great Depression, the Federal Reserve has shown increased willingness to respond to disruptions in financial market functioning outside the banking sector, and the Fed's responses to episodes from 1970 to 2000 in many ways anticipated some of its responses to the recent crisis. For instance, the Fed's response to the problems in the commercial paper market during 2007–2009 built on the actions taken during 1970. In the earlier episode, the Fed lifted deposit interest rate ceilings to provide a means by which banks could fill a funding gap caused by collapse of the commercial paper market. In the recent crisis, the Fed again sought to enable banks to backstop the money market mutual fund industry and thus indirectly the commercial paper market (which was under pressure as a result of the run on the money market mutual fund industry) through the AMLF. However, given the pressures that banks already faced, the Fed also opted to provide direct support to the commercial paper market through the CPFF. This type of assistance to nonfinancial institutions did not have precedence in the response to financial crises since 1970, but does resemble the lending conducted in the 1930s through the Section 13(3), Section 13(13), and Section 13(b) programs arranged at that time.

During previous episodes of market stress, such as following the 1987 stock market crash, the Federal Reserve had eased terms related to lending securities from the system open market portfolio. These prior experiences provided the foundation for easing terms of lending during the most recent crisis and for programs such as the TSLF.

The Fed's willingness to provide extraordinary support to individual financial institutions when it was thought that their failures could destabilize financial markets or spill over to other financial institutions is evidenced by the responses to Franklin National and Continental Illinois. These two troubled firms were both depository institutions and Federal Reserve System members, which made assistance more straightforward. The Federal Reserve response to LTCM demonstrates a concern about threats posed by large non-bank financial institutions. In that case, private actors had the capacity to conduct the rescue. With AIG, however, the Fed determined that private institutions lacked the capacity to respond. Rescues of individual institutions, such as AIG, are well understood to be problematic. Fed officials acknowledged the problems of too-big-to-fail and moral hazard, but contended that without another means of resolving the failures of firms that pose systemic risk, they had little choice but to protect creditors from taking losses in order to avoid catastrophic consequences for the financial system and economy (e.g., Bernanke 2009a). The Dodd–Frank Wall Street Reform and Consumer Protection Act of 2010 responded to these concerns by authorizing the FDIC to resolve systemically important institutions. The Dodd–Frank Act also prohibits the Fed from lending to individual non-depository institutions under Section 13(3) except as part of a program to provide liquidity to a class of institutions or markets.

OBSERVATIONS AND LESSONS FROM THE HISTORICAL EPISODES

Since 1970, the Fed has demonstrated a willingness to respond to financial disturbances that officials believe ultimately threaten to disrupt economic activity. In the cases of Penn Central and LTCM, Fed officials believed that nonfinancial firms might lose access to funding. In the Franklin National episode, the Fed was concerned about potentially detrimental impacts on the economy resulting from potential exchange rate volatility. The wide-ranging disruptions to financial intermediation in the recent financial crisis and concerns about the impact on the economy were clearly important in motivating Fed actions in 2007–2009.

The Fed has employed a range of tools in responding to financial disturbances. The discount window has been a part of the response in most, but not all episodes. The discount window has also been used in different forms: the window was used to provide broad liquidity support to the banking sector via the TAF auctions during the recent episode and to the banking sector as it stepped in to replace commercial paper in the Penn Central episode. The window was also used to provide support to specific institutions such as Continental Illinois and AIG.[44] Open market operations were

---

[44] Loans to AIG were soon restructured as credits to newly formed limited liability companies, Maiden Lane II LLC and Maiden Lane III LLC. Further details are included in

used to provide additional liquidity to the financial system in response to the stock market crash and market disruptions in 2007–2009. (Monetary policy was also used to respond to concerns about the economy amid the financial crises.) Public announcements have also figured prominently in the Fed's responses as policymakers sought to reassure markets. Finally, in several cases, part of the Fed's response involved working with market participants to solve coordination problems, as in the wake of the 1987 stock market crash.

How Should a Central Bank Provide Liquidity?

A longstanding debate in academic and policy forums concerns how a lender of last resort should provide liquidity, and in particular whether the lender of last resort should ever lend directly to individual financial institutions. Bordo (1990) nicely describes several approaches that have been advocated. He notes that the classical position (as articulated by Thorton and Bagehot) is to lend freely at a high interest rate. As a variation on the classical view, Friedman and Schwartz (1963) advocate the use of a penalty rate during normal times but a non-penalty rate during a crisis to maintain the money stock (see Nelson 2011 for further discussion). A second approach, advocated by Kaufman (1991), Goodfriend and King (1988), and Schwartz (1992), among others, is that the lender of last resort should provide liquidity support using open market operations to keep the stock of high-powered money from falling, but generally avoid lending directly to individual institutions. They argue that using the discount window to provide direct support to individual financial institutions, or to address crises originating in the financial sector, can increase moral hazard and cause distortions by removing decisions about credit risk from private markets. Moreover, in an effort to guard against a crisis, policymakers may be inclined to lend freely at any sign of trouble, which could exacerbate moral hazard and thereby increase financial instability.[45]

An alternative view holds that targeted lending to individual financial institutions may be the appropriate response to financial instability. Goodhart (1999) argues that targeted lending to affected financial firms

the Appendix on Federal Reserve Initiatives to Address Financial Strains to the Federal Reserve's Monetary Policy Report for February 2009.

[45] Goodfriend (2012) argues that wide operational and financial independence gives the Federal Reserve an incentive to lend expansively in an effort to avoid financial crises, but that doing so has the capacity to create ever-greater boom and bust cycles. By contrast, he argues that as a private, profit-maximizing institution, the nineteenth century Bank of England had an incentive to lend during a crisis on only high-quality collateral at a level that maintained the stock of high-powered money, which limited distorting credit allocation.

may be necessary to keep financial instability from spreading because it is often impossible to determine reliably the relative importance of illiquidity and insolvency during a crisis. Once the situation has stabilized, insolvency concerns can be dealt with more readily. Rochet and Vives (2004) argue that there are situations in which failures in market coordination can result in liquidity shocks that are best dealt with through discount window lending.[46]

Stern and Feldman (2004) suggest an approach that retains the possibility of supporting individual institutions while addressing concerns about moral hazard and institutions that are too-big-to-fail. Stern and Feldman (2004) argue that in a crisis, policymakers should allow the first large financial institution to fail, that is, not protect the firm's creditors from loss, but then take extraordinary measures to support remaining firms – even potentially insolvent ones – to prevent contagion. By explicitly allowing the failure of at least one large firm, the lender of last resort policy suggested by Stern and Feldman (2004) would limit moral hazard while protecting the banking system from contagion.

Corrigan (1990) suggests another strategy for limiting moral hazard, known as "constructive ambiguity." Corrigan argues that lending to individual firms may be necessary to stem a crisis, but ambiguity about when and which firms would receive bailouts would limit moral hazard. Although constructive ambiguity has appeal ex ante, some have suggested that this policy is not effective ex post. For instance, Meltzer (2009b) argues that the recent financial crisis was worsened by the apparent inconsistent treatment of the creditors of Bear Stearns and Lehman Brothers. In this instance, however, ambiguity may have arisen because of legal constraints on the Fed's ability to lend because, unlike Bear Stearns or AIG, Lehman lacked sufficient collateral to post for a loan from the Fed (Bernanke 2008).

The historical experiences described here illustrate some challenges in using open market operations alone to respond to financial crises. Financial crises are associated with heightened uncertainty about counterparty risks, collateral values, and the capacity of certain borrowers to repay their obligations, all of which increase demand for liquidity and risk-free assets.[47] Open market operations, which are conducted with a relatively small set of institutions, are unlikely to alleviate a crisis unless interbank markets are functioning reasonably smoothly, which has not been the

---

[46] Bordo (1990) also notes that some have argued against any lender of last resort but instead advocate allowing free currency issue by commercial banks.

[47] Indeed, one reason for the TSLF was to allow institutions to substitute less liquid and slightly riskier collateral for higher quality and more liquid collateral (for a small fee and with a haircut).

case in many crises. For example, following the 1987 stock market crash, the willingness of financial intermediaries to provide credit to each other was impaired, and encouraging them to extend credit was a key part of the Federal Reserve response. Similarly, the Fed introduced the TAF in December 2007 after determining that open market operations and the Fed's more conventional discount window programs were failing to alleviate strains in interbank funding markets (Bernanke 2009b).

In several of the crises reviewed here, the Fed sought to ensure that financial institutions had ample liquidity to support markets under strain: commercial paper following Penn Central, bank funding market investors after Continental Illinois, and securities dealers during the 1987 stock market crash. Importantly, in these cases, the Fed believed that liquidity problems had the potential to contribute to deterioration in solvency of various institutions, including those removed from the immediate crisis.[48] Thus, these episodes suggest that provision of liquidity to institutions affected by the crisis either directly or indirectly may be quite important in limiting the spread of crises, preventing asset fire sales, and for allowing a more timely resolution of solvency concerns. On the other hand, it is impossible to know how these crises would have played out if the Fed had not intervened, or simply committed to maintaining the stock of high-powered money or an inflation target.

Our review of the Fed's history as lender of last resort illustrates how the regulatory environment and the scale of the shadow banking system also affect how the lender of last resort responds to crises. Following the bankruptcy of Penn Central in 1970, the banking system, with support from the Federal Reserve, was able to provide credit to institutions shut out of the commercial paper market in part because that market was not large. By 2007, however, the nonfinancial commercial paper market and asset-backed commercial paper market had become quite large. The Federal Reserve established facilities such as the AMLF to channel liquidity through banks to support money market mutual funds and the commercial paper market in a manner broadly similar to what had occurred in the earlier episode. Without such support, banks likely would have been unable to provide loans to replace the substantial drop in commercial paper (or bring the asset-backed commercial paper programs onto their own balance sheets) without becoming highly leveraged or significantly altering the composition of their assets.

---

[48] Calomiris (1994) argues that providing backup protection for financial markets is perhaps the main justification for discount window lending. He also argues that the Fed's response to the failure of Penn Central of taking a more open stance toward use of the discount window was, in fact, consistent with a classical approach of providing liquidity support to the market while leaving credit decisions in the hands of the private market.

The commercial paper market is only a small part of the shadow banking system that was experiencing liquidity difficulties during the crisis. The growth in the size of the shadow banking system has made it is more difficult to provide liquidity support to the financial sector through the banking system. This was apparent during the recent crisis when the Fed determined that it was necessary to establish a number of facilities such as the PDCF and TSLF to support nonbank financial intermediaries that in turn supported many parts of the shadow banking system (Madigan 2009). The fact that the shadow banking system provides many services that were traditionally done within the banking sector – such as maturity transformation and payment services – adds a further complication to the discussion of what types of institutions ought to have access to the lender of last resort.[49] Moreover, as noted by Bernanke (2009b), the nonbank financial sector outside the shadow banking system, such as the corporate bond and syndicated loan markets, is also quite important in the United States, adding further to the challenges faced by the lender of last resort in responding to threats outside the commercial banking system.

Another characteristic we observe in the crisis episodes described here is the concern about spillovers. Franklin National was rescued because of concerns that its failure would roil foreign exchange markets (and thus threaten other financial institutions and the economy). Continental Illinois was rescued partly because of the potential impact its failure could have on wholesale funding markets on which other banks depended. AIG was rescued largely out of concern about the potential impact its failure would have had on commercial paper, other public debt markets, and insurance products to millions of customers (with associated impacts on other financial institutions and on the economy) (Bernanke 2009a). In each case, these institutions were provided extraordinary financing when they lost access to private funding. Institution-specific rescues such as these increase moral hazard.[50] The enhanced resolution strategy contemplated under the Dodd–Frank Wall Street Reform and Consumer Protection Act of 2010 is intended to provide an alternative that will reduce the need for such rescues going forward. Only time will tell whether these measures will prove effective.

---

[49] Still further, Madigan (2009) argues that troubles at shadow banks can affect funding markets, which in turn can impact traditional banks. For example, he notes that money market mutual funds are important purchasers of commercial paper, which in turn is an important source of funding for some banks. Troubles at money market funds and a reduction in their ability to buy commercial paper could thus increase bank funding costs. Madigan argues that these connections ought also to be considered by the lender of last resort.

[50] See, for example, Reinhart (2008) for more detailed list of concerns related to the moral hazard issue, particularly where it concerns providing support to nonbank financial firms.

CONCLUSION

The authors of the Federal Reserve Act intended the Federal Reserve to serve as lender of last resort to the banking system, and in so doing end banking panics in the United States. However, the banking panics and near collapse of the banking system during the Great Depression demonstrated that the Fed as originally established did not guarantee an effective lender of last resort. The Federal Reserve Act failed to re-create the financial environment that enabled the Bank of England and other European central banks to perform effectively as lenders of last resort. In its early years, the Fed was also hamstrung by leadership failures, poor understanding of the appropriate role of a lender of last resort, and statutory limitations on its ability to support the banking system through its discount window.

As a result of the Great Depression, the Federal Reserve System was reorganized and its emergency lending powers were greatly enhanced. Subsequent to the Great Depression, the Federal Reserve demonstrated a much greater willingness to intervene to stem what it perceived were threats to financial stability (which in turn were viewed as threats to economic stability). As these threats to financial stability materialized within an evolving financial system, the Federal Reserve responded with a range of initiatives and actions. The scale of the Fed's response to the financial crisis of 2007–2009 was unmatched in the Federal Reserve's history, but many of the types of programs introduced then had parallels with methods the Fed used to address earlier crises. The legislative response to the financial crisis of 2007–2009, the Dodd–Frank Act, in some ways enhanced the Fed's authority still further, for example, by indicating that the Federal Reserve, at the direction of the Financial Stability Oversight Council, should assume an oversight position of institutions considered to pose a systemic threat. The Dodd–Frank Act also changed the Fed's authority for lending under unusual and exigent circumstances such that the Fed can no longer extend credit to individual firms other than through a program with broad-based eligibility; this change was intended to ensure that such emergency lending programs are geared toward providing liquidity to the financial system as a whole, but in limiting the Fed's ability to support individual firms the change may reduce the Fed's flexibility in responding to an unfolding crisis.[51]

More broadly, the history of the Fed's responses to crises illustrates the importance of government policy toward the banking and broader financial systems. The overall regulatory environment affects the likelihood

---

[51] However, it should be noted that the Dodd–Frank Act did expand access to the discount window for designated financial market utilities to support the functioning of market payments and settlement systems.

that a central bank will be needed as a lender of last resort and whether the central bank is likely to be effective in that role. For example, strict limits on branch banking probably made the U.S. banking system more crisis prone in the nineteenth century and for most of the twentieth century, which increased the likelihood that lender of last actions would be required. The size and nature of the shadow banking sector and its relation to the traditional banking sector and importance to the overall economy have clearly shaped the Fed's response to crises. The size and importance of the largest financial intermediaries, and the ability of the regulators or courts to unwind them, also has an effect on lender of last resort policy.

The Fed's history as lender of last resort does not fully answer some important questions. For example, it remains an open question whether a central bank can serve effectively as lender of last resort solely by using open market operations to maintain the level (or growth) of high-powered money, as argued by Goodfriend and King (1988), Schwartz (1992), and others. In the Great Depression, the Fed neither maintained adequate growth of high-powered money nor responded to banking panics with a liberal lending policy. Since then, the Fed has used a variety of methods to respond to financial disturbances, including currency depots, liberal discount window lending, and special lending facilities to provide liquidity to nonbank firms and markets, but never relied solely on open market operations. The Fed has always viewed its lender of last resort mission as distinct from its monetary policy mission. Policymakers have usually determined that other tools are more effective than open market operations for dealing with a financial disturbance. However, they may have also seen a conflict between aggressively countering a crisis with the tools of monetary policy and maintaining control of inflation or achieving other monetary policy objectives. Using only open market operations to respond to the financial crisis of 2007–2009 would likely have been exceptionally challenging given the breakdown of interbank funding markets, a substantial disruption in what had become a very large shadow banking system, and severe troubles in other key segments of the financial system. The determination by the Fed that it could not resolve the crisis by supplying liquidity solely through open market operations, or even through its traditional discount window facility, resulted in the establishment of various facilities to channel funds to specific markets and types of firms. Moreover, until it could no longer do so, the Fed reduced its holdings of Treasury securities to prevent its lending from increasing the size of its balance sheet. Given the disruptions in interbank funding markets and the heightened demand for Treasury securities during the crisis of 2007–2009, it seems unlikely that the Fed could have fully resolved the crisis by competing with private firms in the open market for Treasury securities. Further, the essence of Bagehot's Rule requires the conversion of *illiquid* assets into liquid assets, not one form of liquid assets (Treasury securities) into another (Fed liabilities).[52] The rapid winding down of the Term Auction Facility and other liquidity programs established by the Fed during the crisis of 2007–2009 suggests that they served their intended purpose of providing liquidity during the crisis without becoming a source of cheap financing for the long term.

The Fed's history also does not fully answer questions about which firms should have access to the lender of last resort. The Federal Reserve Act originally limited access to the Fed's discount window to member banks, which was problematic during the Great Depression when banking panics and failures were more prevalent among nonmember banks. The Monetary Control Act of 1980 opened the Fed's discount window to all depository institutions. However, the financial crisis of 2007–2009 originated in the "shadow banking" system comprised of investment banks and other financial firms outside the traditional banking sector. These firms created liquidity by issuing short-term, seemingly high-quality claims against holdings of long-term assets, which made them vulnerable to run-like phenomena. In assisting in the acquisition of Bear Stearns and in providing loans to AIG, the Fed determined that the disorderly failures of these institutions threatened the broader financial system and economy. Bernanke (2008), in particular, argued that AIG was simply too large and complex to allow to fail in a disorderly manner during an ongoing crisis and noted several concerns about potential impact on the economy from such a bankruptcy. Although the Fed had not previously provided financial assistance to prevent the failure of a nonbank financial firm, it has a long history of responding to disruptions outside the banking system, beginning with the New York Fed's response to the 1929 stock market crash, and including the Fed's responses to the Penn Central crisis, 1987 stock market crash, and the near failure of LTCM. Further, the Fed's actions were not unlike those of J. P. Morgan in 1907, when he helped facilitate loans to prevent the failures of several trust companies that stood outside the regulated banking system but were active in the same markets as banks. However, extending lender of last resort protection beyond the traditional, regulated banking system would foster moral hazard and encourage the growth of a shadow banking system. It is important, therefore, for policymakers to determine in advance how far lender of last resort protection should extend beyond the traditional banking system, and to impose regulations or other measures to limit moral hazard by all firms that enjoy lender of last resort protection.

---

[52] Indeed, this conversion was the purpose of the TSLF, which allowed institutions to borrow Treasury securities in exchange for posting less liquid collateral (for a small fee). Thus the facility increased the liquidity of financial institutions without affecting the size of the Federal Reserve's balance sheet.

Since its creation in 1913, the Fed's crisis response has evolved as it has rethought its role as a lender of last resort, as that role has been altered by Congress, and as financial industry itself has evolved. Many of the important debates about the proper role of a lender of last resort remain to be solved and are likely to become only more complicated as the financial industry becomes more complex. Nevertheless, the lessons illustrated by the past 100 years of crisis responses do provide useful insights that help inform those debates.

REFERENCES

Bailey, J., T. Carrington, and D. Hertzberg. (1984). "Continental Illinois Gets Rescue Package of $4.5 Billion in Record Bailout Attempt." *Wall Street Journal*, May 15, p. 3.

Bailey, J., and J. Zaslow. (1984). "Continental Illinois Securities Plummet Amid Rumors Firm's Plight Is Worsening." *Wall Street Journal*, May 11, p. 3.

Bernanke, Ben. (2008). "Federal Reserve Policies in the Financial Crisis." Speech at the Greater Austin Chamber of Commerce, Austin, Texas, December 1, 2008.

(2009a). "Reflections on a Year of Crisis." Speech at the Federal Reserve Bank of Kansas City's Annual Economic Symposium, Jackson Hole, Wyoming, August 21, 2009.

(2009b). "The Crisis and the Policy Response." Stamp Lecture, London School of Economics, London. Speech dated January 13, 2009.

Bordo, Michael D. (1990). "The Lender of Last Resort: Alternative Views and Historical Experience." *Economic Review* FRB Richmond, Jan/Feb 1990:18–29.

(1993). "The Gold Standard, Bretton Woods and Other Monetary Regimes: A Historical Appraisal." *Federal Reserve Bank of St. Louis Review* March–April 75(2):123–191.

Bordo, Michael D., Rockhoff, Hugh, and Angela Redish. (1994). "The U.S. Banking System from a Northern Exposure: Stability versus Efficiency." *Journal of Economic History* 54:325–341.

Bordo, Michael D., and David C. Wheelock. (2013). "The Promise and Performance of the Federal Reserve as Lender of Last Resort 1913–1933." In Michael D. Bordo and William Roberds (eds), *The Origins, History, and Future of the Federal Reserve: A Return to Jekyll Island*, pp. 59–98. Cambridge: Cambridge University Press.

Brimmer, Andrew. (1976). "The Federal Reserve and the Failure of Franklin National Bank: A Case Study of Regulation." In Jules Backman (ed), *Business and the American Economy, 1776–2001, pp. 108–140.* New York: New York University Press.

Broz, J. Lawrence. (1997). *The International Origins of the Federal Reserve System.* Ithaca, NY: Cornell University Press.

Burns, Arthur. (1971). Statement before the Committee on Banking, Housing, and Urban Affairs, United States Senate, June 16, 1971.

(1974a). Testimony before the Joint Economic Committee, October 17, 1974.

(1974b). Information submitted for the record of the hearing of the Joint Economic Committee on October 1974, in response to additional questions asked by Representative Reuss.

Calomiris, Charles. (1994). "Is the Discount Window Necessary? A Penn Central Perspective." *Federal Reserve Bank of St. Louis Review* 76(3):31–55.

Calomiris, Charles, and David Wheelock. (1997). "Was the Great Depression a Watershed for American Monetary Policy?" *NBER Working Paper* 5623. Cambridge, MA: National Bureau of Economic Research.

Carlson, Mark, Kris Mitchener, and Gary Richardson. (2011). "Arresting Banking Panics: Federal Reserve Liquidity Provision and the Forgotten Panic of 1929." *Journal of Political Economy* 119(5):889–924.

Carlson, Mark, and Jonathan D. Rose. (2011). "Credit Availability and the Collapse of the Banking Sector in the 1930s." *Federal Reserve Board Finance and Economics Discussion Series* No. 2011–38.

Chandler, Lester V. (1971). *American Monetary Policy 1928–1941*. New York: Harper and Row.

Clark, Truman A. (1986). "Interest Rate Seasonals and the Federal Reserve," *Journal of Political Economy* 94(1):76–125.

Conover, C. (1984). "Statement and Comments of C.T. Connover, Comptroller of the Currency." In Inquiry into Continental Illinois Corporation and Continental Illinois National Bank. U.S. Congress, House of Representatives, Subcommittee on Financial Institutions Supervision, Regulation, and Insurance of the Committee on Banking, Finance and Urban Affairs. Hearing, 98 Congress 2 Session. Washington, DC: Government Printing Office.

Corrigan, E. G. (1990). "Statement before United States Senate Committee on Banking, Housing and Urban Affairs." Washington, DC.

Corrigan, T., and W. Lewis. (1998). "Merrill Lynch Details Contacts with LTCM." *Financial Times* October 31, p. 19.

Curtiss, Frederic. (1933). Letter from Frederic Curtiss (Chairman of the Board of the Federal Reserve Bank of Boston) to the Federal Reserve Board dated February 14, 1933.

Delong, J. Bradford. (1997). "America's Peacetime Inflation: The 1970s." In Christina Romer and David Romer (eds), *Reducing Inflation: Motivation and Strategy*, pp. 247–278. Chicago: University of Chicago Press.

Dunbar, N. (2000). *Inventing Money*. New York: John Wiley & Sons.

Edwards, Franklin. (1999). "Hedge Funds and the Collapse of Long-Term Capital Management." *Journal of Economic Perspectives* 13(2):189–210.

Eichengreen, Barry. (1992). *Golden Fetters: The Gold Standard and the Great Depression, 1919–1939*. New York: Oxford University Press.

Euromoney (1981). "Banker of the Year." October, 116–140.

Federal Deposit Insurance Corporation (FDIC). (1997). "Continental Illinois and Too Big to Fail." In *History of the Eighties–Lessons for the Future*, pp. 235–257. Washington, DC: Federal Deposit Insurance Corporation.

Federal Deposit Insurance Corporation (FDIC). (1998). "Continental Illinois National Bank and Trust Company." In *Managing the Crisis: The FDIC and*

RTC Experience, pp. 545–565. Washington, DC: Federal Deposit Insurance Corporation.

Federal Open Market Committee (FOMC). (various). Transcripts of the Federal Open Market Committee. Washington: Federal Reserve System.

Federal Reserve Board. (1934). "Currency Depots." Memorandum by the Division of Bank Operations dated July 13, 1934.

Federal Reserve Board. (1938). *The Establishment and Operation of Branches, Agencies and Currency Funds of Federal Reserve Banks.* Washington, DC: Board of Governors of the Federal Reserve System.

Federal Reserve Board. (1943). *Banking and Monetary Statistics, 1914–1941.* Washington, DC: Board of Governors of the Federal Reserve System.

Federal Reserve Board. (1976). *Banking and Monetary Statistics, 1941–1970.* Washington, DC: Board of Governors of the Federal Reserve System.

Federal Reserve Board. (1984). Plan of Assistance to Continental Illinois National Bank and Trust Company of Chicago and Related Plan of Restructuring of Continental Illinois Corporation, Vol. 1, Sec. 22. Washington, DC: Federal Reserve System.

Federal Reserve Board. (2008). Press release dated September 16. Retrieved from http://www.federalreserve.gov/newsevents/press/other/20080916a.htm

Fettig, David. (2002). "Lender of More Than Last Resort." *The Region, Federal Reserve Bank of Minneapolis* December. Retrieved from http://www.minneapolisfed.org/publications_papers/pub_display.cfm?id=3392

Flood, Mark. (1992). "The Great Deposit Insurance Debate," *Federal Reserve Bank of St. Louis Review* July–August, 74(4):51–77.

Friedman, Milton, and Anna Schwartz. (1963). *A Monetary History of the United States, 1867–1960.* Princeton, NJ: Princeton University Press.

Gilbert, R. Alton. (1998). "Did the Fed's Founding Improve the Efficiency of the U.S. Payments system?" *Federal Reserve Bank of St. Louis Review* 80(3), May/June:121–142.

Gilbert, R. Alton, Kliesen, Kevin L., Meyer, Andrew P., and David C. Wheelock. (2012). "Federal Reserve Lending to Distressed Banks During the Financial Crisis, 2007–2012." *Federal Reserve Bank of St. Louis Review* 93(2), May/June:221–242.

Goodfriend, Marvin. (2012). "The Elusive Promise of Independent Central Banking." Institute for Monetary and Economic Studies, Bank of Japan, Discussion Paper No. 2012-E-9.

Goodfriend, Marvin, and R. King. (1988). "Financial Deregulation, Monetary Policy, and Central Banking." In W. Haraf, and R. Kushmeider (eds), *Restructuring Banking and Financial Services in America*, pp. 216–253. Washington, DC: American Enterprise Institute.

Goodhart, Charles. (1999). "Myths about the Lender of Last Resort." *International Finance* 2(3):339–360.

Green, Richard, and Susan Wachter. (2005). "The American Mortgage in Historical and International Context." *Journal of Economic Perspectives* Fall, 19(4):93–114.

Greenspan, Alan. (1988). "Statement and Comments of Alan Greenspan, Chairman of the Federal Reserve." In "Black Monday," The Stock Market

Crash of October 19, 1987. U.S. Congress. Senate. Committee on Banking, Housing, and Urban Affairs. Hearing, 100 Congress 1 Session. Washington, DC: U.S. Government Printing Office.

(1994). "Statement and Comments of Alan Greenspan, Chairman of the Federal Reserve." In Banking Industry Regulatory Consolidation. U.S. Congress. Senate. Committee on Banking, Housing, and Urban Affairs. Hearing, 103 Congress 2 Session. Washington, DC: U.S. Government Printing Office.

(1998). "Statement and Comments of Alan Greenspan, Chairman of the Federal Reserve." In Hedge Fund Operations. U.S. Congress. House of Representatives. Committee on Banking and Financial Services. Hearing, 105 Congress 2 Session. Washington, DC: U.S. Government Printing Office.

Grossman, Richard S. (2010). *Unsettled Account: The Evolution of Banking in the Industrialized World since 1800*. Princeton, NJ: Princeton University Press.

Hackley, Howard H. (1973). *Lending Functions of the Federal Reserve Banks: A History*. Washington, DC: Board of Governors of the Federal Reserve System.

Hafer, R. W., and David Wheelock. (2003). "Darryl Francis and the Making of Monetary Policy 1966–1975." *Federal Reserve Bank of St. Louis Review*, March/April, 85(3):1–12.

Isaac, W. (1984). "Statement and Comments of William Isaac, Chairman, Federal Deposit Insurance Corporation." In Inquiry into Continental Illinois Corporation and Continental Illinois National Bank. U.S. Congress, House of Representatives, Subcommittee on Financial Institutions Supervision, Regulation, and Insurance of the Committee on Banking, Finance and Urban Affairs. Hearing, 98 Congress 2 Session. Washington, DC: U.S. Government Printing Office.

Janssen, R. (1970). "Avoiding Shock to Economy Termed a Bigger Factor that Maintaining Service." *Wall Street Journal*, June 10, p. 3.

Janssen, R., and C. Stabler. (1970). "Cash Shortage Causes Worry That Big firms Could Face Collapse." *Wall Street Journal*, June 12, p. 1.

Kaufman, George. (1991). "Lender of Last Resort: A Contemporary Perspective." *Journal of Financial Services Research* 5:95–110.

Kilborn, P. (1984). "Harrowing Week-long Race to Rescue Continental Bank." *New York Times*, May 21, p. 1.

Lipin, S., M. Murray, and J. Schlesinger. (1998). "Bailout Blues: How a Big Hedge Fund Marketed Its Expertise and Shrouded Its Risk." *Wall Street Journal*, September 25, p. A1.

Lowenstein, Roger. (2000). *When Genius Failed*. New York, Random House.

Madigan, Brian F. (2009). "Bagehot's Dictum in Practice: Formulating and Implementing Policies to Combat the Financial Crisis." Speech at the FRB Kansas City Annual Economic Symposium, Jackson Hole, WY, August 21, 2009.

McDonough, W. (1998). "Statement and Comments of William McDonough, President of the Federal Reserve Bank of New York." In Hedge Fund Operations. U.S. Congress. House of Representatives. Committee on Banking and Financial Services. Hearing, 105 Congress 2 Session. Washington, DC: U.S. Government Printing Office.

Meltzer, Allan H. (2003). *A History of the Federal Reserve*, Vol. 1. Chicago: University of Chicago Press.

(2009a). *A History of the Federal Reserve*, Vol. 2. Chicago: University of Chicago Press.

(2009b). "What Happened to the 'Depression'?" *Wall Street Journal*, August 31, 2009.

Miron, Jeffrey A. (1986). "Financial Panics, the Seasonality of the Nominal Interest Rate, and the Founding of the Fed." *American Economic Review* March, 76(1):125–140.

Moody's Investors Service. (1981). "*Bank and Finance Manual*," pp. 87–100.

Moody's Investors Service. (1983). "*Bank and Finance Manual*," pp. 153–167.

Morgenson, G. (1998). "Hedge Fund Bailout Rattles Investors and Markets." *New York Times*, September 25, p. A1.

Morris, J., S. Sansweet, and J. Williams. (1970). "Saunders, Bevan Resign Under Fire From Penn Central; Perlman to Quit." *Wall Street Journal*, June 9, p. 3.

Mufson, S., and I. J. Dugan. (1998). "Toll of Fund's Bad Bets is Emerging." *Washington Post*, September 25, p. A1.

Murray, A. (1987). "Fed's New Chairman Wins a Lot of Praise on Handling the Crash." *Wall Street Journal*, November 25, p. 1.

Murray, R. (1971). "The Penn Central Debacle: Lessons for Financial Analysis," *Journal of Finance* 26(2):327–332.

Nelson, Edward. (2011). "Friedman's Monetary Economics in Practice." Federal Reserve Economics Discussion Paper 2011–26.

Owen, R. (1919). *The Federal Reserve Act, Its Origins and Principles*. New York: The Century Company.

Presidential Task Force on Market Mechanisms. (1988). *Report of the Presidential Task Force on Market Mechanisms*. Nicholas Brady (Chairman). Washington, DC: U.S. Government Printing Office.

Raghavan, A., and M. Pacelle. (1998). "To the Rescue: A Hedge Fund Falters and Wall Street Giants Ante Up $3.5 Billion." *Wall Street Journal*, September 24, p. A1.

Reinhart, Vincent. (2008). "Fallout from a Bailout." *Washington Post*, May 22, 2008.

Richardson, Gary, and William Troost. (2009). "Monetary Intervention Mitigated the Banking Panics during the Great Depression: Quasi-experimental Evidence from a Federal Reserve District Border, 1929–1933." *Journal of Political Economy* 117(6):1031–1073.

Rochet, J.-C., and X. Vives. (2004). "Coordination Failures and the Lender of Last Resort: Was Bagehot Right After All?" *Journal of the European Economic Association* 2(6):1116–1147.

Romer, Christina. (1992). "What Ended the Great Depression?" *Journal of Economic History* December, 52(4):757–784.

Romer, Christina, and David Romer. (2002). "A Rehabilitation of Monetary Policy in the 1950's." *American Economic Review* May, 92(2):121–127.

Rowe, J. (1984). "The Grapevine that Caught Continental." *Washington Post*, May 27, p. F1.

Schadrack, F., and F. Breimyer. (1970). "Recent Developments in the Commercial Paper Market." *Federal Reserve Bank of New York Monthly Review*, pp. 280–291.

Schwartz, Anna J. (1992). "The Misuse of the Fed's Discount Window." *Federal Reserve Bank of St. Louis Review* 74(5):58–69.

Securities and Exchange Commission. (1988). *The October 1987 Market Break.* Washington, DC: The Securities and Exchange Commission.

Siconolfi, M., A. Raghavan, and M. Pacelle. (1998). "All Bets Are Off: How Salesmanship and Brainpower Failed at Long-Term Capital." *Wall Street Journal*, November 16, p. A1.

Sinkey, Joseph F. (1975). "Franklin National Bank of New York: A Portfolio and Performance Analysis of Our Largest Bank Failure." FDIC Working Paper 75–10.

Spero, Joan E. (1980). *The Failure of the Franklin National Bank, Challenge to the International Banking System.* New York: Columbia University Press.

Spong, Kenneth. (2000). *Banking Regulation: Its Purposes, Implementation, and Effects.* Kansas City: Federal Reserve Bank of Kansas City, Division of Supervision and Risk Management.

Sprague, I. (1986). *Bailout: An Insider's Account of Bank Failures and Rescues.* New York: Basic Books.

Stern, Gary, and Ron Feldman. (2004). *Too Big to Fail: The Hazards of Bank Bailouts.* Washington, DC: Brookings Institution Press.

Temin, Peter. (1989). *Lessons from the Great Depression.* Cambridge, MA: MIT Press.

Todd, Walker F. (1993). "FDICIA's Emergency Liquidity Provisions." *Federal Reserve Bank of Cleveland Economic Review* 29(3):16–23.

Volcker, Paul. (1984). "Statement and Comments of Paul Volcker, Chairman, Federal Reserve." In *Federal Reserve's Second Monetary Policy Report for 1984.* U.S. Congress, Senate, Committee on Banking, Housing, and Urban Affairs. Hearing, 98 Congress 2 Session, Washington, DC: U.S. Government Printing Office.

Wall, L., and D. Peterson. (1990). "The Effect of Continental Illinois' Failure on the Financial Performance of Other Banks." *Journal of Monetary Economics* 26:77–99.

Wall Street Journal (WSJ). (1970). "Reserve Suspends Interest Limits on Some Big Deposit Certificates." June 24, p. 3.

Wall Street Journal (WSJ). (1984). "Customers of Continental Illinois Shored by Guarantees, Stay Loyal." May 25, p. 6.

Wall Street Journal (WSJ). (1987a). "Trade-Gap News Sends Stock Market Reeling Into a Record Tailspin." October 15, p. 1.

Wall Street Journal (WSJ). (1987b). "The Day the Dow Fell: Brokers Trade Stocks, Fists; Bulls and Bears Are Joined by Ducks and Chickens." October 19, p. 15.

Warburg, Paul M. (1910). *The Discount System in Europe.* National Monetary Commission, U.S. Senate Document No. 402. Washington, DC: U.S. Government Printing Office.

Wheelock, David C. (1992). "Seasonal Accommodation and the Financial Crises of the Great Depression: Did the Fed 'Furnish an Elastic Currency?'" *Federal Reserve Bank of St. Louis Review* November/December, 74: 3–18.

Wicker, Elmus. (1966). *Federal Reserve Monetary Policy 1917–1933*. New York: Random House.

(2005). *The Great Debate on Banking Reform: Nelson Aldrich and the Origins of the Fed.* Columbus: Ohio State University Press.

Winkler, M. (1987). "Interest Rates Fall Again as Banks Cut Prime Rate, Fed Seems to Keep Easing." *Wall Street Journal*, October 23, p. 39.

Zuckerman, G. (1998). "Treasury's Prices Show Solid Rise." *Wall Street Journal*, August 17, p. C1.

5

Close but Not a Central Bank

The New York Clearing House and Issues of Clearing House Loan Certificates

Jon Moen and Ellis Tallman

> The clearing-house system is becoming a definitely recognized power in the financial methods of the United States. It is as yet in its infancy, and the powers that the various clearing-houses possess are capable of development and expansion to an indefinite degree. The clearing-house, which was begun simply as a labor saving device, has united the banking interests of various communities in closer bonds of sympathy and union, and has developed into a marvelous instrumentality for the protection of the community from the evil effects of panics and of bad banking. Clearing-houses are gradually becoming a welding force that ultimately will bring to the banking business of this country the centralization which it so greatly needs.
>
> (Cannon 1910, p. 24)

The New York Clearing House developed several tools that aided member banks in dealing with panics and runs on deposits.[1] One particularly central bank–like tool was the provision of clearing house loan certificates (CHLCs), which were IOUs backed by collateral and used by banks in place of specie and legal tender to settle accounts between banks during the check clearing

An earlier draft of this chapter was presented under the title "Reluctant Central Bankers" at the conference entitled "Economic and Historical Perspectives on Interbank Payments Networks" at Columbia University, June 15, 2012. The authors thank Elmus Wicker and David Weiman for clearing house loan data from 1907 and 1873, respectively. We have benefited from conversations with Christopher Hoag, James Thomson, and David Weiman. In addition, the authors thank Mirjana Orovic and Sujit "Bob" Chakravorti of the Clearing House, Inc. for access to the archival materials from the New York Clearing House Association.

[1] Contemporaries such as O. M. W. Sprague cited the sudden desire of out of town correspondent banks to liquidate their deposits in New York City national banks as a main source of disruption during panics, at least in New York.

process at the New York Clearing House.[2] As a result, CHLCs effectively freed up cash to pay depositors, buy up loans, facilitate gold imports, and preserve liquidity in the payments system.

Most previous research on the issuance of CHLCs during the National Banking Era (1863–1913) depends on aggregate measures of their use in New York and on the informative analysis of Cannon (1910). Relying on Cannon's description and on aggregated measures of CHLCs alone suggests that the Clearing House banks engaged in a united approach to fight panics during the National Banking Era. Our analysis based on bank-level data indicates that was likely not the case.

The big New York City national banks held the largest volume of cash reserves in the banking system and were the lynchpin of the reserves system during the National Banking Era. The pyramid of reserves and correspondent banking funneled reserves to the big New York City banks, which were also able to add liquidity to the financial market in the United States, as James Cannon optimistically anticipated in the preceding quote. The New York Clearing House would allow illiquid member banks to borrow CHLCs, thereby providing liquidity to the banks that needed it. The entire Clearing House membership would honor the CHLCs as (a temporary) final payment. But the larger New York City national banks, during the National Banking Era, could also affect liquidity indirectly and thereby aid illiquid banks by borrowing CHLCs, substituting them temporarily as clearing balances, thereby releasing cash from its clearing balances to the banking system in New York. In this way, the large, New York City national bank would be providing liquidity with a conscious appreciation for improving market liquidity, a positive externality. Although this conventional story is implicit in Cannon (1910), it is unclear whether incentives were sufficient to encourage the large New York City banks to borrow in this way.

The central banking powers of the private clearing house system in the United States were limited. For example, the issues of CHLCs were imperfect substitutes for cash (they could not pass as hand–to–hand currency). One frequent criticism of CHLC issues in New York City is that volume of issuance was perceived as too small to make a big difference in financial market liquidity during a panic, and we agree. That observation likely arose from the passive method of issuance – banks had to borrow them and post adequate collateral against them. Further, the New York Clearing House was not a separate financial entity – it was unable to issue its own liabilities as central banks could. Hence, the New York Clearing House was unable to conduct "open market operations" and offer the financial market cash. Given such limitations to its power, it should not be surprising that

---

[2] See Timberlake (1993), Gorton (1985), and Tallman and Moen (2012). CHLCs were used by other clearing houses as well.

the New York Clearing House was incapable of effectively alleviating panics during this period. Yet the perspective of Cannon still permeates the analysis of the period and conveys a sense of a united clearing house membership engaged in a coordinated effort to forestall the panic. Although we find some evidence consistent with this conventional view, we also find much that is not.

We have created a new data set of bank-level observations from the daily minutes of the New York Clearing House Loan Committee for the panics 1873, 1884, 1890, 1893, and 1907. These data indicate the volume of the CHLCs requested, the bank identity, the exact date of the issues, and the date of cancellation of the certificates. The bank-level data on CHLCs contribute to our understanding of the behavior of individual banks during the panic. This in turn helps clarify the overall performance of the New York Clearing House as a private lender of last resort.

This chapter focuses on the borrowing behavior of the big New York City national banks as well as that of the biggest borrowers of CHLCs in each panic. The bank-level data indicate great variation in the responses of individual New York banks to each panic. We find no explicit evidence of preconceived effort from the New York Clearing House in providing liquidity to the banking system. Depending on the panic instance, some large banks borrowed substantially, other large banks not at all. Although we do not yet know the reasons why particular banks issued loan certificates and others did not, we suspect that bank-specific liquidity needs rather than concerns about the general stability of the banking system explain the changing participation in loan certificate issues. In summary, we find little evidence to indicate coordination of loan certificate issues by the New York Clearing House and its members.

CENTRAL BANK-LIKE TOOLS AND SOME HISTORY

Interior banks deposited cash in New York City national banks, and those deposits qualified as reserves meeting reserve requirements established by the National Bank Acts. Chicago and St. Louis had become central reserve cities in 1887, reducing the proportion of bankers' balances in New York. Nevertheless, New York was still the key central reserve city (Sprague 1910, p. 125), and the reserves held in New York City also had become increasingly concentrated at the big banks. Because the big New York national banks sat at the top of the pyramid of reserves, their ability to rearrange reserves, combined with the supervisory capabilities of the New York Clearing House over its members, presented them with nascent central bank powers.

Clearing House Loan Certificates

The borrowing of CHLCs was a mechanism to allocate temporary liquidity to member banks, and active participation in honoring loan certificates as final payment was an obligation of New York Clearing House members. Therefore, by honoring the payment by CHLC, the accepting bank was effectively lending to the borrowing bank. Further, the membership agreed in advance to abide by their loss-sharing rules, which specifically described how the membership would share losses from clearing house certificates of banks that failed to repay them. New York Clearing House member banks were exposed to losses arising from unpaid CHLCs, so their private equity capital was placed at risk by any issuance of CHLCs.[3]

The New York Clearing House was the issuer of CHLCs for the borrowing member banks. Member banks would borrow them after having put up collateral suitable to the Clearing House Loan Committee. Usually the CHLCs would be issued at 75 percent of the value of the pledged collateral, although it could be higher or lower. Member banks were obliged to accept CHLCs in lieu of cash during settlement, although the accepting bank would earn 6 percent interest paid by the bank that borrowed them. The New York Clearing House kept track of interest payments. Although the certificates bore the name of the borrower, the membership of the New York Clearing House nevertheless guaranteed them, and the guarantee was an important support to the required acceptance for payment.[4]

CHLCs were not a net increase in cash reserves. Rather, the loan certificates were a temporary substitute for specie or legal tender used to settle final payment balances at the New York Clearing House among the member banks.[5] On the balance sheet, the CHLC represents an asset for the receiving bank available for payment and as a liability in the form of a loan from the New York Clearing House membership, or more accurately, from each member bank that accepted it as final payment. The liability in the form of CHLCs could also be transferred from one bank to another at par during settlement. We emphasize that CHLCs were a transferable liability and not a single loan between two specific banks. Rather, as a transferable liability, the CHLC implicitly involved a loan from the holding bank to the borrowing bank. Because they could not circulate outside of the Clearing House and be issued to the public, CHLCs were an imperfect (and inferior) substitute for legal tender.[6]

---

[3] Losses on CHLC issues to New York Clearing House members were shared among the membership and assessments to cover loss amounts would be made relative to member bank capital.

[4] The arrangement for CHLCs resembles the modern triparty repurchase agreement with the Clearing House Loan Committee managing the asset used as collateral.

[5] In some ways CHLCs resembled discount window loans at the Federal Reserve, although a Clearing House Loan Committee had to be assembled to authorize formally and oversee their issue, while the discount window facility is a standing facility.

[6] National bank notes were never accepted at the New York Clearing House for final payment, whereas CHLCs were designed to serve that purpose during a panic. A stock of national bank notes would have allowed banks to offer currency to depositors withdrawing

Other Tools

Suspension of the convertibility of deposits into cash was a drastic tool used in panics to stem deposit withdrawals. Payment suspensions were imposed only during the most severe panics (not in 1884 or 1890). When implemented, they took hold usually near the time CHLCs were authorized, as in 1873 and 1907, but they were imposed more than a month later during the Panic of 1893. Contemporary observers such as O. M. W. Sprague criticized payment restrictions/suspension as an unnecessary response, one that usually added to panic; Wicker (2000) concurs. On the other hand, Friedman and Schwartz regarded restrictions of convertibility as a reasonable response to a panic, thereby limiting the drain of reserves. Individual depositors were most affected by payment suspensions, because the big banks continued to send reserves to interior correspondent banks during a panic. One side effect of payment suspensions was a premium on currency over deposits. The currency premium would induce gold inflows if the country was maintaining the gold standard (1893 and 1907), and the additional supply of gold eventually would add to bank reserves more durably than CHLCs.

According to Elmus Wicker (2000), another tool, reserve pooling, had been abandoned after successful applications in the Panic of 1873 (and the earlier panics associated with the Civil War).With a pooling arrangement, the Clearing House Committee was also authorized to equalize legal tender reserves when CHLCs were authorized.[7] In effect, the reserves of the member banks were united into one pool. In cases where a bank was falling dangerously low in actual reserves, the other members could be assessed and reserves would be directly provided to the troubled bank from the pool. It is not surprising, though, that the apparently successful practice was abandoned; the reserve providers were likely uninterested in offering an uncompensated subsidy to the banks short liquidity.

Selective information provision was also a tool used by the New York Clearing House to subdue panic conditions. The *Commercial and Financial Chronicle* published weekly a subset of key balance sheet items of the New York Clearing House member banks; during panics, the New York Clearing House suppressed publication of individual bank data and instead reported only aggregate data to the public. The aggregate balance sheet typically reflected some stress in the banking sector, but avoided the isolation of a bank with a weak or weakening balance sheet.

---

cash, and they contributed to the eventual recovery in 1907. But national banks note issues took nearly three weeks from request to delivery. CHLCs could be issued more quickly.

[7] Commercial and Financial Chronicle, September 27, 1873, pp. 410–411.

CHLCs and Big New York Banks

Of the tools available to the New York Clearing House to alleviate panics, the issuance of CHLCs most closely resembles central bank action to expand liquidity during a crisis. The New York Clearing House banks used clearinghouse loan certificates in all of the major banking panics during the national banking era. Previous studies have had to rely on the aggregate volume of certificates issued during a panic. Our analysis of CHLCs uses a new data set drawn from the minutes of the New York Clearing House Loan Committees from the 1873, 1884, 1890, 1893, and 1907 panics. We focus on the use of CHLCs by the big New York banks during panics because those banks controlled a large proportion of assets among New York Clearing House members and thereby had the greatest capacity to increase liquidity in an orderly and central bank–like manner.

During the major panics, the New York Clearing House would appoint a subcommittee of member bank officers to oversee the issuance of loan certificates to forestall or in anticipation of widespread depositor withdrawals. The minutes of the committee compiled by the Clearing House contains, among other valuable records, the volume of loan certificates issued and canceled (withdrawn) by each New York Clearing House member bank in 1873, 1884, 1890, 1893, and 1907.[8] Thus, we are able to identify the specific banks that were most actively borrowing CHLCs and how quickly they reacted to the onset of a panic.

We supplement the CHLC data with balance sheet information by bank taken from the Annual Reports of the Comptroller of the Currency of the United States for the national banks and from the New York Superintendent of Banks for the state banks that were Clearing House members.[9] The information from the Comptroller helps us to identify characteristics of banks that would make them more likely to request CHLCs from the New York Clearing House. A bank's connection to the correspondent banking system, for example, as measured by the volume of deposits due to other banks, might be an important correlate with the volume of loan certificates issued by a bank. We also use weekly statements of the New York Clearing House banks published in the

[8] We include the certificates issued by state chartered banks that were members of the Clearing House. Although the membership was dominated by national banks, it was not restricted to national banks, nor were national banks required to be members of the New York Clearing House, as they were of the Federal Reserve System.

[9] We use the call report date that is closest to the start of each panic because panics are transient and yet severe events, so we want to get measures that are temporally close to the event.

Commercial and Financial Chronicle; these statements include a subset of balance sheet items such as net deposits, specie, and legal tender.[10]

Evidence of Central Bank Behavior in a Counterfactual World

We seek evidence of coordinated effort on the part of the Clearing House member banks to fight a panic. We expect unified or coordinated behavior by the Clearing House banks to provide liquidity during a panic, generously, if at a high rate of interest, if it were following Bagehot's advice. We also expect to see the New York Clearing House members intentionally taking on central bank functions. Note that these are ideal behaviors of a central bank.

Reserve pooling, as in the Panic of 1873, might be such an action from a system-focused entity like the New York Clearing House. One can think of reserve pooling as maximizing the value of liquidity provision at the margin and thereby avoiding inefficiencies such as reserve hoarding by individual banks. That said, the absence of reserve pooling in the responses to panic conditions in 1884 through 1907 suggests that the New York Clearing House banks with sufficient reserves were unwilling to share them without compensation. In contrast, CHLCs has an implicit compensation scheme distinguishing it from reserve pooling.

Banks requesting CHLCs were trying to increase their liquidity, and the creditor banks accepting them were agreeing to share the risk of default if a member bank could not redeem its loan certificates. Borrowing loan certificates was at the discretion of the individual bank, and although member banks had to accept loan certificates as payment, there was no provision to compel member banks to borrow them in the first place. In a counterfactual world of an active lender of last resort, we would expect some obligation on the part of all member banks to issue them, and that is the sense one gets from reading Cannon (1910, p. 79):

Others regard it (requesting clearing house loan certificates) as in no way prejudicial to their interests, but rather *as a patriotic movement in which all the banks should engage, both for the purpose of assisting their fellow-members and for the welfare of the community as a whole.*
The members of the New York Clearing House Association especially have distinguished themselves in this regard. Up to 1907, when only about 60 per cent of the members found it necessary to take out certificates, *it has been the almost universal rule for all the members to take loan certificates whenever the occasion demanded such action on the part of any of the banks, and this, too, without regard to how strong*

---

[10] These weekly reports display fewer aggregates and do not allow a rigorous examination of bank conditions. That said, they can offer useful information as interim reports of bank balance sheet items between call dates.

they may have been or how easily they might have gotten on without using them. (italics added)

Our evidence does not support this characterization.

Coordinated issues of CHLCs would display volumes in proportion to each bank's assets, reserves, bank clearings or net banker balances, which would require orchestration and/or coercion by the New York Clearing House. Banks refusing to issue loan certificates might find themselves fined or expelled from the clearing house. This counterfactual assumes only the tools and supervisory authority that the New York Clearing House actually had at the time to establish a baseline for evaluating its observed behavior relative to that of a central bank. In short, could the New York Clearing House have reasonably altered its behavior to be more like a lender of last resort if the evidence indicates that its actual behavior had fallen short?[11]

Aggregate Measures

Before looking at bank level information, we present aggregate information for all New York Clearing House member banks in New York. Table 5.1 presents the total volume of CHLCs issued, a selection of standard balance sheet items, and several ratios for all New York Clearing House member banks in the five major panics. The first contradiction of Cannon's conventional view is the percentage of Clearing House member banks that borrowed CHLCs. We find that the percentages for 1873, 1893, and 1907 are approximately the same at between 53 and 55 percent. Notably, the percentage of participation was highest in 1907, the crisis that Cannon noted as having only about 60 percent of the banks borrowing.

The volume of "due tos" or deposits from other banks held by the New York national banks reflects the exposure of national banks to withdrawal risk from correspondent banks located predominantly in the interior of the country. The aggregates reveal growth in deposits from individuals and other banks (due tos) with the most noticeable increase coming between the Panics of 1893 and 1907. Deposits held by the New York City banks at other banks (due froms) also expand noticeably between 1893 and 1907. These movements are consistent with New York's importance in the correspondent banking system, and the increase in the interconnections throughout the country through correspondent relationships. The correspondent relationships between banks in New York City and the banks in the other two central reserve cities (after 1887) – St. Louis and Chicago – became particularly important.

---

[11] James Cannon (1908) proposed an emergency currency issue from the Treasury for which CHLCs could be deposited with the Treasury as collateral during a panic. Aldrich–Vreeland Emergency Currency embodied his central ideas, but the approval process eschewed CHLCs as collateral.

Table 5.1. Selected Balance Sheet Items and Ratios: New York National Banks (millions $)

	1873	1884	1890	1893	1907
Total loan certificates	25.82	24.92	16.56	41.48	100.91
Maximum CHLC	23.20	21.89	15.47	38.28	88.42
Outstanding					
(date of maximum)	Oct. 10,	May 24,	Dec. 22,	Aug. 29,	Dec. 16,
	1873	1884	1890	1893	1907
Deposits					
Individual	167.40	191.63	283.65	254.34	532.69
Due to banks	90.40	133.73	178.51	211.29	498.03
Due from banks	17.78	22.83	30.94	34.73	188.73
Net due to banks	72.63	110.89	147.57	176.55	309.30
Net deposits	240.03	302.52	431.22	430.89	841.99
Assets	389.49	457.22	569.73	601.26	1364.72
Reserves	36.05	67.39	77.30	95.21	218.79
Reserve ratio	0.15	0.22	0.18	0.22	0.26
NYCH member banks	60	65	66	70	56
Banks taking CHLCs	32	20	24	38	31
Participation (%)	53.33%	30.77%	36.36%	54.29%	55.36%
Various ratios					
Net due tos/assets	0.19	0.24	0.26	0.29	0.23
CHLC/net due tos	0.32	0.20	0.10	0.22	0.29
CHLC/assets	0.07	0.05	0.03	0.07	0.07
Reserves/all deposits	0.14	0.21	0.17	0.20	0.21
Reserves/net due tos	0.50	0.61	0.52	0.54	0.71
CHLC to reserves	0.64	0.32	0.20	0.40	0.40
CHLC to net deposits	0.10	0.07	0.04	0.09	0.11

Source: Calculated from the Clearing House Loan Committee Minutes for each panic. Balance sheet data for aggregate New York Clearing House member banks are from available Annual Reports of the Comptroller of the Currency for national banks and from Annual Reports of the Superintendent of Banking of the State of New York for state chartered member banks. Reserves are specie plus legal tenders.

We examine the issuance of CHLCs relative to key balance sheet items across the five panics in Figures 5.1 and 5.2. Figure 5.1 presents the ratios of loan certificates to cash reserves and to net due tos. Figure 5.2 presents the ratios of CHLCs to net deposits and to total assets. The ratios indicate some important differences in the balance sheet conditions of the New York City banks in certain crisis periods. However, the differences do

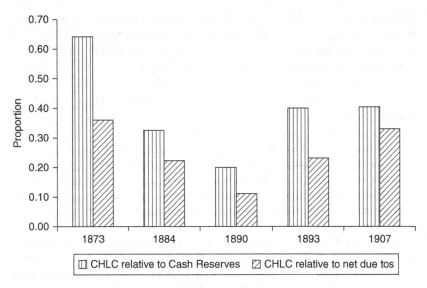

Figure 5.1. Clearing house loan certificates to cash reserves and net due tos.

Source: Minutes of the New York Clearing House, Annual Report of the Comptroller of the Currency, *Commercial and Financial Chronicle* (various issues).

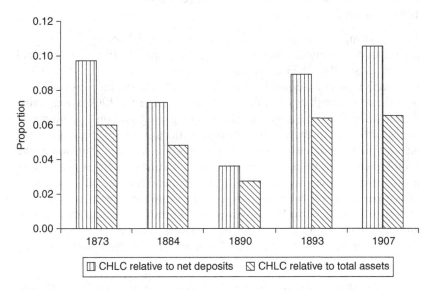

Figure 5.2. Clearing house loans certificates to net deposits and total assets.

Source: Minutes of the New York Clearing House, Annual Report of the Comptroller of the Currency, *Commercial and Financial Chronicle* (various issues).

not indicate substantial changes in the behavior of the New York banks across the panics. For example, the ratio of total loan certificates issued to cash reserves is highest in 1873, at around 65 percent, with the next highest (40 percent) observed in both 1907 and 1893. The Panics of 1873 and 1907 posed the greatest direct threat to the New York banks. The Panic of 1893 was severe in the interior of the country, but Wicker (2000) notes that the panic in New York City was less severe. The ratios for all four measures are lower in 1884 and 1890, the less severe crises.

Looking at the CHLCs to net due tos ratio, we note that the ratio is nearly 30 percent higher in both 1873 and 1907 relative to the other panics. The subsequent drains on deposits – perhaps related to the level of net due tos – likely determined the degree of CHLC issuance. The aggregate figures indicate that the New York Clearing House banks were responding to the severity of panics, at least as viewed from New York.

Figure 5.1 illustrates how CHLCs were used most intensely to increase liquidity during panics that most directly affected the New York Clearing House banks (1873, 1907, and 1893 to a lesser extent). Aggregate-level data present a benign view of the New York Clearing House's response to panics, providing liquidity in proportion to the severity of each panic, at least from the perspective of New York City.

Who Issued Loan Certificates – the Larger Panics: 1873, 1893, and 1907

Making comparisons across 1873 to 1907 is complicated by the fact that the ranks of the biggest banks changed. For example, the First National was rather small in 1873 as measured by volume of assets; by 1907 it was the fourth largest. National City Bank, James Stillman's bank in 1907, was only the seventeenth largest in 1873; it was the largest in 1907. We examine the behavior of the six largest banks in each panic based on the volume of assets and then on the volume of loan certificates issued; these were the banks that had the most to lose if the financial markets shut down. We rank banks based on assets and total loan certificates issued because we presume that if New York Clearing House members behave like a lender of last resort, it will be most pronounced among the largest banks taking the lead during panics. We examine the "Big Six" banks in each panic, although there is no theoretical or structural reason for choosing the six largest banks.[12] Note also that the proportion of New York Clearing

---

[12] In 1907 the Big Six were National City Bank, National Bank of Commerce, Hanover National Bank, National Park Bank, First National Bank, and Chase National Bank (Sprague 1910, p. 267). This is the traditional definition of the Big Six. Myers (1931) also follows the convention of examining the six largest banks. In 1873 the six largest banks were the Fourth National Bank, the National Bank of Commerce, National Park

House member bank assets accounted for by the biggest six banks varies over time.[13]

We focus first on the largest panics –1873, 1893, and 1907 – as each was unique in how New York was affected and how the Clearing House banks reacted. Following Sprague (1910) and Wicker (2000), we return to 1884 and 1890 as two examples of how the New York Clearing House banks handled panics when their private interests were immediately threatened, but not as seriously as in the larger panics. Furthermore, we look only at the mix of banks, ranked by volume of assets and loan certificates issued, participating in issuing loan certificates.

The Panic of 1873

The Panic of 1873, like the Panic of 1907 and unlike the one in 1893, was centered in New York. It began with the failure of Jay Cooke and Company, a well-regarded merchant bank in New York. Cooke was overexposed to several investments in railroad bonds, most notably the Northern Pacific. A stock market panic soon followed and the New York Stock Exchange was shut down for two weeks. The New York Clearing House Committee authorized the issue of CHLCs and imposed the equalization of reserves of the Clearing House member banks on September 20 and partially suspended payments on September 24.[14] Wicker points out that the New York City banks continued to pay legal tender currency to their correspondents even in the presence of suspension.[15]

The New York City banks varied their responses to the authorization of CHLC issues. While the larger banks tended to request loan certificates, there were notable exceptions. The state-chartered banks requested more than 15 percent of all loan certificates in New York. The big national banks along with other intermediaries were borrowing CHLCs and thereby adding temporarily to the liquidity of the New York City financial market. There was no sense, however, that all the biggest banks were in dire need of liquidity.

Bank, the Bank of New York (never a big correspondent – more of a wholesale bank), the Metropolitan National Bank, and the Importers and Traders National Bank.

[13] We could choose a threshold proportion of New York Clearing House bank member assets or deposits as the condition for the large players in New York City banking and we may pursue that route in future work.

[14] September 20, 1873 was the last date the *Commercial and Financial Chronicle* published bank specific balance sheet information of the New York Clearing House banks until the official release of the bank specific balance sheet information for publication resumed on December 13, 1873.

[15] Gold coin did not circulate and currency did not become convertible to gold until 1879, although specie could be used as reserves by banks.

Table 5.2. Loan Certificate Issues, New York City Banks Ranked by Asset
Volume, 1873

Bank	1873	Percent	CHLC to Reserves (%)
Fourth National	4.88	19	164
National Bank of Commerce	0	0	0
National Park Bank	3.37	13	116
Bank of New York	1.30	5	67
Metropolitan National	1.50	6	195
Importers and Traders National Bank	0.50	2	25
Total, other NY national banks	13.74	55	—
Total, all NY banks	25.29		64

Source: Minutes of the Clearing House Loan Committee of the New York
Clearinghouse, September 20 through November 2, 1873. *Commercial and Financial
Chronicle* (CFC), *Banker's Gazette*, p. 412, Vol. 17, September 20, 1873 and September
28, 1873.

Tables 5.2 and 5.3 present the volume and percentages of CHLCs borrowed by banks in 1873. Table 5.2 presents only the largest member banks
ranked by volume of assets, and the biggest six banks represented about
40 percent of New York Clearing House member assets. Note that even
though National Bank of Commerce did not issue loan certificates and
Importers and Traders issued only $500,000, the Big Six banks contrib-
uted CHLCs in about the proportion to their share of New York Clearing
House member assets (45 percent of CHLCs issued). Further, as emphasized previously, the contribution of liquidity through CHLCs is a combination of borrowing loan certificates and having member banks accepting
them as payment, thereby playing the role of creditor. Any member bank
holding the CHLC of another member bank was therefore effectively a
lender. Those banks with balance sheets unencumbered with borrowing
CHLCs were effectively the underwriters of the implicit guarantee for
issued CHLCs, precisely because they did not issue any.

Table 5.3 ranks all New York Clearing House member banks by volume
of loan certificates issued. Both state and national banks were New York
Clearing House members and issued loan certificates. The banks listed in
Table 5.3 reveal that the banks other than the largest national banks were
willing to borrow large volumes of loan certificates. Of all banks borrowing
loan certificates in 1873, the Bank of North America is ranked fourth, and
it was a state-chartered bank.[16] In addition, the Bank of North America

---

[16] It had switched its charter and was a national bank by 1893. We note also that we lack
explicit balance sheet data for the state banks in all panics except 1907. We will address

Table 5.3. Loan Certificate Issues, New York City Banks Ranked by Borrowing Volume, 1873

Bank	1873	Percent	CHLC to Reserves (%)
Fourth National	4.88	19	164
National Park Bank	3.37	13	116
Central National Bank	2.38	9	175
Bank of North America(state bank)	2.08	8	465
Metropolitan National	1.50	6	195
Bank of New York	1.30	5	67
SUM	15.51	60	—
Total, other NY banks	9.78	40	—
Total, all NY banks	25.29		64

Source: Minutes of the Clearing House Loan Committee of the New York Clearinghouse, September 20 through November 2, 1873. *Commercial and Financial Chronicle* (CFC), *Banker's Gazette*, p. 412, Vol. 17, September 20, 1873 and September 28, 1873.

borrowed CHLCs in an amount that was nearly 60 percent of its loans and discounts as of September 20, 1873.[17] This is notable because the Clearing House Loan Committee typically limited the CHLC issues to 75 percent of the fair market value of collateral. State bank members borrowed about 16 percent of the total CHLCs borrowed in 1873.

The big New York Clearing House member banks requested CHLCs in a proportion comparable to their share of member assets – approximately 40 percent. The large banks that did not borrow – National Bank of Commerce, American Exchange, and Merchant's National – could be considered creditors for the borrowing banks. These large banks and the other banks not borrowing CHLCs in 1873 – comprising about 35 percent of New York Clearing House assets – were the effective creditors (and guarantors) for banks such as Central National, Fourth National, and the Bank of North America. The larger New York national banks shared the creditor role with a number of smaller banks that did not borrow CHLCs.

The Panic of 1893

The Panic of 1893 started in the interior of the country and did not threaten the New York banks directly. The lack of an imminent threat to the liquidity

this shortcoming in a future revision. Until then, we use the limited numbers from the weekly listing of New York Clearing House members from the *Commercial and Financial Chronicle*.

[17] *Commercial and Financial Chronicle*, September 27, 1873, Vol. 17, p. 412.

Table 5.4. Loan Certificate Issues, New York City Banks Ranked by Asset Volume, 1893

Bank	1893	Percent	CHLC to Capital and Surplus (%)	CHLC to Loans (%)	CHLC to Reserves (%)
National Park Bank	3.48	9	68.31	16.53	39
Chemical National Bank	0	0	0	0	0
First National Bank	4.00	10	51.75	19.51	76
Fourth National Bank	1.59	4	30.35	9.67	31
Importers and Traders	0	0	0	0	0
National Bank of Commerce	2.00	5	23.08	10.92	52
Total, other NY banks	30.41	73			–
Total, all NY Banks	41.48				40

Source: Minutes of the New York Clearinghouse, June through August, 1893. Annual Report of the Comptroller of the Currency, 1894. *Commercial and Financial Chronicle*, June 17, 1893.

of New York Clearing House banks is revealed in both Tables 5.4 and 5.5. Table 5.4 shows that the six largest banks borrowed only 27 percent of the loan certificates, which was about the same as their share of New York Clearing House member capital and surplus (27 percent); the same banks combined accounted for about 30 percent of New York Clearing House bank loans.

As noted previously, the borrowing reveals a potential for the larger banks to play the creditor role to borrowing banks. The biggest borrowers of loan certificates took out 42 percent and the banks that borrowed were relatively large, ranking from third to eighteenth on the basis of total assets. The New York banks issued a larger total volume of loan certificates than in 1873 (and in 1884 and 1890). Mercantile National borrowed CHLCs in an amount greater than 20 percent of its total assets and in an amount that was more than 125 percent of its capital and surplus, signaling that it faced a serious liquidity crunch. But the total amount of borrowing by Mercantile was not sufficient to threaten the solvency of the membership; the CHLCs of Mercantile were almost 40 percent of its loans, far below the nearly 60 percent of loans taken by the Bank of North America in 1873. State bank members borrowed 15 percent of the total of CHLCs in 1893; that ratio is comparable to what was observed in 1873 (16 percent) even though no state bank was listed among the largest borrowers in 1893. It is notable that Chase, Park, and First National took out CHLCs in amounts greater than 50 percent of their capital and surplus, with Chase taking out more in CHLCs than it had as capital and surplus.

Table 5.5. Loan Certificate Issues, New York City Banks Ranked by Borrowing Volume, 1893

Bank	1893	Percent	CHLC to Capital and Surplus (%)	CHLC to Loans (%)	CHLC to Reserves (%)
First National Bank	4.00	10	51.75	19.51	76
National Park	3.48	9	68.31	16.53	39
American Exchange	3.00	8	41.12	17.91	81
Mercantile National	2.81	7	125.26	39.05	123
Chase National	2.00	5	117.74	18.2	44
National Bank of Commerce	2.00	5	23.08	10.92	51
Total, other NY banks	24.19	58			
Total, all NY banks	41.48		26.21	10.01	40

Source: Minutes of the New York Clearinghouse, June through August, 1893. Annual Report of the Comptroller of the Currency, 1894. *Commercial and Financial Chronicle*, June 17, 1893.

The Panic of 1907

The Panic of 1907, although centered on the trust companies, still presented a grave threat to the New York Clearing House member banks. If the call loan market had frozen up and the stock market collapsed, the New York Clearing House member banks could have been dragged down with the trust companies. Five of the Big Six banks borrowed more loan certificates, collectively and individually, than they had in earlier panics (Tables 5.6 and 5.7). The exception is Hanover National, which therefore played a creditor (and guarantor) role. The "borrowing five" of the largest banks were also the top five in terms of volume of loan certificates borrowed. Mechanics and Traders Bank, a state bank, came into the panic with a large volume of certificates outstanding. It had been subject to bank runs focused on the banks associated with Heinze–Morse–Thomas chain of banks in the week before the run on the trust companies started. The New York Clearing House had successfully stamped out the run on these banks in the week prior to the panic.

The Big Six banks borrowed 53 percent of the CHLCs issued, and comprised just over 50 percent of the total assets of the New York Clearing House membership.[18] Chase National borrowed an amount of CHLCs in excess of its capital and surplus, more than 20 percent of its loans, and close

---

[18] They also comprised 52 percent of capital and surplus and 52 percent of the loans of the New York Clearing House banks.

Table 5.6. Loan Certificate Issues, New York City Banks Ranked by Asset Volume, 1907

Bank	CHLCs	Percent	CHLC to Capital and Surplus (%)	CHLC to Loans (%)	CHLC to Reserves (%)
National City Bank	17.00	17	35	10.7	42
National Bank of Commerce	5.75	6	14.4	4.20	21
First National Bank	10.00	10	33.69	10.83	52
National Park Bank	9.70	10	81.27	13.4	46
Hanover National	0	0	0	0	0
Chase National Bank	10.50	10	108.91	20.55	72
Total, other NY banks	47.96	47	34.4	9.19	
Total, all NY banks	100.91				40

Source: Minutes of the New York Clearinghouse, October 26 and on, 1907. *Commercial and Financial Chronicle*, September 28, 1907.

Table 5.7. Loan Certificate Issues, New York City Banks Ranked by Borrowing Volume, 1907

Bank	CHLCs	Percent	CHLC to Capital and Surplus (%)	CHLC to Loans (%)	CHLC to Reserves (%)
National City Bank	17.00	17	35	10.7	42
Chase National Bank	10.50	10	108.91	20.55	72
First National Bank	10.00	10	33.69	10.83	52
National Park Bank	9.70	10	81.27	13.4	46
National Bank of Commerce	5.75	6	14.4	4.20	21
Mechanics and Traders (State Bank)	4.49	4	152.4	28.31	105
Total, other NY banks	43.48	43	34.4	9.19	
Total, all NY banks	100.91				40

Source: Minutes of the New York Clearinghouse, October 26 and on, 1907. *Commercial and Financial Chronicle*, September 28, 1907.

to 15 percent of its total assets. Mechanics and Traders State Bank borrowed an amount greater than 150 percent of its capital and surplus, nearly 30 percent of its loans, and 20 percent of its total assets. The highest proportion of borrowing relative to total assets was more than 23 percent by New

Amsterdam National Bank, another Heinze–Morse–Thomas bank. Of the Heinze–Morse–Thomas associated banks, those that were Clearing House members borrowed loan certificates at a high ratio.[19]

Preliminary investigation of the ledger book of the New York Clearing House has suggested a mundane explanation for the pattern of borrowing CHLCs during the Panic of 1907. The ledger books are a daily record of payments to and payments from the major banks as cleared through the New York Clearing House. We accumulated the net debit/net credit balances for the membership starting in October 1907 (one starting on October 14 and another on October 21). The accumulated balances as of November 9 when correlated with the outstanding CHLCs borrowing at that date generates a correlation coefficient of –0.55 and –0.7 (relative to October 14 and October 21 accumulations, respectively), signaling that the banks with the largest accumulated debit balances at the New York Clearing House borrowed the most CHLCs. We have these data available only for 1907 at this time, but the finding is consistent with the idea that the banks facing their own liquidity shortage took out the most CHLCs.

Comparing 1893 and 1907

In the Panics of 1893 and 1907, most of the same New York banks took out CHLCs. Although it is well known that the sources of the panics were quite different, the aggregate statistics display fairly similar proportionate borrowing among New York Clearing House banks across the two panics. The Big Six banks in 1893 issued 27 percent of the CHLCs commensurate with their share of capital and surplus among the Clearing House membership; in 1907, the Big Six banks issue 52 percent of CHLCs, comparable to their 52 percent share of capital and surplus at the New York Clearing House. Essentially, the Big Six banks just got bigger between 1893 and 1907 and borrowed CHLCs commensurate with their share of the New York Clearing House.

O. M. W. Sprague, perhaps the most famous observer of the panic, criticized the New York banks for delaying in issuing CHLCs until Saturday, October 26, four days after the run on the Knickerbocker Trust and then the Trust Company of America had started. Had they been issued immediately, Sprague claims that the banks could have avoided the unfortunate step of suspending cash payments, which occurred almost immediately after loan certificates were issued. Wicker (2000) also suggests that an earlier issuance of CHLCs may have avoided the haphazard

---

[19] We display the maximum volume of CHLCs outstanding for each of these three panics to assess the largest potential exposure and the largest borrowings. These observations likely did not happen simultaneously, and are meant only to highlight the extent of borrowing during each panic.

arrangements necessary to provide for cash at the New York Stock Exchange on October 24, 1907. Indeed, J. P. Morgan was reluctant to authorize the issuance of loan certificates early in the panic, fearing that depositors would interpret the issuance as a sign of weakness among the banks (Wicker 2000, p. 94).

Who Issued Loan Certificates – the Lesser Panics: 1884 and 1890

Wicker (2000) views the Panics of 1884 and 1890 as true success stories on the part of the New York Clearing House. Its prompt actions prevented full-scale panics from erupting out of financial disturbances in New York. In 1884 the largest banks issued 26 percent of loan certificates, slightly less than their share of loans (31 percent) in the New York Clearing House (Table 5.8). The panic-based withdrawals were focused on Metropolitan National Bank, which was rumored to have been caught in a large amount of fraudulent speculation in railroad stocks, rumors that were not confirmed by the Comptroller (Wicker 2000, pp. 36–37). One third of all loan certificates issued in 1884 were borrowed by Metropolitan National Bank (Table 5.9). Bank of New York borrowed CHLCs in an amount greater than 40 percent of the loans on its balance sheet. Six banks accounted for 89 percent of all loan certificates issued.

Metropolitan borrowed CHLCs to an amount that was nearly 70 percent of the loans on its balance sheet as of May 10, 1884. The amount verged on its limit for collateral at the New York Clearing House because CHLCs were issued at 75 percent of the market value of the assets offered as collateral. By allowing Metropolitan National Bank to request an enormous volume of CHLCs, the member banks of the New York Clearing House were effectively lending to a bank that was suffering a run. Given that six banks borrowed the majority of the CHLCs, there was a lot of capacity for offering credit to these banks from the remainder of the New York Clearing House member banks. There was no widespread restriction of convertibility of deposits into cash, suggesting that only one specific bank was struck with panic withdrawals. Metropolitan was voluntarily liquidated in November 1884 following extensive withdrawals through the summer. The New York Clearing House required nearly two years to resolve the outstanding CHLCs with Metropolitan, indicating the unusual amount of the borrowing.

The success of the response to the financial distress of 1890 relies heavily on the active Treasury intervention in the financial market earlier in August and September in amounts that dwarf the issues of CHLCs (see Sprague 1910, pp. 387–399 and Wicker 2000, pp. 44–45). That said, the issues of CHLCs in November 1890 were still pertinent for the New York City banks to avoid a more disruptive financial crisis.

Table 5.8. Loan Certificate Issues, New York City Banks Ranked by Asset Volume, 1884

Bank	CHLCs	Percent	CHLCs/Loans	CHLC to Reserves (%)
Fourth National	3.00	13	19	71
Importers and Traders	0	0	0	0
National Park	3.00	13	15	56
National Bank of Commerce	0	0	0	0
American Exchange	0	0	0	0
Chemical Bank	0	0	0	0
Total, other NY banks	16.59	74		
Total, all NY		22.59	7.5	32

Source: Minutes of the New York Clearinghouse, May 14 and on, 1884. *Commercial and Financial Chronicle*, May 17, 1884.

Table 5.9. Loan Certificate Issues, New York City Banks Ranked by Borrowing Volume, 1884

Bank	1884	Percent	CHLC/Loans	CHLC to Reserves (%)
Metropolitan	7.54	33	68	320
Bank of New York	4.00	18	41	207
Fourth National	3.00	13	19	71
National Park	3.00	13	15	56
Hanover	1.65	7	17.2	61
Mercantile National	1.03	5	14.4	56
Total, other NY banks	2.46	11		
Total, all NY banks	22.59		7.5	32

Source: Minutes of the New York Clearinghouse, May 14 and on, 1884. *Commercial and Financial Chronicle*, May 17, 1884.

The pattern of loan certificates issued in 1890 indicates that the largest national banks did not participate heavily in issuing loan certificates; only two of the six issued any CHLCs at all (Table 5.10). In addition, in 1890, several state banks participated by requesting CHLCs, unlike in 1884 (Table 5.11). The most notable aspect for 1890 is that the largest borrowers of CHLCs practically borrowed an amount of temporary liquidity that was about the volume of their cash reserves. The figures provide a strong indication of a severe liquidity crisis for these banks. Only in 1873 was a similar set of characteristics displayed.

Table 5.10. Loan Certificate Issues, New York City Banks Ranked by Asset Volume, 1890

Bank	1890	Percent	CHLC to Reserves (%)
Fourth National	0	0	0
Chemical	0	0	0
National Bank of Commerce	1.00	6	32
Importers and Traders	0	0	0
American Exchange	2.40	15	104
National Park	0	0	0
Total, other NY banks	12.72	79	
Total, all NY banks	16.12		20

Source: Minutes of the New York Clearinghouse, November–December 1890.
Commercial and Financial Chronicle, June 28, 1890.

Table 5.11. Loan Certificate Issues, New York City Banks Ranked by Borrowing Volume, 1890

Bank	1890	Percent	CHLC to Reserves (%)
Bank of New York	2.88	18	92
American Exchange	2.40	15	104
Bank of North America (state bank)	1.45	9	138[a]
Mechanics and Traders (state bank)	1.09	7	177[a]
Chatham National	1.00	6	76
National Bank of Commerce	1.00	6	32
Total, other NY banks	6.30	39	
Total, all NY banks	16.12		20

[a] *Commercial and Financial Chronicle*, June 28, 1890.
Source: Minutes of the New York Clearinghouse, November–December 1890.

Clearing House Loan Certificates and Liquidity Needs

The ratio of loan certificates to reserves (or legal tender and specie) helps reveal the extent to which loan certificates were used to increase liquidity at banks facing large clearing debits and depositor withdrawals. In 1873 the ratio is in general much higher for the big banks than in subsequent panics, reflecting mainly the weak reserve position of New York City at the beginning of the panic as well as lower reserves present in the early National Banking period. There was also a lesser degree of concentration in banking in New York in 1873 when compared to 1907. Further, as emphasized in Wicker (2000, p. 32), legal tender reserve in New York Clearing House banks became extraordinarily low even after the imposition of suspension of convertibility. For the New York City banks, it was closer to reserve depletion than they would ever again experience during the National Banking Era. In 1884, 1890, and 1893 the ratio was lower, and fewer of the large national banks even participated in issuing loan certificates.

Specific banks also issued exceptionally large volumes of loan certificates. Metropolitan Bank in 1884 is a prime example. Metropolitan had been linked to alleged speculation in railroad stocks and experienced a severe depositor run. The New York Clearing House authorized an issue $7 million of CHLCs to Metropolitan National Bank likely because it had significant correspondent deposits. This was by far the largest amount issued to any bank in 1884, amounting to more than three times its reserves of legal tender and specie. The Bank of New York also borrowed a large volume of loan certificates, twice its reserves. Although the Bank of New York was not in danger of failure, it apparently borrowed heavily owing to its prominent position in the correspondent banking system. State banks were also important borrowers of loan certificates in 1890, particularly Mechanics and Traders and the Bank of North America. These two banks were aided directly by nine large New York banks under the supervision of J. P. Morgan, but they also took out large volumes of loan certificates.

The ratio of loan certificates to reserves reveals clearly several things we already suspected. First, the big banks were more likely to take out loan certificates in general if the New York market was under threat, as in 1873 and 1907. It also identifies more closely banks that were in immediate need of reserves, like Bank of North America in 1873 and Metropolitan in 1884.

DISCUSSION

We suggest that issuing CHLCs could not be counted on to deliver reliable liquidity during many of the panics. The main weaknesses were structural. The flaws of CHLCs were (1) the liquidity provision mechanism was passive, relying on the demand from the borrowing banks and on the volume and quality of borrowing bank collateral, (2) CHLCs were not a good substitute for base money liquidity because they were not allowed to pass as currency between non–clearing house banks (much less the public), and (3) there was apparently no way for the New York Clearing House to offer liquidity to the market directly by compelling member banks to borrow loan certificates. They were designed to free up clearing balances and cover clearing debits and led to an increase net liquidity indirectly. That said, they were better than nothing.

The operation of a private association of banks as the lender of last resort institution was also part of the complication. By using CHLCs as substitutes for cash reserves, the New York Clearing House member banks expose their equity capital to risk of losses during a panic. The risk of loss arises especially if the bank borrowing CHLCs could not pay them back. A frequent criticism of CHLC issues as a solution to panics during the National Banking Era is that the aggregate issues were insufficient. It is possible that the fear of capital losses to the New York Clearing House membership limited the aggregate size of the CHLC issues during the largest crises. A more mundane explanation may surround the simple fact that the New York Clearing House could not issue CHLCs unless banks borrowed them.

James Cannon (1910) hints that banks recognized the positive externality of providing for more liquidity to "other" banks when a given bank takes out CHLCs. Recall the quote above citing that banks would request CHLCs "for the purpose of assisting their fellow-members and for the welfare of the community as a whole." Still, it is possible that there was an imperfect understanding of CHLCs across banking institutions. If so, the perception that CHLCs were issued in insufficient amounts may arise because an insufficient amount of bankers thought it was valuable, hence missing the externality value of liquidity. Also, banks could request and borrow CHLCs and not circulate them, thereby not paying interest on them. The only way CHLCs get circulated is if a bank uses them to settle accounts at the New York Clearing House in lieu of legal tender or specie. Some estimates of the percentage that circulated hover between 60 and 75 percent.

CONCLUSION

The New York Clearing House had nascent central bank powers, but we have not uncovered evidence of a consistent application of a lender of last resort policy. There is scant evidence of coordination of loan certificate issues by the Clearing House as counterfactual Clearing House might have done. Although we do not yet know the reasons for why particular banks issued loan certificates and others did not, bank specific interests rather than concerns about the general stability of the banking system seem to be reflected in the changing participation in loan certificate issues.

Relying on Cannon's description and on aggregated measures of CHLCs alone suggests a united approach among New York Clearing House banks to fight panics during the National Banking Era. We show that there was notable variation in the responses of individual New York banks to each panic, and there appears to have been little preconceived effort from the Clearing House in providing liquidity to the banking system. Some large banks participated substantially, and other large banks not at all. Even if there was a generally consistent proportional participation of the big banks in most panics, the severity of the panics suggested that the aggregate liquidity provision through CHLCs was insufficient. The system had to rely on gold imports and suspension of convertibility rather than a deeper use of loan certificates. Whether the shortfall was a result of insufficient quantity borrowed/issued or that the temporary liquidity medium itself was too limited is a question left for future study. Cannon's optimism was cut short by the Panic of 1907. The centralization of the banking business in the United States was accomplished by the Federal Reserve System, not the clearing houses.

REFERENCES

Annual Report of the Comptroller of the Currency, 1874, 1885, 1894, and 1907.
Cannon, James G. (1908). "Clearing Houses and the Currency (Loan Certificate Plan)." In E. R. Seligman (ed), *The Currency Problem and the Present Financial Situation, pp. 95–118.* New York: Columbia University Press.
   (1910). *Clearing Houses.* Publications of the National Monetary Commission, Vol. 32. Washington, DC: U.S. Government Printing Office.
Commercial and Financial Chronicle, various issues, Google Books online.
Gorton, Gary. (1985). "Clearing Houses and the Origins of Central Banking in the United States." *Journal of Economic History* 45(2):277–284.
Myers, Margaret. (1931). *The New York Money Market: Origins and Development.* New York: Columbia University Press.
Minutes of the New York Clearing House Committee, 1873 and on.
Sprague, O. M. W. (1910). *History of Crises under the National Banking Era,* National Monetary Commission. Washington, DC: U.S. Government Printing Office.
Tallman, Ellis, and Jon Moen. (2012). "Liquidity Creation without a Central Bank: Clearing House Loan Certificates in the Banking Panic of 1907." *Journal of Financial Stability* 8:277–291.
Timberlake, Richard H. (1993). *Monetary Policy in the United States: An Intellectual and Institutional History.* Chicago: University of Chicago Press.
Wicker, Elmus. (2000). *Banking Panics of the Gilded Age.* New York: Cambridge University Press.

6

Central Bank Independence

Can It Survive a Crisis?

Forrest Capie and Geoffrey Wood

> The key point to remember is that giving the central bank
> independence is the best method for governments to tie their
> own hands and prevent them from misusing monetary policy
> for short-term political reasons.
>
> (Waller 2011, p. 293)

> ... my frustration was that I could not in practice order the
> Bank to do what I wanted. Only the Bank of England can put
> the necessary funds into the banking system ... The fact that
> we had given the Bank independence had a downside as well
> as an upside.
>
> (Darling 2011, p. 23)

In recent years it became fashionable for countries to give their central
banks "independence." Although not the first "independent" central bank,
the example of New Zealand, whose statute changed in 1989, was often
cited in discussions and appraisals of these revised constitutions.

"The Reserve Bank of New Zealand Act is a landmark piece of legislation. The reforms contained in it are unique, and have attracted widespread interest internationally amongst official, banking, and academic
communities" (Dawe 1990).

It was made obligatory for countries that wished to join the Eurozone
first to make their existing central bank independent – a curious requirement in view of how they ceased to be central banks the moment the euro
was adopted but nonetheless a requirement. And for all countries, not
just those about to adopt the euro, independence was given either in calm

We are indebted to the members of the Monetary History Seminar held at Rothschild
and Co. London, on September 28, 2012, for their most useful comments and questions.
Subsequent drafts have benefited from the comments of Charles Calomiris, David Mayes,
Paul Tucker, and the members of a seminar held at the Winton Institute for Monetary
History, Oxford University, on February 13, 2013.

times, or in times when it was believed that stress was almost over and calm about to come. The question we address in this chapter is whether that much-vaunted change, one that economists as well as politicians generally commend, can withstand stress. Can independence survive a crisis?

We start our approach to that question by considering what "central bank independence" could mean, and then setting out the sense of the phrase embodied in most "independent" central banks. Then we turn to the instructions given to these banks, and why the instructions took the form they did. That leads naturally to a discussion of the recent pioneer – perhaps better re-pioneer – of independence, the Reserve Bank of New Zealand, in which we note both the circumstances that led to its being made "independent" – these were actually quite unusual – and its instructions, which differed in important details, and indeed in the amount of detail, from those of most other central banks. This amount of detail is important to our argument, and for that reason we spend some time on the New Zealand example. There is also, inevitably and usefully at this point, discussion of economic openness and the exchange rate regime in constraining (or freeing) the central bank in its whole range of actions, including those extending beyond the conduct of monetary policy.

Having set out these key issues, we then move to important examples of changes, overt or implied, in central bank–government relations. These examples are drawn from the experience of the United Kingdom and the United States. Then we come to very recent U.K., U.S., and European Central Bank (ECB) experience, looking at how the crisis developed and how it drove the Bank of England into the arms of the government, albeit perhaps rather reluctantly and possibly temporarily, and at the other cases more briefly. The chapter concludes by using these individual examples together with the analytical discussion of the earlier part of the chapter to make some general observations on the effects of crises on central bank independence.

ECONOMISTS ON INDEPENDENCE

Numerous economists have written on central bank independence, but always paying attention to how to measure some undefined notion of independence rather than discussing what the term might actually mean. The context was the relationship between degree of independence, somehow measured, and inflation. This was raised in two papers by Robert Barro and David Gordon (1983a, 1983b). Their papers demonstrate that a politically determined monetary policy will produce high inflation. Hence a recommendation followed that political influence should be removed from monetary policy by giving the central bank "independence." There were criticisms of their model, as it showed that politicized monetary policy would produce high and steady inflation rather than the fluctuating inflation that is much more commonly seen in practice. This criticism was advanced by, for example, Philip Cagan (1986), who then went on to show that a desire not to subordinate low unemployment to an inflation objective can, with appropriate lags, lead to the kind of inflation usually observed. But the relationship between too high (and possibly variable) inflation and politically controlled monetary policy survived in theory. All that had changed was the behavior of the inflation that politicized monetary policy was predicted to produce. The question of whether the relationship between low inflation and independence survived in practice remained of interest.

The pioneers in addressing this were Bade and Parkin (1987). Subsequent studies typical of the approach were Masciandaro and Tabellini (1988) and Alesina (1988, 1989). Bade and Parkin classified central banks into four groups, depending on their estimate of degree of government influence over them. Two types of influence were examined: "financial type" and "policy type." The former refers to the level of government interference in selecting members of the board, the setting of salaries, the determination of budgets, and the distribution of profits. The latter referred to the extent of interference in meetings of the board (or whatever the policy-deciding body is) and whether government has the final decision over policy. Subsequently Capie and Wood (1991, reprinted 2012) reconsidered the issue using a wider range of measures of independence and a longer data period. Broadly speaking, the findings of this work were unanimous: independence did correlate negatively with inflation, albeit, as Capie and Wood (1991) note, in some countries inflation was low regardless of the status of the central bank.[1]

None of these studies, however, spent much time on what independence actually meant. Freedom to take policy decisions seemed an obvious concept, and that was taken as being clear and detailed enough to be satisfactory for the purpose at hand. In a much earlier paper, however, one that concluded by recommending not central bank independence but a monetary rule as the best guarantee of price stability, Milton Friedman (1962) devoted some time to considering the meaning and inevitable corollary of independence. He writes, "The device of an independent central bank embodies the very appealing idea that it is essential to prevent monetary policy from being a day-to-day plaything ... of the current political authorities" (p. 178).[2] He then went on, "A first step in discussing this notion critically is to examine the meaning of 'independence' of a central bank.

---

[1] In a novel study Posen (1993) reversed the argument and maintained that central bank independence was an endogenous consequence of a low-inflation–desiring system. Independence came with rather than led to low inflation.

[2] All page references to this Friedman article are to the 1968 reprint.

There is a trivial meaning that cannot be the source of any dispute about the desirability of independence. In any kind of bureaucracy, it is desirable to delegate particular functions to particular agencies" (p. 179). At this point Friedman gives the example of the Bureau of Internal Revenue as an "independent bureau" within the U.S. Treasury. As he said, "This is simply a question of expediency and of the best way of organising an administrative hierarchy" (p. 179).

What he called a more basic meaning of independence is that "...a central bank should be an independent branch of government coordinate with the legislative, executive, and judicial branches, and with its actions subject to interpretation by the judiciary"[3] (p. 179).

That is the meaning that most writers have implicitly applied to the concept of an independent central bank. Friedman was concerned about the democratic accountability of such an institution. But these were not his only grounds for rejecting the proposal. Independence might, he said be "only a matter of words" if the bank's authority were narrowly defined and its policies tightly specified. This of course raises the question of whether he would have regarded an inflation–targeting bank (such as the Bank of England) as independent. It would, however, be an aside from our theme to pursue that question.[4] For we have reached the point where the importance of his discussion for this study becomes clear. If the central bank is to be independent in the sense in which, say, the judiciary is independent, then it requires a set of instructions to follow just as judges require a set of laws to implement. Further, as is desirable with laws (but not always attained) the instructions must be sufficiently clear that the legislature's intentions are either carried out, or, if they are not, it is clear that they have not been.

WHAT INSTRUCTIONS?

Here it is useful to return to Friedman's paper, for the context in which he places his discussion of central bank independence leads very straightforwardly to the kinds of instructions that have in recent years been given to "independent" central banks. He reviews three proposed solutions for the problem of ensuring that so long as government is responsible for money it cannot by debasement abuse that responsibility. He considers the following three solutions: an automatic commodity standard, an independent central bank, and a rule binding the conduct of policy. An automatic standard, such as gold, has tended to develop toward a "mixed" system with

---

[3] Recently both the ECB and the Bank of England have had their actions reviewed by the judiciary, albeit over very different issues. We briefly discuss these incidents in the text that follows.

[4] His other objections are also well worth discussing, but are not relevant in an essay on the present subject.

a substantial fiduciary component. Further, it is not now feasible: "...the mythology and beliefs required to make it effective do not exist" (p. 177).

That point is supported by the well-known quotation often attributed to Ramsay McDonald, the prime minister in the government immediately before that which took the decision,[5] on Britain's leaving the gold standard in 1931: "No-one told us we could do that."

Many advocates of an independent bank recognize the current impossibility of a commodity standard, and view an independent bank as an alternative way of getting price stability. Hence, together with the widespread acceptance that inflation is not desirable, we have central banks given instructions to focus on maintaining some measure of price stability.

Such instructions, sufficiently simple that their attainment can be monitored, have in the recent past proved troublesome and led to considerable difficulties. But before looking at that recent experience, it is helpful to examine the Reserve Bank of New Zealand, which both illustrates a set of instructions and shows why such changes tend to come about.

THE RESERVE BANK OF NEW ZEALAND

The Reserve Bank of New Zealand was established as a privately owned bank in 1934, but nationalized only two years later by New Zealand's recently elected (and first) Labour government. This nationalization was accompanied by a new and very wide ranging set of instructions, in the Reserve Bank of New Zealand Amendment Act of 1936. Of these instructions, David Archer (1992, unpublished) wrote, "Given such fundamental design flaws in the structure for decision-making, it would have been fortuitous if price stability had eventuated." Throughout the postwar period, New Zealand's growth rate was below the OECD average.

The economy was one of the most highly protected in the Organisation for Economic Co-operation and Development (OECD) area. Effective tax rates were high, and the government (via its control over monetary policy) regularly accommodated external shocks, so that the inflation rate was both high (by OECD standards) and variable. New Zealand became what was described as a "cost plus economy" (OECD 1993).

Monetary policy regularly switched between objectives – from the reduction of inflation to the lowering of (nominal) interest rates so as to encourage "growth." Policy relied increasingly on direct controls of a regulatory nature. There were both interest rate and exchange controls. The main financial institutions were constrained by reserve asset ratios, public sector debt requirements, and lending ceilings. There were income policies, price

---

[5] McDonald's saying that was subsequently rejected by him and by some of his acquaintance. The remark was then passed around several of the ministers of his government, but the parcel has not yet found a definite home.

controls (at a detailed level), quantitative import restrictions, and so forth. By mid-1984, a crisis was believed to have arrived. (Knight, then Deputy Governor of the Reserve Bank wrote of "... a disastrous outcome for the New Zealand economy by the mid-1980s" [1991].) Following the change of government, there was widespread acceptance of the need to change both the nature and the direction of economic policy. A sustained program of reform, affecting the institutions that designed and implemented policy as well as the policies themselves, was launched.

To quote the OECD (1993 p. 13), "These reforms created one of the least distorting tax systems in the OECD area, the lowest OECD producer subsidy equivalent in agriculture, substantial trade liberalisation, and a more efficient public sector." On the financial reforms, Knight (1991) wrote: "The whole financial system was thus remodelled in a remarkably short time, perhaps illustrating that you do not have to have a crisis to bring about major economic reforms, but it certainly helps" (p. 141).

As part of these reforms of policy, the "mechanics" of the public sector itself were reformed. Clear objectives were established for public sector organizations; accountability for the attainment of the objectives was assigned; and performance-based contracts were given to the chief executives of the organizations, who were given much increased management and financial freedom within a framework of agreed policies and total budgets.

The Reserve Bank Act reforms readily fitted into that framework. Monetary policy had been notably politicized and notably short term in New Zealand. Though this had changed, the changes were still dependent for their remaining in place on political whim. The government therefore sought ways of improving the credibility of their monetary commitment.

Almost simultaneously, some theoretical literature (noted previously) was redirecting the attention of economists to the conclusion that many years before had been reached, albeit informally, by Otto Niemeyer, who had played a central role in setting up the Reserve Bank, and many others. A revision of the Reserve Bank Act was (yet again) undertaken. This revision was the initiative of Roger Douglas, the new Minister of Finance. Douglas "... came to the Bank in November 1985 and suggested that the Bank explore ways for it to achieve some autonomy in the conduct of monetary policy. The main aim was to prevent a reversion to the kind of policy followed by former Minister Muldoon" (Knight 1991, p. 142).

After some detailed study of central banks that had been more successful than average in delivering low and steady inflation, the Act was drafted, passed with bipartisan support in December 1989, and became effective on February 1, 1990.

The Reserve Bank was given a clear statutory objective. The primary function of the Bank is to formulate and implement monetary policy directed to the economic objective of achieving and maintaining stability in the general level of prices (Reserve Bank Act 1989, Section 8). That is the primary, not the only, function. But it is the only macroeconomic function. (The Bank, in a contrast with the Bank of England, which appears to have been rather important [see later], retained regulatory and supervisory responsibilities.) A single macroeconomic responsibility was assigned for a number of reasons. It was recognized that in the long run money influences only prices; that determined the objective. It was also recognized that monetary policy, a single instrument, could have only a single objective; and it was feared that having several objectives would lead to conflicts over what to do and thus undermine credibility. The Act therefore assigned to the Bank authority to implement a monetary policy consistent with its price stability objective. The Bank's discretion is limited, however; it is limited by its statutory objective and by the requirement under the 1989 Act for the Governor and the Minister of Finance to negotiate *and publish* a "Policy Targets Agreement" (PTA). The measure of the inflation rate used in the PTA is the consumer price index. This was chosen not because it was thought to be better in some sense than various others, but because it was and remains the most widely known. An above-zero range (0–2% per annum) for inflation was chosen in light of a "... judgement ... that 1 percent inflation is consistent with stability in the general level of prices" (Archer 1992, unpublished). The PTA can be overridden by the government, but doing so requires an Order in Council, which must be tabled in Parliament, and which can last for a maximum of one year. This provision was underpinned, like the decision to introduce the Act, by both "political" and "economic" reasoning. The "political" reasoning was that it ensured that monetary policy was ultimately a government responsibility rather than that of unelected officials. The "economic" reasoning was the belief that by allowing explicitly for an override, *long-run* credibility could be enhanced. This latter possibility existed because without such a provision a bank/government conflict could lead to the Act itself being amended, perhaps after a governor's resignation.[6]

New Zealand has a floating dollar. There are provisions for the Bank to intervene in the foreign exchange market – but such interventions can

---

[6] The ECB's statutes exemplify the lack of explicit channels of democratic override (see Wood 2001). The consequences of this may have started to emerge in 2012. Some might nonetheless say that democratic control has its downside, of course. In New Zealand no PTA has lasted for its designed five years – that is, the term of appointment of a governor. The principal reason is that each new minister of finance has felt obliged to sign a new PTA. On most occasions there have been only minor changes – the range has crept upward and the time horizon has lengthened and some of the rather specific caveats have disappeared.

occur only on the basis of a written *and published* directive. If there is a conflict between such a directive and the objective agreed in the PTA the governor is obliged to notify the minister of finance of this, and is not required to implement the directive unless the PTA is amended to ensure consistency.

There are no limits on the central bank's ability to finance the government. It may seem curious that there should be no restrictions on debt monetization, particularly as New Zealand had in the past experienced inflation because of such monetization. Legislation against this was, however, thought to be both unnecessary and undesirable. It was unnecessary in view of the full-funding commitment the government had previously adopted. It was undesirable because it could constrain actions undertaken for, say, liquidity management or in the course of a lender of last resort operation.

That completes the description and explanation of the relevant details of the Reserve Bank Act and the associated PTA. It is now time to consider some details of the PTA.

The PTA does not specify simply an inflation target; there are exemptions for certain events that can cause shocks to the price level. These shocks comprise changes to the terms of trade (very important for a small open economy such as New Zealand) and changes in taxes that affect the price level at least for a time. The rationale behind allowing exemptions is that as the price level is not perfectly flexible, a shock that changes relative prices can initially affect also the price level and thus the measured rate of inflation over some time period. Because of price stickiness, an attempt to prevent this effect on inflation would (if the shock were positive) cause recession, and if it were negative lead to a boom that might well be hard to stop. The act aims to allow accommodation of the impact of the shock, but non-accommodation of any subsequent-round effects.

Note the detail of the act – and there is much that we have omitted. We return to the significance of this detail for our argument later.

But despite the care embodied in the act's design, there is a fundamental problem with the kind of target chosen, a price level (or inflation target). The problem was set out by Milton Friedman in *A Program for Monetary Stability* (1960 [with many reprints] pp. 186–188), and again in less detail in his 1967 presidential address to the American Economic Association. His argument can be summarized as follows. (The following draws on the earlier and more detailed exposition.) The central bank does not and cannot control the price level. It *can* control the stock of money. This distinction is important because although the stock of money is systematically related to the price level *on the average* (emphasis in original), the short-run relationship is variable, especially for mild movements, and further, the lags between money and inflation are highly variable. The evidence, he wrote,

"... is sufficient to pin the *average* lead with a narrow range" (p. 88). But, he went on "it is the highly variable behaviour for the individual episode with which policy must be concerned" (p. 88).

Before a central bank can hit an inflation (or price level) target, it is therefore necessary for it to predict for a considerable time ahead the effects of nonmonetary factors on the inflation rate (or price level), the length of time monetary actions will take to have effect, and the size of the effect of alternative monetary actions. Without such ability, there is danger of missing the target and, indeed, of swinging about it with increasing amplitude as the instruments of policy are used more and more aggressively in a desperate attempt to achieve the goal. (Some of these problems are discussed in Taylor 2012.)

LESSONS FROM NEW ZEALAND

The first lesson emerges from a comparison with the United Kingdom. Both the United Kingdom and New Zealand have a majoritarian form of government – that is to say, a majority in parliament gives close to unchecked authority. There are few "veto points" where a change can be blocked. Hence it is perhaps no surprise that a new government in the United Kingdom, which took office in 2010 after the financial crisis, made substantial changes to the structure of regulation and to the relationship of the Bank of England to that structure. Changes to the inflation mandate were not considered, and concerns about the Bank's internal government essentially ignored. No changes took place in New Zealand after the crisis.[7] This reflects several factors, and it is not possible to separate them. There was of course no widespread financial crisis in New Zealand – there were substantial problems, but in one part of the finance sector only, and that a part outside the remit of the Reserve Bank. (See Mayes and Wood 2012.) But it is also worth remarking that the Reserve Bank had a constitution that actually encouraged it to think about financial stability and the role of lender of last resort.[8] That was, explicitly, the reason that there were no restrictions on Reserve Bank purchases of government debt. Hence the specification of the Reserve Bank Act had been such as to make the institutions it produced more robust. It did not, however, deal with all eventualities. This can be seen by considering the recent (almost) worldwide crisis.

---

[7] Nonetheless, toward the end of 2012 the opposition parties in the New Zealand parliament tabled a bill to add further objectives in the U.S. style to the Reserve Bank of New Zealand's inflation mandate. It failed by one vote, with voting along party lines.

[8] Nonetheless New Zealand mimicked Australia by introducing two temporary measures in October 2008. The first was a wholesale funding guarantee and the second a crown deposit guarantee scheme. In Australia this latter scheme has become permanent while in New Zealand it lasted two years, dragged on for a further year for half a dozen nonbanks, and ended in 2011.

Banking crises can be of two types, although they rapidly merge into one another. The classic banking crisis is that which lender of last resort evolved to deal with – a sudden surge in the demand for liquidity by the entire banking sector.[9] The New Zealand act was consciously framed both to direct the attention of the Reserve Bank to the possible need for this operation and to allow it to take place.

But there is another type of banking crisis, much rarer in the whole run of recorded banking history but one that has occurred twice in comparatively recent years – one due to a shortage of capital not in one bank but across all or most of a banking system. This was the source of Japan's banking problems and also the original difficulty in the recent crisis (see, e.g., Lastra and Wood 2010).

There is no provision in the Reserve Bank Act to deal with a "capital" crisis. There could have been. For although there could be no instruction for the Reserve Bank to provide capital when needed – like for all central banks its balance sheet is too small to allow that – there could have been formal procedures under which it could approach government to request capital support under certain circumstances. This provision was not there. It was not there because it was thought such crisis could never happen, nor was its absence due to a desire to allow banking system failure under such circumstances. Rather it was due to no more than lack of complete foresight, and thus the inability to write a complete contingent contract dealing with all possible states of the world.

And that is fundamental problem, if a problem it is. It is impossible to design a contract so complete that nothing ever happens to require its being rewritten, thereby letting the government of the day tame or at the least reshape the central bank. That is the basic reason for almost every financial crisis leading central banks into the arms of government, for assistance, relaxation of law, or some other form of support or guidance. This point is supported by examples in the following sections of this chapter. It is not, however, the only reason for crisis compromising independence. Others are shown by example.

INTERNATIONAL COMPLICATIONS

Despite the aforementioned complications, central bank independence is widely regarded as the best means of delivering the best outcome on inflation. However, it is not simply something that, once the merits have been accepted, can and should be adopted with certainty of success. The major international complication is that the exchange-rate regime matters – essentially whether it is a fixed or a floating regime. It should therefore be

[9] See Wood (2000) for a detailed description of the evolution of lender of last resort.

no surprise to find that central bank independence began to get the attention of economists in the 1970s when floating exchange rates reappeared
after a long period of other regimes. Fixed and floating regimes can be seen
as alternatives (in the sense that either one delivers balance of payments
equilibrium), the adoption of which depends on the confidence there is in
the monetary authorities to behave properly. A floating exchange rate is
more readily adopted by a country with a reputation for sound monetary
management. A fixed rate may be more appealing to a country seeking to
establish such a reputation. For a small country under a floating exchange
rate there is no exchange-rate policy and monetary policy can be used.
Under truly fixed rates the exchange rate is the target and there is no monetary policy, with the monetary policy determined through the balance of
payments. Under either of those regimes there are no balance of payments
crises.

It was for these kinds of reasons that the first studies of central bank
independence began to appear in the 1980s after there were some data on a
period of floating rates. Bade and Parkin (1987) examined twelve countries
over the period 1973 to 1986, the starting point being what they took to be
the beginning of the new period of floating rates. Only then, they argued,
did national policymakers have the freedom to reveal their inflationary
preferences and how central bank constitutions may constrain them.

But Friedman (1953) showed that there was another kind of regime.
That was the one that came with Bretton Woods, and could be described as
fixed-but-adjustable rates, sometimes called pegged exchange rates. Under
that regime there can be some attempt at monetary policy at the same
time as the exchange rate is being targeted. With this regime the monetary
base has both domestic and foreign components. And indeed this was the
case that was effectively implicit in the working of the various Exchange
Equalisation Accounts that had been established. Under these, if capital
inflows were considered excessive there would be an attempt at sterilizing
the inflow. And when there are capital outflows and the central bank over-
compensates by supplying too much domestic money a balance of payments crisis could blow up.

As is frequently the case, the real world is not easily squeezed even into
that rather more complex framework. So, for example, in the British case in
the 1950s to the 1970s there was a fixed-but-adjustable regime in place. But
even if that regime were seen as a fixed one, the United Kingdom might
have had some freedom to exercise its own monetary policy. The reason is
that the United Kingdom was not a small country. It was not a big country either. It was an intermediate-sized country. Things were further complicated by its once having been a big country, and it was accustomed to
behaving like a big country. Furthermore, there were exchange controls in
place. And to make things more difficult still, sterling was still a reserve

currency. So, even if there had been a fixed exchange-rate regime in place, for this period there was some scope for Britain to have an independent monetary policy while operating with an exchange-rate target. (The fact that almost everyone in Britain who thought about the subject, including within the Treasury and the Bank of England, did not believe monetary policy to be important is another story.)

In other words, when thinking about central bank independence, its implications, and the design of an appropriate contract, the international setting of the country concerned may well make the specification of a complete contract difficult, perhaps impossible, even apart from the not trivial problem resulting from the absence of perfect foresight.

HISTORICAL EXPERIENCE

We next review some historical experience in two of the world's major central banks, the Bank of England and the Federal Reserve. We concentrate on these two because they were the models for many other central banks, and also because they illustrate many aspects of the problems we discuss.

The Bank of England was founded in 1694 out of the needs of the state to finance war. In return, the Bank was given a charter from the state that gave it a privileged position in banking in the country. The renewal of the charter clearly rested on the Bank's satisfying the state's requirements. And so began a relationship of dependency. The state needed the Bank and the Bank relied on the state for its privileges. When the Bank's charter was renegotiated in 1697, for ten years, it was given protection from competition from rivals; and its position was strengthened further in the renewal of 1708 when a fresh loan was required from the Bank. On that occasion other banks were restricted to six partners or fewer, and the Bank was given a monopoly of note issue in joint stock banking, in effect a joint stock banking monopoly. At the renewal of 1715 its privileged position was further enhanced when it was given the job of managing the government's debt. The Bank's position depended on its fiscal usefulness to the state.

As Britain was at war for more than half of the years between 1688 and 1815 the relationship between Bank and government grew ever closer and stronger. The state needed finance for war and the Bank either provided it or organized it, so that by the end of the eighteenth century the government saw the Bank as an essential component of its war finance program. In the wars with France at the end of the eighteenth century the government would take bills in large volumes to the Bank for discounting. The Bank would huff and puff a great deal but there was no question of it not complying with the state's wishes. In 1797 sterling's link with gold was suspended (a suspension believed from the start to be only temporary) and greater monetary expansion was made possible. If at any stage the

Bank showed any inclination to support a resumption of cash payments government quickly slapped it down. It supported the Bank through the heavy criticism it suffered in these years and then rewarded it by giving the Bank's notes de facto legal tender status in 1811 (de jure in 1816). In the world after the Napoleonic wars the Bank's fiscal usefulness was in decline and so the case for the monopoly in joint stock banking was eroded, and it was soon abandoned.

THE NINETEENTH CENTURY

In the nineteenth century, even in the age of laissez faire when there was free trade, sound money, and small government, the Bank's independence was still limited. In the first place the Bank's essential function was management of the gold standard and so it was heavily constrained by the rules of the gold standard and particularly so after these were redefined in the legislation of 1844. The main objective was to maintain convertibility of the currency into gold and the main control instrument was the short-term interest rate. The interest rate was made effective by discounting bills and, increasingly as time passed, by open market operations. These were all things the Bank became expert in and it was left to get on with the job without political interference.

However, a financial crisis that involved a scramble for cash presented a serious problem. In the crisis of 1825 the government instructed the Bank to pay out to the last penny (Feaveryear 1963). Instruction was thought to be needed as it was feared the still privately owned bank might otherwise have looked after its immediate profits due either to insufficient heed to the long term or to caution over its own survival. (Alistair Darling was not the first Chancellor of the Exchequer to have doubts about the universal virtues of central bank independence.) The 1844 legislation made it difficult for the Bank to perform its key role in a crisis, that of lender of last resort. The act needed to be suspended and that required a letter from the governor to the chancellor seeking the necessary exemption. That happened in the crisis of 1847 and again in the crisis of 1857. Then again at the height of the Victorian boom in 1866 crisis struck again in the famous case of Overend Gurney. The Chancellor agreed that it was "requisite to extend their discounts and advances upon approved securities, so as to require issues of notes beyond the limit allowed by law." But he continued: "No such discounts or advance, however, should be granted at a rate of interest less than 10 per cent, and Her Majesty's Government reserve it to themselves to recommend if they should see fit, the imposition of a higher rate" (quoted in Fetter 1965, 1978; see also Gregory 1929, 1964).

So when crisis struck the rules were such that government again dictated how the Bank should behave. Fetter concluded for the nineteenth century, "the Bank and the Government ... continued the fiction of official independence" (Fetter 1965, 1978, p. 280).

That was true again in 1914. At the outbreak of war in August 1914 there was a major crisis. The governor was invited to a meeting in Downing Street and told to sign a statement and to promise that during the war "the Bank must in all things act on the direction of the Chancellor of the Exchequer whenever in the opinion of the Chancellor the national interests are concerned and must not take any action likely to affect credit without previous consultation with the Chancellor" (Sayers 1976, pp. 99–107). Cunliffe, the governor, initially refused to sign and had the support of the Bank, where they believed, "it was impossible for the Bank thus to renounce its functions." But some face saving was allowed and Cunliffe agreed to comply.

For the interwar years the Bank of England was of the view that it should be "operationally and institutionally distinct from government" regarding this as independence, but "it should accept Treasury control of policy" – which was an implicit target regime on the exchange rate (p. 15). The governor throughout the interwar years, Montagu Norman, made it clear that ultimate authority rested with the Treasury. "I assure Ministers that if they will make known through the appropriate channels what they wish to do in furtherance of their policies they will at all times find us willing with good will and loyalty to do what they direct, as though we were under legal compulsion" (Collins 2012, p. 294). Norman went further than that when he told a meeting of Commonwealth bankers, "I am an instrument of the Treasury." Following the Great Depression when the blame fell on bankers, both central and commercial, their room for maneuver became further circumscribed.

POST–WORLD WAR II

It is often assumed (or asserted) that after the Bank was nationalized by the Labour Government in 1946 everything changed and the Bank thenceforth became a subsidiary of the Treasury. But in fact very little changed. Although there were complex drafting requirements to specify the functions, powers, and purposes of the new public corporations being formed after the war, in the case of the Bank this was unnecessary because there was "never any question that it should not continue doing what it had been doing for a very long time" (Chester 1975, p. 196).

The fact that little had changed following nationalization so irritated the Labour Party when in opposition in the 1950s that it was instrumental in getting the Radcliffe Committee established to enquire into the nature of the monetary system. It was particularly concerned to bring the Bank to heel and have the Treasury clearly dictate the terms.

The question of Bank Rate setting was partly one of principle and partly symbolic. The Bank took a strong line from which it never deviated: this was an operating rate and only the Bank knew which way it should be moving. This was largely accepted by government. The Bank delegated its power to set Bank Rate to the governors, with the chancellor giving formal approval to any change. And that was essentially what happened. The Bank would, primarily for external reasons, decide that a change in the rate was required. It would notify the Treasury of its view and expect to have the decision rubber-stamped. There are some isolated examples of disagreement for political reasons or for timing but generally these simply took the form of the Treasury suggesting a delay of a week or some such trivial alteration.

How central banks are financed also matters for independence. There are essentially three ways in which a central bank can be financed: it could be done straightforwardly out of taxation; it could be allowed to retain seignorage; or it could be done by placing a levy on the financial institutions. The first two means present problems in terms of independence. The third raises far fewer objections in this respect.[10] The last of these was how the Bank of England was (and still is) financed.

THE EXCHANGE-RATE TARGET

Across the period from the 1950s to 1980 the Bank operated with considerable freedom, what it liked to think of as independence.[11] Its principal function of defending the exchange rate was restored. Things were as they had been in the golden age before World War I. Many actions were taken but most important was the use of its oldest instrument – Bank Rate. Bank Rate was regarded as primarily of use for external purposes. And movements in Bank Rate were not merely executed but determined by the Bank. The Bank argued that knowledge of interest rates was a key part of their expertise and they knew better than any other part of government where interest rates should be and when they should be changed. Whenever there was a developing threat to sterling, the governor would tell the chancellor that a rate change was proposed on a particular date. The chancellor's reply was simply a one-line memo of approval. There were only a few isolated cases of resistance or postponement (see Capie 2010, chapters 4–6). The relative freedom began to come under serious pressure in the 1970s following the loss of the explicit exchange-rate target, and when monetary targets were in place monetary policy was increasingly politicized and politicians and civil servants had a simple number that they wanted to see met or be told why it was not.

---

[10] This is the case because it is being financed by a body other than government, and with which it has interests in common.

[11] See Capie (2010).

Thus it can be seen that from the Bank of England's founding a dependent relationship with government was accepted. Because the country was at war more often than it was not between 1688 and 1815 and the state needed funds it needed the Bank and the Bank depended on the state for preservation of its privileges. In the nineteenth century whenever crises flared, under the gold standard the Bank needed government approval to act in the necessary way and that came with conditions. In the first half of the twentieth century war dictated much of what happened; again the Bank responded to the needs of the state. There was a brief period after World War II when another exchange-rate target was in place and the Bank enjoyed relative freedom of action, but that all came to an end in the debacle of the 1970s. The next attempt at restoring some independence in 1997 has lasted only as long as there was no crisis.

THE UNITED STATES

When the Federal Reserve was founded in 1914 financial stability was its chief focus, and it was intended that the bank be independent of political influence. It was founded after a long period of peace but war broke out soon after and the Fed was almost immediately involved as the Treasury's banker. (Further, indicating another level of independence, the twelve district banks were free to operate independently of each other.) The Federal Reserve Act was quickly amended so that banks could borrow from the Fed using government securities as collateral. Inflation followed but the Fed could not raise its discount rate without Treasury approval. So it did not get off to a good start in terms of either independence or inflation control and it took some years after the war before it returned to its intended path of being an independent institution. In the years after the War and particularly following the recession of 1920–1921 the Fed discovered open market operations and the Open Market Investment Committee was established. The New York Fed became the dominant bank under the leadership of Benjamin Strong.

Hardly had the postwar adjustment taken place before new problems confronted the Fed, at the end of the 1920s, and its actions and its failures to act resulted in the Great Depression (Friedman and Schwartz 1963). Following the Great Depression and the criticisms, subsequent and sometimes consequent, that were made of banks and central banks the Federal Reserve Act was again amended, by the Emergency Banking Act of 1933. That act, among other things, gave the president powers to regulate credit, whatever that may mean. But calls for greater reform were strong and a new Banking Act was designed, for implementation in 1935. Initially the principal aim had been to provide a small but flexible monetary authority with its independence restored. The vague mandate that the Fed had been given in 1913 was, however, preserved in the 1935 Act. Further, in the

1930s if the Fed did not stay in line with the Treasury's wishes it was readily brought back into line by the Treasury acting through the new Exchange Stabilization Fund or other Treasury accounts. Meltzer (2009) is critical of the chairman of the time, Marriner Eccles, who, he said, failed to defend the Fed's independence under Roosevelt.

In any case, within a matter of a few years there was war again and in war the Fed was obliged to support the prices of government securities. It was an instruction in time of crisis. Tensions arose immediately between the Treasury and the Fed, with the Treasury seeking low rates to support the sales of bonds for war finance. In 1942 Federal Reserve banks were authorized by government to buy government securities directly from the Treasury. The dangers this gave rise to remained in place for years after the war. Throughout the period of low interest rates commercial bank reserves grew hugely and the inflationary dangers rose with them.

These tensions between the Fed and the Treasury over interest rates came to a head in 1950 and there broke out what has been called the "greatest battle in the history of central banking" (Davis 2012). Sproul of the New York Fed was sufficiently worried after the outbreak of the Korean War in 1950 to force the issue. In what he saw as a dangerously inflationary situation he thought it was time to exercise some independence. So the Board of Governors announced rate increases and indicated they would take further action if required to restrict credit.

The turning point came in January 1951. There was a special meeting between the Federal Open Market Committee (FOMC) and the president. That meeting was a direct consequence of an instruction by the Treasury to the Fed to buy government bonds at a specified price. The Treasury released a public statement after the meeting that suggested that the Fed would do as it was told. This so enraged Eccles, still a board member though a former Chairman, that he broke confidentiality rules and gave the press the Fed's record of the meeting. The Fed's record had suggested no such thing. Discussions then began in earnest between the parties. These led to the Accord of March 1951. The Chairman (McCabe) resigned soon after and his replacement was William McChesney Martin Jr., the Treasury assistant undersecretary who had conducted the meetings on the Accord. This might have looked like a cynical Treasury move but subsequent events indicate otherwise. Some see the Accord as the turning point in the Fed's history, the point at which it became a truly independent central bank. How true that is will continue to be debated. What it does for our purposes is remind us of how fragile independence can be. When any kind of emergency appears the dangers are that the response to these circumstances will be legislation that seems at the time entirely appropriate to the problem. But it then weakens the central bank's position when normality is restored. Although Martin went on to become the longest serving chairman of the Fed, and is generally credited with maintaining the Fed's independent position, he still held a slightly ambiguous view of independence. He liked to repeat the words of Sproul that the institution should be "independent within government not independent of government." Does that match Friedman's favored definition of independence? It might, but then it might not.

So, just as the preceding section showed that the inability to write complete contingent contracts ensures that independence is compromised in a crisis, this section demonstrates one route by which that compromising occurs – emergency legislation whose scope after the crisis turns out to be greater than had been realized at the time.

Reactions to the recent crisis may turn out to be an example of that; but whether they are or not, they certainly exemplify how a crisis can thrust a central bank into the arms of its government.

THE BANK OF ENGLAND AND THE RECENT CRISIS

At the time the Barings failure of 1890 the Bank of England was still a bank in the full sense of the term. Among other things it dealt in the money markets, and thus was aware before Barings actually came to it that the quality of the business Barings was doing was slipping. The Bank was nevertheless still surprised by the timing when Barings came to them; but they had been aware that things had not been going as well as heretofore. Then, when the failure occurred, the Bank did not have to go to the government for capital. They put in some of their own, and organized a consortium of other banks to do the rest. This was possible because there were then more banks than now, and there was more of a view than there appears to be now that there was much common interest between them. And, of course, while Barings was still a big name it was no longer a huge bank.

In contrast, when Northern Rock ran into difficulties the Bank no longer supervised banks either formally or informally, so, unless someone told them, which the Financial Services Authority (FSA) did not, they had no way of knowing the peculiar nature and high risk of Northern Rock's business model. In addition, their eye was off the "financial stability ball." Inflation had been the primary concern for some time, and there had been no financial stability problems for many years. And finally, even had other banks been willing to support Northern Rock (which their behavior in markets had clearly indicated they would not be enthusiastic about), events happened so quickly that there was no time to ask, and the call had to be on the government. The Bank had to go to its owner and ask for funds, and this had to be done in an ad hoc manner, and in haste.[12] As the report

---

[12] Why it was decided to support Northern Rock rather than follow the nineteenth century course and let it fail, and then providing liquidity to the market as needed to prevent a contagious run, is discussed in detail in Milne and Wood (2009).

of the Treasury Select Committee of the House of Commons made clear, there was plenty scope for things going wrong and a serious banking run starting at many stages in the process. Why did this unhappy combination of events occur?

There was an obvious information problem. Central banks need to be sure they are getting information on the health of banks. One way would of course be for central banks once again to engage in daily or more frequent transactions with banks, dealing in commercial paper as well as government paper, so as to get a feeling for how banks were trading and of the quality of their business. This is after all a long-standing tradition. When banks first emerged, they invariably required deposits and a relationship before they would make loans. That was the best way of getting to know their customers. It was a natural extension of how goldsmiths had behaved as they gradually drifted into the business of banking.

Another problem that emerged is that banks got into difficulties because they suddenly lost large amounts of capital when the value of assets they had bought collapsed precipitately. One response to this was that central banks should target asset prices as well as inflation. A less interventionist version of this is that central banks should monitor these prices, and intervene in asset markets when there is a bubble. This is of course in contrast with the traditional view that asset prices matter for central banking only when these prices collapse *and then cause problems for the banking system.*

It has to be said on that last point that it is a slight exaggeration of how central banks operated in the past. When countries were on the gold standard, rising commodity prices were automatically restrained by an increasing shortage of gold, as more went into circulation and some drained abroad. Rising asset prices had a similar effect. Some cash drained from the system. But this, it must be stressed, provided only a modest restraint. Should central banks go further?

If asset price bubbles can be identified, what can be done about them? If the bubbles are the result of "irrational exuberance," it is hard to see what central banks can do apart from make speeches. Tightening money would have surely very limited influence against irrationality. There is, however, a problem that may be more tractable. What if we have easy money but very limited inflation in the price of goods and services in general? And what if this easy money is associated with rising prices of a range of assets? What, in other words, if we are in the kind of situation that preceded the recent crisis? But be all that as it may, when the crisis struck thoughts became focused on dealing with it, and capital was required.

There also appeared to be two lessons for the conduct of monetary policy, neither of them new. The first is to ask why, if any series is behaving in a way that is slightly surprising, it is doing so. In the run up to the crisis inflation was low despite a sustained economic boom and by many measures easy money. Had this question been asked, it might well have been answered that although measured inflation was low, this was the product of a sustained relative price change, the fall in the prices of consumer durables as a consequence of Brazil, China, India, and other developing countries emerging as major exporters of consumer goods.[13] Such a relative price change could not go on forever, and the low inflation that was being produced by that means might well have triggered a reconsideration of the stance, and perhaps even the goals, of monetary policy. The second lesson for monetary policy is that this has been yet another demonstration of the folly of ignoring the monetary aggregates. These are certainly not an exact, day-to-day or even quarter-to-quarter, guide to future inflation (no one has ever claimed they were, of course, except those who wanted to attack their use in policy), but sustained rapid monetary growth is invariably a sign of future inflation.

The crisis thus not only made it necessary for the Bank to call on government support, but it also brought to light inadequacies in the previous set of instructions laid down by the government. It became necessary to reconsider central bank mandates.[14]

Nothing was changed in the United Kingdom, as far as inflation was concerned, as the Bank had de facto given up on inflation targeting and rather was trying to boost the real economy by monetary ease. This monetary ease, it must be emphasized, was carried on well beyond providing liquidity during the crisis, and was justified by, inter alia, continually forecasting that inflation was in the future going to fall to within its target range. To date (spring 2013) it has continued not to do so. Whether or not one interprets this as giving in to the desire of the government, it was certainly convenient for the government. Not only did the government appear to be "doing something," but the policy involved the Bank's buying up a large proportion of the debt issued by the government.

It was after the crisis clearly necessary to ensure that market information and financial stability are both recognized as important. This can follow in part from the Bank's mandate, but internal structure is also important. When the Bank of England, for example, dealt in the money markets it did so through the discount office, so called because it dealt with the Discount Market, the market that developed both as an intermediary between commercial banks and as an intermediary between them and the Bank of England, through dealing in (discounting) bills of exchange and

---

[13] In the United Kingdom at least another indication would have been that although consumers in general were experiencing low inflation, some groups – notably the elderly, who do not buy many consumer durables – were complaining about high inflation.

[14] The implications for the conduct of monetary policy with regard to inflation are obvious. Central banks should not rely exclusively or primarily on measures of the output gap and of inflation expectations in making their forecasts and the subsequent policy decisions. How to get them to do so is a different matter.

trade bills. These discount houses were small, and very highly geared. One precaution they took against failure was to know their customers well. The Bank of England in turn gained information from them both about their customers through regular meetings. Hence if we are not to allow central banks to return to banking, substitutes for this detailed and timely information must be devised.

That leads us very conveniently back to the central bank's relations with its owner, for the owner of course determines what the bank is allowed to do. A crisis, then, can affect central bank–government relations by showing that the contract of ownership, in both its informal and its formal aspects, was in some ways inadequate.

The crisis exposed weaknesses in the mandate given to the Bank of England, as well as defects in how the Bank (and the FSA) responded to the crisis. This inevitably required not only action from the government to deal with the crisis, but also changes in the mandate. The former plainly compromises central bank independence. Does the latter? The changes have concentrated authority in the Bank, but of course a consequence of this is that there is more that can go wrong and affect the Bank's reputation and thus its authority.

There are some similarities with the Federal Reserve. Much of Allan Meltzer's history of the Fed is concerned with its independence. 'The purpose of independence is to prevent government from using the central bank to finance its spending and budget deficit" (2009, p. 1256). But Meltzer argues, following Friedman, that independence needed to be defined in law. Because it was not, its interpretation was left to its chairmen and Board of Governors. A fundamental problem according to Meltzer was the failure of the Fed ever in its history to set out its lender of last resort policy. On some occasions it would respond in one way and on another in another way depending on the views being taken at the time by either the chairman or the board, thus generating uncertainty. Nowhere was this more evident than in the recent crisis.

Meltzer (2009) argues that in the years 2007–2009 the Fed has lost much of the independence it had regained in the 1980s. "(Bernanke) worked closely with the Treasury and yielded to the pressures from the chairs of the House and Senate Banking Committees and others in Congress" (p. 1243). And further, he "has acted frequently as a financing arm of the Treasury" (p. 1256).

In 2008 the Fed almost trebled its balance sheet, much of it in illiquid assets. The policy of ignoring inflation, and claiming to be concerned solely with unemployment, the other goal of the Fed, continued into 2012. The dual mandate allowed something that was politically convenient, but, as Taylor (2012) argues, far from obviously either effective or even worth trying.

If ever a central bank were designed to be independent in the sense of entirely free of political influence it was the ECB using the Bundesbank as the template. It was quite explicit that political interference would not be tolerated. But in the current crisis the behavior of the ECB can surely only be described as political. It has bought government debt not in the conduct of monetary policy, but to finance governments. The falsity of the ECB's denials of this is shown by its concentrating on buying the debt of governments seen as bad risks. This violates the prohibition on its financing governments. There is a justification given for this – it is intended to make the monetary transmission mechanism work across the whole area, a phrase interpreted by the ECB as keeping rates on all government debt within a narrow corridor. But that justification is not robust. For a major reason that debt markets and banks in certain countries are shunned is not shortage of liquidity but doubts about solvency. Again, independence has not withstood a crisis. Rather the central bank adopted a politically chosen goal other than the one it was given, under extensive and well reported pressure.

CONCLUSION

It appears tempting to conclude by constructing a counterfactual, so as to consider what a "truly independent" central bank might have done in the recent crisis. But we resist that temptation, as the whole argument of our chapter is that such a creature cannot exist. There is, however, another and more fruitful way of getting close to the question. What might a central bank guided by and adhering to the principles set out by Thornton, Bagehot, and Hawtrey have done in these circumstances? The answer is clear. They would have provided liquidity until the liquidity aspect of the crisis was over. They would have had nothing to do with the provision of capital to support individual banks – not their responsibility, beyond their balance sheet capacity, and a contradiction of the principles guiding lender of last resort action. As for buying almost all the debt the government cared to issue, that would certainly not have been done – the harm to price stability that would follow had been abundantly illustrated during the Napoleonic Wars. An altogether different approach was chosen in every country we have examined.

In a recent report in the *Financial Times* (September 10, 2012), James Bullard, president of the Federal Reserve Bank of St. Louis, is quoted as saying "I am a little – maybe more than a little bit – worried about the future of central banking. We've constantly felt that there would be light at the end of the tunnel and there'd be an opportunity to normalise but it's not really happening so far."

That really describes well what has happened in every major Western economy to its "independent" central bank. It happened of manifest necessity in the United Kingdom. There were obvious failures in how the financial regulatory and supervisory system had been constructed, and these required correction. The correction involved a much greater concentration of responsibility in the Bank of England, undoubtedly increasing its importance but also increasing of course its areas of accountability to its owner. At the same time the Bank certainly appeared to compromise its independence over inflation by consistently failing to achieve its target, a failure always accepted by the chancellor, and carried out a policy of financing the government's budget deficit. Meanwhile, the problem of how to get capital into a failing bank to prevent contagion was dodged by seeking to put in place measures to make retail banks failure-proof. This is a misguided endeavor - see Wood and Kabiri (2012) and the numerous references therein – and is in addition not guaranteed to succeed.

In the Eurozone, the ECB switched from control of inflation by monetary policy to a policy of buying government debt to keep the zone together at least long enough for further political changes to be implemented in the European Union. That this has not threatened inflation so far is an accidental by product of the severe recessions in a substantial part of the Eurozone. Despite that it represents a complete change in the objective of the ECB. The ECB has been politicized under the pressure of numerous heads of government.

And finally the Federal Reserve. That institution in the course of the crisis worked erratically and unpredictably along with the Treasury, in ways not consistent with its mandate, and also, as Meltzer (2009) put it, changed from protecting the value of the dollar to being the "financing arm of the Treasury."

This is all deplorable, but it should not be a surprise. So long as we have had central banks governments have used them at times of crisis, and have not hesitated to override whatever set of rules supposedly constrained the central bank. This is a consequence of several factors. First there is the inescapable fact that uncertainty makes it impossible to write complete contingent contracts for central banks. Second, even if it were possible to write such contracts, there are few countries where a constitution could prevent them being overridden were doing so to be temporarily convenient. Rules constrain men only so long as they believe the rules cannot be broken.

The ultimate consequence of that is that Friedman's "Program for Monetary Stability" is still incomplete, and perhaps will always remain so.

REFERENCES

Alesina, Alberto. (1988). *Macroeconomics and Politics*. NBER Macroeconomic Annual 1988. Cambridge, MA: MIT Press.
    (1989). "Politics and Business Cycles in Industrial Democracies." *Economic Policy* April: 55–98.

Archer, David. (1992). "Organising a Central Bank to Control Inflation." Unpublished manuscript.

Bade, R., and M. Parkin. (1987). "Central Bank Laws and Monetary Policy." University of Western Ontario Department of Economics Discussion Paper.

Barro, Robert, and David Gordon. (1983a). "A Positive Theory of Monetary Policy in a Natural Rate Model." *Journal of Political Economy* 91(4) :589–610.

(1983b). Rules, Discretion and Reputation in a Model of Monetary Policy. *Journal of Monetary Economics* 12(1):101–122.

Cagan, P. (1986). "Conflict between Short and Long Run Objectives." In Colin D. Campbell and William R. Dougan (eds), *Alternative Monetary Regimes*. Baltimore: Johns Hopkins University Press.

Calomiris, Charles. (2011). "Banking Crises and the Rules of the Game. In Geoffrey Wood, Terence C. Mills, and Nicholas Craft (eds), *Monetary and Banking History*. London and New York: Routledge.

Capie, Forrest. (2010). *The Bank of England; the 1950s to 1979*. Cambridge: Cambridge University Press.

Capie, Forrest, and Geoffrey Wood. (1991). "Central Banks and Inflation: An Historical Perspective." Published in two parts in *Central Banking*, Autumn 1991 and Winter 1990, and reprinted in *Money over Two Centuries*, by Forrest Capie and Geoffrey Wood (Cambridge: Cambridge University Press, 2012).

Chester, N. (1975). *The Nationalisation of British Industry, 1945–51*. London: Her Majesty's Stationary Office.

Collins, M. (2012, reissue). *Money and Banking in the UK: A History*. London: Croom Helm.

Darling, Alistair. (2011). *Back from the Brink: 1000 Days at Number 11. London:* Atlantic Books.

Davis, Gavin. (2012). "How the Fed Defeated President Truman to Win Its Independence." *Financial Times*, January 20.

Dawe, Stephen. (1990). Reserve Bank of New Zealand Act 1989. *Reserve Bank Bulletin* 53(1):29–36.

Feavearyear, Sir Albert, (1963). *The Pound Sterling; A History of English Money*. Oxford: Clarendon Press.

Fetter, F. W. (1965, 1978). *Development of British Monetary Orthodoxy*. Cambridge, MA: Harvard University Press, reprinted by Augustus Kelley.

Friedman, Milton. (1953). "The Case for Flexible Exchange Rates." In M. Friedman. *Essays in Positive Economics*, pp. 157–203. Chicago: University of Chicago Press.

(1962). "Should There Be an Independent Monetary Authority? In Leland B. Yeager (ed), *In Search of a Monetary Constitution*. Cambridge, MA: Harvard University Press.

Friedman, Milton, and Anna J. Schwartz. (1963). *A Monetary History of the United States*. Princeton, NJ: Princeton University Press for National Bureau of Economic Research.

Gregory, T. E. (1929, 1964). *Statutes Documents and Reports Relating to British Banking, 1832–1928*, Vol. 2. London: Oxford University Press.

Knight, R. L. (1991). "Central Bank Independence in New Zealand." In P. Downes and R. Vaez-Zadeh (eds), *The Evolving Role of Central Banks*, pp. 140–146. Washington, DC: International Monetary Fund.

Lastra, Rosa, and Geoffrey Wood. (2010). "The Crisis of 2007–2009: Nature, Causes, and Reactions." *Journal of International Economic Law* 13 (3):531–550.

Masciandaro, D., and Tabellini, G. (1988). "Monetary Regimes and Fiscal Deficits: A Comparative Analysis." In Hang-sheng Cheng (ed), *Monetary Policy in the Pacific Basin Countries*. New York: Kluwer Academic.

Mayes, David, and Geoffrey Wood (eds). (2012). *Reforming the Governance of the Financial Sector*. London and New York: Routledge.

Meltzer, Allan. (2009). *A History of the Federal Reserve, 1970–1986*, Vol. 2, Book 2. Chicago: Chicago University Press.

Milne Alistair, and Geoffrey Wood. (2009). "Shattered on the Rock? British Financial Stability from 1866 to 2007." *Journal of Banking Regulation* 10:89–127.

Organisation for Economic Co-operation and Development (OECD). 1993. *OECD Economic Surveys: New Zealand*, Paris: OECD.

Posen, Adam. (1993). "Why Central Bank Independence Does Not Cause Low Inflation: There Is No Institutional Fix for Politics." In Richard O'Brien (ed), *Finance and the International Economy*, Vol. 7, pp. 40–65. Oxford: Oxford University Press.

Reserve Bank of New Zealand Act, Public Act 1989 No 157, 20 December 1989. Retrieved from http://www.legislation.govt.nz/act/public/1989/0157/latest /DLM199364.html?search=ts_act_Reserve+Bank+Act+1989_resel_25_a&p=1

Sayers, Richard. (1976). *The Bank of England, 1891–1944*. Cambridge: Cambridge University Press.

Taylor, John B. (2012). *First Principles: Five Keys to Restoring America's Prosperity*. New York and London: W. W. Norton.

Waller, Christopher J. (2011). "Independence + Accountability: Why the Fed Is a Well-Designed Central Bank." *Federal Reserve Bank of St. Louis Review* September/October, 93(5):293–302.

Wood, Geoffrey. (2000). "The Lender of Last Resort Reconsidered." *Journal of Financial Services Research* 18(2/3):203–227.

(2001). "Is the European Central Bank Too Independent?" In Jens Hoschler (ed), *50 Years of the German Mark: Essays in Honour of Stephen F. Frowen*, London: Palgrave.

Wood, Geoffrey, and Ali Kabiri. (2012). "Firm Stability and System Stability: The Regulatory Delusion." In David Mayes and Geoffrey Wood (eds), *Reforming the Governance of the Financial Sector*. London and New York: Routledge.

7

Politics on the Road to the U.S. Monetary Union

Peter L. Rousseau

A recurring theme in discussions of challenges facing the Eurozone is the feasibility of a successful monetary union in a region that lacks a full political one. The early United States often arises in this context as a textbook example of a political union, forged by the Federal Constitution ratified in 1789, paving the way for future monetary stability (Rousseau 2006; Rousseau and Sylla 2005; Sargent 2012). This view holds strong elements of truth, but is misleadingly simple as a policy prescription. Indeed, the U.S. historical record indicates that politics interacted with the monetary and financial systems in an organic manner and that a stable monetary union, if defined as a system with a uniform currency and adequate safeguards against systemic risk, eluded the nation until well after the Civil War and probably not until the founding of the Federal Reserve. Moreover, monetary stability in the United States arose from the dual advantages of a decentralized system of banks under a firm central authority, a notion somewhat removed from the Federalist vision of 1789.

Seen from this perspective, the early United States was not much more of a "political union" in 1790 than today's European Union, though it did enjoy the advantages of a common culture and language early on. If history offers insights for the future, perhaps monetary stability in the European Union will also arise through a sequence of informed trial and error across political and monetary actors, though knowledge of the past may accelerate the time frame this time around.

This is not to say that the Federal Constitution was unimportant. The lack of even a rudimentary political union among the thirteen colonies prior to their independence allowed, for example, individual colonies in New England to undermine a loose regional currency zone, and the weak political union that emerged with the Continental Congress during the Revolution (1776–1781) and then under the Articles of Confederation (1781–1789) aggravated problems of monetary control. Moving to a single unit of account in the dollar, privatizing the money creation process, and

ceding some fiscal authority to the federal government after 1789 represented a leap toward a well-functioning monetary union, but the process
by no means ended there. Rather, political struggles shifted the balance
of power between centralist and decentralist influences in the government
and produced a patchwork of institutions and monetary practices that
ended up being codified in the compromise that was the Federal Reserve
Act of 1913.

The Federalist vision of banking was far from universally held in the
1790s. The anti-Federalist opposition attempted to stop the formation of
a central bank – the First Bank of the United States – on constitutional
grounds, and worried that excessive central control over monetary affairs
through a quasi-private bank would sacrifice general prosperity in favor
of "moneyed interests." They lost the first round in the conflict and the
Bank began operations, but turned the tables two decades later when an
act to renew the Bank's initial twenty-year charter failed by a single vote
in both chambers of Congress. The victory was short lived, with the needs
of war and financial stress leading to the chartering of a Second Bank of
the United States in 1816, but it too failed to have its twenty-year charter
renewed. The United States would proceed to go without a central bank
until 1914.

The pivotal point in this second and more serious unraveling of the
Federalist plan in 1832 occurred when the same sentiments expressed by the
opposition in 1810 truly took root following President Jackson's election
in 1828. Though ending in the nation's second largest cyclical downturn,
the Jackson presidency left a legacy that saw many more banks created by
1860 and with them an increased density of banking services that would
not have occurred as rapidly under the earlier regime. Note issue fell into
the hands of individual banks with often inadequate regulation at the state
level, and though the unit of account remained intact, it was manifested
in literally hundreds of different currencies in circulation. The surviving
monetary union, if one could call it that, was dealt another blow during
the political unrest of the Civil War with the uncoupling of paper money
from its backing. Following resumption of the previous system of convertibility at full face value in 1879, the system was undermined again and
again by financial crises through the start of World War I.

Today's U.S. monetary union would look quite different had the
Federalist plan gone off without a hitch. In this chapter I lay out the broad
history of how political and economic forces interacted up to the founding
of the Federal Reserve, emphasizing how a basic political union was insufficient for having a stable monetary union, and how the two evolved side
by side. In this respect, optimism about the European Union's prospects
for emerging in the end as a true political and economic union does not
seem misplaced.

THE COLONIAL PERIOD

The thirteen colonies, as individual possessions of the British Empire, comprised a union only in the sense that their geographic proximity allowed people and goods to move across them, and to the extent that the mother country addressed concerns about their governance with some degree of consistency. Political control of each colony resided in the hands of a governor appointed by the crown, and there was no single legislature to represent the colonies as a unit until the Second Continental Congress began to act as a provisional government for the fledgling United States in 1775.

Located on the Empire's periphery, the colonies were not well integrated politically with England, and were largely viewed by Parliament as a store of natural resources meant for extraction. Spanish and other coins circulated in the colonies, but their scarcity seemed to serve more as a vehicle for financial repression by the crown than a problem for the Empire to solve. The metallic nature of the monetary base led to problems of divisibility for small transactions (Sargent and Velde 2003). Disagreements between colonial legislatures, their governors, and the crown about managing these shortages eventually led to makeshift monetary systems of foreign coins and paper monies known as "bills of credit." These systems enlarged the stock of money but were inadequate for the volume of desired transactions. Classical monetary theory would predict domestic prices to fluctuate proportionately with the supply of money, yet the ability of an expanded stock of paper money to replace transactions formerly accomplished with barter or bookkeeping allowed the real stock of money to rise in many of the colonies (Rousseau 2007; Rousseau and Stroup 2011).

The main problem with these independent systems was an inability of the colonies to act collectively to control the total supply of money, given that the crown would surely resist any attempt to form a political or monetary block. This led to inconsistent monetary policies across colonies and often violent fluctuations in exchange rates among their currencies, with each denominated in its own "pounds" and quoted against each other and against the English sterling. This increased transactions costs and inefficiency, which were higher when informational and other frictions kept automatic stabilizers from working.

The New England colonies before 1750 offer an interesting and paradoxical example. Each colony in the region issued its own bills of credit that somehow circulated throughout New England at a common value. The system was thus an early de facto currency zone even though the four separate colonial legislatures (Connecticut, Massachusetts, New Hampshire, Rhode Island) controlled their individual money supplies. Indeed, there was no political union in place. Rhode Island, however, discovered early on that it could issue additional bills that would circulate at par with the other

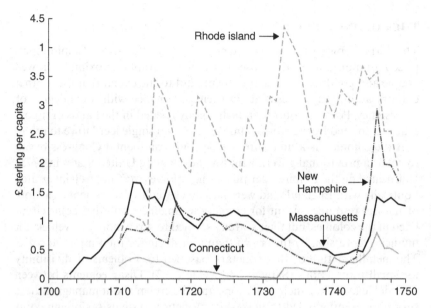

Figure 7.1. Bills of credit per capita in the New England colonies, 1703–1749.
Source: Reproduced from Rousseau 2006, p. 104.

New England currencies and at worst devalue the bills of the collective as a whole. This was nothing short of an inflation tax that Rhode Island imposed upon its neighbors.

Figure 7.1 shows the time path of the paper money stock in each New England colony, with all quantities expressed in per capita sterling.[1] It is clear that Rhode Island, with one-sixth the population of Massachusetts, had generated a per capita supply of bills that was three times that of its neighbor. When the other colonies began to sharply increase issues in the 1740s, rapid inflation commenced that saw prices in Massachusetts rise more than threefold between 1740 and 1749 (Rousseau and Stroup 2011, p. 604).

There is no doubt that lack of a central monetary authority in New England allowed a disproportionate share of the seigniorage to accrue to a single small colony, and it is in this sense that the region's natural experiment supports the view that a successful monetary union is not possible

---

[1] The quantities of outstanding bills of credit for the New England colonies are from Brock (1992, table 1). Colonial populations are from U.S. Bureau of the Census (1975, p. 1168, series Z-3, Z-6, Z-7, Z-11) and use constant growth rates to interpolate between decadal benchmarks. Sterling exchange rates are annual averages of local pounds per 100 pounds sterling from McCusker (1978, table 3.1, pp. 138–145).

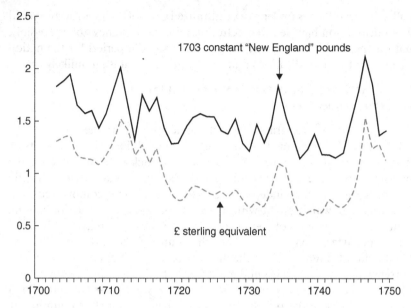

Figure 7.2. Per capita money supply in New England, 1703–1749.

without a viable political one first. But is this too strong an interpretation? After all, the real money stock did rise in New England as a whole by an average annual rate of 14.2 percent (7.6 percent in the 1710s, 9.6 percent in the 1720s, 10.4 percent in the 1730s, and 36.2 percent in the 1740s), and Rousseau and Stroup (2011) show that this development was growth promoting.[2] Even Figure 7.2, which shows the per capita stock of money in the region deflated by the local price level and in sterling equivalents, indicates that Rhode Island's emissions helped to stabilize money balances in the region as a whole compared to the wide fluctuations shown for the individual colonies in Figure 7.1.

Did the New England colonies actually see some success in their early monetization without a political union in place? Perhaps the strength that these colonies showed in even a loose collective action gave the crown reason to put an end to fiat paper money with the Currency Act of 1751 and effectively place New England on a specie standard for the remainder of the colonial period.

This begs the question of whether the situation in New England would have been different had it stood as a single political unit rather than a

---

[2] Growth rates are computed by dividing the total money stock in New England by the price level in Massachusetts (see Rousseau and Stroup 2011, p. 604) and averaging across each decade.

collection of colonies under weak centralized control an ocean away. Would a political union have led to a better functioning currency zone? Possibly, but one need only turn to the immediate post-1776 period for the nation as a whole to find indications that this counterfactual is an unlikely one.

THE REVOLUTIONARY WAR AND ARTICLES OF CONFEDERATION

On signing of the Declaration of Independence in 1776, the colonies were officially a self-proclaimed political union, but still lacked components of many successful ones. One deficiency was the lack of a mandate for the national legislature (i.e., the Continental Congress) to tax citizens directly to finance the war of independence that immediately commenced with England. The war brought with it a need for coordinated action among states, and some parts of the young United States, and particularly those along its eastern coast, would bear the brunt of the early assaults. The Continental Congress solved the direct taxation problem by issuing paper currency to pay for soldiers and munitions. The $38 million "continentals" placed into circulation between 1775 and 1777, which rose to $200 million by 1780 (Grubb 2008, p. 286), entitled the bearer to a stated number of Spanish milled dollars, if one believed what was printed on the face of the bill, but there were no stated provisions for their conversion into coin. This meant that the continentals were backed only by the firmness of beliefs that they would be redeemed in hard money if the young nation were to win the war.

Without a clear physical backing, the continentals plunged to near worthlessness by 1781, with most of the decline complete as early as 1778. Figure 7.3, which shows the nominal and real stock of continentals outstanding between 1776 and 1781, illustrates the course of the decline.[3] The real stock of continentals kept pace with the nominal through much of 1776, but additional issues were unable to raise the real stock of bills, instead setting it back further. Did the lack of immediate convertibility to specie precipitate the decline? In some respects the answer is yes, as an adequate physical backing could have substituted for a lack of credibility in controlling the supply of notes in the short term. In contrast, consider the dollar of today, which remains relatively stable without a specie backing due to a credible commitment by the U.S. monetary authorities to control its supply. Its success lies in the "backing" implied by the "full faith and credit" of the United States.

---

[3] The solid line in Figure 7.3 cumulates the issues of continentals documented in table 1 of Grubb (2008, p. 286), and the dashed line divides these totals by the paper-to-specie exchange rates reported in table 2 of Calomiris (1988, pp. 57–58).

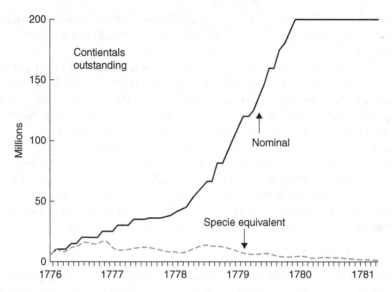

Figure 7.3. The rise and fall of the continentals.

Yet it is exceedingly difficult for a weak or young political union to establish the full faith and credit of its own citizens, let alone the international community. The tenuous nature of the political union that was the young United States therefore explains why the currency failed. After all, from the start it was not at all clear that the United States would emerge victorious in the conflict with England. And even if it did, it remained unclear whether the Continental Congress had come to view the continentals as an indirect form of taxation for a federal government that lacked the ability to impose direct taxes. As such a notion took hold, there would be ever decreasing confidence in the continentals being redeemed (Calomiris 1988). It is perhaps at this point that the real money stock began the free fall that saw it officially devalued at 40:1 in 1780 and then again at 100:1 in 1790 as part of the Funding Act.

This is not to say that the new political union failed to make a show of it for a time, with continentals used to meet expenses in the early stages of the Revolutionary War, but in the end the continentals paid for only 40 percent of the conflict (Calomiris 1988, p. 58), and it took assistance from domestic as well as French and Dutch investors to ensure that the war could be financed and ultimately won. It is therefore safe to say that the nation lacked the confidence of the public in its coordinated efforts for some time into its early history. It is also important to note that the nation had these problems even though its citizens spoke the same language and had similar cultural roots. This suggests that such differences in the European Union may be overemphasized as reasons why their political union is less than complete.

After the war, the nation continued under a treaty-like arrangement among the states – The Articles of Confederation – in which the states agreed to act collectively, and some states such as Pennsylvania began issuing paper money with some success once again. But depreciation of these new state notes, though never reaching anything near the severity experienced with the continentals, was still unacceptably high. The young nation could in general be characterized as a vulnerable and weak state, with its political union designed primarily for mobilizing defenses in case of foreign attack. This vulnerability was recognized by the Founding Fathers, and created an urgency to overcome opposition that feared central authority in favor of the sea change that was the Federal Constitution.

THE FEDERALIST ERA

The early Federalist period is rightfully recognized by a growing group of scholars as the time when the United States made leaps toward achieving the monetary union that persists in some form to this day. Sylla (2002) and Rousseau and Sylla (2003, 2005) emphasize a change in the nation's growth trajectory after 1815 that can be plausibly linked to earlier developments championed by the nation's first Secretary of the Treasury, Alexander Hamilton (1789–1795). These changes included stronger public finances, support for a variety of banks, some form of a central bank, and active securities markets. The new institutional structure created an environment conducive to entrepreneurship, especially in the major population centers. At the same time, the relative monetary stability established in 1790 came at the price of "re-booting" the nation's failed financial system. This took the form of delivering the final blow to the continentals and restructuring U.S. government securities, many of which were held outside of the United States. In other words, whether expected for some time or not, the nation forged a monetary union in the wake of repudiation.

The Federalists' decision to default, however, was the right one. As mentioned previously, the continentals had already fallen to near worthlessness by 1778, were officially devalued on a generous 40:1 basis in March 1780, and were mostly hoarded by individuals or purchased by speculators in the hopes of eventual redemption at par. Of the nearly $200 million in continentals outstanding at the start of 1780, some $80–88 million remained in the hands of the public in 1789 (Grubb 2012, p. 160). So redemption was likely to benefit speculators rather than soldiers and others who had watched the value of their currency vanish and had long parted with it. Indeed, it would be impossible to identify those who once held these bearer instruments when their value fell. At the same time, the bond holders who had financed the later part of the war also saw the value of their assets fall to pennies on the dollar over the 1780s, and there was speculation in these instruments as well.

Why did Hamilton and the Federalists give priority to holders of state and federal bonds over those with domestic currency? They did it because the scheme restored some confidence in the United States and its commitment to meet its medium and long-term obligations. Given that the commitment to redeem the continentals at par had always been vague, the young nation as a result became better able to attract capital from abroad.

The early financial markets were largely centered in New York, Philadelphia, and Boston. Cowen (2000) and Sylla, Wright, and Cowen (2009) characterize the nation's first securities markets crisis in 1792 as a result of speculative excesses, and emphasize how the Bank of the United States injected liquidity into the New York money market to calm the selling frenzy. The example demonstrates what the quasi-central bank could potentially do to avert a financial crisis, but hardly represents a systematic response to a nationwide disaster. Rather, it spared a small number of wealthy investors in New York from realizing large losses. The nation's population was still concentrated in the Northeast and the restricted reach of the financial sector had not yet come under the pressure that was to rise to a fever pitch some thirty years later.

At the same time, there is also little doubt that the monetary union forged by the Federalists brought order to a chaotic system of state currencies through more centralized handling of monetary affairs. It is also clear that the beginnings of the banking system observed today took shape over the period of the First Bank's charter. The inability of Congressional Federalists to renew that charter in 1811 under President Madison's ambivalent watch proved nearly disastrous as the War of 1812 called for a unified monetary response to England's attempt to regain control of its former colonies. But by the time a new and even more powerful central bank – the Second Bank of the United States – received a federal charter in 1816 and came under the firm control of Nicholas Biddle in 1823, it was becoming clear that there were limits to how far a monetary union could be built through hubris rather than cooperation among its members.

The available data themselves point to the weaker long-term aspects of the Federalist plan. Although Rousseau and Sylla (2005) document a sharp rise in securities available for trading in the major financial centers, potential investors outside of these centers had considerably less access to the capital market. The First Bank did establish eight branches when some legislators sought to relocate some control over loans and discounts away from the main bank in Philadelphia, yet the Bank and its branches were still often viewed as constricting the supply of money by redeeming notes of other banks whose currency issues they deemed excessive, thereby

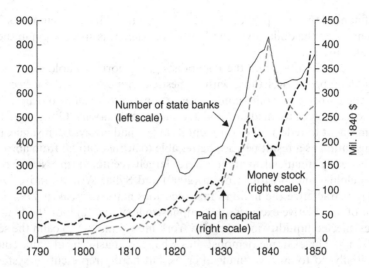

Figure 7.4. Monetary and banking aggregates, 1790–1850.

lowering total credit.[4] Some other members of Congress argued vociferously to this effect as the Bank's initial charter was considered.[5]

Hamilton's own statements in 1790 demonstrate a reluctance to embrace a system of branches, but more for the possibility of mismanagement than for their inability to distribute credit widely.[6] For a country that had just experienced hyperinflation during the Revolutionary War, caution was prudent at the time, yet it is telling that the aggregate money stock, number of banks, and bank capital all took a sharp upturn after the nation's first round of Federalism came to a close in 1828. Figure 7.4 shows these time paths through 1850.[7] Although the number of state banks did increase

---

[4] Branches were formed at first in Boston, New York, Baltimore, and Charleston (1792), and later in Norfolk (1800), Washington and Savannah (1802), and New Orleans (1805). In total, the Bank had apportioned 38.5 percent of its $10 million in capital to the branches in 1800 and 53.8 percent by 1809 (Wettereau 1937, p. 278).

[5] Representative Michael Stone of Maryland, for example, stated on February 5, 1790 that "by this bill a few stockholders may institute banks in particular States, to their aggrandizement, and the oppression of others. It will swallow up the State banks" (Wettereau 1942, p. 71).

[6] Hamilton writes "the argument against it [i.e., branching] is, that each branch must be under a distinct, though subordinate direction, to which considerable latitude of discretion must of necessity be entrusted. And as the property of the whole institution would be liable for the engagements of each part, that and its credit would be at stake, upon the prudence of the directors of every part" (Wettereau 1942, p. 70).

[7] Estimates of the number of banks and their paid-in capital are from Rousseau and Sylla (2005), who build these series from data in U.S. Bureau of the Census (1975) and Fenstermaker (1965a, 1965b). Rousseau and Sylla (2005, pp. 22–24) provide details on the construction of the money stock.

rapidly in the 1810s, their number was low during the time of the First Bank's charter and the series flattens during the 1820s as Biddle took control of its successor.[8] The stock of money and bank capital also developed at a modest pace until rapidly rising with the number of banks in the latter half of the 1820s.

These expansions, of course, came to a spectacular conclusion in 1837, but nonetheless raise the question of whether banking could have grown and spread more rapidly without a quasi-private central bank, and whether subsequent financial development benefited from the Bank's demise. In terms of achieving a currency zone with monetary and financial services distributed in proportion to the population, the first Federalist period can claim many successes, but by 1828 financial system had come under the same strains that surfaced twenty years earlier as democratic forces once again agitated against the central bank and its influence over monetary affairs.

JACKSON AND HIS LEGACY

Few periods in the U.S. monetary history are more maligned as examples of politics and monetary policy at their worst than the Jackson years (1829–1837). The stage was set on the Democrats' return to the White House as rhetoric from the president escalated about the dangers of centralized monetary control and misuses of the public funds as allegedly practiced by the Second Bank.[9] Although Jackson's early statements were firm but moderate, politicization of the Bank issue led to the famous "Bank War" and Jackson's 1832 veto of legislation to renew the Bank's federal charter on its expiration in 1836.[10] Some consider this event and all

---

[8] The data show a sharp decline in the number of banks in the wake of the Panic of 1819, yet the recovery was slow in the early Biddle years compared to after 1828.

[9] Jackson raised concerns about the constitutionality of the Bank and its privileged position in lending public monies in his 1829 and 1830 annual messages to Congress. At the same time he urged Congress to "in the spirit of improvement and compromise which distinguishes our country and its institutions it becomes us to inquire whether it not be possible to secure the advantages afforded by the present bank through the agency of a Bank of the United States so modified in its principles and structure as to obviate constitutional and other objections" (Second Annual Message, December 6, 1830).

[10] In his Sixth Annual Message to Congress on December 1, 1834, Jackson makes his views on the resuscitation of the Bank clear: "the bold effort the present bank has made to control the Government ... are but premonitions of the fate which awaits the American people should they be deluded into a perpetuation of this institution or the establishment of another like it. It is fervently hoped that thus admonished those who have heretofore favored the establishment of a substitute for the present bank will be induced to abandon it, as it is evidently better to incur any inconvenience that may be reasonably expected than to concentrate the whole moneyed power of the Republic in any form whatsoever or under any restrictions."

that followed in the 1830s a serious setback for the U.S. monetary union, but its longer term consequences can easily be cast in a more positive light.

Indeed, there was a lofty and unassailable goal that Jackson and the Democrats had in mind when they pushed back against Biddle's control of the money creation process. Perhaps it was a more equitable distribution of monetary resources among the public that Jackson sought when he removed the government's deposits from the Second Bank in 1833 and 1834, scattering them into a system of depository banks (i.e., "pet" banks) that would become the government's new fiscal agents. The "Specie Circular" of June 1836, which was an executive order requiring all government lands sold to the public to be paid for in specie, was also consistent with this goal. I say this because the Specie Circular, though purportedly issued to slow land sales in areas inundated with an expanded stock of paper money, actually ended up directing coin out of the eastern cities and to points in the West and South (Rousseau 2002, pp. 473–477). The Deposit Act of 1836, sometimes referred to as the "Distribution of the Surplus," also relocated government deposits away from the eastern money centers and to the South (Rousseau 2002, pp. 463–473).

Was it Jackson's view that less centralized control of reserves and money creation would lead to more localized and independent lending decisions that would promote development more effectively in areas outside of the major population centers? This does not seem to have been the immediate result, which may explain some of the negative views that historians typically hold of Jackson's policies. Yet after the downturn of 1837–1843, a more distributed banking system did begin to emerge and gather strength over the next two decades, some of which occurred under a series of "free banking laws" passed by individual states in the 1850s. These laws set more uniform standards for bank entry and allowed them to start up more quickly.

It is fair to say that the Federalist banking system worked well at a time when the nation's population remained largely concentrated to the east of the Appalachians, but that the system did not fully anticipate the nation's growth potential and by the mid-1840s had become constrictive. Since early in the Federalist era, organizers seeking to start a bank need to obtain a state charter to operate through a special legislative act. This meant that acquiring a state charter was tedious and approval depended on political influence as much as financial resources (Bodenhorn 2006; Hammond 1957, p. 574). Seeking to advance their political and economic fortunes, legislators protected existing banks and prevented the market from expanding, leading to an intense need for liquidity in developing areas.[11]

---

[11] As quoted by Bodenhorn (2003, p. 188), A. C. Flagg, a former comptroller of New York State, recalls that merchants, manufacturers, and bankers regularly appealed to politicians

Whether the new free banks met this intense need and explicitly contributed to growth in their localities is an open question and recent evidence in Jaremski and Rousseau (2013) suggests that they did not. But immediate impact is not always the appropriate gauge with which to measure success. It is notable that President Tyler had an opportunity to put an end to any Jackson banking legacy in 1843, but chose not to do so. Perhaps he deserves more credit for broadening the banking system than history has given him. Bodenhorn (2000, pp. 155–156) shows that commercial paper rates were progressing toward convergence across New York, New Orleans, Charleston, and Cincinnati by 1845. If measured by the integration of the short-term capital market and the diffusion of financial services, important steps toward an inclusive monetary union were made without the discipline of a central bank.

Politics were a central ingredient in the evolving monetary union. Sylla (2010) and Bordo (2012) consider the type of central bank that might exist today had Jackson signed the 1832 bill to recharter the Second Bank, and speculate that it could be a European-style central bank quite different from the Federal Reserve that emerged in 1914. This counterfactual could well have occurred had politics not forced Jackson's hand prematurely. To see this, consider the stance of an earlier iconic Democrat, Thomas Jefferson, who opposed chartering the First Bank of the United States in 1790 and remained a critic of the Bank after his election as the nation's third president in 1800. Yet even Jefferson over eight years in office came to appreciate the usefulness of the Bank – so much so that he could be considered a supporter by 1808. His successor, former Federalist turned Democrat James Madison, also held this view. Though the First Bank did not prevail despite these sentiments, it is interesting to consider what the Second Bank's fate could have been had its recharter not been forced onto the legislative agenda by the Whigs four years prior to expiration and turned into a political issue in the 1832 election. Indeed, Jackson, like his Democratic predecessors, may also have come to a better understanding of the Bank's functions and reached some compromise with Congress as to what the Bank's lending policy should be and how the government's deposits should be handled. Jackson's early statements on the subject seemed to allow some room for common ground (see footnote 9).

Although many of Jackson's policies were disruptive, Temin (1969) shows that the inflation and recession of the 1830s were not entirely due to his missteps. External specie inflows from Mexico and points south expanded the monetary base and the state banks multiplied these reserves at existing ratios, leading to the credit boom and inflation. This ended in

---

for more banks. Delegations were often led by powerful and well-respected individuals such as Albert Gallatin, the nation's longest-serving Secretary of the Treasury (1801–1814).

a spectacular crash, but two decades of expansion in the banking system followed that took its size to unprecedented heights and led to a more equitable distribution of banking activity across the nation's land mass. Certainly the Whigs who succeeded Jackson were unable to alter and were ultimately forced to embrace the new wave in financial and banking structure that followed in his shadow. Even Bray Hammond (1936, p. 184), a pointed critic of Jackson's policies, conceded that:

Free banking is a direct heritage from Jacksonian democracy. The interest of Jackson himself in banking was mainly destructive, but the people who gave him his following – the mass of rugged individualists imbued with what Gallatin called with dismay the fierce spirit of enterprise – wanted not to stop with the destruction of the Bank of the United States, but beginning with that to erect thousands of local banks owned by local capitalists. They wanted to destroy the monopoly and make banking open to all.

THE RETURN OF THE WHIGS AND FREE BANKING

When William Henry Harrison defeated incumbent Martin Van Buren (Jackson's vice president and successor) in his 1840 bid for a second term, the White House returned to the Whigs and it was widely anticipated that many of the changes to the banking system brought about by Jackson would be reversed through the reestablishment of a central bank. Harrison's untimely death after a month in office did not alter these expectations at first, as most assumed that his successor John Tyler would pursue the Whig agenda, but hope was quickly lost as Tyler twice vetoed legislation to establish a new central bank by the early autumn of 1841.[12] Though the political fallout from this ended in Tyler's expulsion from the Whig party, the nation would nonetheless emerge in 1843 from its five-year recession and render the vetoes of little immediate economic consequence. When the Democrats returned to power in 1844 with the election of James K. Polk, the banking system once again began to expand. And by the early 1850s, under the final Whig Millard Fillmore's watch, a system of "free banks" quickly increased the density of banking services.

It is interesting to consider the potential impact of the Fillmore presidency had Jackson not vetoed the bill for the Second Bank's recharter in 1832, since the decision about the next charter renewal would likely have fallen into Fillmore's hands. As a Whig, we can only assume that he would have supported such a bill, leaving the United States with some version

---

[12] Tyler was a former Democrat and always an advocate for state's rights, so his opposition to chartering a third central bank should not have been an enormous surprise to the Whigs in Congress and in his cabinet who had supported his somewhat controversial accession to the "full" presidency only months before.

of Biddle's bank well into the 1870s. In this case it is unlikely that anything like free banking or the National Banking System would ever have emerged.

Free banking involved states passing their own laws that allowed virtually anyone to form a bank so long as it adhered to state requirements regarding capital, reserves, collateral, and note issuance. Although free banking was thus far from "laissez-faire," banks could now enter the industry at relatively low cost and with a minimum of legislative barriers. Free banks expanded rapidly in the 1850s, and by 1860 there were 1,371 state banks (including free banks) operating in the United States, more than twice the number in operation in 1845 (Weber 2006, p. 35).

Starting with Michigan in 1837 and continuing through 1860 in Pennsylvania, free banking laws replaced legislative processes for starting banks with a defined set of capital, reserve, and note issue requirements that varied from state to state. Most laws permitted entry with low administrative barriers and small sunk costs. Banks and liquidity could then expand with population and demand without political interference. In total, eighteen states passed free banking laws, but most were not passed until the early 1850s (Rolnick and Weber 1983, p. 1082).

Despite establishing liquidity on the frontier, it is not clear that free banks promoted development in their immediate locations, and free banks had a greater propensity to close than charter banks (Jaremski and Rousseau 2013). Such closures would sometimes occur before free banks could have a positive effect on their communities. Rolnick and Weber (1983) show that this was not because free banking was an inherently unstable institutional arrangement, but rather a result of fluctuations in the value of collateral bonds required by individual states for securing notes. Because the quality of bonds acceptable for securing notes varied across states, with some even allowing nongovernment bonds such as railroad securities to secure notes, free banks in states with looser collateral standards were more vulnerable to negative business cycle fluctuations or particular industry-specific shocks.

The expansion of banking during the Jackson and free bank eras distributed banks across the country and furthered integration in the early capital market. Figure 7.5 illustrates the density of banking in 1832 (left panel), the year in which the Bank War culminated, and in 1859 (right panel) on the eve of the Civil War. In contrast to the dominating cluster of northeastern banks in 1832, by 1859 banks had spread throughout the Midwest, the Upper Midwest, and the mid-South, bringing more widely diffused banking services along with them.

The greater geographic reach of both charter and free banks was consistent with promoting a monetary union, but in some respects represented a step backward. The Federalist system did allow for a wide range

166

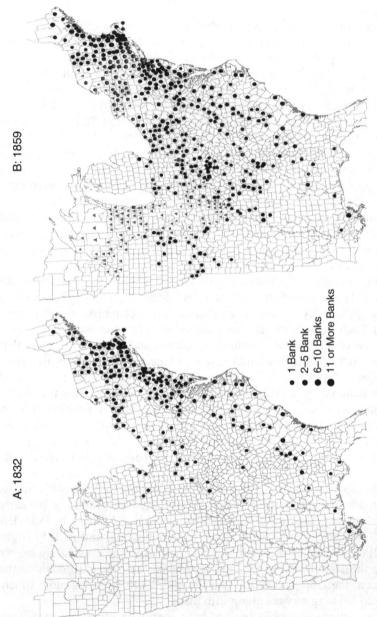

Figure 7.5. The distribution of free and charter banks, 1832 and 1859.

of notes issued by individual banks under the general control of the First and Second Banks, but the expansion after the Second Bank's demise generated an unprecedented multiplicity of notes. With it came problems with counterfeiting and asymmetric information regarding the condition of banks that issued notes. When a note would circulate far from the bank of issue (i.e., the only place required to redeem the note in specie), there were considerable costs involved with returning the note to that particular bank, including the possibility that the bank that had issued the note would be closed (Gorton 1996). This led to notes of different banks trading at discounts against each other and based on the location of a particular note holder.

The nonuniformity of the currency led to regular publications in the major cities – called "bank note reporters" – that listed various known bank notes along with their value with respect to specie. This was not as straightforward as it may seem when considering discounts for notes issued at great distances or from remote locations. One problem with reporters was that there were considerable lags in updating information about particular notes so that it would never be clear how much a note would be worth on its return to the issuing bank. This would not affect the ability of distant notes to trade at their reported values in the major cities so long as there were no systematic biases in the discounting errors, but the uncertainty generated discounts that could be quite deep.

One way to think of conditions by the late 1850s was that Hamilton's unit of account had indeed prevailed, but that a uniform currency circulating at values consistent with that unit of account had not. This caused confusion and inefficiency in the monetary system. When free banks began to close in large numbers in Indiana, Minnesota, Wisconsin, and other states, the problems with the system and the lack of a common currency backed by a nationwide and uniform set of acceptable collateral reached the fore, but the Civil War intervened to delay a resolution (Jaremski 2010).

These facts suggest that the National Banking Acts of 1863 and 1864 sought to retain the enabling aspects of free banks but with improvements in capital adequacy and in the quality and uniformity of collateral required for note issue. By eliminating note discounts across locations, these changes represented further progress toward monetary union. Sylla (1969) and James (1978) note that the restrictiveness of some of these regulations had negative effects on the availability of credit later in the nineteenth century, but it was the legacy of free banking that allowed conditions under the National Banking System to develop to the point where the rules could bind. In other words, the establishment of free banks in areas that had previously gone without banks generated conditions where National Banks could start up knowing that there was a demand for their services. Though the original free banks themselves may not have had much of an immediate and direct impact on growth, they left a footprint of banking in rural areas that would eventually be filled by national banks and later by a second wave of state banks that brought the age of deposits with them.

THE CIVIL WAR AND NATIONAL BANKING SYSTEM

The free bank and the National Banking eras were punctuated by the largest political upheaval in U.S. history, which led to the succession of eleven southern states in 1861 and the nation's bloodiest war. The Union lacked the resources needed to prosecute the war, and could not float bonds among domestic and foreign investors at interest rates that were sufficiently low. It was in the midst of these difficulties that the Union began to issue paper money – the greenbacks – through the Legal Tender Acts of 1862 and 1863. The $450 million in greenbacks issued by 1864 were not payable on demand in specie and quickly began trading at discounts from gold, with the exchange ratio peaking at about 2:1 in 1865 (Kindahl 1961, p. 36).

One might consider this as a continental-like experience all over again, but the federal government was able to maintain confidence in its ability to redeem the greenbacks at a rate reasonably close to par. In late 1865 (shortly after the conclusion of hostilities) the Treasury announced a policy of retiring greenbacks and the Congress passed a resolution approving this policy, yet progress slowed within a few years with only 10 percent of the greenbacks retired by 1868 (Kindahl 1961, p. 45). The Public Credit Act of 1869 transformed the informal commitment to retire the greenbacks into law, but it took the Resumption Act of 1875 to establish a firm schedule of par convertibility. In the end, resumption went off smoothly in 1879 not because the government retired the greenbacks but rather because it allowed the nation to grow into the new money supply. Some bolstering of specie reserves in 1878 and 1879 headed off any remaining doubt about a return to convertibility.

In the meantime, the National Banking Acts improved the safety of the financial system by imposing minimum capital requirements for those starting National banks, and by clawing back outstanding notes issued by state banks through a prohibitive 10 percent tax on them.[13] Note issues were also controlled more rigorously under the new Office of the Comptroller of the Currency, which replaced state-determined collateral requirements with national ones that called for the deposit of federal bonds in return for privilege of issuing notes. The stringent collateral

---

[13] The original legislation required national banks in communities with fewer than 3,000 persons to have at least $50,000 in capital. National banks were also to hold at least one-third and no less than $30,000 of their paid-in capital in federal bonds. The 10 percent tax on state bank notes took effect on July 1, 1866.

requirements, however, coupled with the tax on state bank notes and the minimum capital provisions, caused many state banks to end their operations and in general kept the number and diffusion of national banks at less than optimal levels. A nationwide ceiling of $300 million on the total outstanding national bank notes also began to bind as early as 1866. By the time the ceiling was lifted in 1875, the prices of the federal bonds required as collateral also rose, making note issue less profitable for banks and making the ceiling a moot point.

The greenbacks were not uninvolved in these developments, as the slower growth in the money supply associated with the new regulations facilitated the deflation required to achieve resumption. By then the nation had finally achieved a uniform currency, with both bank notes and government notes trading at par with gold. The bank notes even looked the same, as the comptroller would receive federal bonds as collateral from national banks and send back notes that were identical across banks other than carrying the name of each particular bank. The comptroller could in turn liquidate the collateral bonds and pay off depositors in full in the event that a national bank was forced to close.

Banks responded to the high collateral requirements for issuing notes by focusing on deposits instead. As the demand for deposits and the services associated with them increased over the latter part of the nineteenth century, state banks also saw a resurgence in the 1880s and 1890s, which corrected some of the deficiencies in the diffusion of banking. State capital requirements were usually lower than those required for national banks, so state banks found that deposits gave them an innovative way to fund earning assets, making note issue unnecessary for having a successful bank. With the passage of the Gold Standard Act in 1900, minimum capital requirements in low population areas were lowered to $25,000 for starting a national bank, and the number of banks saw another surge.

Even though the capital market was becoming increasingly integrated by 1900 as evidenced by narrowing differentials in regional interest rates (Davis 1965), the banking system in the National period was vulnerable to liquidity squeezes. Sprague (1910) describes the major disturbances that occurred in 1873, 1893, and 1907, along with less severe ones in 1884 and 1890. Given that the nation lacked a lender of last resort, which was a direct consequence of going without a central bank for so long, it fell on private associations of bankers to operate clearinghouses that could pool resources and keep markets liquid in times of strain. These systems more or less worked in the earlier crises but the system exhibited excessive strain in 1907. Even with a uniform currency, there were inadequate mechanisms for handling systemic risks and so the nation remained still somewhat removed from full monetary integration.

CONCLUSION

The founding of the Federal Reserve in 1914 and all that came with it was a watershed event in the establishment of the U.S. monetary union. Though the U.S. political union had been fractured only fifty years earlier, the Federal Reserve arose in a period of relative political stability – a situation that for the most part continues to the present. The Federal Reserve was formed as a quasi-public bank with power distributed among twelve regional branches, and this regional emphasis seems to reflect the Jacksonian concern about excessive centralization. In some ways, however, the Federal Reserve can also be considered a variant of how the First Bank of the United States ended up. Even though Hamilton initially opposed branching, his bank did create them. So did the Federal Reserve, but it also allowed for an adequate system of affiliated banks and avoided the problem of these banks issuing their own nonuniform currencies. In other words, the structure of the Federal Reserve can be seen as a compromise of Federalist and Democratic leanings – one that tried to take advantage of the best features of each.

The Federal Reserve was formed with adequate powers for handling systemic crises, and so its unwillingness to use these levers during the Great Depression is not so much a fault of the system's design as it was a misunderstanding of how the tools at hand could be deployed in times of crisis. The locus of power shifted to the Board of Governors after the Depression and away from the regional banks, returning to a regime where control of the money supply and monetary affairs was more centralized, but the result still had a wide range of member banks and did not concentrate decision making to the extent that the Federalists imagined. Complaints by the public about the Federal Reserve today often involve perceived policy shifts toward more centralized control, but indeed banking and financial services are distributed and the central bank is ready and able to act strongly to head off systemic risks.

These advantages did not come quickly to the young United States, and if they were in any sense a result of the political union formed in 1789, they did not follow directly from it. The political and monetary equilibrium settled on in 1790 was a temporary one that has been subjected to shock upon shock along both dimensions for more than two centuries. This is not to say that ratification of the Constitution was less than a defining moment for the nation, or that Hamilton's financial system was less than a leap forward, but to suggest that the establishment of the political union ensured the course of future events is clearly an overstatement. The U.S. financial system that we observe today was not the result of a "big bang," but rather derives from a fluid, ever-evolving, and organic process of improvement, misstep, and improvement driven by interactions between political and monetary forces. It seems likely to this observer that similar forces will interact gradually to bring about monetary and political union in Europe as well, but that unlike the historical case of the United States, it will require less than a century to achieve.

REFERENCES

Bodenhorn, Howard. (2000). *A History of Banking in Antebellum America: Financial Markets and Economic Development in an Era of Nation-Building.* New York: Cambridge University Press.

(2003). *State Banking in Early America: A New Economic History.* New York: Oxford University Press.

(2006). "Bank Chartering and Political Corruption in Antebelllum New York." In Edward Glaeser and Claudia Goldin (eds), *Corruption and Reform: Lessons from American History*, pp. 231–257. Chicago: University of Chicago Press.

Bordo, Michael D. (2012). "Could the United States Have Had a Better Central Bank? An Historical Counterfactual Speculation." *Journal of Macroeconomics* 34(3):597–607.

Brock, Leslie V. (1992). "The Colonial Currency, Prices, and Exchange Rates." *Essays in History* 34, Retrieved from http://etext.virginia.edu/journals/EH /EH34/brock34.htm.

Calomiris, Charles W. (1988). "Institutional Failure, Monetary Scarcity, and the Depreciation of the Continental." *Journal of Economic History* 48: 47–68.

Cowen, David J. (2000). "The First Bank of the United States and the Securities Market Crash of 1792." *Journal of Economic History* 60(4):1041–1060.

Davis, Lance. (1965). "The Investment Market, 1870–1914: The Evolution of a National Market." *Journal of Economic History* 25(3):355–399.

Fenstermaker, J. Van. (1965a). *The Development of American Commercial Banking: 1782–1837.* Kent, OH: Kent State University Press.

(1965b). "The Statistics of American Commercial Banking, 1782–1818." *Journal of Economic History* 25:400–414.

Gorton, Gary. (1996). "Reputation Formation in Early Bank Note Markets." *Journal of Political Economy* 104:346–397.

Grubb, Farley. (2008). "The Continental Dollar: How Much Was Really Issued?" *Journal of Economic History* 68(1):283–291.

(2012). "State Redemption of the Continental Dollar, 1779–90." *The William and Mary Quarterly* 69(1):147–180.

Hammond, Bray. (1936). "Free Banks and Corporations: The New York Free Banking Act of 1838." *Journal of Political Economy* 44(2):184–209.

(1957). *Banks and Politics in America: From the Revolution to the Civil War.* Princeton, NJ: Princeton University Press.

James, John. (1978). *Money and Capital Markets in Postbellum America.* Princeton, NJ: Princeton University Press.

Jaremski, Matthew. (2010). "Free Bank Failures: Risky Bonds versus Undiversified Portfolios." *Journal of Money, Credit and Banking* 43(8): 1565–1587.

Jaremski, Matthew, and Peter L. Rousseau. (2013). "Banks, Free Banks, and U.S. Economic Growth." *Economic Inquiry* 51(2):1603–1621.

Kindahl, James K. (1961). "Economic Factors in Specie Resumption in the United States 1865–79." *Journal of Political Economy* 69(1):30–48.

McCusker, John J. (1978). *Money and Exchange in Europe and America, 1600–1775: A Handbook.* Chapel Hill: University of North Carolina Press.

Rolnick, Arthur J., and Warren E. Weber. (1983). "New Evidence on the Free Banking Era." *American Economic Review* 73(5):1080–1091.

Rousseau, Peter L. (2002). "Jacksonian Monetary Policy, Specie Flows, and the Panic of 1837." *Journal of Economic History* 62(2):467–488.

    (2006). "A Common Currency: Early US Monetary Policy and the Transition to the Dollar." *Financial History Review* 13: 97–122.

    (2007). "Backing, the Quantity Theory, and the Transition to the U.S. Dollar." *American Economic Review* 97, Papers and Proceedings, 266–270.

Rousseau, Peter L., and Caleb Stroup. (2011). "Monetization and Growth in Colonial New England, 1703–1749." *Explorations in Economic History* 48: 600–613.

Rousseau, Peter L., and Richard Sylla. (2003). "Financial Systems, Economic Growth, and Globalization." In M. Bordo, A. Taylor, and J. Williamson (eds), *Globalization in Historical Perspective,* pp. 373–413. Chicago: University of Chicago Press.

    (2005). "Emerging Financial Markets and Early U.S. Growth." *Explorations in Economic History* 42:1–26.

Sargent, Thomas J. (2012). "Nobel Lecture: United States Then, Europe Now. *Journal of Political Economy* 120 (1), February, 1–40.

Sargent, Thomas J., and François R. Velde. (2003). *The Big Problem of Small Change.* Princeton, NJ: Princeton University Press.

Sprague, O. M. W. (1910). *History of Crises under the National Banking System.* Washington, DC: U.S. Government Printing Office.

Sylla, Richard. (1969). "Federal Policy, Banking Market Structure, and Capital Mobilization in the United States, 1863–1913." *Journal of Economic History* 29: 657–686.

    (2002). "Financial Systems and Economic Modernization." *Journal of Economic History* 62:277–292.

    (2010). "What Price Did the USA Pay for Abolishing Its Central Bank in 1836?" In J. Morilla et al. (eds), *Homeaje a Gabriel Tortella,* pp. 685–693. Madrid: LID Editorial Empresarial S.L., University de Alcald.

Sylla, Richard, Robert E. Wright, and David J. Cowen. (2009). "Alexander Hamilton, Central Banker: Crisis Management During the U.S. Financial Panic of 1792." *Business History Review* 83:61–86.

Temin, Peter. (1969). *The Jacksonian Economy.* New York: W. W. Norton.

U.S. Bureau of the Census. (1975). *Historical Statistics of the United States: From Colonial Times to 1970.* Washington, DC: U.S. Government Printing Office.

Weber, Warren E. (2006). "Early State Banks in the United States: How Many Were There and Where Did They Exist?" *Federal Reserve Bank of Minneapolis Quarterly Review* 30(2):28–40.

Wettereau, James O. (1937). "New Light on the First Bank of the United States." *The Pennsylvanian Magazine of History and Biography* 61:263–285.
(1942). "The Branches of the First Bank of the United States." *Journal of Economic History* 2:66–100.

8

U.S. Precedents for Europe

Harold James

As Michael Bordo pointed out in an article with Carlos Végh (2002), under Alexander Hamilton the United States developed a model of debt management which allowed a credible fiscal response to emergency situations – notably large-scale military conflict – involving tax-smoothing: in other words, borrowing during the emergency when taxation of labor income would reduce work effort at the time of greatest need and retiring the debt after the war by raising taxes. Bordo and Végh conclude with a speculation that had Hamilton been an Argentinean, that country might have had better institutions, and a better inflation and indeed growth performance.

A great deal of the discussion of how European integration might operate – both in the past and in the future – has been driven by thoughts of how precedents on the other side of the Atlantic have worked. At the highest political level, such reflection concerns the constitution, where the U.S. precedent has driven European leaders to contemplate (up to now rather unproductively) the possibility of realizing a European constitution. At the time of independence in 1776, the thirteen former colonies were widely thought of as independent and sovereign entities, and Americans did not want the United States simply to be another conventional state like France or Britain. The constitution was drawn up only in 1787, and really completed only in 1791 with the Bill of Rights. Modern European attempts to follow the eighteenth century U.S. constitutional path were suspended after the proposed constitutional treaty was rejected in referenda in France and the Netherlands in the summer of 2005. That was not, however, the end of the discussion. In the wake of the financial crisis, some – including Chancellor Merkel – suggested that in the long run, a new constitutional settlement is the only acceptable way of defining the claims and obligations of member states. This argumentation is convincing. If the path laid out in this section is taken, in which monetary union is followed by the development of some measure of fiscal federalism, a constitutional solution laying out clearly the extent and limits of states commitment would be an essential condition.

The aftermath of the recent financial crisis has driven another sort of European reflection on how a workable federal fiscal system arose in the United States: that came, again with a considerable lag after the Declaration of Independence, in 1790. Fiscal federalism actually took much longer to work its nation-building magic. It was not until the middle of the nineteenth century that "the United States is" became the accepted grammatical form (rather than "the United States are"). The federal state expanded beyond a rather modest peacetime share of 3 percent of gross domestic product (GDP) only in the middle of the twentieth century. Strikingly, that ratio of 3 percent was the size of the European Union budget envisaged by European Commission President Jacques Delors at the time of the Maastricht Treaty, at a moment when the actual size of the budget was the 1 percent where it still lies.

Those who (like Jacques Delors) would like to see Europe moving in a federal direction see the long (and often tumultuous) development of the United States as a precedent. But is it a helpful example or rather a grim warning? Each episode in the creation of a modern federal U.S. state holds analogies in the painful and politically contentious road to European integration.

This chapter investigates two of the most widely debated aspects of U.S. fiscal and financial integration: (1) the responsibility of the federation for state-level debts and for the creditworthiness of states; and (2) the working of a federal central bank. Today's fiscal federalism in the United States is relatively robust, but the road from 1790 was rocky; and the first two decades of the Federal Reserve were equally filled with monetary mistakes.

ASSUMPTION OF STATE DEBTS

The search for solution to Europe's post-2008 debt crisis has whetted European interest as to American precedents for federal finance. As a result, Alexander Hamilton has become the hero of contemporary Europe. Hamilton's 1790 negotiation of a federal assumption of the high levels of state debt in the aftermath of the War of Independence looks like a tempting model for European states groaning under unbearable debt burdens. It has been cited as a helpful precedent in Thomas Sargent's Nobel Prize Acceptance speech (2011). The background to the assumption was a no-blame principle. The thirteen states had not been responsible for the poor fiscal performance: that was a consequence of the external circumstances of the War of Independence. It might plausibly be argued that at least some of the European debt problems (especially for countries such as Spain and Ireland with a strong precrisis fiscal performance) are also not the consequence of bad policies but of a global financial crisis.

Hamilton's eventually successful proposal for the assumption of state debt arising out of the War of Independence was certainly a decisive initial step in the creation of a real Union – and it accompanied the constitutionalization of the American experiment. But assumption did not produce a responsible system of state finance, and within the subsequent half century there were numerous state-level defaults and a debate about new debt assumptions and/or new ways of blocking state indebtedness. The irresponsibility of states also gravely damaged the reputation of the federal government and made external borrowing prohibitively expensive.

Hamilton argued – against James Madison and Thomas Jefferson – that the war debt accumulated by the states in the War of Independence should be assumed by the federation. There were two sides to his case, one practical, the other philosophical. Initially the most appealing argument was that a federal takeover of war-related state debt was an exercise in providing greater security and thus reducing interest rates, from the 6 percent at which the states funded their debt to 4 percent. Hamilton (1790) emphasized the importance of a commitment to sound finance as a prerequisite to public economy. "When the credit of a country is in any degree questionable, it never fails to give an extravagant premium upon all the loans it has occasion to make." Reduced borrowing costs and a lower drain on resources by the need to service debt would allow the state governments to "furnish new resources," to uphold public order and protect the security of the union against foreign attacks. There would be concrete benefits, accruing "to every member of the community." Land values would increase from their postwar lows. The historical case looks like an attractive precedent for the Europe of today, where proponents need to sell a solution as holding out gains for both debtors and creditors.

Hamilton also insisted on a stronger reason for following good principles than merely the pursuit of expediency. There existed, he stated, "an intimate connection between public virtue and public happiness." That virtue consisted in honoring commitments. Extended in a political body, it would build solidarity. Those principles made the fiscal union what he called "the powerful cement of our union" (Hamilton 1790). The promise to honor obligations had already been clearly set out during the War of Independence as a foundation of a new American identity: in Congress's address to the states of April 18, 1781, it had stated that: "A bankrupt, faithless Republic would be a novelty in the political world, and appear, among reputable nations, like a common prostitute among chaste and reputable matrons" (*Journals of the American Congress from 1774 to 1788*, p. 357).

The state debt (estimated at $25 million) at this time was smaller than the federal debt (also incurred almost entirely as a result of the war), with $11.7 million foreign-owed federal debt (on which at that time default was unthinkable) and $40.4 million domestically owned (for comparison, a modern estimate of 1790 GDP is $158 million: Mitchell 1983).

The condition for success in the American case was that the Union raised its own revenue, initially mostly through new excises and federally administered customs houses that generated an amount equivalent to 10 percent of imports or around 2 percent of GDP (Bordo and Végh 2002; Perkins 1994). The logic of a need for specific revenue applies also in modern Europe, where the sources of funding for bank rescues or for a recapitalization fund should be clearly spelled out. This consideration has produced an initiative to impose a small levy or tax on financial transactions. In the longer horizon, the analogy with Hamilton's system would require a more extensively reformed fiscal system that might include a common administration of customs or of value added tax (with the additional benefit in both cases of eliminating a great deal of cross-border fraud).

Would an expansion of European federal fiscal capacity represent a massive transfer of power from member states to EU authorities? It is significant that the 1790 assumption of state debt occurred in the context of an understanding that federal powers should be few and limited. In Federalist paper 46, James Madison had made clear that central authority should be carefully circumscribed, and had concluded that "the powers proposed to be lodged in the federal government are as little formidable to those reserved to the individual States, as they are indispensably necessary to accomplish the purposes of the Union" (Madison 1788).

There were two problems with the Hamilton proposals, both of which gave rise to immediate and violent political controversy. First, state debt had been extensively traded on a secondary market at a deep discount. Relatively few of the original purchasers, who had acted out of patriotism, still held the debt; instead, the debt had been bought up by speculators – financial intermediaries – who hoped that something like the Hamilton scheme might be realized. A settlement that imposed no haircut and treated the debt at nominal value would in effect be a reward for speculation. James Madison disliked the idea of what would be in effect a subsidy for northern financiers. But Hamilton argued that any discrimination between creditors based on the moment when they had bought debt would be a breach of contract.

Second, some states had already made great efforts to pay down their wartime debt and would not benefit from the federal bailout. Virginia and Maryland in particular had largely paid off their debt, and the Virginian representatives in Congress consequently pressed for a precise calculation of the level of state debt outstanding (Mitchell 1962, p. 70). Madison in particular pressed for a compensation for states that had already discharged their debt. Politically, a straightforward debt assumption was unworkable.

Initially, assumption was rejected by Congress, with potentially cat-astrophic consequences. Thomas Jefferson, who was opposed to the Hamilton proposal, wrote to his fellow Virginian James Monroe about the possibility of failure as Congress was split. "Unless they can be reconciled by some compromise, there will be no funding bill agreed to, our credit will burst and vanish, and the States separate" (Mitchell 1962, p. 81).

Eventually the Union was bought, at a price, and there was a compro-mise. Because the financial arrangement favored the northern states, the South and its landed elite needed a symbolic but also practical compensa-tion. There were financial clauses that limited the liability of the southern states. The exposure to the common liability of Virginia, the most politically powerful state in the Union, was limited with a ceiling. Only this induce-ment moved Madison to drop his opposition and agree to assumption. But there was also a symbolic and political concession. The historic compro-mise also led to the capital being moved to the new site of Washington, on the border of Virginia and Maryland, rather than staying in Philadelphia. Some states, such as Georgia, opted out of the assumption.

Conclusions from this Section

1. The federalization or mutualization of state debt depended on the creation of a fiscal mechanism producing a stream of revenue to ser-vice the debt.
2. The 1790 compromise might be seen as a precedent for limiting the liabilities of the northern European surplus countries in the case of the creation of a common European bond or Eurobond.

PROBLEMS OF STATE DEBT

The U.S. experiment in federalized finance was not immediately successful from the point of view of driving economic growth in the young republic. Two important parts of Hamilton's financial architecture were not realized, or only realized imperfectly. He proposed a model of joint stock banking on a national scale, which ran into immediate opposition, and which curi-ously was much more influential in Canada than in the U.S. Second, the proposal for a national central bank, based on the model of the Bank of England, was eventually blocked by political opposition. The charter of the First Bank of the United States was allowed to lapse in 1811; then, one generation later, the charter of the Second Bank of the United States was successfully opposed by Andrew Jackson after 1832.

The fiscal side did not bring long-lasting relief, either. Yields on U.S. government debt fell immediately, showing the new confidence pro-duced by the debt arrangement (see Figure 8.1). By the beginning of 1792,

Figure 8.1. Yield of ten-year U.S. federal bonds, 1790–1914.

they had fallen to 4.6 percent; but after that the cost of borrowing rose sharply again.

Neither did the Hamiltonian scheme of federal finance guarantee a peaceful commonwealth in the longer term. The immediate consequence of the new excise was a revolt in Pennsylvania (the Whiskey Rebellion of 1794 and four years later the Fries Rebellion). States were in the longer run divided over the shape of tariffs, which southern states saw as disadvantageous to them because they relied on cotton exports and the import of British manufactures. In fact, the fiscal union proved to be explosive rather than cement, because the tariff dispute by the 1830s was turned into a constitutional struggle in which southern states claimed that the constitution was merely a treaty between states and that the South could resist federal laws that they deemed to be unconstitutional. The fiscal mechanism designed to allow servicing of a common liability raises inherently explosive distributional issues.

The distributional consequences between states of a fiscal mechanism would also be a potentially divisive mechanism in contemporary Europe. The most popular suggestions in discussion today are a general financial transactions tax, which would fall heavily on major financial centers (and for this reason is resolutely blocked by the United Kingdom); or a European payroll tax, which would raise problems of different implementation and coverage in the various European states.

The fiscal union was also dangerous because it allowed states to recommence their borrowing. As with the dispute over the tariff, the problem became very apparent in the 1830s. As international capital markets developed in the first decades of the nineteenth century, American states used their newfound reputation to borrow on a large scale, and quite soon ruined their creditor status. At first, the North American states looked to British banks and investors as more appealing debtors than the newly independent South American republics, which wanted to borrow just to buy weapons. Agents of the American states swarmed over Europe in order to sell their debt. A key part of the argument for the foreign investors was that the American state borrowing was sanctioned and approved by the U.S. government. A characteristic statement was that of the London *Morning Chronicle* in 1839 and 1840 that "persons desirous of investing money in any of the principal American securities will find on inquiry that we have never over-rated the honor and good faith which have always been shown by the United States government." Even "the newest and smallest states" were satisfactory for Washington (McGrane 1933, p. 677).

In addition, the difficulties of the states became acute because of banking issues. In the long-standing conflict about the Hamiltonian concept, President Andrew Jackson launched a Bank War, in the course of which he vetoed the rechartering of the Second Bank of the United States, but also encouraged other banks to seek charters. The result was successful in achieving Jackson's immediate objective, in that it decentralized credit. But then the new banks immediately started to expand their lending, above all to the states and the political elites that had facilitated their establishment. The upshot was an orgy of bank credit to individual states, often structured in a complex way so that debt securities could be repackaged and sold on foreign markets.

When in 1841 the first state, Mississippi, reneged on its debt, disingenuously claiming that its law allowing state bond issuance had been unconstitutional, the major British bank involved in the issuance of American state debt in London, Barings, counseled against a panic response: "Is it wise for this single instance of dishonesty in a remote and unimportant state to endeavor to brand the whole of the United States as wanting in good faith? We think not" (McGrane 1933, p. 683). But the foreign creditors also tried to push the U.S. government into a new federal assumption of state debts, and the case was actively pushed by the Whigs (whereas Jacksonian Democrats saw the campaign as a conspiracy to get the American taxpayer to bail out individual states but above all the foreign creditors).

The practice of default spread in 1841–1842, with Florida, Michigan, Pennsylvania, Maryland, Indiana, Illinois, Arkansas, and Louisiana all announcing their unwillingness or inability to pay. At this time, a whole palate of responses was contemplated, ranging from the expulsion of defaulters from the Union to the repetition of the Hamiltonian assumption. The situation was so precarious because of the international consequences: not just exclusion from the European capital markets needed to finance American development but also a real security threat. The federal government could not even sell bonds yielding 6 percent, while – as the U.S. Treasury bitterly complained, "nations with not a tithe of our resources, and with large public debts, have been able to effect loans at three per cent per annum" (Bolles 1885, p. 580). But the consequences of default also included the risk of international conflict, as Britain was widely thought to be willing to use naval and military power to enforce credit claims. As a response to the danger of military conflict with the principal creditor country, Congressman John Quincy Adams even introduced a proposal to make the repudiation of any debt to foreigners "a violation of the Constitution of the United States" and that any state involved in a war as a consequence of repudiation should cease to be a state of the Union (Scott 1893, pp. 248–249).

Inevitably, the Hamiltonian option was floated again. In 1843, a Congressional committee recommended a new assumption, on the grounds that the debts incurred had been mostly for infrastructure which was "calculated to strengthen the bonds of union, multiply the avenues of commerce, and augment the defenses from foreign aggression" (Scott 1893, p. 251). But this proposal was rejected, primarily on moral hazard grounds: if states were freed of present debt, they would only be likely to get into debt very quickly again. The measure also would have imposed a clear and heavy cost on the nonindebted states. The outcome of the 1840s debate was laissez-faire: no federal intervention to punish defaulters, but also no bailout.

The question of how the Union should respond to a state default inevitably hinged around the degree of responsibility of the defaulters. Subsequently, it was sometimes claimed that the U.S. crisis had come about because of tightening credit conditions in Europe and especially because of the hiking of interest rates by the Bank of England (Temin 1969). Econometric analysis however shows that the surge in state yields in 1841–1842 occurred first on the domestic U.S. markets and only with a lag (because of the then slow communications technology) on European exchanges (Kim and Wallis 2005).

There are strong parallels between the development of American states in the 1830s and that of modern Europe. The American states that borrowed most heavily and then ran into problems were the less developed states that saw borrowing as a way of financing development infrastructure, especially in transport. The borrowing states were also keen to encourage the development of domestic financial institutions to stimulate growth and development. When problems appeared, there could be a debate as to whether they were due to external circumstances (a crisis in the world's financial center, the United Kingdom then, the United States now), or to a flawed development strategy, or to governance problems and corruption in state governments as well as in banks. These issues were extensively debated in the 1840s, and a contrast was made with the position of state finances in the aftermath of the War of Independence. In the case of the state defaults of the early 1840s, as in that of contemporary Greece, the problems stemmed primarily from misguided policies, and cannot be blamed on external circumstance such as war or global crisis.

One generation after the era of defaults, in the 1860s, the country was torn by Civil War as a result of what was in large part a dispute about states' rights and about the character of financial burdens. In attempting to end the immoral practice of slavery, Abraham Lincoln originally proposed that the slave-owners should be compensated by the public purse. But such a buy-out would have been unacceptably expensive for the non-slave states. So in the end, the Virginians (and the rest of the South) were expropriated by the Union – at least that is the way they saw things. The Civil War arose out of long-standing tensions between the North and the South, in large part driven by southern hostility to the revenue stream chosen to service the federal debt (the Hamiltonian tariff, which protected northern manufacturers and penalized southern exporters), as well as by the deeply problematic issue of whether and how slave-owners might be compensated for abolition.

A second wave of state defaults occurred in the 1870s in the South (and in Minnesota), in the aftermath of the Civil War and of Reconstruction. Some southern policymakers – and the broader public – took as their example the Fourteenth Amendment to the Constitution, which repudiated debts that had been contracted in the interest of rebellion. Southerners disliked the new debt incurred in the process of Reconstruction – the more so because it was owed to northern creditors. In addition, interest payments had risen during the war and accrued interest increased the overall debt levels, while tax revenues had collapsed. For the most severely affected of the states, Arkansas, bonds were trading at 7 percent of their nominal value by the end of the 1870s (see Figure 8.2). Unlike the defaults of the early 1840s, the problems of a specific group of southern states no longer affected the cost of borrowing of other states or of the United States.

The eventual solution lay in the adoption of debt restraint or balanced budget laws. At the end of the nineteenth century, many states set a very low ceiling on permissible state debt, and other states limited indebtedness to a (small) share of total taxation. Only northern states (New Hampshire, Vermont, Massachusetts, Connecticut, and Delaware), which had never really experienced the debt problem, allowed their legislatures to contract unlimited debt. By the early twenty-first century, such legislation limits state indebtedness in all but one of the fifty states.

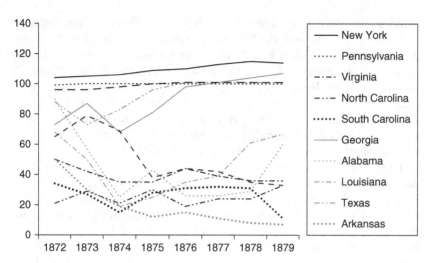

Figure 8.2. State bond prices.

Conclusions from this Section

1. The choice of the fiscal mechanism to service a federalized debt potentially raises deeply divisive issues about the distributive effects of the tax or tariff on the constituent states.
2. A commitment not to renew the assumption of state debts is a condition for stable financial and political development of the union.

FEDERAL CENTRAL BANKING

How centralized should the operation of a central bank be? The early central banks – in Sweden, England, and France – were unitary institutions that corresponded precisely to unified and centrally directed states with a powerful capital that was also the main financial center. The models for federal central banking came rather later, with Germany (1875), Switzerland (1907), and the United States (1914). Such a federal central bank required complex rules to ensure that there was no direction by the federal government, and that policy operations reflected the diverse conditions of a federation.

The central banking side of the U.S. federal model, the Federal Reserve System, has often been held up as a model for the European System of Central Banks. Indeed the Federal Reserve had an impact on the development of European central banking in two ways: first, indirectly, in its influence on German central bank design. Allied suggestions on how to reform German central banking and free it from its previous dependence on the central German state (the *Reich*) drew on the U.S. model and shaped banking law during the allied occupation. The Deutsche Bundesbank evolved out of a federal *Bank deutscher Länder*. It retained that federal organization, in which a board (*Direktorium*) met with regional heads of the *Landeszentralbanken* in the policymaking Bundesbank Council (*Zentralbankrat*). Because of the Bundesbank's successful policy, especially in providing for a greater degree of price stability than any European central bank except for the Swiss National Bank, the Bundesbank's design of the in turn heavily influenced the debate on the governance and policy orientation of the future European Central Bank (ECB).

There was also a direct impact of the U.S. model. When it came to designing European institutions, European federalists also consistently looked directly and explicitly to the American model. In the 1960s, the vice president of the European Commission, Robert Marjolin, who had pushed for the institutionalization of a Committee of European Central Bank Governors, saw that body as the "embryo of a Community Federal Reserve Board." German Economics Minister Karl Schiller in 1970 drew up a four-stage plan for increasing economic and monetary coordination that he believed would lead to a "sort of Federal Reserve System." The 1970 Werner Plan envisaged two parallel Community "organs" as indispensable for European stability: a center of decision for economic policy and a Community system for the central banks. When in 1972, in accordance with the Werner recommendations, a European Monetary Cooperation Fund was established its designers talked ecstatically about it becoming a new Federal Reserve, even though in practice the new body had only very limited routine tasks. In the early 1990s, the Federal Reserve System, and its relationship to federal political authority in the executive branch and the legislature, was conceived of as an explicit model for European emulation. The European Commission, in particular, in the early 1990s liked to refer to the future European central bank as a "Eurofed" (James 2012).

Both the European Commission and the existing national central bankers saw an attraction in the U.S. institutional model. The board or council of the central bank had a permanent core, as well as some way of securing an alternation of National Central Bank (NCB) representatives analogous to that of the Federal Reserve districts, whose presidents all attend but do not all vote in the Open Market Committee (there is a rotating voting system, for all except the president of the New York Bank). As at the time of drawing up the ECB draft statute and negotiating the Maastricht Treaty it was unclear how many countries would initially participate in the monetary union (and that number might have been relatively small), no solution involving a rotation of committee members was adopted. By the time the Eurozone had increased to a membership of seventeen, the large number of NCB representatives had become a problem for the effective operation of the ECB Council.

The interest in learning from the Federal Reserve and its policy stance remains intense. By 2012, with the new ECB government bond purchasing program, many commentators suggested that the ECB had at last become more like the Fed. For some, this meant praise of institutional flexibility; for others, the meaning was rather that central banking principles had been replaced by politically driven expediency.

The Federal Reserve System

As in the case of fiscal federalism, the American precedent is filled with a legacy of policy mistakes and of bitter controversies. The question of the relationship of a central federal bank to local banking systems – and to the patronage systems built up by local elites – has always been a highly contentious issue in American politics from the beginning. The feeling that local interests would be sacrificed to a Massachusetts and New York banking elite was a strong driver of opposition to Alexander Hamilton's plans of 1790. It was also at the core of Andrew Jackson's campaign against Nicholas Biddle and the Second Bank of the United States in the 1830s and his attempt to establish an alternative banking system, answerable to and controlled by local elites (the so-called "pet banks").

Initially, as a response to the U.S. financial panic of 1907, the National Monetary Commission looked at the models of the leading institutions of the time, the Bank of England, the Banque de France, and the Reichsbank, and recommended a federally dominated state central bank (in the form of the Aldrich bill). That proposal was rejected by the Democrats. The alternative scheme – which was eventually adopted – was engineered to give a great deal of power and autonomy to the Reserve Banks in the individual Reserve districts, whose boards banks were largely chosen by the regional banks. Until 1933, the power of the Washington Board was very limited, and it met and interacted relatively rarely with the Committee of Governors representing the individual Reserve Banks. After 1933, a more centralized system relied on the Open Market Committee as the key policymaking organ.

The Federal Reserve System relied on a complicated governance system that was designed to preserve checks and balances, and to ensure that the system could not be dominated either by the powerful East Coast financial community or by the federal government in Washington. The regional Federal Reserve banks corresponded to what were felt to be logical economic area, which did not necessarily overlap with state boundaries. A separate Reserve Bank for each state would have created an overcomplicated system, with a large and unwieldy central committee (originally termed the Federal Reserve Advisory Council). The majority on the boards of the Reserve Banks were selected by the local nationally chartered banks that composed the U.S. financial system and that were required to subscribe to the capital of the Reserve Bank. This principle continues to the present. Three directors were chosen by the banks of the district to reflect the financial community, and another three to represent the general community ("commerce, agriculture, or some industrial pursuit"), with a final group of three being selected by the Washington Board. The seven-member Board in Washington was the political counterpart, and five members were appointed by the president with the advice and consent of the Senate. In the original Federal Reserve Act, the Treasury Secretary and the Comptroller of the Currency were also members of the Board. The twelve regional banks represented coherent regional economies. The Reserve Banks were required to pay a 6 percent dividend on the capital subscribed by the banks, but profits above this level (and potential losses) went to the federal government, which in this sense becomes the ultimate backstop of the system. To highlight the surprising character of this feature, a mental experiment might be helpful. A modern European equivalent to the Federal Reserve would be to create private sector based regional central banks, for instance with Alpine, Baltic, North Sea, Atlantic, Danubian, and Mediterranean banks.

The original (1914) Federal Reserve System in many ways resembles more the interaction of national central banks in the international system of the gold standard. The system as a whole was not a bank with its own balance sheet. The twelve Reserve Banks controlled their own operations, and had their own discount policy. Any transactions with other Reserve Banks were required to be settled in the same way as the foreign central banks would. Section 17 of the 1913 Act deterred the individual Reserve Banks from issuing each other's notes by imposing a fine, and notes from one bank were to be returned to the issuing bank: "Whenever Federal reserve notes issued through one Federal reserve bank shall be received by another Federal reserve bank they shall be promptly returned for credit or redemption to the Federal reserve bank through which they were originally issued. No Federal reserve bank shall pay out notes issued through another under penalty of a tax of ten per centum upon the face value of notes so paid out.... The Federal reserve agent shall hold such gold, gold certificates, or lawful money available exclusively for exchange for the outstanding Federal reserve notes when offered by the reserve bank of which he is a director. Upon the request of the Secretary of the Treasury the Federal Reserve Board shall require the Federal reserve agent to transmit so much of said gold to the Treasury of the United States as may be required for the exclusive purpose of the redemption of such notes." The mechanism was known as the Gold Settlement Account.

The individual banks were also required to hold gold to allow clearing of debit balances. The loss of gold would affect their reserve ratio, with the result that presumably they would also need to reduce credit to banks and would thus shrink the regional money stock. In this regard, the system seemed to reproduce the pre-1914 characteristics of the National Banking Era (following the 1863 banking act), which in practice made for regional contractions as banks contracted loans when their reserves fell (these were maintained by law at very high levels, as 15 or 25 percent of deposits). A similar mechanism operated for one episode in the history of the Fed, in the severe deflation at the end of World War I in 1920–1921. The agricultural districts were worse affected than the industrial districts, and payments to farmers were slow and at low prices. The consequence was a balance of payments deficit. As the reserves fell, the district Reserve Banks were under pressure, but they borrowed from other reserve banks with large surpluses so as to minimize the impact. There was thus substantial interdistrict bank borrowing, but the outcome was still that credit restrictions were believed to have hit the agricultural areas and made for a faster recovery from the deflation in the manufacturing districts (Goldenweiser 1925, p. 36). By the time of the Great Depression, however, when a similar effect might have been expected to operate, the district shortfalls as a result of regional balance of payments deficits were made good, not by interdistrict accommodation, but by federal fiscal transfers made through the Federal Reserve System (Burgess 1936, pp. 123–124). The Federal Reserve System in practice during the Great Depression also moved away from the previous practice of limiting loans to credit secured by commercial bills (the so-called real bills or Burgess–Riefler doctrine) to operating much more with government securities as collateral, and then to the direct purchase of government securities. The expansion of the federal budget avoided the need for big financing operations by the central bank through the interdistrict settlement account, and the alteration in the credit practice of the System in practice removed monetary policy from being driven by regional imbalances. Large interdistrict surpluses and deficits appeared again only after 2008, in the aftermath of the failure of the private interbank market. Then, as in Europe, the Federal Reserve System substituted for a failure of private sector bank intermediation.

Immediately after the entry into force of the Federal Reserve Act, the outbreak of the European war made the question of international gold movements highly sensitive, and the most important financial figure in dealing with international issues, the New York Governor Benjamin Strong, pressed for a centralization of reserves, and New York in practice became the dominant holder of gold assets in the U.S. system. The Board was pleased with the easing of interest rates in the United States after 1915 and claimed that it was the result of the new institutional regime (Meltzer 2003, pp. 79–80).

Like national central banks in the international gold standard order, the various American Reserve Banks had their own discount policies and applied different rates – especially at moments of strain. Globally, despite the theoretical possibility of capital being sent over vast distances to other parts of the world, much capital remained local. Creditors and banks often preferred to do business with known borrowers, and where local jurisdictions could settle disputes. In particular, a critical part of the international gold standard was that individual national central banks set their own interest rates, with the aim of influencing the direction of capital movements. This became the central feature of the gold-standard world: a country that was losing gold reserves would tighten interest rates to attract money. Central bank discount rates (the policy rate) in France and Great Britain, major capital exporters, were constantly lower than in Germany, which had no major current account surplus, even though there was never any market expectation of a parity alteration. France and Britain in practice placed a floor under rates, and their choices affected other countries because of the possibility of arbitrage. Italy, where there were expectations of parity changes in the 1870s and 1880s, needed much higher rates.

We can see the same differentiation of interest rates in the early history of the Federal Reserve System. Individual Reserve Banks set their own discount rates (see Figure 8.3). Under Section 14(b) of the 1913 Federal Reserve Act, their rates were "subject to review and determination of the Federal Reserve Board." The Board also (Section 13) had the "the right to determine or define the character of the paper thus eligible for discount." The individual Reserve Banks had different collateral requirements and accepted differing kinds of securities. In smooth or normal times, the rates tended to converge. But in times of shocks, they could move apart. In the summer of 1929, at the height of the credit boom, New York tightened, while the other banks left rates unchanged; in 1932, New York went much faster and further in lowering rates than other banks. There was thus a space for big policy conflicts. In 1919 the Attorney General ruled that the Board could change rates for a Bank; and in 1929 there was an acute conflict when the Board voted 4:3 to impose a reduction on the Chicago Bank (Chandler 1958, p. 44; Meltzer 2003, pp. 221–224).

By the late 1930s, the rate differences were disappearing, but they vanished completely only during World War II, for the simple reason that operating with federal bills (a single instrument) in open market operations, rather than with a multiplicity of differently valued private securities, became the primary tool of U.S. monetary policy. When it came to monetary policy instruments, the designers of the ECB took the practice of the postwar Federal Reserve, and assumed that the debt instruments of different member states could fill the monetary policy role of a single financial instrument (federal government securities) in the case of the Federal Reserve's open market policy.

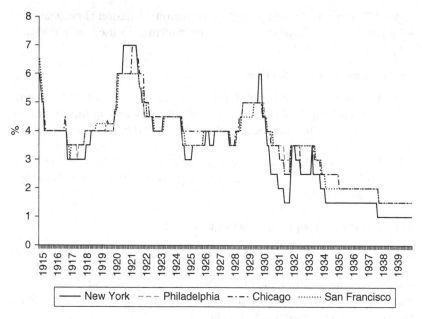

Figure 8.3. Federal Reserve discount rates, 1915–1939.

The gold-standard rules look very different from the modern practice of monetary union, which relies on a single uniform interest rate. That one-size-fits-all approach meant that in the 2000s interest rates in southern European countries were too low, and too high in northern Europe. Identical nominal rates with divergent real rates produced unsustainable credit booms in the south. By contrast, a gold-standard rule would have produced higher rates for the southern European borrowers, which would have attracted funds to where capital might be productively used, and at the same time acted as a deterrent against purely speculative capital flows. A modern equivalent to the gold standard/early Federal Reserve approach would require differing (higher) levels of collateral requirement for central banks operating in countries with a housing and credit boom (pre-2007 Spain or Ireland) than in countries with no credit boom (pre-2007 Germany) (Brunnermaier 2012).

The early history of the Federal Reserve is rarely seen as a productive source of lessons for central bank policy because it is overshadowed by dramatic policy mistakes that did not follow automatically from its design, but were probably intensified because of the governance structure and the conflicts of the different powerful Reserve Banks (especially New York, as the international financial center and Chicago as the hub of the domestic trading system). In 1920–1921 and more disastrously in 1930–1933, the

Federal Reserve System engineered a pernicious deflation (Friedman and Schwartz 1963). Reform suggestions consequently focused on coordinating policy more centrally.

Conclusions from this Section

1. Designing a central bank for a very large area is a complicated process, and requires some measure of flexibility to respond to local or regional circumstances, as well as checks and balances in the governance structure.
2. Initially, the design of a new central bank may not be a perfect fit for evolving policy demands, and some process of institutional redesign becomes necessary.

REFORM OF THE FEDERAL RESERVE SYSTEM

It was only in the 1930s, with the new Bank Law of 1933, that the Federal Reserve System really started to act as a modern central bank. That legislation was the result of the Great Depression, a profound disruption of economic life in which it was generally felt that both American banking and American central banking had failed.

The mechanism of settlement changed in the 1930s, and was renamed from the Gold Settlement Account to the Interdistrict Settlement Account (ISA). The change in nomenclature was necessary in that the dollar value of gold or gold certificates was arbitrarily set after 1933 by the U.S. Treasury. In April 1975, with much larger international transactions occurring through New York, the Federal Reserve Open Market Committee agreed to institute an annual settlement (in April) of the ISA balances of the Federal Reserve Banks. From the 1970s to 2008, the balances were of small size and limited importance, because interdistrict transfers occurred primarily through the interbank market. After 2008, with the seize-up of the interbank market, the ISA became very significant.

As in the case of the ECB, the settlement mechanism did not appear as problematic or controversial until the 2008 financial crisis. After 2008, large and persistent imbalances appeared, however, with large liabilities of the San Francisco and Richmond banks, and large asset balances of New York. The highest levels of deficits for San Francisco were $67 billion (February 3, 2010) and $66 billion (December 28, 2011); and the maxima for the New York surpluses were $270 billion on November 12, 2008, in the aftermath of the Lehman collapse, and $368 billion on January 12, 2012. These are relatively small figures compared with the overall expansion of the Federal Reserve System's balance sheet, but they are not insignificant. They are comparable to European TARGET2 imbalances in that they arise from very large movements of funds out of some commercial banks that operate across the whole of the United States but have their headquarters (and thus their financial location) in a particular place within one of the twelve Federal Reserve districts. The most plausible explanation involves the head office location of large banks in the San Francisco district (Wells Fargo) and in the Richmond district (Bank of America), with the Federal Reserve Bank keeping claims against these banks rather than selling them in the settlement process. Because the ISA imbalances reflect fundamentally changing market perceptions of U.S. private financial institutions, they do not display the permanence that has characterized their European equivalents, where banks in deficit countries are paralyzed because of the ties between banks and sovereigns (with banks holding the paper of the sovereigns that bail them out). While there are pronounced differences between the U.S. and the European settlement process (highlighted in Sinn and Wollmershäuser 2011), they arise fundamentally out of the central fact that the Federal Reserve System as a whole has a sovereign as a counterpart, while the ECB does not (Garber 2010). Profits and losses from the specified penalty rate of interest of 6 percent on the ISA have no policy impact, because the system is underwritten by the U.S. government. In that sense, making the European system more like that of the U.S. would also require some move to fiscal federalism.

Conclusion from this Section

1. In the post-2008 Great Recession, there was a widespread failure of the interbank market, which raised novel problems for central banks. A central bank that finances large transfers in the aftermath of a general failure of the banking system and of the interbank market is assuming functions that are potentially fiscal, and logically requires underwriting from a governmental institution that can raise taxes.

SUMMARY

The U.S. example is often cited to make the sensible point that in the long run any monetary union also requires some sort of a fiscal union. That demand appeared frequently in political rhetoric of the early 1990s, when the German government in particular insisted that economic and monetary union needed to be accompanied by political union. The interconnections of state debt and (private) banking sector liabilities produce intense conflicts about who – which political authority – is the ultimate debtor. Without a political mechanism for allocating fiscal responsibility, it is hard to think of long-term stability.

Sometimes a move to political union is suggested simply as a pragmatic solution to the borrowing incapacity of some states. In an extreme example, early in World War II, the Russian Imperial government believed that it would be able to borrow if it declared a union with its political allies France and Great Britain. The proposal was absurd, and merely highlighted absurd incompatibilities of very different political systems. The political union can succeed only on the basis of a constitutionalization, as in the American example, which in turn depends on the recognition and acceptance of common identity as well as of some shared interests.

There is certainly an interest-based case to be made for greater integration. At the time of European monetary union, no adequate provision on a European basis existed for banking supervision and regulation, which, like fiscal policy, was left to rather diverse national authorities. An explosion of banking activity occurred simultaneously with the transition to monetary union and may well have been stimulated by the new single money. A "banking glut" led to a new challenge to monetary policymaking. Neither of these problems, fiscal and banking, was a uniquely European one, but the complexity of interaction between different levels of authority and different interests produced a coordination problem that was uniquely difficult to deal with in the European context.

In this context, it is not surprising that Europeans turn to examples of how political institutions evolved elsewhere that solve the problem of federalism (as well as looking to the history of European federal systems, such as that of the German state system since 1806). But it is a mistake to think that the United States holds out a very simple or easy to apply model. American history shows how difficult and obstacle-filled is the path to federalism. As Bordo and Végh showed, one crucial determinant of success is the relative paucity of wars or unexpected surges of expenditure: with many more wars, or a sustained strained fiscal regime, even Hamilton's institutions couldn't have saved the United States.

REFERENCES

Bolles, Albert A. (1885). *The Financial History of the United States from 1789 to 1860*, New York: D. Appleton & Co.
Bordo, Michael D., and Carlos A. Végh. (2002). "What if Alexander Hamilton Had Been Argentinean? A Comparison of the Early Monetary Experiences of Argentina and the United States." *Journal of Monetary Economics* 49:459–494.
Brunnermeier, Markus. (2012). "Macroprudential Regulation: Optimizing the Currency Area." In *The Great Financial Crisis: Lessons for Financial Stability and Monetary Policy*. Frankfurt: European Central Bank.
Burgess, W. Randolph. (1936). *The Reserve Banks and the Money Market*. New York: Harpers.
Chandler, Lester. (1958). *Benjamin Strong, Central Banker*. Washington, DC: Brookings Institution Press.

Friedman, Milton, and Anna J. Schwartz. (1963). *A Monetary History of the United States: 1867–1960*. Princeton, NJ: Princeton University Press.

Garber, Peter. (2010). *The Mechanics of Intra Euro Capital Flight*. Deutsche Bank Economics Special Report, December 10, 2010.

Goldenweiser, E. A. (1925). *Federal Reserve System in Operation*. New York: McGraw-Hill.

Hamilton, Alexander. (1790). Report on Public Credit, January 9. Retrieved from http://press-pubs.uchicago.edu/founders/documents/a1_8_2s5.html

James, Harold. (2012). *Making the European Monetary Union*. Cambridge, MA: Harvard University Press.

Journals of the American Congress from 1774 to 1788, Vol. 3, 1823 p. 357. Washington: Way and Gideon.

Kim, Namsuk, and John Joseph Wallis. (2005). "The Market for American State Government Bonds in Britain and the United States, 1830–1843." *Economic History Review* 736–764.

Madison, James. (1788). (Publius). "The Influence of the State and Federal Governments Compared." Federalist Paper No. 46. Retrieved from http://avalon.law.yale.edu/18th_century/fed46.asp

McGrane, Reginald. (1933). "Some Aspects of American State Debts in the Forties." *American Historical Review* 38(4):673–686.

Meltzer, Allan H. (2003). *A History of the Federal Reserve I: 1913–1951*. Chicago: University of Chicago Press.

Mitchell, Brian. (1983). *International Historical Statistics: The Americas and Australasia*. London: Macmillan.

Mitchell, Broadus. (1962). *Hamilton: The National Adventure, 1788–1804*. New York: Macmillan.

Perkins, E. J. (1994). *American Public Finance and Financial Services 1700–1815*. Columbus: Ohio State University Press.

Sargent, Thomas J. (2011). "United States Then, Europe Now." Nobel Prize speech. Retrieved from http://www.nobelprize.org/nobel_prizes/economics/laureates/2011/sargent-lecture.html

Scott, William A. (1893). *The Repudiation of State Debts*. New York: Crowell.

Sinn, Hans-Werner, and Timo Wollmershaeuser. (2011). "Target Loans, Current Account Balances and Capital Flows: The ECB's Rescue Facility." NBER Working Paper 17626. Cambridge, MA: National Bureau of Economic Research.

Temin, Peter. (1969). *The Jacksonian Economy*. New York: W. W. Norton.

9

The Limits of Bimetallism

Christopher M. Meissner

Bimetallism vanished as a monetary framework in the late nineteenth century. By 1885 nearly all nations in the world had pegged their currency exclusively to either gold or silver, while a small minority operated a fiat money regime. This is surprising. From at least Roman times, many countries had sanctioned the unlimited monetary use of both silver and gold at a stable fixed exchange rate. This chapter investigates the strikingly rapid disappearance of bimetallism that began in the 1870s, and its relation to the international monetary system.

In 1872 Germany de-monetized silver and adopted the gold standard. In 1873, France, the largest bimetallic country in the world, limited silver coinage in a bid to avoid the consequences of Gresham's law (i.e., "swallowing" German silver and losing its entire gold circulation). This was a departure from strict adherence to bimetallism. And though from 1873 until 1876 French officials said that they were very likely to return to full-fledged bimetallism, that hope hinged on the possibility of reviving bimetallism in the face of the subsequent move to the gold standard by many other countries.

But because of this international shift to the gold standard, a return to bimetallism would have exposed France to Gresham's law. In this chapter I ask how long it would have taken for the French decision of 1873 to become irreversible from an economic standpoint. Essentially I investigate how widespread the adoption of the gold standard had to be to expose France to a complete drain on its gold circulation.

The point of no return depended crucially on the size of the bimetallic bloc. The size of this bloc was directly related to the ability to use silver and gold reserves to cushion changing global precious metal demands at a fixed silver/gold mint ratio. For decades, France was the buyer and seller of last resort of both silver and gold, managing to peg the silver price of gold at 15.5 to 1. Few other countries of such size maintained bimetallism. The United States abandoned bimetallism in 1873 by de-monetizing silver, but for domestic political reasons it initiated the International Monetary Conference of 1878. The goal was to create a global accord to revive bimetallism. I also ask if the United States, in partnership with France, could have pegged the world price of silver at the old international mint ratio and made bimetallism viable. I argue that such a partnership would have been infeasible.

Contemporaries and Velde and Weber (2000) argued that bimetallism's strength and value was its ability to generate greater price stability than a monometallic regime. On the other hand, bimetallism might be theoretically inefficient when compared to a gold or silver standard if both precious metals have nonmonetary uses (Velde and Weber 2000). If this is true, then bimetallism's failure shows how an efficient institution (i.e., the gold standard in Europe) can displace an inefficient institution. On the other hand, if the sole function of a monetary system is to maintain price stability, the disappearance of bimetallism was a negative outcome.

I emphasize that the end of bimetallism, and the subsequent geography of the international monetary system, was path dependent. Its ultimate contours were the result of historical events and systematic misperceptions about future possibilities by policymakers. History matters for the evolution of the international monetary system. More broadly, this is an excellent case study of new institutional theoretical arguments that suggest that the past heavily influences the long-run evolution and the current state of the economy and its policies and institutions (e.g., North 1997). Using the end of bimetallism as a case in point, it is worthwhile to show how these concepts have empirical salience.

To show how long France could have waited after 1873 and still have been capable of reinstating bimetallism, I use an elegant model of bimetallism pioneered by Flandreau (1996). Flandreau used his model to ask if German de-monetization of silver could have sealed bimetallism's fate. His answer was negative. I ask if France could have continued to peg the silver price of gold while *many other nations* de-monetized silver and moved to the gold standard. The answer uses readily available data on the demands for precious metals for monetary purposes and world stocks of specie.

I find that bimetallism would have become a de facto silver regime by around 1875. That is, had France eliminated its quantitative restrictions on silver coinage after this year, it would have faced a complete drain on its gold circulation at the historical mint ratio of 15.5 to 1. And although my result supports Flandreau (1996) and Oppers (1996), who find that Germany's de-monetization of silver could not have destroyed bimetallism, I go further and pinpoint the year in which the allegedly temporary suspension of bimetallism became permanent. Moreover, my finding appears to be reasonably robust to imperfections in the precious metals data. Finally I present what is, to my knowledge, the first evidence based on a precisely specified model, that the United States and France could not have resuscitated bimetallism in 1878.

I begin with an introduction to the historical events surrounding the end of bimetallism and then I propose and analyze the counterfactual. The second section provides the analytical mechanics based on the seminal theoretical model of Flandreau (1996). The third section uses the model to simulate how long it might have taken for the French decision to become irreversible. The fourth section investigates whether the disappearance of bimetallism could have been remedied by including a larger coalition in the bimetallic bloc. I conclude by discussing the similarities between recent events in the European Monetary Union and the last days of bimetallism.

BIMETALLISM IN THE LONG AND SHORT RUN

Until recently, scholars asserted that Germany's de-monetization of silver in 1872 was largely responsible for sharply and surprisingly causing silver to fall in value relative to gold (Friedman and Schwartz 1963). A second version of the story argued that German de-monetization of silver threatened the viability of bimetallism in France. France reacted by de-monetizing silver, thus reinforcing the price effects of Germany's initial move. The idea that the German move threatened bimetallism in France has been rejected by Flandreau (1996) and Oppers (1996).[1]

Bimetallic regimes follow Gresham's law. Concurrent circulation of both metals is impossible if the price of gold in terms of silver is not roughly equal in specie markets and at the government mint. When the market ratio and the mint ratio diverge, the depreciating metal will displace the other metal from the bimetallic country.[2] If the shock is small enough, arbitrage transactions would equalize world prices and the mint ratio, but the bimetallic country would be left with a higher proportion of the once-depreciated metal in its money supply (Flandreau 1996). However, a large shock to the demand or supply of either metal could end up causing the depreciated metal to make up the entire circulation before the market has reequilibrated.

French bimetallism apparently did not succumb to Gresham's law for at least 20 years prior to 1872. Flandreau (1995) provides evidence that gold and silver circulated continuously in France during these years despite the gold discoveries of California. Figure 9.1 shows the market price of gold in terms of silver hugged the mint ratio of 15.5 to 1 from as early as 1840. Oppers (2000) and Flandreau (1996) have both concluded that France was

---

[1] According to Flandreau, France held 90 percent of the precious metal stocks in the bimetallic bloc. In the text that follows I use France as representative of the entire bimetallic bloc.

[2] See Rolnick and Weber (1986) for a dissenting view. They challenge the notion that Gresham's law exists.

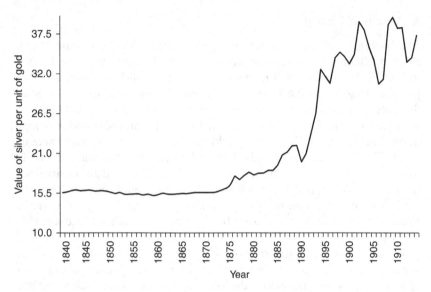

Figure 9.1. The silver–gold exchange rate, 1840–1914.

large enough to peg the market price and that there was a concurrent circulation of both metals in France.[3]

But the global move to gold put bimetallism to the test. The German Empire was the first European country to adopt the gold standard after the monetary conference of 1867. The Germans then attempted to swap their silver reserves for gold with the aid of the bimetallic pledge in France to purchase all silver at a fixed exchange rate. As of 1872 Germany held nearly one-third the amount of specie in France. As a matter of economic principle it should have been easy for France to purchase nearly all of the German silver. Oppers (1996) and Flandreau (1996) have looked more closely at the historical debate, and using theoretical models calibrated to the data, they reject this thesis on historical grounds.[4]

---

[3] Velde and Weber (2000) investigate whether changes in world precious metals supplies endangered bimetallism. Their answer for the 1870s is no. In a finding more closely related to this chapter, Velde and Weber also note that the secular fall in the value of silver associated with the rise of the gold standard led to a monometallic (gold) equilibrium by the 1880s. Their model suggests that in any bimetallic equilibrium the market ratio equals the mint ratio which from 1873 was not the case, and yet bimetallism "survives" in their model for another decade. The quantitative restrictions on silver coinage imposed by France from 1873 would move actors off their first-order conditions in this model, but this is not discussed in Velde and Weber.

[4] Friedman (1990) claims that the United States could almost have resurrected bimetallism at the mint ratio of 16 to one after 1878. Friedman finds U.S. bimetallism would have resulted in a reasonably constant market ratio just above 16 to 1 after about 1900. Why

A Current of Change

The harbinger of the scramble for gold came in 1872 and early 1873. Sweden, Denmark, Norway, Holland, and the United States all decided in late 1872 or early 1873 to de-monetize silver. Still, Flandreau (1996) proposes that it was the *French* suspension of unlimited silver coinage in September 1873 that caused the silver price of gold to rise and not German de-monetization. The argument is that French action prevented arbitrage in precious metals markets that would have stabilized the market value of silver. Flandreau asserts that the French limited silver purchases partially to frustrate their rival's attempt to switch regimes. Residual animosity from the recently concluded Franco-Prussian war no doubt partially contributed to French decision making. By limiting the free coinage of silver in France, Bismarck's regime change became more difficult. France was able to protect its financial stability and its domestic gold circulation as well as avoid being handed capital losses on silver. But Flandreau emphasizes that some French policymakers perceived the limitation of silver coinage as a "precautionary and transitory decision" and bimetallism with unlimited silver coinage would soon return. In the end it turned out to be a misperception that the French could return to bimetallism. But the French also called their policy a "wait-and-see" policy, which suggests some contingency planning in the event that the rest of the world moved to gold or bimetallism became unsustainable.

The notion that this move was temporary, whether held by the French themselves or others beyond France, was very likely based on a faulty or incomplete cognitive model, and no one at the time appears to have been able to truly gauge the ability of the bimetallic system to resist shocks to the demands for precious metals. Moreover, and more crucially, French authorities who thought that the policy was only temporary seem to have misread the international strategic setting in which their actions and strategies were being set. Their actions and words seem to ignore the facts on the ground, already evident by January of 1873, that all of France's major trading partners would soon be on the gold standard. Flandreau (1996) argues that the limitation on silver coinage was seen as a signal by the markets and policymakers in other nations of a noncredible commitment to bimetallism in the long run. Consequently, French action solidified the preference for gold in Scandinavia, Holland, and the United States, among other nations. These countries preferred to conform to the regimes of their

the Americans could have been more successful than the French has to do with the lower valuation of silver at the mint and the rapidly increasing size of American demands for specie after 1879 associated with rapid growth of overall GDP. The focus of this paper is on France as the key anchor of the bimetallic system in the 1870s and 1880s. I also focus on the French mint ratio of 15.5 to 1.

trading partners and to avoid a potential capital loss on their silver reserves in the event of French unwillingness to put a floor on the value of silver. In the case of the United States, a forward-looking policy anticipating gold and the lack of silver made for the "Crime of 1873." And because at this point Germany was set on gold, while France appeared likely to give up bimetallism, many nations opted for gold.[5]

The proximate reason that German and French decisions catalyzed the global mobilization toward gold has to do with the strategic complementarities inherent in the trading and financial systems of the time. Flandreau (1996), Eichengreen and Flandreau (1998), and Meissner (2005) provide evidence that nations both declared it to be, and did indeed act as if the greater the proportion of their gross domestic product (GDP) was devoted to trade with countries that were on gold, the more beneficial it would be to join the gold standard This network effect existed because coordination on monetary regimes decreased the transaction costs associated with international trade and capital movements. The transaction costs were eliminated in direct proportion to the number and size of a nation's economic partners already on gold.[6]

Germany's move to gold led indirectly to the same decision by the countries of northern Europe. Further, this switch, along with France's probable abandonment of bimetallism, had a global resonance partially responsible for sending the United States (1879), Holland (1875), and Scandinavian countries (1874–1875) onto gold. This policy change also pushed Holland and Austria-Hungary to de-monetize silver. Belgium, Switzerland, and Italy, as part of the Latin Monetary Union, were forced to follow France and limit silver coinage in 1873. Japan, along with many other nations, also began to seriously contemplate moving to gold in the mid-1870s.

And so the original policy in France and Flandreau's finding lead us to a question. If bimetallism was a viable system in the face of the German de-monetization of silver, what sealed bimetallism's fate, and how long did it take for this decision to become irreversible? How many other countries had to switch to gold to make the "transitory" decision permanent?

---

[5] From the International Monetary Conference of 1867, policymakers learned that France was *not* totally opposed to moving to a monometallic gold standard.

[6] Not only is the econometric evidence from Meissner (2005) consistent with such a theory, but in addition Flandreau (1996) dismisses many of the competing theories on the emergence of the gold standard as incompatible with the historical record. Meissner (2005) finds evidence that coordination on other regimes such as silver, or even bimetallism, would have diminished the relative gains from moving to gold, as would the numerous switching costs. Meissner (2005) also finds that the following were related to the decision: the need to establish credibility in capital markets, the level of GDP per capita, and other domestic considerations such as the desire to achieve (or inability to avoid) high inflation via inconvertible paper currency.

The End of Bimetallism as a Case Study in Institutional Change

In terms of lessons for institutional change, this historical episode is an extraordinary moment. Velde and Weber (2000) argue that bimetallism was inefficient (i.e., welfare dominated by a monometallic standard). The argument relies on a microfounded model of bimetallism with a cash-in-advance constraint and a nonmonetary role for precious metals. Assuming an appropriate utility function (e.g., constant elasticity of substitution between metals), the use of one commodity for money dominates the use of both concurrently.[7] From a macro-historical perspective, bimetallism, an inefficient institution, was seemingly viable for a long time. But this regime suddenly came to be replaced by a more efficient arrangement. And though some calculation went into the disappearance of bimetallism, human error and historical circumstance seem to have played a large role.

This historical episode is an example of how mental models, perceptions, and historical accidents produce economic outcomes. Douglas North argues "ideas matter and different perceptions produce different choices ... the result is that multiple equilibria can ensue." And more to the point:

It is belief systems that are the underlying determinant of path dependence ... (organizations) arise as a result of a given institutional structure (and) have a vested interested in perpetuating that institutional structure ... The way the institutions evolve reflects the ongoing belief systems of the players ... Path dependence conceived of in this way, can account... for those occasions when abrupt changes in the path of a society do occur. The latter will occur when the belief system is perceived to be inconsistent with the outcomes predicted by that belief system.

The feedback system being described is the transition path from one equilibrium to another, and it is extremely salient in understanding the end of bimetallism.[8] French policymakers initially seem to have believed that bimetallism was viable in the long run – no matter what – even after temporarily suspending the unlimited coinage of silver. Ex post this seems

---

[7] On the other hand, they also suggest bimetallism brings about greater price stability because an increase in one metal would have to be accompanied by a decrease in the other commodity money in order to hold the market ratio at the mint ratio.

[8] One question, if we are interested in understanding the regime changes and strategies after 1873, is whether the beliefs and actions might represent a plausible (sequential) equilibrium in the game theoretic sense. A sequential equilibrium requires that beliefs on and off the equilibrium path are consistent or "sensible" and that strategies be rational given those beliefs. Roughly speaking, a set of strategies has to be sub-game perfect (i.e., credible) and beliefs on and off the equilibrium path must be correct according to the dictates of rationality and Bayes' rule. The question hinges on whether the French abandonment of bimetallism was an unexpected outcome. More precisely, the question hinges on what probability French policymakers put on reaching a point where they would have to quit bimetallism because of the rest of the world moving to gold.

like a misperception. French policymakers seemingly underestimated the chances countries would move to gold all together and overestimated the ability of the French monetary system to withstand these changes. French bimetallism, solid for so many years, expired in the wake of these events. In 1876 the Bank of France, facing a massive capital loss on its sizable silver reserves, sponsored the law that fully suspended silver coinage. French officials had determined by then that reintroducing actual bimetallism would be economically risky. In a new and highly relevant paper, Flandreau and Oosterlinck (2012) argue that until 1875 market participants acted as if bimetallism was viable. From 1875, the market became increasingly convinced that bimetallism would fail and the gold standard would reign. The question is then exactly how long after 1871 did it take for bimetallism to become fundamentally nonviable for France?

The next section formally investigates a counterfactual where France attempts to go back to full bimetallism in the face of the global adoption of gold during the 1870s. It turns out that France's "temporary" policy became permanent (and full bimetallism became nonviable) by about 1874. The worldwide shift to gold ensured this was so, and the United States' return to gold convertibility in 1879 made a later reversal all the more difficult.

A MODEL OF THE BIMETALLIC SYSTEM

This section formally investigates whether France could have reinstated bimetallism at the official mint ratio of 15.5 to 1 at any point between 1870 and 1885. I use Flandreau's model of bimetallism, which outlines key relationships in precious metals markets. The strategy is to derive a long-run equilibrium condition on the supply and demand of precious metals under which bimetallism remains intact. By adjusting the demands for specie appropriately (i.e., taking into account the given regime changes in the 1870s), I can analyze the consequence of changes in these conditions for the viability of bimetallism. I show that if France had reinstated free silver coinage it would have become a de facto silver standard country after 1874.

The world has two precious metals used for monetary purposes: gold (G) and silver (S). There are three types of countries according to their monetary standard: gold (g), silver (s), and bimetallic (b). Each bloc has an ad hoc monetary specie demand equation as follows:

$$M_G^g p_G = k^g p Y^g \tag{9.1}$$

$$M_S^s = k^s p Y^s \tag{9.2}$$

$$M_G^b p_G + M_S^b = k^b p Y^b \tag{9.3}$$

where M_j^i is the monetary specie demand for metal j, $j \in \{G,S\}$, for standard i, $i \in \{g,s,b\}$, k^i is a parameter, Y^i is real output in bloc i, p is the price of output, and p_G is the price of one unit of gold in terms of silver. Flandreau's model also allows for nonmonetary demands for precious metals but I will abstract from these demands, assuming them to be constant throughout.[9] The setup in its current state takes world money supplies and incomes as exogenous. Money demands can be justified in a cash-in-advance setup.

In addition, assume that gold, silver, and bimetallic countries have a constant ratio of real output such that

$$Y^g = \beta_G Y^b \text{ and} \tag{9.4}$$

$$Y^S = \beta_s Y^b. \tag{9.5}$$

Finally, assume that total supply of precious metals is the sum of monetary demands across the different blocs:

$$G = M_G^g + M_G^b \text{ and} \tag{9.6}$$

$$S = M_S^s + M_S^b \tag{9.7}$$

where G and S are the total world supplies of monetary gold and silver respectively.

Using equations (9.6) and (9.7), the model can be solved by adding up demands for both metals and making the appropriate substitutions. This leads to two useful parameters on gold and silver demands:

$$m_g^m = k^g \beta_G \tag{9.8}$$

$$m_s^m = k^s \beta_S. \tag{9.9}$$

Letting $k = k^b$, $Y = Y^b$, and G_b equal to the bimetallic demand for gold, S_B equal to bimetallic silver demands, and $G_n(S_n)$ equal to gold (silver) bloc demands for gold, we can write the following equations:

$$G_n = m_G^m \left(\frac{p}{p_G} \right) Y \tag{9.10}$$

---

[9] In discussion, Velde showed that the share of gold in nonmonetary demands fluctuated between 0.57 and 0.52 from 1870 to 1880 and for silver the range is 0.765 and 0.73.

$$S_n = m_S^m pY \tag{9.11}$$

$$kpY = p_G G_B + S_B \tag{9.12}$$

$$G_B + G_n = G \tag{9.13}$$

$$S_B + S_n = S \tag{9.14}$$

These five equations give rise to two key conditions that describe how the specie stock in the bimetallic bloc adjusts to shocks in the demand for precious metals and world supplies of specie. They are

$$p_G G_B = p_G G(1 - m_G) - Sm_G \tag{9.15}$$

$$S_B = -p_G Gm_S + (1 - m_S) \tag{9.16}$$

where $m_G = \dfrac{m_G^m}{k + m_G^m + m_S^m}$ and $m_S = \dfrac{m_S^m}{k + m_G^m + m_S^m}$.

Condition (9.15) shows, for example, that the gold stock in the bimetallic bloc would increase by $(1 - m_G)$ units for every one-unit increase in the world supply of gold. In addition, equations (9.15) and (9.16) also provide a useful set of boundary conditions that must be met if both silver and gold are to be in circulation in the bimetallic country.

A proper bimetallic equilibrium requires that both metals circulate in the bimetallic bloc or $p_G G_B > 0$, and $S_B > 0$. This gives rise to the following inequalities:

$$\frac{m_G}{(1 - m_G)} < \frac{p_G G}{S} < \frac{(1 - m_S)}{m_S}. \tag{9.17}$$

The inequalities from (9.17) yield upper and lower bounds on the relative levels of silver and gold in the world. Flandreau (1996) estimated m_G and m_S for the years 1850 to 1870 as 0.37 and 0.39 respectively. Before 1871, the ratio of gold to silver ($p_G G/S$) was well within the structural limits imposed by the model prior to Germany's de-monetization of silver (Flandreau 1996). However, the worldwide shift to the gold standard after 1871 had a large impact on those boundaries.

To analyze the situation where France maintains bimetallism and the rest of the world moves to gold, we assume that p_G is held fixed at the historical French mint ratio of 15.5 and that unlimited silver coinage is allowed. When a country moves to the gold standard from the silver standard, it thrusts the lower boundary of condition (9.17) up toward the world specie stock ratio. As the demand for monetary gold rises, it has to be sat-isfied by a transfer of gold from the bimetallic bloc. This change would then make bimetallic countries more sensitive to additional increases in the world stock of gold. Whether France could have revived bimetallism is the same as asking if the worldwide shift to gold pushed the lower boundary above the ratio of world gold to silver stocks.

Comparative Statics for a Shift to Gold from Silver

To assess the shocks to the boundary there are two cases to consider. The first is a move from silver to gold and the second is a move from an incon-vertible currency to a gold standard, as in the case of the United States.[10] Flandreau analyzes the case when a country joins the gold standard and departs from a silver standard. Assume that this brings a rise in the demand for gold equal to the fall in the demand for silver, which in turn equals the entire stock of monetary silver prior to the change. Germany, Holland, and the Scandinavian countries fall into this category of change. This type of switch affects the parameters on the specie demands such that we have

$$\bar{m}_G^m = m_G^m + k_d^g \beta_d \tag{9.18}$$

for the gold demand parameter and

$$\bar{m}_S^m = m_S^m - k_d^s \beta_d \tag{9.19}$$

for the silver demand parameter. The subscript d indexes the identity of the defecting country or countries. In this case we assume that there was a constant relationship between the bimetallic and the defecting country's demand for specie such that $\alpha = \dfrac{k_d^s \beta_d}{k}$. If so, the consequence of the defec-tion can be found easily by using the old parameters m_G^m and m_S^m. This yields new expressions for the parameters after defection:

$$\bar{m}_G = m_G + \alpha(1 - m_G - m_S) \tag{9.20}$$

$$\bar{m}_S = m_S - \alpha(1 - m_G - m_S) \tag{9.21}$$

Expressions (9.20) and (9.21) can be used to find the lower and upper boundaries after such defections. All one needs to know is the ratio of specie

---

[10] I consider only the counterfactual where France maintains free coinage of silver through-out and therefore p_G is fixed at 15.5. I focus only on the lower boundary because a move to gold forces the upper boundary away from the critical region of breakdown.

demands for the defectors relative to France and the coefficients m_G and m_S. The new boundaries substitute $\bar{m}_G(\bar{m}_S)$ for $m_G(m_S)$ in the boundary conditions.

Comparative Statics for a Shift to Gold from a Fiat Currency

There is a second type of move to the gold standard not analyzed by Flandreau but that is relevant. In this case a nation adopts gold but was not previously on a silver standard. The consequence of such a defection for the bimetallic country will not be as large because there is presumably little silver this country would "sell" to the bimetallic nation. The effect from this country comes purely through gold demands. This case is applicable for the United States, which officially moved from its greenback regime to the gold standard in 1879.[11]

We can see how such a defection changes the lower boundary condition for bimetallism by performing slightly more involved operations than above. Let W be the new lower boundary after the non-silver country has gone to gold so that $W \equiv \dfrac{\bar{m}'_G}{(1 - \bar{m}'_G)}$. Note that

$$W = \frac{m_G^m + \alpha k}{k + \alpha k + m_G^m + m_S^m}\cdot\left(1 - \frac{m_G^m + \alpha k}{k + \alpha k + m_G^m + m_S^m}\right)^{-1} = \frac{m_G^m + \alpha k}{k + m_S^m}. \qquad (9.22)$$

Similar to expression (9.18) we use the fact that the defection causes m_G^m to increase by αk but has no effect on m_S^m.

Using the expressions for m_G and m_S, observe that we can write $l = \dfrac{m_G}{1 - m_G} = \dfrac{m_G^m}{k + m_S^m}$ and $u = \dfrac{m_S}{1 - m_S} = \dfrac{m_S^m}{k + m_G^m}$. Consequently we have

$$W = l + \frac{\alpha k}{k + m_S^m} = l + \frac{1}{1 + \delta}\alpha. \qquad (9.23)$$

The last equality is obtained by solving for m_S^m and m_G^m using the expressions for m_G and m_S above to find $m_S^m = k\delta$, where $\delta = \dfrac{1 + l}{u - l}$.

This expression can be used to find out how a country like the United States affected the lower boundary in Figure 9.2. Because δ comes from the boundary before the U.S. switch, all we need is P (i.e., the ratio of American

---

[11] The specie stock of the United States grew threefold between 1877 and 1881 but was constant or declining from 1870 to 1876.

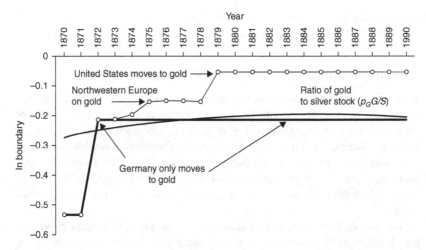

Figure 9.2. The structural limits of bimetallism, 1870–1885. The figure depicts the limits of bimetallism under two scenarios: only Germany moves to gold and Germany, Western Europe, and the United States move to gold. The limits are derived from the model presented in the text. Sources for gold and silver stocks are the Report to Congress of the Commission the Role of Gold in the Domestic and International Monetary Systems (1982) and Warren (1935).

specie demands to French demands). The average value of P from 1878 to 1885 was about 0.4.[12]

The aforementioned theoretical model demonstrates how changes in demands for precious metals resulting from regime changes affect the boundary conditions that defined veritable bimetallism. Increased demand for gold from nations transitioning to a gold standard from a silver standard had to be fulfilled by buying gold from the bimetallic bloc while excess silver had to be sold to the bimetallic country.[13] A simple calculation using condition (9.23) and data on gold and silver stocks shows that defectors to the gold standard from the silver standard must have had a demand for specie, α, of about 31 percent the size of France to make bimetallism inviable. In fact, Germany's specie demand was roughly 27 percent of France's, which made bimetallism sensitive to regime changes. This differs from Flandreau (1996), who concluded that the French monetary system would have been robust to the German switch. His assessment of the ratio of

---

[12] That value increased from 0.23 to 0.56 between 1879 and 1885 as the United States outgrew its fiat currency episode, established credibility in the capital markets, and attracted a large gold reserve.

[13] Arbitrage on precious metals would ensure that excess demands were ultimately satisfied in the bimetallic country that held a constant mint ratio.

world gold stocks (valued at 15.5:1) to silver stocks in 1873 is roughly 1.3. I use data from Commission on the Role of Gold (1982) for gold stocks and from Warren (1935) for silver stocks and find a ratio of 0.77. An intermediate value of 1 was published in Oppers (1996). The next section uses the model with data on specie demands to show that owing to changing specie demands by 1875 bimetallism would have become a monometallic, silver standard.

THE RISE OF GOLD AND THE DEMISE OF BIMETALLISM

In this section I use data on α (i.e., the ratio of specie demands in different blocs to France) for the countries that moved to gold after 1871. I show how the diffusion of the gold standard affected the viability of bimetallism in France. Table 9.1 gives a list of countries, the dates at which they adopted gold convertibility, their previous monetary regime, and the average amount of specie holdings in those countries relative to France (α). Individually, many nations had quite small specie holdings relative to France. Germany, and the United States were the two largest countries to make an impact on gold markets. In fact, Table 9.1 understates the U.S. relative specie demand since by 1885 this ratio equaled more than 50 percent that of France. Table 9.1 emphasizes that *aggregate* holdings might have been large enough to drain France of all its gold had it reinstated unlimited silver coinage in any year after 1875.

Up to 1878 I use expression (20) to derive the changes on the lower boundary from the model. In 1879 when the United States adopted the gold standard, I use expression (9.23) and the lower bound from 1878 to show how the American resumption made French bimetallism obsolete.

Figure 9.2 shows graphically the effects of the increasing demands for gold during the 1870s. The lower boundary (i.e., $m_G/(1-m_G)$) continually shifted up as each new country joined the gold standard from 1873 to 1879.[14] Given my data on precious metals stocks, the lower boundary is *above* the ratio $p_G G/S$ by 1872 implying France would have held only silver in that year had it reversed or failed to implement its so-called transitory policy. By 1875, the inability of France to maintain bimetallism is definitive.[15]

---

[14] I do not plot the upper boundary as precious metal production was relatively inconsequential compared to the changes in demands. In any case, that boundary was shifting upward.

[15] In each case where there is a defection to the gold standard I use the value of α in the given year and the formulas to adjust to boundaries. I continually adjust the boundaries as the levels of α change. I interpret these regime changes as one-time shocks to the long-run equilibrium parameters m_G and m_S, so year-to-year noise in the level of specie demands should not have a large impact on the main parameters.

Table 9.1. Money Demand for Various Countries in the Year of Adoption of the Gold Standard

Country	Date of Adoption of the Gold Standard	Previous Standard	Ratio of Specie Demands to France (α)	
			Oppers and Jones and Obstfeld Data	Flandreau Data
Germany	1872	Silver	0.31	0.27
Norway	1873	Silver	0.006	—
Sweden	1873	Silver	0.002	—
Denmark	1873	Silver	0.002	—
Holland	1875	Silver	0.045	—
Finland	1877	Silver	0.002	—
United States	1879	Paper	0.23	—

Notes: Dates of adoption and previous regimes come from Meissner (2000). Estimates of specie demands come from Flandreau (1996), Jones and Obstfeld (2000), Muhleman (1895), Oppers (1996), and Soetbeer (1886).

If Germany had been the only country to switch regimes, the boundary labeled "Germany moves to gold" corroborates Flandreau (1996) and Oppers (1996) but only after 1877. This is largely due to a small rise in the relative abundance of gold stocks. Before then, there is a period where bimetallism might have been at risk had unlimited coinage been allowed. It might indeed have been prudent to limit silver coinage. Even after 1877, the difference between the boundary and the stock is not large, and it implies a very fragile bimetallic equilibrium. However, because the rest of the world also went to gold, bimetallism at a mint ratio of 15.5 to 1 was doomed. By 1875 at the latest, the new demands for gold would have been too heavy for France to continue to support bimetallism unilaterally. These estimates are sensitive to my data on the world's gold and silver stocks. Using Flandreau's (1996) implied ratio of precious metal stocks would have made bimetallism robust through 1885 despite a massive increase in demand for gold induced by the U.S. return to convertibility. Using figures from Oppers (2000) would have made bimetallism sustainable until the United States adopted gold convertibility in 1879.[16]

France could not have revived bimetallism after 1873. Policy spillovers that ran between nations' actions sealed bimetallism's fate. France's policy

---

[16] At this time I am unable to reestimate Flandreau's regressions that provided the original bounds on bimetallism and that relied on his data on world precious metals stocks. Unless the annual *changes* in the different estimates of the stocks are highly correlated then different bounds might arise and the conclusions stated above could be different.

partially persuaded countries such as Sweden, Norway, Denmark, Holland, Belgium, Switzerland (the latter two part of the Latin Monetary Union), and even the United States that the time was ripe to move to gold. In the mid-1870s, countries acted on the belief that the major players of Europe and the United States would all be monometallic gold in the future. These regime changes shifted precious metals demands and endogenously limited the viability of bimetallism.

Throughout the 1870s, the French called their actions temporary. However, the strategic consequences and the inadequate size of French metallic demands in the face of changing global demands led to an ostensibly unanticipated outcome. Historical events led to a seemingly small change in French policy in late 1873 (i.e., limiting silver coinage in 1873). If it is true that the French policymakers believed they could reverse course and move again to unlimited silver coinage, these beliefs did not square with how events ultimately unfolded. When the dust settled, France was forced to completely suspend silver coinage leading the Latin Monetary Union to negotiate a move to the gold standard in 1878.

THE RESUSCITATION OF BIMETALLISM?

Owing to the immense changes in the demand for gold in the 1870s, the French could not reverse course after 1875. The French reacted to events by suspending all silver coinage in August 1876, which Flandreau and Oosterlinck (2012) interpret as the permanent abandonment of bimetallism. But some policymakers and interest groups, especially those in the United States, clung to the hope of an internationally coordinated revival of bimetallism. Activists conjectured that global cooperation on a bimetallic system would stabilize the world silver price by raising demand for silver and dampening demand for gold. The subsequent attempts to manage regime coordination in the international monetary system provide the building blocks for a case study in international cooperation – or the lack thereof. To assess the economic feasibility of such a program, assuming nations can credibly commit to their actions, we can use the model of the second section. Specifically we can check if France and the United States could have established enough demand for silver to make bimetallism feasible at a given mint ratio.

Showing that the economics of the situation made bimetallism nonviable is one thing, but it does not imply that the politics of making such a deal were propitious. Beginning in 1876, a tide of support for silver awakened in the United States. Extensive discussion was held in Congress and was documented in the Report of the United States Monetary Commission. Nevada senator, and silver miner, John P. Jones chaired the commission and carried his pro-silver bias into the final draft of the report. The committee strongly supported rehabilitating bimetallism or at least providing a monetary use for silver.[17] In hearings, the commission aimed to find experts that would testify on the feasibility of bimetallism despite silver's massive depreciation and the nearly complete abandonment of silver's monetary role in Europe. Specifically, the commission inquired about the strategic ramifications of a U.S. return to bimetallism. The commission asked eminent U.S. economist H. C. Carey "...if the United States were to establish the double standard (bimetallism) do you think it would have the effect of confirming France, Italy, Belgium and the other nations ...in their present policy of employing silver as an unlimited tender?" Carey responded affirmatively, and he also suggested that Great Britain might even be convinced by such a move.

The outcome of these turbulent years, the first of a series of battles between "hard" money advocates and "inflationists," was the Bland–Allison Act of 1878. The Bland–Allison Act is remembered as the act that mandated the government purchase between two and four million dollars of silver each year.[18] An amendment was also inserted into the act calling for an international monetary conference. The goal of the conference was to persuade other nations of the world to reinstate bimetallism.[19] To this end, twelve nations met in Paris in 1878 to discuss the resuscitation of bimetallism.

Reti (1998) and Russell (1898) give an account of the political impediments blocking the revival of bimetallism after 1878. They classify countries into three main policy positions. The Scandinavian countries, England, and then Germany (the last of which refused the American invitation to attend the conference in 1878) immovably advocated gold monometallism.[20] On the other hand, France and the Latin satellites along with Austria-Hungary clung to their "attitude of expectancy," and so did not want to reinstate bimetallism until the Germans committed to stop silver sales. Only Italy and one of the two Dutch delegates allied themselves with the Americans in advocating international bimetallism.

---

[17] The 44th congress elected in 1874 was divided with a democratic majority in the house and a Republican majority in the senate. Jones, a Republican, might have followed the party line in favor of gold had he not been from Nevada and had silver mining interests. Richard Bland, democratic representative of Missouri, after whom the Bland-Allison silver support bill would be named, also served on the commission.

[18] Recall that in 1871 Germany held about 400 million dollars' worth of silver specie.

[19] The irony is that anti-silver forces actually proposed the amendment to hold the conference as a tactic to appease the more rabid free-silver activists and to make it appear as if the president and the Treasury were more sympathetic than they were to their demands.

[20] This sentiment would change later. Germany is noted for having more sympathy for silver in the early 1890s. Political gains by the junker class in the early 1890s led to speculation that Germany might re-monetize silver. Germany's financial panic of 1893 is attributed, in part, to such speculation (Bordo and Eichengreen 1999).

As history shows (see earlier), the French attitude appears to have been based on the misconception that an "attitude of expectancy" could be reversed at any time. Even at the monetary conference in August 1878 the French delegate Leon Say disavowed that France would be adopting the gold standard, and he added that if conditions were right France would probably return to bimetallism. But the model shows this was overly optimistic if France stood alone in trying to reverse course. It stands to reason, however, that bimetallism would have been feasible given some sort of an accord between France and the United States (the two major actors and countries with an historic bimetallic tradition).

At one point, the English economist and bimetallic advocate Stanley Jevons argued that a large bimetallic bloc could stabilize the market price of silver (Reti 1998, p. 81). And bimetallic advocates wanted to attract as many participants to the bimetallic bloc as possible (Reti 1998, p. 89). The largest countries with an historical tradition of bimetallism were the United States and France, and so it is interesting to look at the possibility of a French-American agreement.

The data and model used in this chapter allow us to gauge the economic feasibility of Franco-American bimetallism in 1878. Supposing that France and the United States had agreed on a mint ratio in 1878, could they have sufficiently dropped the lower boundary condition to bring back bimetallism?

Of course, one of the principal political problems in reaching an agreement in 1878 was agreement on the proper mint ratio. The United States proposed 16 to 1 ("the dollar of our daddies") while France preferred its historical ratio of 15.5 to 1. Not coordinating would have left France with silver and the United States with gold because of an obvious arbitrage possibility. I assume that this disagreement was overcome and the historical French mint ratio was agreed on.

To see the effect of a bimetallic treaty, I assume that U.S. demands for specie are part of the bimetallic bloc after 1878. I also assume that this change does not alter the coefficients in equations (9.15) and (9.16). Figure 9.3 shows that the upper boundary is now just even with the relative specie supply line that determines if a given mint ratio is viable. Bimetallism might have survived, but such attempts would have been tenuous. Any small amount of speculation in the financial and precious metals markets could have given rise to the destruction of such an equilibrium, as would small shocks to the relative supplies and demands of gold and silver. Alternatively, a mint ratio of 16 to 1 instead of 15.5 to 1 would have increased the likelihood of survival of international bimetallism. Of course, U.S. demand for specie rose briskly in the early 1880s, which would have put further downward pressure on the lower boundary, making bimetallism more robust.

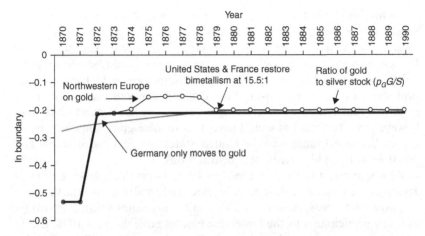

Figure 9.3. A revival of bimetallism? France and the United States both bimetallic after 1878. The figure depicts the limits of bimetallism under the scenario: Germany and Western Europe move to gold while the United States and France restore bimetallism. The limits are derived from the model presented in the text. Sources for gold and silver stocks are the Report to Congress of the Commission the Role of Gold in the Domestic and International Monetary Systems (1982) and Warren (1935).

How should we understand the failure to resuscitate bimetallism if the fundamentals were in place? Using Flandreau's values for the ratio of specie stock would change my conclusion. With his estimates for world precious metals stocks, international bimetallism would have been viable. A solid Franco-American commitment to bimetallism might have altered the regime choices of countries sitting on the fence like Spain, Austria-Hungary, Russia, and possibly even Italy. But the commitment to bimetallism was not entirely credible in all states of the world. No one nation could trust another to stay the course of bimetallism. Prior experience, and especially the years between 1872 and 1875, generated doubt about how solid the bimetallic cushion was even when France, with its enormous reserves, was at the center of the system. Any nation agreeing to adhere to bimetallism could easily be exposed to capital losses on reserves held in the depreciating monetary metal if other nations did not cooperate and honor the pledge to fix the silver price of gold. It would be hard to imagine a binding international accord among sovereign nations of the requisite size in the 1870s that could have maintained bimetallism.

CONCLUSIONS AND "LESSONS" FROM HISTORY

French bimetallism failed after 1874 owing to unprecedented monetary changes. Historical events, French misperceptions, and the strategic interaction between nations all combined to bury bimetallism. Leftover rivalry from the Franco-Prussian war limited French willingness to buy German silver during its transition to gold. This limitation on silver coinage partially fed into other nations' strategic calculations. Network externalities pushed many countries in Western Europe, America, and Asia onto the gold standard, and provided a radical shift in precious metals demands. After this, France was not large enough to peg the price of silver at the mint despite its large endowment of precious metals. Had France reversed its original policy, it would have shortly become a silver standard country. It is unlikely that the French (mis-)perception that bimetallism could return would have been validated by an international coalition. Even if the United States had gone back to bimetallism in 1879 instead of finally committing to the gold standard, the world's demands for gold were too strong to make bimetallism viable.

This story is one of long-run institutional change. Napoleon I had instituted bimetallism in 1803, and that system appears to have worked reasonably well until 1872. As we have seen, bimetallism quickly became obsolete after 1874. North's theoretical argument that misperceptions can quickly lead to surprisingly important changes in the institutional environment appears reasonable in this case. Bimetallism disappeared partially because of the lack of a true model of how the international monetary system functioned. Once bimetallism was out of the set of rational strategy space for French policymakers, it was on them to decide for a replacement regime. Ultimately they decided on the gold standard, as did nearly all other nations after the 1870s.

Finally, it is worth pondering the parallels between the 1870s and recent events in the European Monetary Union. Greece, Spain, Ireland, Portugal, and Italy all ran significant current account deficits in the run-up to the 2007–2008 financial crisis. The strains of readjustment within the confines of the single currency have been felt since then. All of the aforementioned countries have been required to impose significant austerity to facilitate the necessary real devaluation that the sudden stop of capital inflows has required. Default is another option, and Greece has already resorted to writing down some of its outstanding sovereign liabilities. By the end of 2011, many commentators projected a Greek exit (grexit) from the monetary union with a very high probability. The ability of other countries to endure has also been questioned.

As pressure in the capital markets mounted (again) in 2012, the European Central Bank and the German chancellor strongly rejected the possibility that countries undertaking adequate reforms would be forced to exit the monetary union. These statements were intended to build confidence in the ability of the European Central Bank and the European Union to resolve the crisis and to maintain the status quo. By and large, policymakers treated the issue almost as if the crisis were one of liquidity. These statements bear a strong resemblance to those of French policymakers who viewed the limitations on silver coinage as temporary measures and argued until 1878 that bimetallism would almost surely make a comeback.

Then, as now, these statements reflected a particular view and assessment of the likelihood of various scenarios. Policymakers were repeatedly optimistic that the status quo was viable in both episodes. In the 1870s, market pressures and policy spillovers led to the collapse of the bimetallic project in spite of some late attempts at international cooperation. The reasons that cooperation failed are unclear. Bimetallism, as it had functioned for decades prior to 1878, yielded fixed exchange rates and presumably provided the same network externalities as a gold regime. Still, as argued previously, bimetallism might not have been a "perfect" equilibrium. The early 1870s led countries to believe that a credible commitment to bimetallism was impossible. Few policymakers of the time (excepting the forces of inflation in the United States and like-minded factions elsewhere) were willing to run the risk of such instability.

As for the European Monetary Union, the crisis boils down first to a distributional issue of who pays for the crisis – the deficit or the surplus countries. History suggests that surplus countries rarely bear the burden of readjustment. Going forward, the issue boils down to international cooperation (within the European Union) on a unified banking regulator that could share and spread the risks of modern banking practices. As of November 2012, this project appears to be in jeopardy owing to the unwillingness of nations to share the potential costs of a foreign banking meltdown. The other alternative is a transfer/fiscal union that could smooth over negative shocks.[21] As in the 1870s, many view this as a problem of moral hazard. How would the self-proclaimed virtuous (Germans and the Dutch in the current case) ensure that the profligate did not overborrow and burden others with significant transfer payments? Once again, the credibility of national commitments is an issue. In this case, it is easy to be pessimistic about the potential for international cooperation. If compromises could be made such that a loss of fiscal sovereignty could be traded off against other benefits, a brighter future for the single currency might be possible. Without such a deal, the European Monetary Union as established in 1999 is very likely to face the fate of bimetallism.

---

[21] Bordo, Markiewicz, and Jonung (2011) discuss the prospects for a fiscal union in historical perspective.

REFERENCES

Bordo, Michael, and Barry Eichengreen. (1999). "Is Our Current International Economic Environment Unusually Crisis Prone?" In David Gruen and Luke Gower (eds), *Capital Flows and the International Financial System*. Proceedings of a Conference held at the Reserve Bank of Australia, August 9–10, 1999, Australia: J. S. McMillan, pp. 18–75. Retrieved from http://www.rba.gov.au/publications/confs/1999/pdf/conf-vol-1999.pdf

Bordo, Michael D., Agnieszka Markiewicz, and Lars Jonung. (2011). "A Fiscal Union for the Euro: Some Lessons from History." *National Bureau of Economic Research Working Paper* 17380. Cambridge, MA: National Bureau of Economic Research.

Commission on the Role of Gold in the Domestic and International Monetary Systems (1982). *Report to the Congress of the Commission on the Role of Gold in the Domestic and International Monetary Systems.*

Eichengreen, Barry, and Marc Flandreau. (1998). "The Geography of the Gold Standard." In Jorge Braga de Macedo, Barry Eichengreen, and Jaime Reis (eds), *Currency Convertibility: The Gold Standard and Beyond.* London: Routledge.

Flandreau, Marc. (1995). "Coin Memories: New Estimates of French Metallic Currency 1840–1878." *The Journal of European Economic History* 24(2):271–310.

(1996). "The French Crime of 1873: An Essay in the Emergence of the International Gold Standard, 1870–1880." *Journal of Economic History* 56(4):862–897.

Flandreau, Marc, and Kim Oosterlinck. (2012). "Was the Emergence of the International Gold Standard Expected? Evidence from Indian Government Securities." *Journal of Monetary Economics* 59(7): 649–669.

Friedman, Milton. (1990). "The Crime of 1873." *Journal of Political Economy* 98(6):1159–1194.

Friedman, Milton, and Anna J. Schwartz. (1963). *A Monetary History of the United States, 1867–1960*. Princeton, NJ: Princeton University Press (for the National Bureau of Economic Research).

Gallarotti, Giulio M. (1995). *The Anatomy of an International Monetary Regime.* New York: Oxford University Press.

Jones, Matthew T., and Maurice Obstfeld. (2000). "Savings and Investment Data for 13 Countries." Retrieved from http://www.nber.org/databases/jones-obstfeld/

Laughlin, James Laurence. (1891). *The History of Bimetallism in the United States.* New York: D. Appleton & Co.

Meissner, Christopher M. (2005). "A New World Order: Explaining the International Diffusion of the Gold Standard, 1870–1913." *Journal of International Economics*, 66(2):385–406.

Muhleman, Maurice L. (1895). *Monetary Systems of the World A Study of Present Currency Systems and Statistical Information Relative to the Volume of the World's Money with Complete Abstracts of Various Plans Proposed for the Solution of the Currency Problem.* New York: Charles Nicoll.

North, Douglass C. (1997). "The Historical Evolution of Polities." Economics Working Paper Archive Working Paper ewp-eh/9411007.

Oppers, Stefan E. (1996). "Was the Worldwide Shift to Gold Inevitable? An Analysis of the End of Bimetallism." *Journal of Monetary Economics* 37:143–162.

(2000). "A Model of the Bimetallic System." *Journal of Monetary Economics* 46(2):517–533.

Reti, Steven P. (1998). *Silver and Gold: The Political Economy of International Monetary Conferences, 1867–1892.* Westport, CT: Greenwood Press.

Rolnick, Arthur J., and Warren E. Weber. (1986). "Gresham's Law or Gresham's Fallacy?" *Journal of Political Economy* 94:185–199.

Russell, Henry Benajah. (1898). *International Monetary Conferences.* New York: Harper and Brothers.

Soetbeer, Adolf. (1886). *Materialien zur Erläuterung und Beurteilung der Wirtschaftlichen Edelmetallverhaltnisse.* Berlin: Putkammer and Muhlbrecht.

Velde, François R., and Warren E. Weber. (2000). "A Model of Bimetallism." *Journal of Political Economy* 108(6):1210–1234.

Warren, George F. (1935). *Gold and Prices*, New York: John Wiley & Sons.

10

The Reserve Pyramid and Interbank Contagion during the Great Depression

Kris James Mitchener and Gary Richardson

> The failure of the Federal Reserve System to prevent the collapse reflected not the impotence of monetary policy but rather the particular policies followed by the monetary authorities and, in a smaller degree, the particular monetary arrangements in existence. The contraction is in fact a tragic testimonial to the importance of monetary forces.
>
> (Friedman and Schwartz 1973, p. 4)

> Since one bank's asset is another bank's liability, interbank deposits cancel when the accounts of banks are consolidated into the accounts of the banking system as a whole.
>
> (Friedman and Schwartz 1963, p. 20)

One-sixth of Milton Friedman and Anna Schwartz's opus, *A Monetary History of the United States: 1867–1960*, focuses on 1929 through 1933, an era that the authors label the Great Contraction (Friedman and Schwartz 1963). During that contraction, output in real terms, the wholesale price level, the stock of money, and the number of commercial banks all fell by more than one third. At the trough in February and March of 1933, unemployment exceeded 25 percent. Banking panics forced authorities in increasing numbers of states to shutter large numbers of financial institutions. Ultimately, President Roosevelt declared a nationwide banking holiday, closing all banks for the week beginning Monday, March 6 and slowly reopening banks thereafter. The contraction afflicted economies around the world. It ranks as the most severe and widespread business-cycle downturn in modern times (Friedman and Schwartz 1973, pp. 3–4).

The contraction profoundly influenced economic thinking. The Federal Reserve's failure to stem the falling tide convinced academics and practitioners that monetary forces played little independent role in economic affairs and that monetary policy could do little to influence the business cycle. "The inference was drawn that policy designed to prevent or moderate economic fluctuations must assign major emphasis to government

217

fiscal policies and direct intervention (1973, p. xi)." This inference led to decades of dominance of Keynesian economic thought and strict regulation of commerce and industry, with the financial sector – commercial and investment banking – particularly targeted for heavy regulation.

According to Friedman and Schwartz, however, these inferences were incorrect. Rather than evidence of the impotence of monetary policy, our depression experience was a "tragic testimonial to the importance of monetary forces (1973, p. xi)." They suggest three key findings based on their reading of the historical evidence. First, the Federal Reserve

... had ample powers to cut short the tragic process of monetary deflation and banking collapse. Had it used those powers effectively in late 1930 or even in early or mid-1931, the successive liquidity crises ... could almost certainly have been prevented and ... Such action would have eased the severity of the contraction and very likely would have brought it to an end at a much earlier date. (1973, p. xi)

Second, numerous individuals in the leadership of the Federal Reserve System understood how the Federal Reserve could and should have employed the policy tools at its disposal. These leaders proposed palliative policies, which were not adopted by the system as a whole, but "very likely would have been adopted under a slightly different bureaucratic structure or distribution of power, or even if the men in power had had somewhat different personalities" (1973, p. xii). Third, the policies necessary and sufficient to counteract the crisis would not have endangered the gold standard even during the international financial crisis in the summer and fall of 1931, and perhaps not during the year that followed.

Friedman and Schwartz's conclusions arose from examining aggregate information about economic activity to the national level to consider how Federal Reserve policies influenced monetary aggregates, prices and production for the economy as a whole. Only occasionally do they refer to the Federal Reserve's federated structure, which left each Federal Reserve district free to pursue policies on its own. Interbank deposits, a key variable of interest in our study, are, in general, an afterthought in the *Monetary History*.[1] Because their narrative aims to link changes in the money supply to the real economy, Friedman and Schwartz appropriately focused on *national* aggregates. Precisely where deposits were held within the system was not important for establishing this relationship. As they note early in their book (p. 20), "since one bank's asset is another bank's liability, interbank deposits cancel when the accounts of banks are consolidated into

---

[1] They mention interbank deposits only once in their analysis of the Great Contraction. They indicate (p. 338) that New York City banks took over brokers' loans and increased lending to others in response to the October 1929 stock market crash. "Some of the loans taken over were for the accounts of out-of-town banks were matched by an increase in interbank deposits of $510 million in New York City weekly reporting member banks."

the accounts of the banking system as a whole." If one's focus is instead aimed at understanding the sources of financial contagion and factors influencing systemic stability, then the structure of deposits *within* the system, rather than aggregate deposits, becomes more salient. Interbank deposits linked the balance sheets of banks to each other, and are one of many network linkages that may transmit financial shocks from one institution to another. Friedman and Schwartz's statistical work – including their calculations of money supply, bank reserves, and the deposit/reserve ratio – excludes data on interbank deposits, which they assert may act as reserves on the balance sheets of individual banks and the minds of individual bankers, but that do not serve as reserves for the system as a whole.

In this essay, we move in a new direction by developing a data set that can be used to analyze interbank deposits' role in the financial system of the 1920s and 1930s, and in particular, how interbank deposits linked distress in the financial hinterland – such as nonmember banks operating in towns throughout America's agricultural and industrial heartland – to financial centers such as New York and Chicago. We calculate that interbank deposits were about 20 percent of the deposits of Federal Reserve member banks in financial centers (both central reserve and reserve cities). More than 90 percent of these interbank deposits came from nonmember country banks (i.e., banks located outside a reserve city that did not belong to the Federal Reserve System). Our analysis shows that during the 1920s, banking distress in the hinterland, which was caused in large part by declining agricultural prices after World War I, appears to have had little influence on interbank balances at the center of the system. Measures of bank distress and flows of interbank deposits were uncorrelated. During the 1930s, however, the pattern changes. Banking distress in the hinterland became highly correlated with flows of interbank deposits. When distress increased in the 1930s, interbank deposits flowed out from financial centers, particularly New York and Chicago. When distress eased, interbank deposits flowed back into financial centers. Interbank financial flows during this period thus became increasingly volatile and unpredictable. They ceased to be seasonal as had been the case in the 1920s. In sum, during the banking panics of the 1930s, interbank deposit flows transmitted financial shocks from the periphery to the core of the financial system.

These flows help to explain the strain placed on the financial centers and the changing portfolio behavior of banks at the center of the monetary system. We document that these changes in interbank deposit flows in turn altered the portfolios of reserve city banks, and precipitated a movement out of loans and into bonds and reserves in the early 1930s. This finding has important implications for our understanding of how the interconnected nature of the banking system may have contributed to the severity of the real contraction.

In the next section of the chapter, we review the relevant literature and describe the historical background, explaining the evolution of the pyramid system of bank reserves during the nineteenth century and the modification of that system after the creation of the Federal Reserve in 1913. The second describes the new data set collected for our study. The third section describes our methods and results. The fourth section discusses the implications of our analysis.

BACKGROUND

Literature on Contagion and Regional Banking Crises during the Great Depression

In recent decades, researchers have exploited micro-level data and variation within regions of the Federal Reserve's system with the aim of confirming or refuting Friedman and Schwartz's conjectures concerning the contraction. Richardson and Troost (2009), for example, test the first conjecture: that the Federal Reserve had the ability to mitigate banking panics in the early 1930s. Richardson and Troost compare outcomes across two districts, the 6th (Atlanta) and 8th (St. Louis), whose policies differed. Atlanta championed counter-cyclical monetary policies and the extension of aid to ailing banks. St. Louis advocated pro-cyclical policies. During the banking crisis in the fall of 1930, Atlanta expedited lending to banks in need. St. Louis did not. In Atlanta's district, banks survived at higher rates, lending continued at higher levels, commerce contracted less, and recovery began earlier. These patterns indicate that the Fed had the ability to alleviate banking panics, as Friedman and Schwartz concluded. Recent papers by Ziebarth (2012) and Jalil (2011) confirm the robustness of these results.

The article by Carlson, Mitchener, and Richardson (2011) reinforces these findings and also sheds light on the second conjecture: that members of the Federal Reserve's leadership understood how to use monetary tools to arrest banking panics and could act quickly and creatively to devise policies appropriate for new and unique circumstances. The article examines the Federal Reserve's reaction to a banking panic in Florida in the summer of 1929 and preceding the onset of the Great Contraction. The panic occurred after an infestation of agricultural pests destroyed citrus crops in central Florida, preventing farmers from repaying loans, and threatening the solvency of banks that extended loans to farmers. Runs on those country banks drained funds from banks in Tampa, the financial hub of the region, leading to runs on those institutions. The Federal Reserve Bank of Atlanta responded by rushing large quantities of cash to the afflicted institutions, piling the cash on the floors of those banks (in an arrangement deemed a currency depot), and promising to provide the funds necessary to repay every depositor at every bank in the city, if necessary. This extraordinary intervention stopped the panic, saved the afflicted institutions and their financial counterparties, restored faith in the financial system, and within twenty-four hours, reversed the flow of funds from the system, convincing the previously panicked public to redeposit the funds that they had withdrawn.

An array of recent research also corroborates Friedman and Schwartz's first and second conjectures. Elmus Wicker's *Banking Panics of the Great Depression* (1996) uses aggregate data to show that Federal Reserve bank failure rates differed from district to district. Districts that advocated procyclical policies tended to suffer higher rates of bank failures. Allan Meltzer (2003, pp. 282, 402–422) shows that, in some districts, the Federal Reserve's leaders adhered to outdated doctrines and monitored misleading indicators of monetary conditions. Meltzer (2003, pp. 266, 408) and David Wheelock (1991, pp. 72–74, 113–117) argue that the Federal Reserve Board lacked leadership and could not coordinate policies among its disputatious districts.

Interbank Deposits and the Reserve Pyramid

The interconnected nature of financial institutions features prominently in descriptions, analysis, and academic work on the recent financial crisis, but these network linkages have received significantly less attention during the Great Depression. This is somewhat surprising because it has long been hypothesized that the "inverted pyramid structure" of the U.S. banking system made the banking system fragile to network-induced runs (James 1978; Meyers 1931; Sprague 1910). The layered structure of the banking system dates back to the nineteenth century, when correspondent networks developed as a response to the geographical growth in the nation, and its burgeoning population outside the industrial and populous Northeast. "Interior banks" sought sources for funds and investment, and correspondent networks facilitated this demand. The national banking acts further cemented the interconnected structure of U.S. banking, permitting country banks to meet their legal reserve requirements by keeping a large portion of their reserves (originally up to three fifths) with reserve-city or central reserve-city banks.[2] By the early twentieth century, central reserve-city

---

[2] Under the initial rules of the act, national banks in small cities and rural areas, so-called country banks, faced a reserve requirement of 15 percent, 3/5ths of which could be held with the aforementioned correspondent banks in reserve cities (initially, cities with populations greater than 50,000) or in central reserve cities (initially, New York, Chicago, and St. Louis). The remaining fraction of required reserves were to be held in lawful money (U.S. notes, specie, gold, and clearing house certificates). National banks located in reserve cities had to hold 25 percent of their deposits as reserves, half of which could be deposits in national banks located in central reserve city national banks. "Central reserve city national banks were required to hold 25 percent of their deposits in lawful money. Country and

banks in New York were holding roughly two thirds of all required reserves, much of which was then invested in the call loan market. Country and reserve-city banks also utilized interbank deposits for portfolio management: that is, they also directly participated in the call loan market to manage the most liquid part of their assets. When call loan rates rose above the standard 2 percent interest paid on interbank deposits, country banks would directly invest in the call loan market, draining interbank deposits from New York City national banks (Bordo and Wheelock 2011).

The relationship between the call loan market and the inverted pyramid structure of reserves was fragile, however. Withdrawals from noncentral reserve-city banks happened regularly, and if they were of sufficient magnitude, it could put pressure on call loan rates to rise and stock prices to fall, triggering panic selling of assets and inducing a financial panic that could reach well beyond New York City.[3] Indeed, all of the major panics of that era were marked by withdrawals of funds by the country and reserve-city banks from New York City (Bordo and Wheelock 2011). Even though the national banking system's reserve requirements created a large potential pool of reserves that could be used at the time of such a crisis, there was no central coordinating mechanism to deploy them. Rather, individual banks, wary of being run, tended to hoard them and feared paying penalties if they fell below the legal requirement. As a consequence, the national banking systems reserves, though large in aggregate, were effectively unavailable for meeting the demands of panicked depositors in crisis periods (Beckart 1922).

The Federal Reserve System was created in response to these and other structural flaws of the National Banking system, with the hope that a formal central bank would be better suited to act as a lender of last resort in times of panic. The authorizing legislation required that national banks and members meet their reserve requirements by carrying deposits at one of the systems reserve banks; it was thought this would reduce the concentration of correspondent balances held in reserve centers and funds invested in the call loan money market (believed to be the source of the earlier era of banking panics). Even with these institutional changes, nonmember banks, still two thirds of all commercial banks and half of all deposits in 1929, satisfied state-mandated reserve requirements using interbank deposits. Moreover, interbank deposits retained their relevance as a

---

reserve-city banks tended to hold the maximum allowable amount of reserves in the form of deposit balances in central reserve cities" (Bordo and Wheelock 2011).

[3] The standard story for explaining why country banks and reserve-city banks withdrew their interbank deposits in this era was due to the seasonal demand for money arising from planting and harvest cycles (See Calomiris and Gorton 1991). The creation of an "elastic currency" that could meet the needs of agriculture was a key principle behind the Fed's founding.

way for all commercial banks to manage their liquid portfolios and offer a broader variety of services to their clientele. Interbank deposits were therefore a key network feature of the American banking system, and a potential source for system distress in the 1930s.

DATA

To understand the reserve pyramid and its relationship to bank lending and distress, we compile information from an array of sources. We focus on the data that are germane to our analysis, discussing its pros and cons as well as how the data could be used in related future work. The principal source for information on the reserve pyramid is *Banking and Monetary Statistics of the United States, 1914 to 1941* (Board of Governors of the Federal Reserve System 1943). Part 2 contains 144 tables that present information on the balance sheets of Federal Reserve member banks aggregated by Federal Reserve District. The tables provide counts of banks in each district as well as assets (15 categories) and liabilities (17 categories) of member banks from 1914 through 1941. The volume also contains more detailed classifications of the loans, investments, and deposits of banks from 1928 through 1941. The tables report information for all banks, for banks located in reserve cities, and for banks located outside of reserve cities (called country banks). For the second and seventh Federal Reserve Districts, we calculate the balance sheets of banks in the central reserve cities of New York and Chicago by subtracting reserve and country banks from all banks. We verify the accuracy of this calculation by comparing the result to data for banks in central reserve cities reported in part 1 of *Banking and Monetary Statistics.*

Data are provided for each call date, which we present in Table 10.1. The nature of the calls deserves attention because the data-generating process determines the useful forms of statistical analysis. Calls typically occurred four times per year, with a maximum of six (in 1915) and minimum of three (in several years, including 1933). In 1933, the low number of calls leaves a large lacuna in the data at a crucial point in time – the year of the federal banking holiday. The last call of 1932 occurred on December 31, a point in time when the slump appeared to have stabilized and a month before events triggered the financial panic preceding the banking holiday. The initial call of 1933 occurred six months later, on June 30, after the collapse of the commercial banking system, the banking holiday, the Emergency Banking Act, and the restructuring of thousands of financial institutions.

The spacing of the calls raises other issues. Calls occurred on average every 96 days, but the standard deviation of that average, 35, was high. One call almost always occurred on the last business day of June. Another call almost always occurred on the last business day of December. Concerning these foreseeable calls, pundits and scholars long complained that bankers

Table 10.1. Call Dates for Federal Reserve Member Banks

Call Date			Days Since Last Call	Call Date			Days Since Last Call	Call Date			Days Since Last Call
Year	M	D		Year	M	D		Year	M	D	
1914	12	31		1923	4	3	95	1932	6	30	182
				1923	6	30	88	1932	9	30	92
1915	3	4	63	1923	9	14	76	1932	12	31	92
1915	5	1	58	1923	12	31	108				
1915	6	23	53					1933	6	30	181
1915	9	2	71	1924	3	31	91	1933	10	25	117
1915	11	10	69	1924	6	30	91	1933	12	30	66
1915	12	31	51	1924	10	10	102				
				1924	12	31	82	1934	3	5	65
1916	5	1	122					1934	6	30	117
1916	6	30	60	1925	4	6	96	1934	10	17	109
1916	9	12	74	1925	6	30	85	1934	12	31	75
1916	11	17	66	1925	9	28	90				
1916	12	27	40	1925	12	31	94	1935	3	4	63
								1935	6	29	117
1917	3	5	68	1926	4	12	102	1935	11	1	125
1917	5	1	57	1926	6	30	79	1935	12	31	60
1917	6	20	50	1926	12	31	184				
1917	12	31	194					1936	3	4	64
				1927	3	23	82	1936	6	30	118
1918	5	10	130	1927	6	30	99	1936	12	31	184
1918	6	29	50	1927	10	10	102				
1918	11	1	125	1927	12	31	82	1937	3	31	90
1918	12	31	60					1937	6	30	91
				1928	2	28	59	1937	12	31	184
1919	3	4	63	1928	6	30	123				
1919	6	30	118	1928	10	3	95	1938	3	7	66
1919	11	17	140	1928	12	31	89	1938	6	30	115
1919	12	31	44					1938	9	28	90
				1929	3	27	86	1938	12	31	94
1920	5	4	125	1929	6	29	94				
1920	6	30	57	1929	10	4	97	1939	3	29	88
1920	11	15	138	1929	12	31	88	1939	6	30	93
1920	12	29	44					1939	10	2	94
				1930	3	27	86	1939	12	30	89

Call Date			Days Since Last Call	Call Date			Days Since Last Call	Call Date			Days Since Last Call
Year	M	D		Year	M	D		Year	M	D	
1921	4	28	120	1930	6	30	95				
1921	6	30	63	1930	9	24	86	1940	3	26	87
1921	12	31	184	1930	12	31	98	1940	6	29	95
								1940	12	31	185
1922	3	10	69	1931	3	25	84				
1922	6	30	112	1931	6	30	97	1941	4	4	94
1922	12	29	182	1931	9	29	91	1941	6	30	87
				1931	12	31	93	1941	9	24	86
								1941	12	31	98

Source: Federal Reserve Board of Governors (1943).

took measures to improve the appearance of their balance sheets around those dates – a practice known as "window dressing." The data may substantiate this practice, as banks' balance sheets on these dates appear to differ in important ways from other call dates (i.e., higher holdings of cash and reserves). Calls on other dates were intentionally unpredictable, with the examiners varying them and notifying banks with short notice. These variable calls may, as intended, provide a more accurate depiction of banks financial health; because the variable calls typically occurred during the spring and fall, it may be impossible to distinguish their impact from other seasonal forces influencing financial institutions.

The long and variable spacing between calls can complicate statistical analysis. Many modern time series tests assume observations arise from stable generating processes with consistent spacing, which is not characteristic of these data. Restricting the analysis to regularly spaced calls, December and June, eliminates more than half the observations from the data set, leaving less than a dozen observations during the Great Contraction – far too few to employ time-series statistical tests based on asymptotic arguments.

Information for non–Federal Reserve member, state-chartered banks comes from *All Bank Statistics, 1896 to 1955*. This publication reports annual balance-sheet data on 14 assets categories and 11 liability categories for state-chartered (member and nonmember) banks as well as national banks aggregated at the state level. Balance sheet figures are described as coming from the call on or as close to the last business day of June. The categorization of many of the assets and liabilities match those for Federal Reserve members from *Banking and Monetary Statistics*, allowing us to integrate these sources into a panel containing information from both member and nonmember banks in each Federal Reserve district at their spring calls. We aggregate information on state-chartered banks into Federal Reserve districts by summing the data for all states that lie entirely in that Federal Reserve district and adding a portion of the data for states that lie partially in that Federal Reserve district. We apportion the data using weights calculated county by county, as counties lie entirely within single Federal Reserve districts. We employ two different county-level weighting schemes, which turn out to be roughly equivalent. One sums total deposits or total assets of the state or national banks in each county. We derive these data from the Federal Deposit Insurance Corporation data on banks in the United States, 1920 to 1936 (ICPSR Study 7). The second uses populations of counties to derive weights. These are from Park and Richardson (2012), which uses United States census of population annual state and county population estimates.

Data on bank suspensions come from several sources. From data in *Banking and Monetary Statistics*, we can calculate annual changes in the number of Federal Reserve member banks in each Federal Reserve District for the period 1914 to 1941. Although this information is consistent over the entire time period, it is a net figure – bank closings minus bank openings – and does not reveal the reasons for banks' change in status, which may have been mergers, voluntary liquidations, nationally chartered banks adopting state charters, or state-chartered banks voluntarily departing from the Federal Reserve. For the same years, we can calculate changes in the number of state-chartered banks from *All Bank Statistics*, but these figures suffer from the same problems as the data mentioned previously; moreover, the number can be calculated only from one spring call to the next.

Some of these problems are solved using data from the September 1937 issue of the *Federal Reserve Bulletin*, which reported on the results of the Board of Governors' bank suspension study. The bulletin reports bank distress by cause – temporary suspension, terminal suspension, voluntary liquidation, and merger forced by bank distress as well as other changes in bank status – for 1921 through 1936. The data are aggregated at the state level, however, and therefore need to be summed to Federal Reserve districts using the county-level weighting methodology described previously. The data are reported by month and must therefore also be aggregated by call dates. When call dates fall within months, we divide monthly failures, using the assumption that failures occurred at the same rate on all business days within the month.

The most accurate source for information about bank failures during this period is the micro-level data from the Board of Governors' bank suspension study. These are described in Richardson (2007a, 2007b, 2008). For the years 1929 through 1932, we can tabulate the micro data by call date and Federal Reserve district, creating an accurate analog for our panel of bank balance sheets by call date. We are currently pushing the micro data project back in time, and will eventually be able to include the 1920s.

The overlap in the various data series permits us to cross check the data. The comparisons are reassuring; all of the series reflect underlying patterns of bank distress, and all series spanning the same place, time, and type of bank appear highly correlated. (Correlation coefficients typically range from 0.85 to 0.95.) Correlations among series representing different districts, however, tend to be lower, which reflects the regional patterns of bank distress during the 1920s and 1930s. For example, all of the bank failure series for the Boston district are highly correlated, but none of those series are highly correlated with the series representing bank distress for the Dallas district.

Combining all these data sources provides us with a new, comprehensive panel, describing all banks in the United States, aggregated at the level of the Federal Reserve district and at each call date (for member banks) and at the June call (for state-chartered banks). We know the number of bank failures between call dates, and have accurate information about bank balance sheets, including data on who made deposits and to whom banks loaned those funds.

For our analysis, we aggregate bank asset information into three categories: (1) lending to businesses (the sum of loans, acceptances, and corporate bonds); (2) lending to the U.S. government (the sum of government securities of varying maturity); and (3) reserves (the sum of cash in the vault and deposits at Federal Reserve banks). We calculate reserves in this manner to conform to the approach used by Friedman and Schwartz, who excluded from their calculations balances at domestic banks (which counted as part of a bank's legally required reserves if deposited in a bank in a reserve or central reserve city) and balances at foreign banks. We also excluded cash items in the process of collection from banks' reserves because the slow pace of inter-city check clearing left these items simultaneously on the balance sheets of multiple banks, leading to a double counting of reserves. During periods of distress, banks found items in the process of collection generally illiquid and uncollectible (see Richardson 2007b for details).

RESULTS

Table 10.2 describes the structure of the reserve pyramid at the peak of the Roaring twenties, using data from the June 1929 call of Federal Reserve member banks and related data from nonmember commercial banks. The table focuses on member banks, whose balance sheets can be accurately aggregated into the categories of central reserve-city (either New York or Chicago), reserve-city, and country bank (i.e., operating outside a reserve or central reserve-city). Rows (a) through (e) examine deposits at member

Table 10.2. Interbank Balances, Deposits, and Reserves in June 1929

		Central Reserve City		Reserve City	Country Bank	All Member Banks
		New York	Chicago			
	Deposits					
(a)	Demand, D	5,689	1,080	6,012	5,523	18,304
(b)	Time	1,116	413	4,697	6,463	12,689
(c)	Interbank, I	1,478	355	1,494	335	3,662
(d)	Total	9,656	2,178	13,675	12,655	38,163
(e)	$I/(D + I)$	0.21	0.25	0.20	0.06	0.17
(f)	I% nonmember	0.93	0.93	0.99	1.00	0.96
	Reserves					
(g)	Primary	841	175	895	882	2,793
(h)	Secondary	1,006	159	1,607	1,383	4,155
(i)	I% Reserves	0.80	1.06	0.60	0.15	0.53

Notes: Row (e) indicates interbank deposits, I, as a share of all nongovernment demand deposits, $I + D$. Row (i) shows interbank deposits, I, as a share of aggregate reserves.
Source: Board of Governors (1943).

banks. Substantial interbank deposits existed in reserve and central reserve cities. In these locations, interbank deposits exceeded 20 percent of all demand deposits (excluding preferred government deposits). The bulk of these deposits came from nonmember banks.[4] This point deserves emphasizing, given the nature of the network we are describing. Ninety-six percent of the interbank deposits in member banks came from nonmember banks. These deposits consisted largely of correspondent balances that nonmember banks placed in reserve cities. These correspondent balances counted as a portion of the nonmembers required reserves. Federal Reserve members deposit few funds in other banks, because the Federal Reserve District banks served as their reserve depository and principal correspondent. Thus, the flows of interbank deposits that we analyze later

---

[4] Our balance sheet data enable us to determine total member and nonmember balances accurately, allowing us to ascertain that 96 percent of all interbank balances came from nonmember banks. Allocating these interbank balances across reserve and central reserve cities requires assumptions. We assume that member country banks place half of their interbank deposits in the nearest reserve city and allocate the remainder between New York and Chicago based on the proportion of interbank balances in those cities. We assume that member banks in reserve cities divide their interbank deposits between New York and Chicago based on those proportions.

in this essay consist largely of flows of funds between nonmember and member banks.

The other rows of Table 10.2 examine reserve holdings. Primary reserves consist of cash in the vault and balances at the Federal Reserve. Secondary reserves include government securities and interbank balances.[5] Interbank balances amounted to a large fraction of the reserves in central and reserve cities. At any point in time, of course, banks lacked direct access to most of these reserves, as laws required banks' to retain minimum legal reserves. The amount above these legal minimums was termed excess reserves. The Federal Reserve began calculating excess reserves for banks in 1929.[6] In June 1929, excess reserves for all banks in reserve cities amounted to a little over $12 million. Excess reserves for all country banks totaled a little over $18 million. Thus, at the end of the 1920s and on the eve of the Great Contraction, interbank balances comprised a large multiple of member banks' excess reserves. As a result, members most likely could meet unexpected declines in interbank balances only by liquidating investments or borrowing reserves from the Fed.

We first examine the trends in interbank deposits from 1920 through 1932. In Figure 10.1, we show time series plots for central reserve, reserve city, and country member banks at call report dates. The curving lines indicate kernel-weighted local polynomial smoothed values of the data. The kernel is Epanechnikov. The bandwidth is set at seven. The smoothed curve helps to illuminate trends in the data that may be difficult to perceive among seasonal and idiosyncratic movements. The first vertical line indicates the date of the stock market crash in 1929. The second vertical line indicates the date on which the closure of Caldwell and Company triggered the initial banking panic of the 1930s.

Figure 10.1 reveals several important patterns. Country banks held few interbank deposits. Those deposits changed little during the 1920s and declined during the early 1930s, although that decline may have been an acceleration of a trend that began in the mid-1920s.[7] Reserve-city banks held substantial interbank deposits. These deposits increased during the early 1920s, plateaued in the later half of the decade, rose rapidly after the stock market crash, and declined rapidly during the period of banking panics. Central reserve-city banks also held substantial interbank deposits, which continued to grow throughout the 1920s, peaked near the onset of banking panics, and on average declined thereafter.

---

[5] Note that cash items in the process of collection, which we do not report, also counted as a portion of banks' legal reserves.

[6] Note: the Fed made these calculations based on monthly averages of daily figures from a process described in Banking and Monetary Statistics (1943). Excess reserve figures do not come directly from call reports.

[7] Note that we have not conducted standard time-series structural break tests on these series owing to the nature of the data described in the third section.

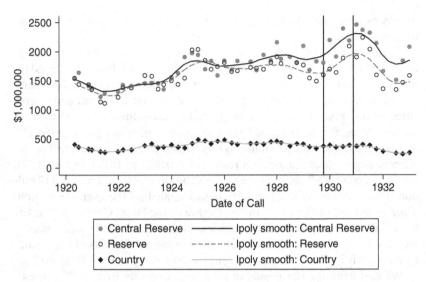

Figure 10.1. Interbank deposits, 1920–1932.

A change in the pattern of interbank deposits, which may be difficult to discern in Figure 10.1, is emphasized in Table 10.3, which describes the variability of interbank deposits. Although interbank deposits on average declined during the period of banking panics, their deposits did not decline uniformly. Instead, interbank deposits became increasingly volatile, flowing out from central reserve and reserve cities at some points in time and flowing back into those cities at other points in time. During the 1920s, inflows and outflows had alternated on a clear seasonal basis. Interbank deposits flowed in during the fourth quarter of the year. Interbank deposits flowed out during the winter quarter. Interbank deposits moved less during the spring and summer. Seasonality declined during the 1930s. Quarters that previously experienced inflows witnessed outflows, and vice versa. Something else – which we show in the text that follows to be bank distress – appears to be propelling interbank flows.

Figure 10.2 provides perspective on the patterns displayed in the preceding figure. It illustrates demand deposits (except interbank and government) aggregated at call dates using the same methods as in Figure 10.1. Demand deposits for central, reserve, and country banks track closely during the 1920s, rising from a trough during the recession in 1921 and plateauing in the later 1920s. The exception is demand deposits in central reserve cities – principally New York. They jumped dramatically as the stock market boomed in late 1928 and early 1929, when funds rushed into the bubbling equity markets, and soared once again after the stock market crash in the fall of 1929, when investors pulled from equity markets

Table 10.3. Volatility of Interbank Deposits, 1925 through 1933

	Central Reserve City		Reserve Cities	Country Banks	All Member Banks
	New York	Chicago			
Standard Deviation					
Millions of Dollars Between Calls					
1925 January	1929 October	218.3	40.9	228.8	58.9	502.1
1929 December	1932 December	250.5	67.2	293.8	97.8	645.0
Standard Deviation					
Millions of Dollars Per Day					
1925 January	1929 October	2.0	0.4	1.6	0.4	3.2
1929 December	1932 December	3.2	0.4	2.6	1.1	5.6

Source: Board of Governors 1943. See the second and fourth sections for details.

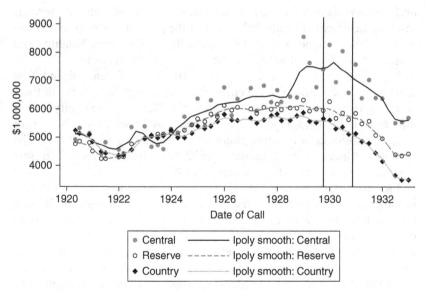

Figure 10.2. Demand deposits, 1920–1932.

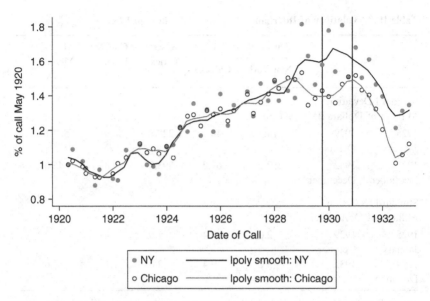

Figure 10.3. Deposits in New York and Chicago.

and dumped them in convenient depositories. Overall, demand deposits reached their zenith in early 1929, around the peak of the economic boom in the 1920s. Demand deposits fall rapidly during the 1930s. Volatility and seasonality change, but much less than for interbank deposits.

Figure 10.3 focuses on deposit flows (the sum of demand and time deposits) in the central reserve cities of Chicago and New York. In these cities, deposits grow continuously during the 1920s. As the equity bubble inflates in 1929, deposits in Chicago plateau, while deposits in New York jump. Deposits in both cities plummet after banking panics begin. The decline continues until the middle of 1932, when balances recover for several months prior to the final cataclysm in 1933.

Figure 10.4 focuses on interbank deposits. Patterns for interbank deposits differed across central reserve cities. Interbank balances in Chicago peaked in the middle of the 1920s, declined slowly until the stock market crash, rose rapidly for one year, and then crashed during the financial crises of 1930, 1931, and 1932. Relative to Chicago, interbank deposits in New York experienced more growth during the later 1930s, particularly when the stock market boomed. They appear to have been highly and increasingly volatile in the late 1920s and early 1930s.

Figures 10.5 and 10.6 illuminate the connection (or lack thereof) between flows of deposits into and out of central reserve cities and bank distress in the rest of the United States. Figure 10.5 plots the number of

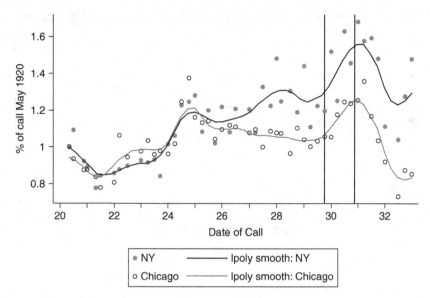

Figure 10.4. Interbank deposits in New York and Chicago.

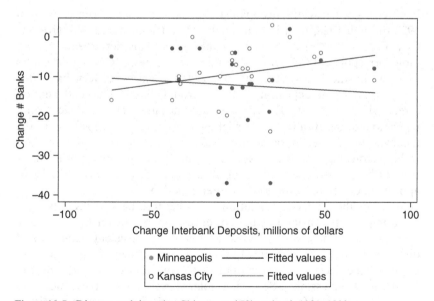

Figure 10.5. Distress and deposits, Chicago and Hinterland, 1923–1928.

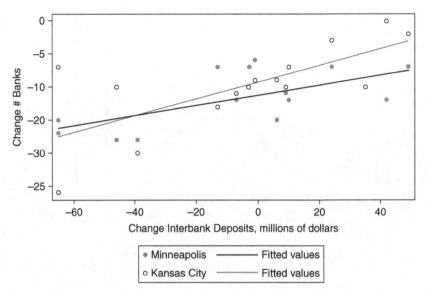

Figure 10.6. Distress and deposits, Chicago and Hinterland, 1929–1932.

bank changes between calls against interbank flows between calls from 1923 through 1928, focusing on the 9th (Minneapolis) and 10th (Kansas City) Federal Reserve districts. For banks in those districts, the most common correspondent link with a central reserve city was Chicago. It shows that, during the 1920s, little or no correlation exists between bank distress and interbank deposit flows to and from Chicago. The coefficient on a regression for the 9th District is slightly negative. The coefficient on a regression for the 10th District is slightly positive. For both coefficients, the null hypothesis that the coefficient equals zero cannot be rejected.

Numerous additional regressions for the 1920s employing other measures of bank distress yield the same result. Bank distress during the 1920s appears uncorrelated with flows of interbank deposits.

It is possible that no correlation exists because bank distress is measured imperfectly during this period, but we doubt this for three reasons. First, we ran hundreds of regressions, found no consistent patterns, and discovered almost no statistically significant coefficients (even before we corrected the decision rule for the fact that we mined the data and ran hundreds of regressions). Second, scholars have analyzed these measures of bank distress and found them to be correlated with many characteristics of bank balance sheets and with economic activity at the state and national level. So, although the measures may be imperfect, they are probably accurate enough to reveal a correlation, if it had in fact existed. Third, a logical explanation for the lack or correlation exists. During the 1920s, thousands of banks failed, but with the exception of a few instances, most of these failures appear to have been due to solvency shocks. A typical example would be a bank in a town on the Great Plains that locked into long-term local loans in the agricultural boom during World War I that failed when borrowers could not repay their loans during the agricultural doldrums of the 1920s. Insolvencies of small banks spread across space and over time seldom triggered large flows of liquid funds from financial centers. In sum, our robust (non) result appears to have a logical explanation.

Figure 10.6 illustrates that circumstances changed during the 1930s. The figure displays the relationship from 1929 through 1932 between bank distress and interbank flows using the same districts and same (admittedly imperfect) measure of bank distress. Both districts exhibit a clear correlation. Large declines in the number of banks coincide with large outflows of interbank deposits. Small declines in the number of banks coincide with inflows of funds.

Figure 10.6 thus suggests that during the banking panics in the Great Contraction, bank distress was closely correlated with interbank deposit flows. A plausible explanation for this correlation is illiquidity. As depositors of banks throughout the nation withdrew funds, those banks in turn needed to withdraw interbank balances, which were a large portion, often more than 50%, of the reserves of nonmember banks throughout the nation.

The final stage of our analysis is the link between interbank deposit flows and bank lending, particularly during the Great Contraction of the 1920s. Table 10.4 aggregates the information into three categories. The first, lending to businesses, is the sum of the loans, acceptances, and corporate securities (predominantly bonds); it corresponds to the asset side of banks' balance sheet. Lending to businesses contracted for all banks, with reserve-city banks contracting slightly more than country banks and central reserve-city banks contracting substantially more than the rest. The second category, lending to government, is the sum of all government bonds on a bank's balance sheet. Lending to government rises for all banks, with reserve cities expanding lending to government at nearly four times the rate of country banks and central reserve city banks expanding holdings of government securities at six times the rate of country banks.

While lending moves in the same direction for all banks, Table 10.4 shows that reserves, the third category, moves in different directions. (Following Friedman and Schwartz [1963], reserves are calculated as the sum of the cash in banks' vaults and the deposits at the Fed.) Reserves rise substantially in central reserve cities; increasing more than 18 percent in New York and 37 percent in Chicago from the onset of banking panics to the end of 1932. In the same period, reserves fell by 19 percent in reserve

Table 10.4. Percentage Changes in Lending and Reserves during the Great Contraction

	NY	Chicago	Reserve	Country
Peak to trough				
Lending to business	–40.6	–51.5	–33.3	–32.9
Lending to government	134.2	96.6	63.3	16.2
Reserves	31.6	66.5	–14.8	–28.2
Onset of panics to end 1932				
Lending to business	–37.3	–54.9	–31.3	–30.6
Lending to government	138.7	44.3	37.1	20.8
Reserves	18.5	37.1	–19.0	–25.4

Note: The peak of assets in commercial banks occurred in the call report immediately following the stock market crash in the fall of 1929; thus we measure peak to trough from call 10/4/1929 to call 12/31/1932. Banking panics began in November 1930, following the call in September of that year; thus we measure the onset of panics to the end of 1932 from call 9/24/1930 to call 12/31/1932.

cities and 25 percent in country banks. Note that the same patterns appear if we include in these figures interbank balances and cash items in the process of collections.

Figures 10.7 and 10.8 examine the changing composition of portfolios of banks in central reserve cities. Figure 10.7 focuses on New York. Lending to business remained relatively steady between the stock market crash (first vertical line) and the onset of banking panics (second vertical line), but fell continuously for two years following the failure of Caldwell and Company and Bank of United States. After the beginning of the banking panics, holdings of government bonds began a steady rise. Reserves slowly increased from the winter of 1932. Figure 10.8 focuses on Chicago. The break in behavior came about at the same time as, or one call date before, the onset of banking panics. After that date, lending to business fell steadily. Lending to government rose quickly, but then gradually trended back toward its old level. Reserves rose gradually over the next two years.

It is worth comparing the gradual changes on the asset side of banks' balance sheets with the volatile flows on the liability side of banks' balance sheets, particularly in central reserve cities (e.g., Figures 10.3 and 10.4). Deposits – particularly interbank deposits – flowed in and out of central reserve cities at increasing rates. Banks accommodated these flows, in part, by borrowing from the Federal Reserve and other financial institutions. This liquidity management proved to be expensive, particularly in periods of rapid deflation and when the Federal Reserve increased discount rates.

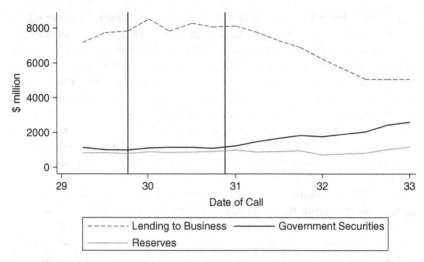

Figure 10.7. Portfolio compositions, New York, 1929–1932.

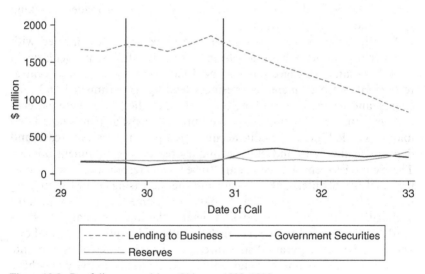

Figure 10.8. Portfolio composition, Chicago, 1929–1932.

DISCUSSION

Our investigation of network linkages across the banking system suggests several interesting findings. First, during the 1920s, bank distress in the hinterland had little or no systematic influence on the central reserve cities. No correlation existed between distress of country banks around the nation and deposit flows in and out of reserve and central reserve cities. Second, this pattern changed during the Great Depression, particularly after the banking panics began in the fall of 1930. When distress increased during banking panics, interbank deposits flowed out of reserve cities, particularly the central reserve cities of New York and Chicago. When panics ebbed and distress eased, deposits flowed back in to the cities at the top of the reserve pyramid. Third, the nature of interbank flows changed markedly. Interbank flows became increasingly volatile and the volatility ceased to be seasonal, as it had been during the 1920s; it became increasingly correlated with bank distress in the heartland of American agriculture and industry.

Plausible explanations exist for these patterns. During the 1920s, bank distress seems driven by fundamental factors, such as the boom and bust of agricultural communities on the Great Plains and changing fates of American industries propelled by technological shocks, such as electrification and internal combustion, which altered the landscape and location of manufacturing and commerce. Bank distress during the 1930s seems driven by new forces, particularly the contagion of fear spreading among depositors and liquidity shocks spreading through the correspondent banking system and the reserve pyramid.

Finally, changes in the nature of interbank deposits coincided with shifts in the allocation of assets in banks' portfolios, particularly in New York and Chicago. During the 1920s, deposit flows into central reserve cities led to increased business lending, government bond purchases, and reserves. During the contraction of the 1930s, these patterns changed. Business lending contracted precipitously, as banks liquidated loans, canceled lines of credit, accumulated primary reserves (cash and deposits at the Fed), and built secondary reserves (government bonds). These changes seem, at least in part, to be logical responses to the increasing volatility of interbank deposits and the increasing cost of managing liquidity by borrowing in a deflationary environment in which monetary authorities raised discount rates to defend the international gold standard. To understand these relationships fully will require additional evidence of the entire pyramid structure, but our initial exploration points to an intriguing channel through which real economic activity may have been affected.

REFERENCES

Allen, F., and D. Gale. (2000). "Financial Contagion." *Journal of Political Economy* 108:1–33.
Beckhart, B. H. (1922). "Outline of Banking History from the First Bank of the United States Through the Panic of 1907." *Annals of the American Academy of Political and Social Science* 99:1–16.

Board of Governors of the Federal Reserve System (U.S.). Committee on Branch, Group, and Chain Banking. (1932). *Dual Banking System in the United States.* Retrieved from http://fraser.stlouisfed.org/publication/?pid=808

Board of Governors of the Federal Reserve System (U.S.). (1943). *Banking and Monetary Statistics 1914–1941.* Washington, DC: Federal Reserve Board. Retrieved from http://fraser.stlouisfed.org/publication/?pid=38

Board of Governors of the Federal Reserve System (U.S.). (1959). *All Bank Statistics 1896–1955.* Washington, DC: Federal Reserve Board. Retrieved from http://fraser.stlouisfed.org/publication/?pid=39

Board of Governors of the Federal Reserve System (U.S.). *Federal Reserve Bulletin,* various issues.

Bordo, Michael D., and David C. Wheelock. (2011). "The Promise and Performance of the Federal Reserve as Lender of Last Resort 1914–1933." NBER Working Paper 16763. Cambridge, MA: National Bureau of Economic Research.

Calomiris, Charles, and Gary Gorton. (1991). "The Origins of Banking Panics: Models, Facts, and Bank Regulation." In R. Glen Hubbard (ed), *Financial Markets and Financial Crises,* pp. 109–174. Chicago: University of Chicago Press.

Carlson, Mark, Kris James Mitchener, and Gary Richardson. (2011). "Arresting Banking Panics: Federal Reserve Liquidity Provision and the Forgotten Panic of 1929." *Journal of Political Economy* 119(5): 889–924.

Craig, B., and G. Von Peter. (2010). "Interbank Tiering and Money Center Banks." Federal Reserve Bank of Cleveland Working Paper No. 10–14.

Federal Deposit Insurance Corporation. (2001). *Federal Deposit Insurance Corporation Data on Banks in the United States, 1920–1936.* Ann Arbor, MI: Inter-university Consortium for Political and Social Research.

Friedman, Milton, and Anna J. Schwartz. (1963). *A Monetary History of the United States, 1867–1960.* Princeton, NJ: Princeton University Press.

(1973). *The Great Contraction: 1929–1933.* Princeton, NJ: Princeton University Press.

Jalil, Andrew J. (2012). "Monetary Intervention Really Did Mitigate Banking Panics During the Great Depression: Evidence Along the Atlanta Federal Reserve District Border." Occidental College Manuscript, July 2012.

James, John. (1978). *Money and Capital Markets in Postbellum America.* Princeton, NJ: Princeton University Press.

Lester V. Chander. (1971). *America's Greatest Depression, 1929–41.* New York: Harper & Row.

Meltzer, Allan H. (2003). *A History of the Federal Reserve,* Vol. 1, *1913–1951.* Chicago: University of Chicago Press.

Myers, Margaret. (1931). *The New York Money Market: Origins and Development.* New York: Columbia University Press.

Park, Haelim, and Gary Richardson. (2012). "Retail Trade by Federal Reserve District, 1919 to 1939: A Statistical History." In Christopher Hanes and Susan Wolcott (eds), *Research in Economic History,* Vol. 28, pp. 151–231. Bingley, U.K.: Emerald Group Publishing Limited.

Richardson, Gary. (2006). "The Records of the Federal Reserve Board of Governors in the National Archives of the United States." *Financial History Review* 13(1):123–134.

(2007a). "Categories and Causes of Bank Distress during the Great Depression, 1929–1933: The Illiquidity-Insolvency Debate Revisited." *Explorations in Economic History* 44(4):586–607.

(2007b). "The Check Is in the Mail: Correspondent Clearing and the Banking Panics of the Great Depression." *Journal of Economic History* 67(3):643.

(2008). "Quarterly Data on the Categories and Causes of Bank Distress during the Great Depression," *Research in Economic History* 25:37–115.

Richardson, Gary, and William Troost. (2009). "Monetary Intervention Mitigated Banking Panics During the Great Depression: Quasi-Experimental Evidence from the Federal Reserve District Border in Mississippi, 1929 to 1933." *Journal of Political Economy*, 117(6): 1031–1073.

Sprague, O. M. W. (1910). *History of Crises Under the National Banking System.* A Report of the National Monetary Commission. U.S. Senate, 61st Congress, 3rd Session, Document 538. Washington, DC: Government Printing Office. Retrieved from https://fraser.stlouisfed.org/publication/?pid=633_

Wheelock, David. (1991). *The Strategy and Consistency of Federal Reserve Monetary Policy, 1924–1933.* Cambridge: Cambridge University Press.

Wicker, Elmus. (1996). *The Banking Panics of the Great Depression.* Cambridge: Cambridge University Press.

Ziebarth, Nicolas L. (2013). "Identifying the Effects of Bank Failures from a Natural Experiment in Mississippi during the Great Depression." *American Economic Journal: Macroeconomics* 5(1): 81–101.

11

Would Large-Scale Asset Purchases Have Helped in the 1930s?

An Investigation of the Responsiveness of Bond Yields from the 1930s to Changes in Debt Levels

John Landon-Lane

The global economic crisis of 2007–2009 has once again focused academic's and the layperson's attention to events of the 1930s. The events of the 1930s (and the 1920s that preceded it) are eerily similar to the events that unfolded during the 1990s and 2000s. Although the recent crisis was not a pure monetary event, a la Friedman and Schwartz, it did have some similarities to the events leading up to the crisis in the 1930s. The Friedman and Schwartz (1963) story is that the financial crisis was precipitated by a contagious banking panic. The recent crisis also contained a financial crisis but this crisis was centered on the shadow banking system that was not regulated by the central bank or by federal deposit insurance. The crisis started in the repo market for mortgage backed securities and moved into an investment bank crisis after the fall of Lehman Brothers in September 2008 (Gorton 2010). Eichengreen (2008) attributed the rapid rise of the shadow banking system to the repeal of the Glass–Steagall Act of 1935.

The resulting recession was not as severe as the one seen in the 1930s but it has lasted a long time – longer than would be expected for a recession caused by a financial crisis. Bordo and Haubrich (2012) attribute this to the most recent financial crisis being associated with a housing crisis. What is similar to the events of the 1930s is that short-term yields on government securities fell to essentially zero, making contemporary observers mimic Krugman (1998) in claiming that the liquidity trap was back. Conventional monetary policy – the buying and selling of short-term government debt to keep interest rates at a predetermined level – in such an environment is difficult. The Federal Reserve (Fed) embarked on three separate attempts to manipulate longer term interest rates via large-scale purchases of assets, which are referred to in the popular literature as quantitative easing (QE) even though in a speech made at the London School of Economics in 2009 Chairman Bernanke refers to it as credit easing.[1]

---

[1] http://www.federalreserve.gov/newsevents/speech/bernanke20090113a.htm

Recent research has shown that the impact of the first two rounds of quantitative easing have had different impacts on long-term yields. The first round of quantitative easing (QE I) was shown to have a larger impact than the second round. This may be due to the first round occurring during the worst of the financial crisis and thus reflecting other factors than just the impact of purchases of longer term debt. It could also be that the first round was novel and by the second round market participants became more skeptical. Research on the impact of QE II and similar programs in the U.S. history, such as Operation Twist in the early 1960s, and similar programs in the United Kingdom and Japan has shown small impacts on longer term interest rates. The impacts, although statistically significant, are small and it is not clear that the effects are economically significant.

The question that this chapter investigates is whether there was room for similar quantitative easing policies in the 1930s and what the magnitude of bond purchases of similar size to QE I and QE II would have been on longer term interest rates for this period. Basile, Landon-Lane, and Rockoff (2011) look at the impact of M2 on longer term interest rates for the 1930s and find that monetary policy did have some traction during this period, at least for the longer maturity interest rates. Basile et al. (2011) show that monetary policy could have had some impact on long-term treasury yields as well as corporate bonds of varying quality. This leads to the question of whether quantitative easing policies could have worked during the 1930s and, if used, whether the impact on interest rates have been large enough to have a significant economic impact on the economy. This chapter aims to do just that by looking at the impact of observed net changes in outstanding debt during the 1930s on various interest rates. An event analysis is performed for periods in which the net change in the amount of outstanding debt is greater than 5 percent of existing outstanding debt and a comparison is drawn to the literature on the effectiveness of quantitative easing for the current period.

The outline of the chapter is as follows. The first section reviews the literature on the effectiveness of various historical and current episodes of quantitative easing. The second section discusses the background and monetary conditions facing the US during the 1930s. The third section introduces the data used in the analysis and describes the empirical strategy employed, the fourth section describes the results, and the fifth section concludes the chapter.

THE IMPACT OF LARGE-SCALE ASSET PURCHASES ON LONG-TERM YIELDS

There is a growing literature on the impacts that the various long-term asset purchase programs had on interest rates, both sovereign and corporate. Meaning and Zhu (2011) review and extend this literature on the effect of purchases of long term assets in the United States (QE I and QE II) and in the UK (asset purchase facility 1 [APF 1] and APF 2). Swanson (2011) looks at another example of manipulation of long-term interest rates – "Operation Twist" from 1961. The results reported in these and other studies show that the impacts on long-term yields were higher in QE I than in QE II and that the results from Swanson (2011) show that the impacts of large purchases of long-term securities on yields were on the small side and were consistent with what other authors found for QE II. Of course there are a number of channels by which the impacts of these asset programs can be measured and the impacts can vary depending on what rates one looks at (Krishnamurthy and Vissing-Jorgenson (2011).

Meaning and Zhu (2011) report impacts using two methodologies: (1) an event study analysis looking at the impact of the announcements and (2) the methodology of D'Amico and King (2010) to measure the impact of actual purchases on yields. The results found in the literature are summarized in the sections that follow.

U.S. Quantitative Easing from November 2008 to March 2009 (QE I)

QE I started off in November of 2008 with an announcement that the Fed would purchase $600 billion of mortgage-backed securities (MBS) and other agency debt. In addition, a further $850 billion of securities and $300 billion of long-term U.S. securities was announced so that the total amount purchased was $1.75 trillion. This amount was 14.5 percent of the total outstanding securities in the market (Meaning and Zhu 2011).

Gagnon et al. (2011), using a high-frequency event study approach, estimate that QE I lowered long-term Treasury yields by 92 basis points. Using monthly data they found the impact to be 52 basis points. The analysis of Gagnon et al. (2011) was repeated by Meaning and Zhu (2011). They found similar results in that five- to ten-year bonds were affected the most. Meaning and Zhu (2011) also find the impact of QE I did not stop at sovereign bonds with the impact of the announcements having significant impacts of the yields of BBB rated bonds – the drop was about 62 basis points. Looking at actual purchases rather than announcements and using the methodology of D'Amico and King (2010), Meaning and Zhu (2011) find that yields dropped between 30 and 50 basis points.

U.K. Quantitative Easing from January 2009 to November 2009 (AFP I)

In January 2009 the Bank of England opened the asset purchase facility (APF) whereby the Bank of England bought high-quality assets, gilts. Starting in January and ending in November the Bank committed to buying £200 billion. This was about 29 percent of the outstanding debt in the market (Meaning and Zhu 2011). The impact of the Bank of England announcements had large impacts on yields across the spectrum. Yields for government securities dropped between 36 to 55 basis points with the larger drops being for the longer maturities. Actual purchases were estimated to have lowered yields for medium-term securities by about 27 basis points and up to more than over 70 basis points for longer term securities. Again the impact was felt across the range of securities with U.K. BBB rated securities falling 55 basis points in one day after announcements. Both QE I and AFP I had significant and far-reaching affects.

U.S. Quantitative Easing from November 2010 to Mid-2011 (QE II)

Starting in November of 2011 the Fed announced the start of another round of quantitative easing (QE II). It announced that it would purchase $600 billion of longer term Treasuries until the end of the second quarter of 2011. This amounted to 7% of outstanding debt (Swanson 2011, table 1). Meaning and Zhu (2011) find the initial impact of the announcement of QE II to be much lower than in QE I. They attribute this somewhat to the novelty of QE wearing off. Using actual purchases rather than announcements Meaning and Zhu (2011) find that QE II impacted yields by about 20 basis points on average, with some longer term assets lowering yields by 100 basis points.

The impact of actual asset purchases for QE II are smaller than for QE I but when one controls for the size of the program the two impacts are closer but still QE II had lesser impacts.

U.S. Operation Twist, 1961

Swanson (2011) looks at the impact of the Kennedy Administration's attempt to lower long-term rates while keeping short-term rates unchanged – Operation Twist. During this period the Fed bought about $8.8 billion of longer term bonds and sold about $7.4 billion of shorter term bonds. The purchase of long-term bonds amounted to about 4.5 percent of outstanding long-term debt. The impact of the announcements was analyzed using a high-frequency event analysis. Swanson (2011) does not find that the impact of Operation Twist is large, finding that the sum of the impacts on yields amounts to only 15 basis points. This impact was statistically significant but not likely to be economically significant (Swanson 2011).

The results of the analyses of the more recent attempts to manipulate yields on long-term debt are somewhat mixed. The biggest impacts are for the first round of quantitative easing in both the United States and United Kingdom. The impact of the second round of U.S. easing is somewhat lower so that the large impact initially might be due to its relative novelty. The results suggest, though, that quantitative easing can impact yields of securities with maturities over 10 years and the impact can extend to corporate bonds as well. This suggests that this tool might have been useful to the Fed during the middle to late 1930s when short-term interest rates were close to 0 and trading in short-term commercial paper had all but dried up. The next section explores the background of the behavior of interest rates during the 1930s and discusses whether monetary policy might have been useful in manipulating medium- to long-term yields.

INTEREST RATES IN THE 1930S

As the Federal Funds Rate fell to near zero during the recent financial crisis there was a reemergence of the debate of whether the U.S. economy fell into a liquidity trap during the latter part of the 1930s. Basile et al. (2011) discusses the literature at length and looks at whether there were interest rates that the Fed could have used for policy purposes. One side of the debate argues that an economy faces a liquidity trap as short-term interest rates fall close to 0. In this case, according to Keynes (1936), the demand for money could become (almost) perfectly elastic as a result of speculators in the bond market. Any attempt by a monetary authority to influence interest rates by buying or selling bonds would be offset by speculators. Thus interest rates would become difficult to manipulate from a policy perspective. This argument worked in theory for any rate but was much more likely as the interest rate approached 0. In such a case monetary policy would become powerless to manipulate interest rates and thus would be ineffective in stimulating investment and growth in the economy.

It is indeed correct that short-term interest rates during the 1930s fell to close to 0 and appear to be unresponsive. Figure 11.1 reports the yield on U.S. Treasury bills from 1929 to the end of 1941. By the end of 1933 the yield had fallen below 1 percent and remained there for the rest of the 1930s. In fact, except for the period during 1937 the yield on Treasury bills stayed below 30 basis points, with most of the time below 10 basis points until the end of 1941. Figure 11.2 shows the amount of Treasury bills outstanding during this period. It is clear that between 1934 and 1937 there was net additions to the stock of Treasury bills but, except for the period at the end of 1936, the yield on the Treasury bill was pretty much unresponsive. After 1937 the stock of outstanding Treasury bills remained pretty constant, which could be the reason why the yield remained constant through to the end of the 1940s.

We will return to analyzing this behavior of Treasury bill yield in the next section but it is not clear whether selling or purchasing short-term Treasury bills would have any action during this period, as the rise of the interest rate during 1936 and its subsequent fall in 1937 does not line up well with the increase in outstanding debt or its subsequent fall. The yield started to fall in October of 1937 whereas the retiring of Treasury bills did not occur until December of 1937.

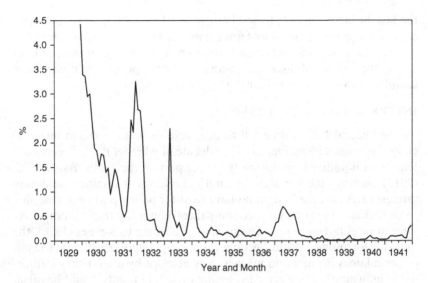

Figure 11.1. Yield on U.S. Treasury bills during the 1930s.

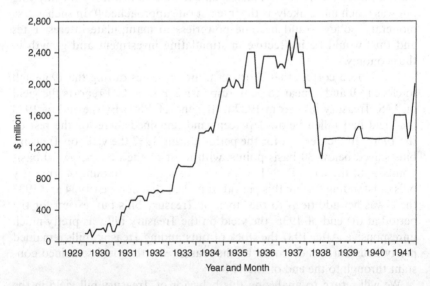

Figure 11.2. Outstanding U.S. Treasury bills during the 1930s.

Of course other important events were occurring during this period (1936–1937) with the Fed's decision to double reserve requirements. Orphanides (2004) stresses this decision and its impact on interest rates. Given the response of short-term government yields during 1936–1937

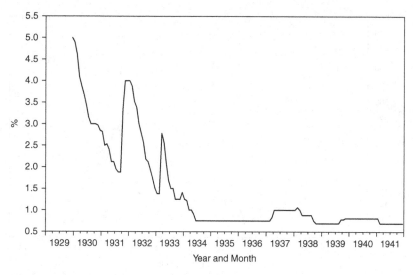

Figure 11.3. Yield on short-term commercial paper during the 1930s.

it is not clear that monetary policy was completely helpless to manipulate short-term interest rates during this period. Of course the actual impact on yields was small in magnitude – only about 10 basis points in total – so monetary policy probably would not have been able to stimulate enough investment to have a significant economic effect on the economy.

Short-term government debt was not the only short-term debt that was affected during this period. Figure 11.3 shows the yield on high-quality commercial paper during the 1930s. Just as in the case for short-term government securities the yield for commercial paper fell precipitously during the first part of the 1930s. After the middle of 1934 the yield pretty much remained unchanged and never rose above 10 basis points the rest of the time. Figure 11.4 shows the amount of commercial paper outstanding during this time. The market for commercial paper fell off in the early 1930s, dropping from a peak of $541 million in May of 1930 to a low of $60 million in May of 1933. The market never fully recovered after 1933 and so it is not clear whether the yields for commercial paper were unresponsive to changes in supply and demand of debt or just that the market became thin and never recovered.

Many authors have question whether the United States was in a liquidity trap during this period. Brunner and Meltzer (1968), Friedman and Schwartz (1963), and even Keynes himself (Keynes(1936)) argue that one needs to look at the full spectrum of interest rates and not just short-term interest rates before determining whether the economy was in a liquidity

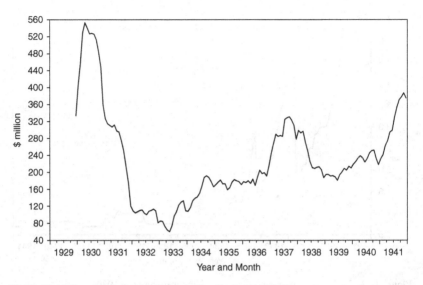

Figure 11.4. Commercial paper outstanding during the 1930s.

trap. Basile et al. (2011) show, using a simple vector autoregression (VAR) that contains a measure of the real economy, M2, and yields on various medium- and long-term securities (including both government securities and corporate bonds of varying quality), that changes in money supply did have significant impacts on medium- and long-term interest rates. The conclusions of Basile et al. (2011) were that as you move away from short-term bonds on the liquidity spectrum there are interest rates that appear to have been sensitive to monetary policy.

Figure 11.5 show the yields on a number of longer term bonds during the 1930s. Reported are the yields on medium-term Treasury notes (three- to five-year maturity), long-term Treasury bonds (10+ year maturity), AAA rated corporate debt, BAA rated corporate debt, and low-quality (Junk) rated corporate debt. The figure shows that yields were certainly responsive during the 1930s, with only the medium-term U.S. Treasury note series dropping below the 1 percent threshold after March 1938. Figure 11.6 depicts the yields for the higher quality bonds: the AAA rated corporate bonds and the two government bond series. All series show a decline in yields over the period but the yields of the long-term government security and the AAA rated corporate bond stayed pretty much above 2 percent for the whole period.

The period for which the short-term interest rates reached and stayed close to 0 covers the period from 1934 to 1940. During this period the Fed was fairly passive in its open market operations. Meltzer (2003) characterizes the Fed's actions during this period under the heading "Delay and

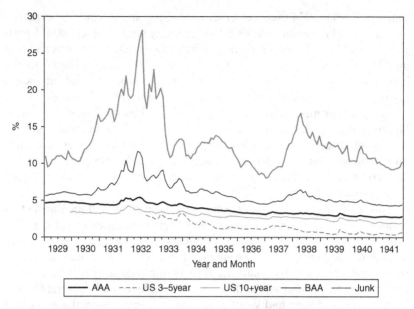

Figure 11.5. Yields on medium- to long-term bonds during the 1930s.

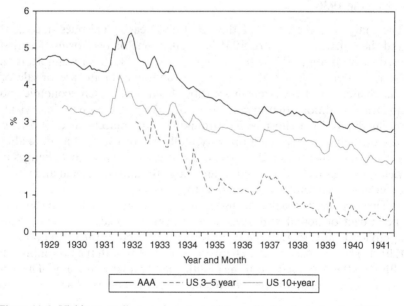

Figure 11.6. Yields on medium- to long-term high-quality bonds during the 1930s.

Inaction." After 1934 excess reserves were rising and it would be expected that this would pressure banks into expanding credit, which would push yields even lower. However, there was little evidence that this was happening. The Federal Open Market Committee (FOMC), in a memo to the board, suggested that it could use open market sales to soak up excess reserves but this approach was rejected by the FOMC on economic and political grounds (Meltzer 2003, p. 493). Thus the Fed did nothing. Discount rates at the member banks were low, around 1.5 percent, and the volume of discounts were below $10 million. Even lower were the rates on commercial paper and banker's acceptances. The discount rates were kept constant until 1937. The volume of discounts remained unchanged throughout the decade.

This leads to the question of what the Fed could have done during this period. The purchasing or selling of short-term securities would not have been helpful if, as Keynes argued, the presence of speculators in the bond market would "crowd-out" the intended impact of open market operations. Instead, could they have tried to manipulate longer term interest rates, and if they could would they have been able to move interest rates in a way that could have had significant economic impacts on the economy? The next section attempts to do just that.

Analyzing the Impact of Net Sales of Debt on Yields during the 1930s

The analysis of the effects of the quantitative easing episodes since 2007 and the Operation Twist of 1961 have taken one of two forms. The first used by Swanson (2011) and Meaning and Zhu (2011), for example, is an event analysis. To isolate the impact of an announced purchase, or sale, of a large amount of government securities from other macroeconomic and financial conditions that happen to be occurring at the same time, yields are analyzed for a short period around the announcement date. In the case of high-frequency data this is typically one or two trading days after the announcement date. It is therefore implicitly assumed that changes in yields during this "short" window are due to the announcement and not to other macroeconomic or financial factors.

The second approach is to use instrumental variables (IV) to estimate the impact of actual purchases, or sales, on the yield of an asset. This approach is used in D'Amico and King (2010) and in Meaning and Zhu (2011). The approach of this chapter is more in line with the first approach although the data used are at the monthly level rather than daily.[2] The second difference is that there are no announcements of purchases to use to

---

[2] Data on yields is available at a weekly frequency but data on debt outstanding are available only at a monthly frequency.

perform the event analysis so the procedure is to look for periods where there were large purchases or sales of bonds and use these dates as the basis of the event study.

For the purposes of this analysis a large transaction is a net change in outstanding debt that is more than 5 percent of the existing stock of outstanding debt. To distinguish from a large net change over a short period (i.e., a shock) and a large net change over a longer period I look at changes in which the average monthly net change is greater than 5 percent. This way I can isolate the impacts of large sudden net changes to the stock of debt outstanding.

DATA

Data on interest rates (yields) were obtained from the Federal Reserve's banking and monetary statistics published in 1943.[3] Short-term government securities before 1930 are represented by the average yield on three- to six-month Treasury notes and certificates. After 1930 the series was discontinued because the yields were always negative. After 1929 short-term rates are the yields on short-term Treasury bills that were sold on a discounted basis. Treasury bills were offered with varying maturities up to nine months but were mostly three-month bills. Initially, offerings of Treasury bills were infrequent and only after 1931 did the offerings of Treasury bills become regular. Also obtained from *Banking and Monetary Statistics* were data on the yields of commercial paper and banker's acceptances.

Medium-term interest rates are the yields on three- to five-year tax-exempt Treasury notes and long-term interest rates are the yield on U.S. government bonds that are due or callable after twelve years. Interest rates on corporate debt are the bond yields on AAA and BAA debt and can be found in *Historical Statistics* (2006, series Cb58 and Cb59). The data on junk bond yields were created by Basile et al. (2011). Junk bonds are defined as bonds that were rated B or lower by Moody's.

Data for total debt outstanding were obtained from *Banking and Monetary Statistics* (Section 12) for commercial paper, and banker's acceptances and data on total debt outstanding for Treasury bills, notes, and bonds were obtained from the *Monthly Statement of the Public Debt (MSPD)*. Data for the years 1929 to 1941 were obtained from the Treasury direct website.[4] Figure 11.7 reports the total amount of debt outstanding during the 1930s. As can be seen, short-term debt was a small proportion of total debt during this period. Long-term debt played a more important role after 1934, with the proportion of total debt being made up by long-term

---

[3] *Banking and Monetary Statistics: 1914–1941*, U.S. Federal Reserve System, Board of Governors, September, 1943.

[4] http://www.treasurydirect.gov/govt/reports/pd/mspd/mspd.htm

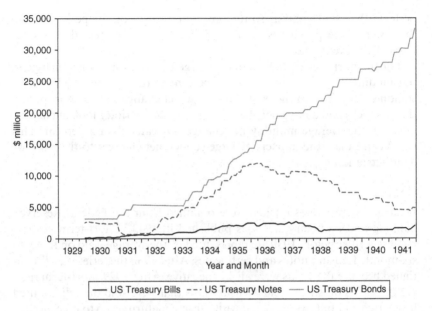

Figure 11.7. Total U.S. government debt outstanding during the 1930s.

debt increasing significantly after the start of 1936. Medium-term debt played an important role until 1936 but after 1936 it declined.[5]

EMPIRICAL RESULTS

The empirical strategy employed is to first look for correlations in the data. Endogeneity issues play an important role here and we do not have enough data to distinguish between supply and demand effects on the price (and hence yield) of the securities or to control for exogenous macroeconomic and financial factors affecting the relationship between the amount of debt outstanding for a security and its yield. In Figure 11.7 we see that the amount of outstanding long-term debt increased over time. Figure 11.6 shows that over time yields on long-term debt fell, suggesting that over the long run demand facts played an important role.

For medium-term and short-term debt yields fell over the whole period but total outstanding debt for both the medium-term and short-term securities did not monotonically increase. Thus there are other factors at play than just increasing (or decreasing) demand for a security. During the latter part of the 1930s the amount of outstanding medium term debt fell but yields continued to fall, on average. This suggests, ignoring other factors, that supply shocks dominated here in the aggregate.

---

[5] Note that this graph depicts total outstanding debt and not debt holding by the Fed.

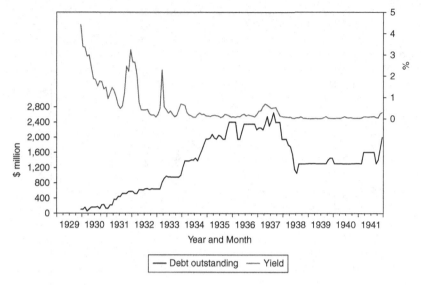

Figure 11.8. Treasury bill data.

However, this doesn't illuminate what would have happened if the Fed had have wanted to purchase securities. To do this a "pseudo" event analysis is performed.[6] During the period that is identified – where outstanding debt changes by at least 5 percent – the change in the yield is calculated starting at the first month of the window and ending two months after the window closed. During this window I calculate the largest change in yield during this time.

Treasury Bills

Figure 11.8 depicts the yield and the total outstanding debt for short-term Treasury bills. Looking at the relationship between the outstanding debt series and the yield it is clear that after 1934 there is little relationship between changes in outstanding debt and yield. This is reinforced by the scatterplot between the one period change in outstanding debt and the one period change in the yield (Figure 11.9). Almost all of the observations are clustered around the *x*-axis, suggesting that net changes to the level of outstanding debt had little impact on the yield for short-term treasury debt during the 1930s.

It is also clear from inspecting the outstanding debt series that there were some periods in which large net changes in outstanding debt occurred.

---

[6] By "pseudo" I refer to the fact that I am identifying certain periods and only looking at the relationship between outstanding debt and yields for that particular window.

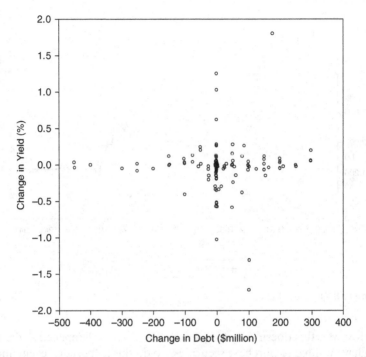

Figure 11.9. Relationship between change in debt and change in yield, Treasury bills.

Table 11.1 reports the dates of these events and the subsequent change in yield associated with these dates. It is clear that, except for the first period in early 1933, the impact of large net changes in the amount of Treasury bills outstanding is low. The elasticities are almost always below 1 in absolute value. All but one of the elasticities are negative, suggesting that the demand side is driving these changes. These results are consistent with the notion that short-term rates were unresponsive to monetary policy during this period.

Medium-Term Treasury Notes

The next set of securities that were investigated was U.S. Treasury notes that had maturities between three and five years (Figure 11.10). Until the end of 1935 the amount of outstanding medium-term debt rose and this coincided, for the most part, with declining yields. However after 1935 the amount of outstanding medium-term debt declined. Again, for the most part yields after 1935 continued to decline.

Figure 11.11 reports the scatterplot between the change in outstanding debt and change in yield. Compared to the same scatterplot for short-term debt there is clearly more responsiveness of yields to changes

Table 11.1. Impact of Large Changes in Debt on Yield: Treasury Bill

Date	Change in Debt ($million)	% Change in Debt	Change in Yield (basis points)	Elasticity
Feb 33–May 33	338.16	52.78	−202.2	−3.83
Nov 33–Feb 34	427.18	44.89	−42.5	−0.95
Aug 34–Dec 34	700.02	50.77	−12.5	−0.25
Sept 35–Nov 35	452.06	23.16	−12.5	−0.54
Feb 36–Mar 36	−452.05	−18.80	10.1	−0.54
Aug 37–Jul 38	−1599.40	−60.29	−43.4	0.72

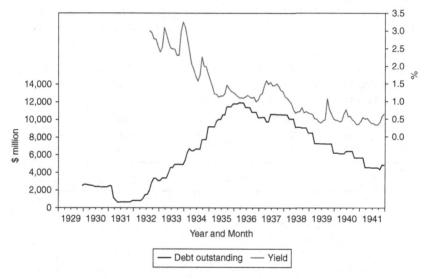

Figure 11.10. Treasury note (3- to 5-year) data.

in outstanding debt suggesting that medium-term securities were not as affected by a liquidity trap as short-term debt. Although the scatterplot is not as concentrated around the *x*-axis as was the case for short-term debt, there is no clear relationship that jumps out at someone from looking at the scatterplot.

Table 11.2 reports the relationship between yield and changes in debt for the identified periods where the amount of outstanding debt changed significantly. In contrast to the results for the short-term debt there are instances where changes in debt levels did have a large impact on medium-term yields. The impacts were not consistent in that one window there might be large impact while in another window close by there was

Table 11.2. **Impact of Large Changes in Debt on Yield: Treasury Notes (3- to 5-year maturity)**

Date	Change in Debt ($million)	% Change in Debt	Change in Yield (basis points)	Elasticity
Apr 32–Oct 32	2,518.2	316.25	–60.00	–0.19
Apr 33–Aug 33	1,550.2	46.25	–78.00	–1.69
Dec 33–Mar 34	1,805.6	37.00	–133.00	–3.59
Aug 34 Dec 34	2,562.3	38.68	–84.00	–2.17
Mar 35–May 35	863.19	9.41	–9.00	–0.96
Aug 35–Sept 35	940.23	8.93	–17.00	–1.90
May 36–Jun 36	–528.88	–4.44	8.00	–1.80
Aug 36–Sept 36	–514.06	–4.52	3.00	–0.66
Nov 36–Dec 36	–619.98	–5.71	23.00	–4.02
Mar 37–Apr 37	–502.36	–4.89	15.00	–3.06
May 37–Jun 37	852.90	8.74	–10.00	–1.14
May 38–Jun 38	–928.96	–9.22	4.00	–0.43
Feb 39–Mar 39	–1,226.80	–14.44	–9.00	0.62
Nov 39–Dec 39	–1,029.00	–14.22	–18.00	1.27
Sept 40–Oct 40	–724.68	–11.35	1.00	–0.09
Feb 41–Mar 41	–1,091.40	–19.33	2.00	–0.10

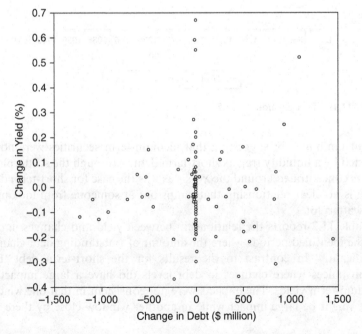

Figure 11.11. Relationship between change in debt and change in yield, Treasury notes.

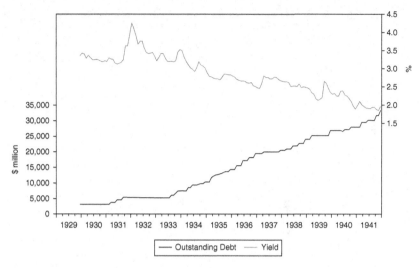

Figure 11.12. Treasury bond (8+-year) data.

not a large impact. Almost half (7/16) of the cases the elasticity is greater in absolute value than 1.5.

Long-Term U.S. Government Bonds

The final category that is looked at is the long-term U.S. bond. Figure 11.12 shows the data. As noted earlier, the big picture is one of declining yields as the level of outstanding debt rose, which is consistent with increasing demand for long-term debt. The scatterplot between changes in debt and changes in yield show this negative pattern as well (Figure 11.13). Again it looks like long-term yields would be responsive to large-scale asset purchases. Table 11.3 reports the impacts on yields for large changes in long-term debt. Here there is a consistent impact of net changes in debt on yield. After early 1934 the elasticity for each of the events is fairly consistent, ranging from –0.48 to –2.28. The average elasticity over this period from 1934 to 1941 is –1.336. Thus the impact of large changes of debt on long-term yields is quite small. A 5 percent change in the debt position would lead to only a 6.7 basis point change in the yield.

To compare this to the results found for the recent episodes we should compare this result to the results based on actual purchases reported by Meaning and Zhu (2011). The results reported here are based on actual changes in debt holdings, so our comparison should be to similar results. Table 11.4 compares the results. This table reports the average results from Table 11.3 for the 1930s and compares them to the results reported above.[7]

---

[7] The reported elasticity is the average elasticity and not the elasticity of the average change in debt and change in yield. That number would be –1.11.

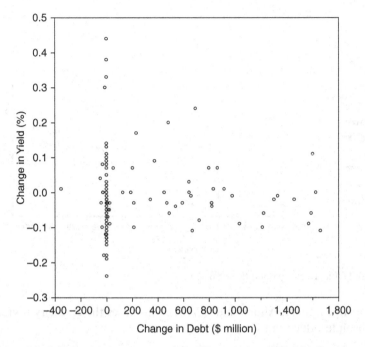

Figure 11.13. Relationship between change in debt and change in yield, Treasury bonds.

The results reported in Table 11.3 are at the low end of the elasticities computed for the large-scale asset purchases that were undertaken after 2008 but are consistent with the elasticity reported for the U.K. AFP program. Could the Fed have undertaken such a program in the 1930s? According to the results presented in Table 11.3 the answer is yes. Long-term government security yields do appear to be responsive to changes in debt positions. The elasticities are small but not that different from what has been calculated for the recent episodes. What the results suggest is that to lower long-term yields by 20 basis points the scale of the asset purchase would need to be of the same size as what we saw in QE I.

Impacts on Corporate Bonds

In Basile et al. (2011) there is a discussion on whether the reaction of interest rates during the 1930s followed Temin's "pebble-in-the-pond" pattern or followed a "tsunami-in-the-sea" pattern.[8] That is, where would you expect to see

---

[8] In the "pebble-in-the-pond" story the ripples of a monetary injection die off the further away from the epicenter you go while in the "tsunami-in-the-sea" story the ripples get bigger the further away from the epicenter.

Table 11.3. Impact of Large Changes in Debt on Yield: Treasury Bonds (12+ year maturity)

Date	Change in Debt ($million)	% Change in Debt	Change in Yield (basis points)	Elasticity
Feb 31–Mar 31	593.81	18.92	–3.00	–0.15
May 31–Jun 31	821.40	22.01	–3.00	–0.13
Aug 31–Sept 31	800.40	17.58	7.00	0.39
Jul 33–Nov 33	2,175.2	41.70	2.00	0.05
Mar 34–Jun 34	1,886.2	25.32	–22.00	–0.87
Nov 34–Dec 34	490.93	5.01	–6.00	–1.20
Feb 35–Mar 35	1,458.9	14.19	–7.00	–0.49
Feb 36–Mar 37	1,223.5	8.54	–11.00	–1.29
May 36 –Jun 36	1,626.7	10.46	–5.00	–0.48
Aug 36 –Sept 36	981.47	5.72	–8.00	–1.40
Nov 36–Dec 36	1,302.7	7.18	–16.00	–2.23
Nov 38–Dec 38	1,332.2	5.87	–6.00	–1.02
Feb 39–Mar 39	1,213.6	5.06	–10.00	–1.98
Nov 39–Dec 39	1,662.4	6.59	–11.00	–1.67
Feb 41–Mar 41	1,571.7	5.62	–9.00	–1.60

Table 11.4. Comparison of Elasticities across Episodes

Episode	% Change in Debt	Change in Yield (basis points)	Elasticity	Source
QE I	14.5	–40	–2.76	Meaning and Zhu (2011)
QE II	7	–20	–2.85	Meaning and Zhu (2011)
AFP I	29	–27	–0.93	Meaning and Zhu (2011)
Operation Twist	4.5	–15	–3.33	Swanson (2011)
1930s	9.1	–10	–1.34	Author's calculations

the impact of monetary policy? Following the "pebble-in-the-pond" pattern you would expect to see the biggest impact on interest rates closest in attribute to long-run government debt. If the "tsunami-in-the-sea" pattern is evident we would expect that purchases of long-term government debt would have impacts a "long way" from the long-term debt market.

To investigate whether manipulating long-term government securities has any impact on corporate bonds the same table as Table 11.3 is calculated for each of the corporate bond classes: AAA, BAA, and Junk.

Table 11.5. Elasticities of Large Changes in Long-Term Debt on Corporate Yields

Date	U.S. Treasury Bond	AAA	BAA	Junk
Feb 31–Mar 31	–0.15	–0.21	0.32	2.06
May 31–Jun 31	–0.13	–0.05	0.95	–0.55
Aug 31–Sept 31	0.39	0.85	3.41	12.74
Jul 33–Nov 33	0.05	0.43	3.26	3.24
Mar 34–Jun 34	0.87	–0.79	–0.79	–1.94
Nov 34–Dec 34	–1.2	–1.00	–2.79	–2.40
Feb 35–Mar 35	–0.49	–0.14	1.76	3.95
Feb 36–Mar 37	–1.29	–0.35	0.70	4.68
May 36 –Jun 36	–0.48	–0.38	–0.38	–1.91
Aug 36 –Sept 36	–1.4	–0.52	–1.40	–7.17
Nov 36–Dec 36	–2.23	–0.70	–0.28	–1.95
Nov 38–Dec 38	–1.02	–0.34	0.68	19.08
Feb 39–Mar 39	–1.98	–0.20	–3.16	–6.72
Nov 39–Dec 39	–1.67	–0.91	1.06	10.02
Feb 41–Mar 41	–1.6	0.36	–0.18	–2.14

That is for each identified period in Table 11.3 the change in yield for each corporate bond is calculated and the elasticity is calculated. These elasticities are reported in Table 11.5 and the data are depicted in Figure 11.14. Evidence in favor of the "pebble-in-the-pond" story would be that movements in long-term government bond interest rates would coincide with higher impact in high-quality corporate debt markets and relatively smaller impacts in lower quality corporate debt markets. The alternative "tsunami-in-the-sea" story would have movements in long-term government debt yields having little impact on high-quality corporate debt and bigger impacts on lower quality debt yields.

The results are more in favor of the second "tsunami" story in that the impacts of changes in long-term government debt interest rates are greater the further away the asset is on the quality spectrum. The slope coefficient estimate for the change in long-term government debt in a simple linear regression that regresses changes in corporate debt on changes in long-term government yields is 0.37** for AAA rated debt, 1.56** for BAA rated corporate debt, and 3.07* for Junk rated corporate debt.[9] The impact of changes in long-term government yields on corporate yields does appear to

---

[9] Here ** means significant at the 5 percent level and * means significant at the 10 percent level.

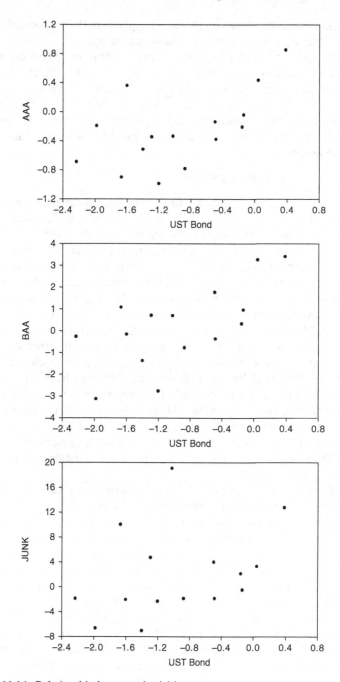

Figure 11.14. Relationship between elasticities.

be stronger the further away on the quality spectrum the corporate bond is situated. This is consistent with the "tsunami" story.

It does appear that shocks to long-term bonds in the 1930s do propagate through to corporate bond yields, with the biggest effect occurring at the low end of the quality scale. This is consistent with the results of Basile et al. (2011), who reported that changes in M2 had bigger effects on low-quality corporate bonds than on high-quality corporate bonds, and the results reported in Meaning and Zhu (2011) for the recent large asset purchase programs.

CONCLUSION AND DISCUSSION

The 1930s was a period in which a financial crisis precipitated a big recession and at the same time short-term interest rates fell to a few basis points above 0. The short-term interest rate stayed there for most of the latter part of the 1930s. There is a large debate as to whether the United States was in a liquidity trap but there is less debate in the literature that manipulating short-term interest rates would have helped stimulate the economy. There is some evidence that interest rates at the long end of the spectrum were sensitive to monetary policy. It was shown in Basile et al. (2011) that changes in M2 did have significant impacts on long-term government securities and corporate securities of varying quality. Given this then it is interesting to ask how effective nonstandard monetary policy would have been if it was used in the 1930s. In particular, could the Fed have had manipulated interest rates at the longer end of the spectrum and if so, how large of an asset purchase program would have been needed to stimulate the economy by enough to have a significant economic impact? Also, if there is evidence that large-scale asset purchases would have been effective the late 1930s what does this evidence suggest about the efficacy of similar programs we see today?

In this chapter data on yields for a wide variety of securities were collected. Interest rate data for short-term U.S. Treasury bills, medium-term Treasury notes, and longer-term Treasury bonds were collected as well as short-term corporate securities such as commercial paper and long-term corporate securities such as long term AAA-rated bonds, BAA-rated bonds, and Junk-rated bonds. Data on the total value of outstanding bonds for each of the Treasury bonds and the short-term corporate bonds were collected from the Treasury's Monthly Statement of Public Debt.

Using these data on the value of outstanding debt, a number of stylized facts emerge. Over the course of the 1930s there was a move away from short-term government securities toward long-term securities – a situation that is mimicked today on the balance sheet of the Fed. Moreover, there are a number of episodes for each of the three types of Treasury securities where there were large net changes in the value of the outstanding debt.

The approach used in this chapter is to use these periods as proxies for large-scale asset purchases by the Fed. The rule that was used was that the net change in the value of outstanding debt had to average 5 percent per month for a period to be considered as a proxy. This number was chosen to try to mimic the size of the quantitative easing that occurred as a response to the global financial crisis of 2007. In the United States, QE I, as it is commonly called, resulted in the Fed purchasing about 14.5 percent of existing debt over the space of 5 months and for the second round of purchases, QE II, the total amount purchased amounted to about 7 percent of existing debt over the space of 6 months. In the United Kingdom, during their AFP I program, the Bank of England purchased assets totaling about 29 percent of outstanding debt over the space of 10 months. Thus the 5 percent per month rule is quite conservative in trying to identify periods that could proxy a large asset purchase program.

The existing literature on the effectiveness of the large-scale asset programs seen today suggests that purchasing longer term assets has a small impact on long-term yields. Various estimates of the impact of QE I, QE II, and AFP I put the impact between 1 and 3 basis points for every 1 percent of existing debt purchased. These results are statistically significant but possibly not economically significant.

It is a difficult problem to correctly compute the impact of asset purchases on yields owing to the endogeneity problem inherent in any system that involves the counteracting forces of supply and demand. Authors such as D'Amico and King (2010) and Meaning and Zhu (2011) try to correct this by using IV estimators using low-frequency time series data. Another approach is to use high frequency data in an event study to reduce the impact of omitted relevant variables and endogeneity. These two approaches yield quite similar results in that the elasticities computed are between 1 and 3.

In this study the lack of data on possible covariates made it difficult to follow the first strand of the literature, and the lack of high-frequency data made it difficult to follow the second approach as well. In the end a "pseudo"-event study (my term) was performed in that I look at the behavior of yields on securities only in a small window around the identified large-scale asset purchase event. Because the data are monthly this leads to the valid criticism that other macroeconomic or financial factors might be mixing with the impact of the asset purchase. There is not much than can be said to mitigate this criticism except to say that, at least for the event windows, the yield series invariable always change direction. It is true that over the whole sample the yields on the U.S. Treasury securities fell but at least locally the yields changed direction. That is, if the trend had been for yields to be rising locally then during the window the yields would fall. In almost 90 percent of all windows the yield time series typically behaved differently from what it was doing before the window. Unless there is an unobserved variable that determines the periods in which the net change of the value of outstanding debt was large it is hard to claim that all of the results reported here are driven by omitted variables.

Events – defined as periods where the net change in the value of outstanding debt was large – were identified for each of the three types of U.S. securities. Using short-term U.S. Treasury bills, it was found that these large net changes in the value of outstanding debt had very little effect on short-term yields. This is not surprising as the yields on the short-term assets were almost 0, and the value of the outstanding short-term debt fell throughout the 1930s. The results for the medium term debt (U.S. Treasury notes with three- to five-year maturities) and for long-term debt (U.S. Treasury bonds with maturities greater than 12 years) were much more interesting. It was found that large expansions and contractions of the value of the outstanding debt did have significant impacts on the yields of both the medium- and the long-term debt.

The elasticities for the medium-term debt were similar in magnitude to the elasticities for the long-term debt but the sign of the impact was not as consistent. For long-term debt, after 1934 all of the event windows yielded a negative elasticity. The size of the elasticity computed for long-term debt is consistent with the results obtained from studies on the large-scale asset programs of the last few years, and the average elasticity (computed for the period from 1934 to 1941) was –1.336, which is at the low end of the estimates for QE I, QE II, and AFP I.

It was also shown that there is evidence that the manipulation of long-term interest rates would also impact long-term corporate bonds. The correlation between the elasticities for the long-term Treasury securities and AAA-rated bonds was 0.58, the correlation between the elasticities for the long-term Treasury securities and BAA-rated bonds was 0.66 and the correlation between the elasticities for the long-term Treasury securities and Junk-rated bonds was 0.33. This result is also consistent with the results reported in the studies of the contemporary large asset purchase episodes.

There is evidence that large-scale asset programs similar to the ones used after the end of the most recent global financial crisis would have given the Fed a tool for monetary policy during the late 1930s. It was possible to manipulate long-term interest rates and this would have had a flow on effect into corporate bond markets. Similar to the evidence for the recent episodes the elasticity on the long-term interest rates is quite small, meaning that the Fed would have had to purchase a sizeable amount of assets to have an economic effect on high-quality corporate yields. Like today, though, asset purchases did have relatively large impacts on the low-quality yields, thus suggesting more impact on the periphery of the economy than in the core.

Finally, what if any are the lessons of this analysis for today? The evidence from the 1930s suggests that the impact of purchasing large quantities of assets would have a statistically significant impact on long-term interest rates but that it may not be economically significant. This is further evidence that large-scale asset programs can work but that the emphasis needs to be on the word *large*. Maybe it shouldn't be surprising that the economic effects of the contemporary large-scale asset programs have been somewhat underwhelming.

REFERENCES

Basile, P., J. S. Landon-Lane, and H. Rockoff. (2011). "Money and Interest Rates in the United States during the Great Depression." In G. Wood, T. C. Mills, and N. Crafts (eds), *Monetary and Banking History: Essays in Honour of Forrest Capie*. Routledge International Series in Money and Banking. London: Routledge.

Bordo, M., and J. G. Haubrich. (2012). "Deep Recession, Fast Recoveries, and Financial Crises: Evidence from the American Record." *NBER Working Paper* 18194. Cambridge, MA: National Bureau of Economic Research.

Brunner, K., and A. H. Meltzer. (1968). "Liquidity Traps for Money, Bank Credit, and Interest Rates." *The Journal of Political Economy* 76:1–37.

Carter, Susan B., Scott Sigmund Gartner, Michael R. Haines, Alan L. Olmstead, Richard Sutch, and Gavin Wright (eds). (2006). *Historical Statistics of the United States: Earliest Times to the Present*. Millennial Ed. New York: Cambridge University Press.

D'Amico, S., and T. King. (2010). "Flow and Stock Effects of Large-Scale Treasury Purchases." Federal Reserve Board Finance and Economics Discussion Series, 2010–52.

Eichengreen, B. (2008). "Origins and Responses to the Crisis." UC Berkeley (mimeo) October.

Friedman, M., and A. Schwartz. (1963). *A Monetary History of the United States 1867 to 1960*. Princeton, NJ: Princeton University Press.

Gagnon, J., M. Raskin, J. Remasche, and B. Sack. (2011). "The Financial Market Effects of the Federal Reserve's Large-Scale Asset Purchases." *International Journal of Central Banking* 7(1):3–43.

Gorton, G. (2010). "Questions and Answers about the Financial Crisis." NBER Working Paper 15787. Cambridge, MA: National Bureau of Economic Research.

Greenwood, R., and D. Vayanos. (2008). "Bond Supply and Excess Bond Returns." *NBER Working Paper* 13806. Cambridge, MA: National Bureau of Economic Research.

Hamilton, J., and J. C. Wu. (2011). "The Effectiveness of Alternative Monetary Policy Tools in a Zero Lower Bound Environment." *NBER Working Paper* 16956. Cambridge, MA: National Bureau of Economic Research.

Keynes, John Maynard. 1965 [1936]. *The General Theory of Employment, Interest, and Money*. New York: Harcourt, Brace & World.

Krishnamurthy, A., and A. Vissing-Jorgensen. (2011). "The Effects of Quantitative Easing on Interest Rates: Channels and Implications for Policy." *NBER Working Paper* 17555. Cambridge, MA: National Bureau of Economic Research.

Krugman, P. R. (1998). "It's Baaack: Japan's Slump and the Return of the Liquidity Trap." *Brookings Papers on Economic Activity* No. 2:137–187.

Meaning, J., and F. Zhu. (2011). "The Impact of Recent Central Bank Asset Purchase Programmes." *BIS Quarterly Review* December:73–83.

Meltzer, Allan H. (1999). "Liquidity Claptrap." *The International Economy* (November/December):18–23.

———. (2003). *A History of the Federal Reserve.* Chicago: University of Chicago Press.

Orphanides, Athanasios. (2004). "Monetary Policy in Deflation: The Liquidity Trap in History and Practice." *The North American Journal of Economics and Finance* 15(1):101–124.

Swanson, E. (2011). "Let's Twist Again: A High-frequency Event-study Analysis of Operation Twist and Its Implications for QE2." *Brookings Papers on Economic Activity* (Spring):151–188.

12

A Tale of Two Countries and Two Booms, Canada and the United States in the 1920s and the 2000s

The Roles of Monetary and Financial Stability Policies

Ehsan U. Choudhri and Lawrence L. Schembri

Financial crises offer an important opportunity for learning lessons, deepening understanding and improving policies. In this vein, this chapter examines the experience of Canada and the United States in the run-up to the two biggest financial crises in global history, in the 1920s and 2000s, and the roles of their central banks. The central bank policy we focus on is monetary policy, but we also consider a broader set of policies that would fall under the heading of "financial stability" policy, which may not be exclusively the purview of the central bank. In this context, the goal of financial stability policy would be to limit systemic risk stemming from pro-cyclical movements in credit, leverage, and asset prices, which would render the financial system and the real economy more vulnerable to an adverse shock.

Canada and the United States experienced a similar boom–bust economic cycle in the 1920s and 1930s and 2000s. Although this occurrence is perhaps not surprising given the close economic and financial relationships between the two countries, they did have very different institutional frameworks for determining monetary and financial conditions over the two periods. In the 1920s, the United States had a central bank, the Federal Reserve, that was responsible primarily for setting monetary conditions, whereas Canada was still in an era of free banking, where note issue and control of monetary conditions were primarily in the hands of the private commercial banks, although the Canadian Ministry of Finance did provide access to a lending window. In the 2000s, the Bank of Canada (BoC) followed an explicit inflation targeting rule, whereas the Federal Reserve (Fed) had a dual inflation and employment mandate. Both countries had

The authors would like to thank Michael Bordo, Owen Humpage, David Laidler, Bennett McCallum, and Eugene White for their helpful comments and Janet Pass for superb research assistance. The views expressed in this chapter reflect those of the authors and not the Bank of Canada.

limited micro- and macroprudential financial regulation and supervision in 1920s, which was greatly strengthened in the 1930s in the aftermath of the crisis.[1] In contrast, in the years before the most recent crisis, Canada stepped up its financial regulation and supervision, whereas the United States deregulated.[2] The recently adopted Dodd–Frank Act, which includes the Volcker rule restricting the capital market activities of deposit-insured banks, undoes some of the recent deregulation and parallels the sweeping financial reforms of the 1930s.

In view of these institutional differences, comparing the Canadian experience to the U.S. experience over both periods is instructive for three reasons. First, during both periods, Canadian monetary policy was somewhat more conservative than U.S. monetary policy and it would be useful to consider the relative economic impact. Second, Canada did not have a central bank in the 1920s; thus, the interesting question is whether this institutional difference led to different monetary conditions over this period. Finally, although both countries suffered the consequences of inadequate financial regulation and supervision in the first period, their experiences during the most recent crisis were very different, and it would be useful to consider the impact of these policies on the credit, asset price, and economic booms.

Recently, there has been much debate about the causes of the recent economic boom (reflected especially in housing prices) that led to the financial crisis of 2008 in the United States. Taylor (2008, 2012) has argued that easy U.S. monetary policy was largely responsible for the boom. He shows that the Fed lowered the interest rates to levels that were significantly below the path predicted by monetary policy rules that were followed since mid-1980s. Bernanke (2010) counters that one reason for the interest rate deviation from the rule was that inflation rates in this

---

[1] In the United States, the Glass–Steagall Act of 1933, the Securities Act of 1933, and the Securities Exchange Act of 1934 were passed. Pecora (1939) provides further details on the investigations leading to these pieces of legislation. In Canada, the Macmillan Commission report (1933) recommended numerous reforms including the founding of the Bank of Canada in 1935. See Table 12.3 for more information.

[2] In Canada, in the wake of two small regional bank failures in 1983, the Northland Bank of Canada and the Canadian Commercial Bank, the Estey Commission Report (1986) recommended the creation of the Office of the Superintendent of Financial Institutions with a stronger mandate and increased independence. Interagency micro- and macroprudential senior-level agencies, including the Financial Institutions Supervisory Committee (FISC), the Senior Advisory Committee (SAC), and the Heads of Agencies (HOA) have also been established. See Financial Stability Board (2012) for more details. In the United States, the Angelides Commission Report (2011, p. xviii) on the financial crisis concluded, "More than 30 years of deregulation and reliance on self-regulation by financial institutions... had stripped away key safeguards, which could have helped avoid catastrophe." See Table 12.3 for more information.

period turned out to be higher than the Fed's forecasts. Another reason was the concern that interest rates were headed toward zero bound and that aggressive policy action was needed to avoid this situation. He also presents some evidence indicating that the monetary policy did not cause the housing boom, but rather that the housing boom and collapse, and the resultant financial crisis, were the consequence of inadequate financial stability policies, notably outdated regulation, lax supervision, and policy interventions that distorted incentives in the housing and financial markets.

Our chapter contributes to this debate by assessing the Bernanke hypothesis. In the first section we compare monetary and financial stability policies in Canada and the United States during the recent boom and examine whether differences in the policies of the two countries can account for the differences in their economic performance. We find evidence consistent with the Bernanke hypothesis. Although Canadian monetary policy was more conservative, likely because of its explicit inflation target, it is the difference in financial stability policies that largely explains the difference in the extent of the financial and economic expansion in the two countries. In the second section, we repeat this exercise for the 1920s. Again Canadian monetary policy is more conservative than U.S. monetary policy, largely because of different approaches to restore the prewar gold standard. This difference helps to explain relative economic performance during the booms, which were similar in both countries. The subsequent busts owe much to inadequate financial stability policies that failed to control the rapid increase in credit that fuelled the housing and stock market booms. Poor post-crisis monetary and exchange rate policies in both countries aggravated the subsequent economic slowdown.

Interestingly, the recent crisis demonstrates that although central banks seem to have learned the lessons from the Depression experience in terms of how to use monetary policy and liquidity provision to respond to a financial crisis, the lessons for financial stability policy were much less absorbed. Central banks, including the Fed and the BoC, responded immediately and boldly to the crisis with aggressive policy rate declines and large and pervasive increases in the provision of liquidity. Exchange rates were also allowed to depreciate to facilitate the adjustment. In contrast, many of the financial vulnerabilities that were realised in the 1920s, because of inadequate micro- and macroprudential regulation and supervision were allowed to reemerge in the run-up to the recent crisis: excess leverage, in part by pyramiding investment strategies; procylical margins and asset fire sales; mortgage securitization and perverse incentives; moral hazard and too-big-to fail; opaque instruments and asymmetric information; and the underassessment and underpricing of risk by uninformed investors, including those from abroad.

RECENT FINANCIAL CRISIS: WHY CANADA FARED BETTER
THAN THE UNITED STATES

Over the recent period in the 2000s, Canada experienced a smaller economic boom and a smaller bust when the global financial crisis hit than the
United States. To see this, consider the U.S. and Canadian macroeconomic
performance in 2000s; Figures 12.1 and 12.2 show the behavior of output gap (expressed as percentage deviation between actual and potential
output) and inflation (expressed as four-quarter percentage change in core
Consumer Price Index) in the two countries. Both countries experienced
low inflation rates (between 1 and 3 percent) throughout the 2000s. There
are important differences, however, in the behavior of output in the two
countries. The U.S. output gap closed faster than the Canadian gap during the expansion from 2003 to 2006 with actual exceeding potential after
late 2004, but fell much below the Canadian levels after the financial crisis
in 2007.

To understand the source of these differences in output movements, we
next consider monetary and financial stability policies in the two countries. Figure 12.3 examines the U.S. interest rate policy during the 2000s. It
shows quarterly values of the federal funds rate, and to illustrate the Taylor
argument, it compares these with values determined by a simple Taylor
rule of the following type:

$$R_t = \bar{r} + \pi^* + \alpha(\pi_t - \pi^*) + \beta \breve{y}_t, \tag{12.1}$$

where R_t denotes the policy interest rate, $\bar{r}$ and π^* represents the natural
real rate and the target inflation rate, and π_t and $\breve{y}_t$ are the (four-quarter)
inflation rate and output gap. As originally proposed by Taylor (1993), we
set $\bar{r} = \pi^* = 2.0$ and $\alpha = \beta = 0.5$ in calculating the rule-determined policy
rate in the figure. As noted by similar comparisons by others, the U.S. policy rate was set well below the hypothetical Taylor rule rate. Of course,
such evidence is sensitive to specification of the Taylor rule and, in particular, to the indexes used to measure inflation and the output gap. Most notably, Bernanke (2010) argues that the gap between the rule and the actual
rate is less if a real-time forecast of inflation is used instead of the actual
rate because U.S. expected inflation was much lower than it turned out to
be (Dokko et al. 2009). Bernanke (2010), however, does not provide an
explanation of these fairly persistent forecast errors.

We next examine how the Canadian monetary policy differed from the
U.S. policy over this period. Figure 12.4 compares the behavior of the policy rates for the two countries. The Canadian target rate generally follows
the movements of the federal funds rate, but during the critical 2002–2004
period of low U.S. interest rates, the Canadian rate remained significantly
higher. Indeed the Canadian–U.S. interest rate differential increased during

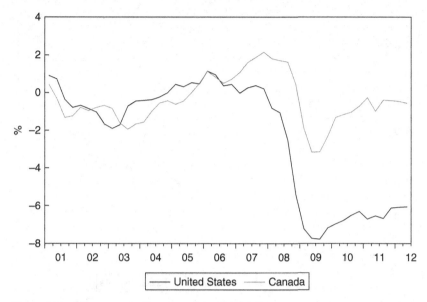

Figure 12.1. Output gap in Canada and the United States.

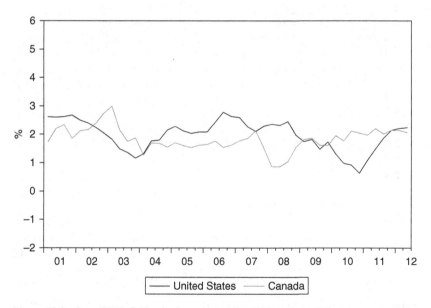

Figure 12.2. Core CPI inflation in Canada and the United States.

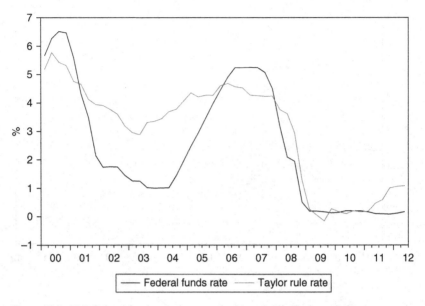

Figure 12.3. U.S. federal funds rate compared with a simple Taylor rule rate.

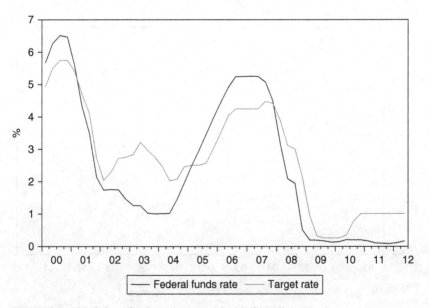

Figure 12.4. U.S. federal funds rate compared with Canadian target rate.

this period and rose to about 2 percent in 2003 Q2. The interest rate comparison also shows that Canadian interest rate did not increase as sharply as the U.S. rate during the 2004–2006 period.

The Canadian interest rate policy rate has also been compared with the policy prescribed by a Taylor rule. In an annual review of the Canadian economy, the Organisation for Economic Co-operation and Development (OECD 2010) argues that the Canadian policy rate was well below the Taylor rule rate during the pre-crisis period, and the loose monetary policy during this period was responsible for the housing boom in Canada.[3] Indeed, estimating the coefficients of Taylor rule equation (12.1) for Canada using quarterly data from 1990 Q1 to 2001 Q4, the Canadian target rate is shown to be significantly below the Taylor rule rate in the pre-crisis period from 2002 to 2007 (see Figure 12.5).[4] The standard rule, however, does not account for the fact that the Canadian policy rate may also be set in response to the U.S. policy rate to avoid large exchange rate movements.[5] We thus also estimated a modified rule that also includes the U.S. policy rate.[6] As also shown in Figure 12.5, the Canadian policy rate does not diverge much from the rate generated by the modified Taylor rule rate over the period 2000–2007. Canadian monetary policy in the 2000s thus does not appear to depart much from its behavior in the 1990s. In particular, the Canadian policy interest rate was correlated with U.S. policy rate over both periods and the inclusion of the U.S. interest rate increases the explanatory power of the Taylor rule equation.[7] However, as discussed previously, the Canadian interest rate movements were more moderate than U.S. movements during the 2002–2006 period.

A key mechanism for the transmission of monetary policy effects is the adjustment in the ex ante real interest rates. This channel is highlighted in the new-Keynesian dynamic stochastic general (DSGE) models.[8] It is,

---

[3] A cross-country study of twenty countries by the International Monetary Fund (Fatas et al. 2009) also suggests that the Canadian interest rate was substantially below the Taylor rule rate.

[4] The Taylor rule rate is calculated based on coefficients obtained by estimating the following form of the rule by OLS: $R_t = c + \alpha \pi_t + \beta \breve{y}_t$, where $c = \bar{r} + (1 - \alpha)\pi^*$.

[5] For example, Lubik and Schorfheide (2007) estimate a general equilibrium model to provide evidence that the Canadian interest rate rule includes the nominal exchange rate.

[6] The modified form of the estimated equation is: $R_t = c + \alpha \pi_t + \beta \breve{y}_t + \delta R_t^{us}$, where R_t^{us} is the U.S. policy rate. The estimation period (1990 Q1–2001 Q4) is the same as in the OECD study and excludes the 1980s, which represent the transition to lower inflation targets. Also, in the augmented Taylor rule, the output gap coefficient is not significantly different from zero, which result may indicate that Canada had an explicit inflation targeting framework, whereas the United States had a dual mandate.

[7] This correlation may, however, be spurious if it reflects similar responses to common external shocks due to omitted variables and may not necessarily reflect the desire to lean against exchange rate movements.

[8] The basic versions (e.g., Clarida, Gali, and Gertler 1999; Woodford 2003) do not assign a prominent role for monetary aggregates. These models, however, do not incorporate

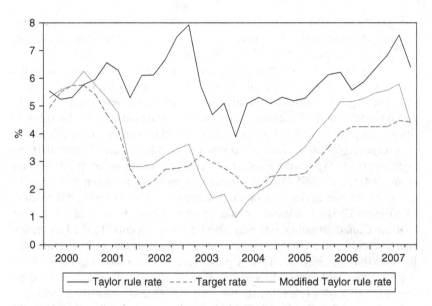

Figure 12.5. Canadian target rate compared with Taylor rule rate.

however, difficult to develop satisfactory measure of expected real rates, as the process determining inflationary expectations is not well understood. Arguably, expected inflation rates depend on both forward-looking (model-consistent) and backward-looking components. We do not attempt to construct an index of the expected inflation rates, but for illustrative purposes, examine the behavior of real policy rate defined simply as the nominal policy rate minus four-quarter core CPI inflation. Figure 12.6 compares the behavior of the real policy rates in Canada and the United States. According to our simple measures, policy real rates in both countries fell sharply in 2001. The U.S. rate stayed below the Canadian rate until 2005 and was negative over most of the period.

As the financial crisis is typically identified with collapse of the U.S. housing boom, there has been considerable interest in assessing the contribution of U.S. monetary policy in generating the housing boom. For example, using a vector autoregression (VAR) model, Jarocinski and Smets (2008) find that low interest rates in the United States had a significant effect on house prices and housing investment. Other studies (e.g.,

financial frictions, and monetary aggregates or interest rate spreads could be an important part of the transmission mechanism in the presence of these frictions (Bernanke, Gertler and Gilchrist 1999; Canzoneri et al. 2008; Goodfriend and McCallum 2007). Also, changes in ex post real interest rates would have distributional effects in nonrepresentative agents' versions.

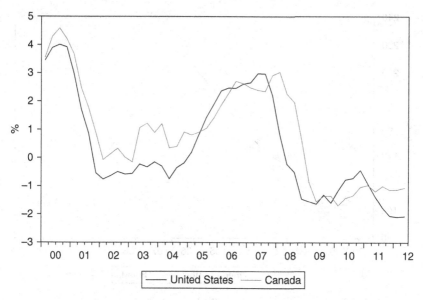

Figure 12.6. Real policy rates in Canada and the United States.

Dokko et al. 2009) suggest that monetary policy was not a major factor in causing the housing boom and subsequent collapse.

To assess this issue further, we compare the experience of Canada and the United States. Figure 12.7 shows the behavior of house prices: three-month moving average of S&P Case–Shiller index for the United States and Teranet index for Canada.[9] This figure shows that the rise in house prices was much steeper in the United States over the period 2000 to 2006. U.S. house prices increased by 100 percent over this period as opposed to 71 percent for Canadian prices. U.S. house prices started declining in 2007. Canadian house prices fell somewhat during the most intense period of the crisis in 2008–2009, but then continued to increase while the U.S. house prices collapsed. It is likely that this stark difference in the behavior of U.S. house prices relative to Canadian house prices does not solely reflect the potential differences in the stance of monetary policy. Although one could argue that U.S. monetary policy was looser as measured by simple Taylor rule gaps, it is unlikely that these differences alone can account for the significant deviation in the house price behavior in the two countries.

The prolonged post-crisis collapse of the U.S. housing market versus the relative strength of the Canadian housing market is consistent with

---

[9] These are comparable price series because they are both quality adjusted and data are drawn from major urban areas.

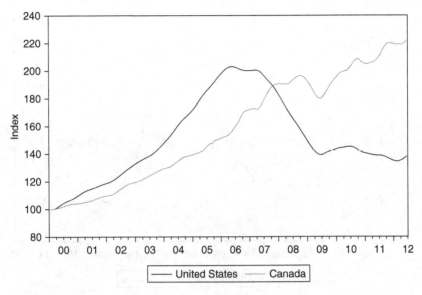

Figure 12.7. House prices in Canada and the United States.

an explanation based on Canada–U.S. differences in financial regulation and supervision and overall government housing policy. In particular, Bernanke (2010) notes that the United States had an explicit policy over this period to promote homeownership, particularly among those families who had not previously had access to mortgage financing. This policy as well as those that deregulated banking to allow deposit-taking banks to participate in higher risk capital market activities and increase leverage, in part through off-balance sheet securitization vehicles exacerbated the risks.[10] These policies and resultant rise in the issuance of subprime mortgages in the United States did not occur in Canada. Moreover, the extent of mortgage securitization was much less; thus the perverse "no skin in the game" or "originate and distribute model" was much less pervasive. As a consequence, the incentives to lower underwriting standards to issue mortgages to high-risk households and then securitize them was much less. In 2007, 15 percent of the U.S. mortgages were subprime versus 3 percent in Canada, and 60 percent of U.S. mortgages were securitized versus 30 percent in Canada (Kiff 2009). Consequently, when the U.S. recession took hold in 2007–2009, house prices collapsed by about 30 percent, mortgage default rates shot up and the value of structured (often subprime) mortgage products declined sharply. Given how much of these toxic assets

[10] Angelides Commission Report (2011, pp. 64–66).

remained on the highly leveraged balance sheets of major U.S. banks, the U.S. banking system teetered on the edge of systemic insolvency and massive government bailouts were required to prevent a total collapse.[11]

Although runs on deposit-taking banks did not occur, largely because of the presence of deposit insurance, and later in the crisis, blanket Federal Deposit Insurance Corporation (FDIC) deposit guarantees, runs occurred in the lightly regulated shadow banking markets, including money market mutual funds and repurchase (repo) markets.[12] Other core financial markets, including the interbank market and over-the-counter derivatives, seized. To fill the bank funding gap, the Federal Reserve and U.S. Treasury stepped in to guarantee money market mutual funds and inject massive amounts of liquidity into the U.S. financial system via a number of different programs.[13] The situation in Canada was very different; house prices declined by about 9 percent in 2008–2009, but then quickly recovered and continued to increase. Canadian banks did not experience significant losses or failures. Despite being universal banks, regulation and effective supervision prevented Canadian banks from becoming too dependent on short-term funding and unduly exposed to the higher risk capital market activities (Ratnovski and Huang 2009). Mortgage underwriting and securitization standards were also higher and generally enforced.[14] Indeed, Table 12.1 shows that Canada went into the 2007–2008 financial crisis with a financial regulatory and supervisory framework that had been significantly strengthened, especially with the creation of the Office of the Superintendent of Financial Institution. In contrast, Fed Chairman Bernanke in his testimony to the Angelides Commission said that "the Gramm-Leach-Bliley requirements made it difficult for any single regulator to reliably see the whole picture of the activities and risks of large, complex banking institutions" (Angelides 2011, p. 55). All in all, the experience of the two countries provides support for the Bernanke Hypothesis. The difference in the behavior of the housing prices in these countries over this period, in particular, the U.S. boom and collapse is more likely due to differences in mortgage market and banking regulation and supervision than to differences in monetary policy.

---

[11] A number of observers including Obstfeld and Rogoff (2011) have stressed the relationship between these financial imbalances in the United States and its current account deficits. Lorenzo Bin-Smaghi (2008) describes them as "two sides of the same coin" as capital flows "searching for yield" flooded into U.S. financial markets and exploited and exposed regulatory weaknesses (Bernanke 2010). Bertaut et al. (2012) provide a more detailed assessment of the role of foreign investors in asset-backed securities.

[12] See Angelides (2011), chapter 2.

[13] See Fleming (2012).

[14] Some government and central bank liquidity support was needed in Canada as global bank funding markets dried up.

Table 12.1. Major Financial Reforms in Canada and the United States: Pre-2007–2008 Crisis

Canada	United States
1968: *Canadian Deposit Insurance Corporation Act* • Established deposit insurance for federally regulated deposit-taking institutions 1987: Revision to the *Bank Act* • Eliminated the prohibition on chartered banks from engaging in investment banking activities 1987: *Office of the Superintendent of Financial Institutions Act* • Merged previous agencies responsible for banks and insurance companies • Gave the superintendent significant powers to oversee these institutions and enforce compliance 1992: Revision to the *Bank Act* • Permitted financial institutions to engage in other financial activities by creating subsidiaries within a financial holding company structure (e.g., an insurance company could have a bank subsidiary) subject to provisions prohibiting conflicts of interest and self-dealing	1980: *Depository Institutions Deregulation and Monetary Control Act* • Deregulated the lending and borrowing of thrift institutions, including promoting the issuance of mortgages that could be securitized by the federal housing agencies 1992: *Federal Housing Enterprise Safety and Soundness Act* • Promoted home ownership by low-income and minority groups through increased securitization by the housing agencies[a] 1999: *Gramm–Leach–Bliley Act* • Repealed *Glass–Steagall Act* • Allowed investment banks to own thrifts, which gave them access to FDIC-insured deposits without supervision of the Fed

During this period the U.S. federal authorities did not act to regulate the immense over-the-counter derivatives (swaps) market despite mounting concerns (Partnoy 2003).
[a] This act reinforced the 1977 *Community Reinvestment Act*, which required banks to lend to their local markets, especially in lower income, predominantly minority areas (Rajan 2010).

ROARING TWENTIES AND THE GREAT DEPRESSION: THE CANADIAN AND U.S. EXPERIENCES

The U.S. experience and the behavior of the Federal Reserve in the economic boom and bust during the 1920s and early 1930s have been studied extensively. It is now generally agreed that, as argued by Friedman and Schwartz (1963), the failure of the Fed to prevent the large decline in the money stock due to bank panics turned a recession into the Great Depression.[15] It is also well recognized (e.g., Bernanke 2002; White 1990a) that tight monetary policy in 1928–1929 caused an economic slowdown that lead to the stock market crash in October 1929 and the subsequent contraction. There is less agreement on whether easy monetary policy in 1924–1925 contributed significantly to economic expansion and the stock market boom in the mid and late 1920s.[16] We explore this question further in the text that follows.

There were significant differences between the periods prior to the economic booms of the 1920s and 2000s. Although the latter period followed more than a decade and a half of stable economic conditions under rule-based monetary policy, the former period represented a transitional state in which the Fed was in its early years and the appropriate rules of monetary policy were being developed and debated, and the gold standard as an international monetary system had not yet been restored. Federal Reserve Banks set the discount rates, but borrowing by member banks at these rates was discouraged and open market operations were also used as a tool of monetary policy. The Fed had enough instruments to control short-term interest rates, and this power was also available even after the world-wide restoration of the gold standard because of its large holding of gold reserves and a significant margin between import and export gold points for Europe.[17]

Figure 12.8 shows monthly values of the New York Fed discount rate and the three-month Treasury bill rate from January 1923 to December 1933, the period after the short boom and bust of 1921–1922. The discount rate was decreased (in a number of steps) from 4.5 percent in April

---

[15] Bernanke (1983) argues that monetary factors alone cannot explain the depth of the Great Depression in the United States. He maintains that the U.S. bank failures not only reduced the money supply, but also disrupted credit intermediation and this exacerbated the economic decline.

[16] Freidman and Schwartz (1963) and Meltzer (2003) view the conduct of U.S. monetary policy during the 1920s as generally appropriate because inflation was low and stable and output growth relatively robust. Hayek, Robbins, and Robertson, however, felt that the Fed policy contributed to excess investment during the 1920s (see Laidler [2003] and Wheelock [1992] for summary of these criticisms of U.S. monetary policy). They argue that given the rapid technological growth over this period, deflation would have occurred in the absence of monetary expansion.

[17] The large stock of gold reserves enabled the Fed to influence money supply and the interest rates in the rest of the world. The gold-point margin arising from transportation costs implied some room for the home-foreign interest rate spread to vary. Indeed, in the presence of this margin, the gold standard could be viewed as a target zone exchange rate system. See Bordo and MacDonald (2005) for evidence on such characterization for the classical gold standard.

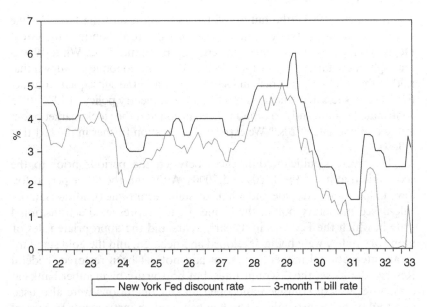

Figure 12.8. The U.S. short-term interest rates.

1924 to 3.0 percent in September 1924 and kept at this level until February 1925.[18] The rate was raised to 3.5 percent in March 1925 and maintained at this value until December 1925. The three-month Treasury bill rate also declined significantly during this period. The monetary policy in this period appears to be largely motivated by the downturn in 1924, but may also have been influenced by the desire to facilitate United Kingdom's return to the gold standard.[19] Given the magnitude of the reduction in the interest rates and the duration over which they stayed at low levels, a case can be made that this easy money episode played an important part in the development of 1920s boom. Although the CPI inflation rate exhibited modest variability in the 1922–1929 period, the average inflation rate

---

[18] The discount rate was also decreased temporarily in the summer of 1927. This decrease was seen as part of a coordinated interest agreement among the Fed, Bank of England, Banque de France, and the Reichsbank to reequilibrate the allocation of gold and stabilize the gold standard (Eichengreen and Michener 2003). Eichengreen (1992, p. 213) describes this agreement as "admirable instance of international cooperation."

[19] The discount rate reductions in the 1924–1925 period were generally viewed (e.g., Meltzer 2003) as appropriate countercyclical measures. The low U.S. interest rates led to an outflow of gold especially to Britain (which set a higher discount rate), and thus also helped strengthened Bank of England's reserve position before the United Kingdom's return to the gold standard (Eichengreen 1992, chapter 7).

in this period was equal to zero. If inflationary expectations during this period were also close to zero, there was a sizable decline in the real interest rates in the 1924–1925.

It is also interesting to examine whether the low interest rates in this period represent an excessive deviation from normal policy similar to the easy money policy of 2002–2004. White (2009) has compared the U.S. policy interest rate (represented by the New York Fed discount rate) with the rate determined by simple Taylor rules (using coefficients suggested by Taylor, but changing the inflation target to zero and the real interest rate to 4 percent) in the 1920s.[20] Movements in the actual rate tend to be smaller than the Taylor rule rate, and the actual rate was below the rule-based rate by about 2 percent during the 1925–1926 period, which was critical for the housing boom that occurred over this period. However, White estimates that a counterfactual policy of raising the interest rate to the levels specified by the rule would not have made a major difference to the housing boom. White attributes the housing boom to excess mortgage credit expansion fueled by inadequate financial stability policies, namely the securitization of mortgages combined with a reduction in lending standards and lax supervision.[21]

We next review Canadian monetary policy in this period and examine how it differed from the U.S. policy and whether these differences had any influence on the macroeconomic performance of the two countries. During the 1920s, Canada operated without a central bank, but the Canadian Ministry of Finance did provide access to a lending window. According to the Finance Act of 1914, the banks could borrow from the Ministry at an interest rate called the "advance rate" against a collateralized line of credit. The lines of credit were generally not a constraint, as actual borrowing tended to be a small proportion of the credit limit (Shearer and Clark 1984). The 1914 Finance Act set a floor of 5 percent for the advance rate (with a provisions for a lower rate for special advances), but this floor was removed in 1923 by a new Finance Act. After the removal of the floor, the advance rate became the primary instrument of monetary policy in Canada, although it was changed infrequently.

Canada was on the gold standard for only a short period from July 1926 to January 1929. Low costs of transporting gold between New York and Montreal implied a narrow interval between gold export and import points. During the gold standard period, the Finance Ministry thus had

---

[20] He also estimates the coefficients of several versions of the Taylor rule equations for the 1922–1929 period, and finds that the response coefficients were reasonable.

[21] Canada also experienced a housing boom in the 1920s, which peaked in 1929. It was largely in housing construction rather than house prices (Firestone 1951).

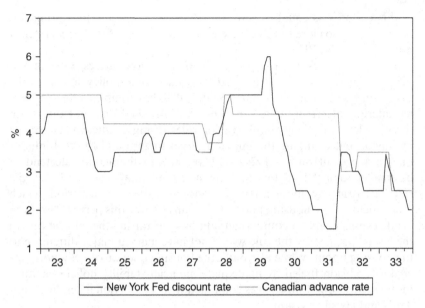

Figure 12.9. The Canadian advance rate and the New York Fed discount rate.

limited room to vary the discount rate relative to the short-term rates in the United States.[22] In pre- and post-gold standard periods, however, Canada had the power to follow an independent interest rate policy. The Canadian authorities, however, appear to have been reluctant to allow the exchange rate to deviate much from parity and tended to respond to short-term U.S. interest rates. The Canadian interest rate policy did deviate significantly from the U.S. policy during certain periods. Figure 12.9 compares the behavior of the advance rate to the New York Fed discount rate from January 1923 to December 1933.[23] The advance rate was not decreased as much in the 1924–1925 episode of easy U.S. monetary policy and was not increased as much in the later 1928–1929 episode of tight U.S. monetary policy. There were also important monetary policy differences during the Great Depression period.

[22] There may also have been significant departures from interest parity because the financial markets in Canada were not well developed at that time and interest rate arbitrage between Canada and the United States may have involved substantial transaction costs.

[23] The figure shows the ordinary advance rate applicable to any eligible collateral. There was also a lower special rate applicable to loans secured by special issues of government securities, but after 1923, this rate was available only for selected periods, from October 1928 to October 1931 and after October 1932 (Shearer and Clark 1984).

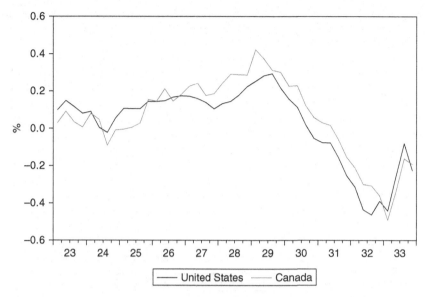

Figure 12.10. Detrended industrial production in Canada and the United States.

To explore the impact of these monetary policy differences on economic activity in Canada relative to the United States, we construct a measure of output gap for the two countries. As estimates of quarterly gross domestic product (GDP) are not available for this period, especially for Canada, we base our measure on industrial production.[24] As an estimate of normal or potential output, we fit a linear trend to quarterly industrial production data from 1919 Q1 to 1939 Q4 for both countries. Figure 12.10 compares the deviation of industrial production from this trend (for the 1923–1933 period) as a rough indicator of the output gap in the two countries. As the figure shows, the industrial production gap in Canada was lower than the U.S. gap during the 1924–1925 episode, and was higher during the 1928–1929 episode. Further evidence on the impact of the monetary policy differences is provided in Figure 12.11, which shows the behavior of four-quarter CPI inflation in the two countries. The Canadian inflation rate was lower than the U.S. rate during the first and higher during

---

[24] An alternative measure could be based on unemployment rates. Although official unemployment data for Canada are not available before 1945, Gower (1992) has estimated Canadian unemployment since 1921. It is difficult to determine how comparable Canadian unemployment estimates are with the U.S. estimates. Gower's estimates do suggest, however, that Canada suffered lower unemployment than United States during the Great Depression (the Canadian and U.S. unemployment rates peaked at 19.1 percent and 25.2 percent respectively).

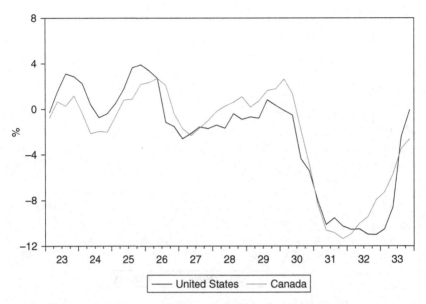

Figure 12.11. Four-quarter CPI inflation in Canada and the United States.

the second episode. Monetary policy differences between Canada and the Unites States over this period are thus reflected in output and inflation outcomes in the two countries.

To examine the role of credit growth and financial leverage in exacerbating the economic boom in the 1920s, we consider the contribution of credit growth to asset prices, primarily stock, and house prices, in Canada and the United States in the 1920s. Eichengreen and Michener (2003, p. 3) argue that in the United States "credit fuelled a real estate boom in 1925, a Wall Street boom in 1928–9 and a consumer durable spending spree spanning the second half of the 1920s." Whereas White (2009) points to securitization and lax lending standards for increases in housing credit,[25] Galbraith (1955) and Eichengreen and Michener identify unregulated investment trusts and margin borrowing as well as innovations in consumer credit for durables purchases as important new sources of credit growth and leverage over the period. Higher leverage was achieved by purchasing stocks on margin for as low as 10 percent and by "pyramiding"

[25] Rajan and Ramcharam (2012) examine the boom and bust in land prices in the United States in the 1920s. They find that credit availability fueled the land price boom and the resulting bust lead to increases in bank failures for those banks that were overleveraged and overexposed to land loans.

Table 12.2. Formation of Investment Companies Prior to 1930

Year of Formation	Number of American Companies Formed	Number of Canadian Companies Formed
1924 and before	37	2
1925	26	1
1926	24	3
1927	89	14
1928	130	9
1929	203	21
Total as of December 31, 1929	509	50

investment trusts (Galbraith 1955).[26] Table 12.2 compares the exponential increases in investment trusts in Canada and the United States over this period. The expansion was significantly greater in the United States given the much greater overall size of the stock market.

In the United States, bank loans increased by 35 percent from 1923 to 1929, whereas in Canada, bank loans, accelerated over the latter half of 1920s, rising by 60 percent over the years from 1923 to 1929. Domestic bank loans, however, explain only part of the story, as there were other forces affecting domestic credit conditions. For example, in the United States there were substantial borrowings from abroad, especially in the latter part of 1929, much of which were intermediated through the New York call loan market. Call loan rates in the New York call money market increased steadily to 12 percent and this drew in funds from nonfinancial U.S. corporations (White 1990b) and also from the rest of the world.[27] Because of the pressure exerted by these gold outflows on its exchange rate, Canada suspended gold convertibility in 1929.

In an effort to capture these different factors, Eichengreen and Michener (2003) constructed a credit conditions index, based on Borio and Lowe (2002), for a set of advanced economies that combines deviations from trends of the ratios of M2, stock prices, and investment to GDP. They find a sharp spike in credit conditions in Canada and the United States in 1928.

[26] Such pyramiding is analogous to the CDO^2 and CDO^3, etc. instruments in 2000s, where CDO refers to collateralized debt obligation. Kindleberger (1978) and Minsky (1986) also stress the pervasive information problems that contributed to the stock market excesses. Such information problems are analogous to those that occurred in the recent crisis; for example, huge counterparty exposures were largely unknown, especially in the over-the-counter derivatives and repo markets.

[27] In this instance, when gold flows are driven by expected capital gains from rapid asset price increases, the gold standard has a pro-cyclical impact.

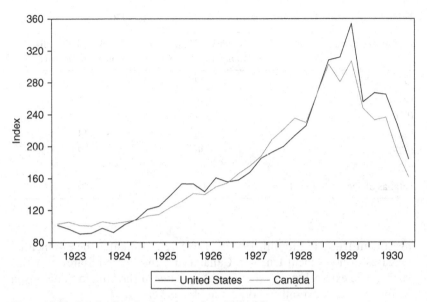

Figure 12.12. Stock prices in Canada and the United States.

They also find evidence that the size of this index, especially in interaction with the stock price index, helps predict the depth of the subsequent economic downturn.

To explore further the impact of this credit expansion on asset prices, consider stock market prices in the two countries (see Figure 12.12). U.S. stock prices rose at a slightly faster pace than Canadian prices until 1925, at a somewhat slower pace until 1928, and then they rose sharply and reached a higher peak than Canadian prices in 1929. The difference in stock market price behavior in 1929 does not appear to reflect monetary policy differences, but is more likely related to the more rapid expansion in U.S. credit.

Because both countries lacked effective financial stability policies, in the form of micro- and macroprudential tools, they resorted to raising policy interest rates in the latter part of this period in attempt to stem the rise in asset prices, and in Canada's case, to help maintain its peg to gold. The resulting stock market crash and severe economic downturn are testament to the bluntness of monetary policy as tool for maintaining financial stability and need for better regulation and supervision to prevent the occurrence of such rapid asset price increases.[28] To address these

---

[28] Galbraith (1955), White (1990b), and Meltzer (2003) examine the Fed's reluctance to raise interest rates sufficiently to restrain the rapid expansion in credit and stock prices. Meltzer explains this behavior as follows: inflation was low, growth was not excessive, and there

shortcomings in financial regulation and supervision, substantial changes were made to laws governing the financial system. In the United States, this includes passing the Glass–Steagall Act and the Securities Exchange Act (see Table 12.3).

Figures 12.10 and 12.11 also show that the decline of output and inflation in Canada during the Great Depression was nearly as severe as in the United States.[29] The transmission of the Great Depression from the United States to the rest of the world has been linked to the gold standard. The United Kingdom and the Scandinavian countries left the gold standard in 1931 and fared better than the United States while France and Germany stayed on the standard beyond 1933 and fared worse (Bernanke 1995; Choudhri and Kochin 1980). Canada was, in fact, the first country to abandon the gold standard, but did not derive any benefits from this policy. There are two possible explanations of this puzzling behavior. One explanation (Betts, Bordo, and Redish 1996) emphasizes the role of common real shocks that produced a contraction in both countries independent of the exchange rate regime. An alternative explanation, based on the presence of nominal rigidities and consistent with the evidence for other countries, argues that Canadian exchange rate regime did not permit sufficient exchange rate flexibility when Canada was off the gold standard.[30]

Figure 12.13 displays the monthly exchange rate (U.S. dollar per Canadian dollar) series. Except for a slight discount during January

were concerns about the international impact. The Fed recognized the speculative use of credit but was "reluctant to use a general instrument to deal with what it regarded as special circumstances" (p. 236). White (1990b) argues that although the New York Fed wanted to raise rates to rein in bank lending to brokers, the Board preferred "direct pressure" on bank members (p. 74). Galbraith writes "Federal Reserve authorities are held to be not so much unaware or unwilling as impotent. They would have liked to stop the boom, but they lacked the means" (p. 34).

[29] Although Canada had a debt crisis like the United States, it did not have a banking crisis because of Canada's branch banking system (Bernanke 1983). Nonetheless, Canada still experienced similar and severe economic contraction (Amaral and MacGee 2002). Bordo (1986), Drummond (1991), and Kryzanowski and Roberts (1993) argue that Canadian government policy also played an important role in preventing bank failures. In particular, Kryzanowski and Roberts maintain failures were prevented by an implicit guarantee on bank deposits and regulatory forbearance. Drummond notes that Canadian banks were also shielded from losses by government guarantees on advances to wheat pools and by government-led support for securities' prices. Canadian banks were also not allowed to issue mortgages and their exposure to the stock market was less. Safarian (1959) stresses the degree of openness of the Canadian economy, which was four times more dependent on exports than the U.S. economy, as the explanation of why the Canadian depression was almost as severe despite the lack of bank failures.

[30] See, for example, Bordo and Redish (1990), who claim that exchange rate did not change until September 1931 as a result of credible policy commitment to parity.

Table 12.3. Major Financial Reforms in Canada and the United States: Post 1929–32 Crisis

Canada	United States
1933: *Ontario Securities Commission* founded[a] • To enforce the 1928 *Securities Fraud Prevention Act*, which included antifraud provisions as well as provisions for the regulation of brokers and salesman 1934: Revision to the *Bank Act* • Phased prohibition of note issue by banks • Removal of super-liability of shareholders • Prohibition of the publication of bank names on corporate prospectuses 1934: *Bank of Canada Act* • Establishment of a central bank with the sole right of note issue and to provide loans/advances to commercial banks and to serve as the government's fiscal agent 1935: *Dominion Companies Act* • Required prospectuses with more disclosure be supplied by underwriters for all federally incorporated corporations and strengthened provisions for disclosure in the annual report and directors' transactions in company's securities[b]	1933: *Banking (Glass–Steagall) Act* • Required the separation of commercial and investment banking activities into distinct corporate entities • Established the Federal Deposit Insurance Corporation • Allowed the Federal Reserve to discount any "sound" asset, not just commercial loans (1935 version of the *Banking Act*) 1933: *Securities Act* • Regulated the offer and sale of securities across state lines; in particular, it required issuers to fully disclose all material information for potential investors via a prospectus 1934: *Securities Exchange Act* • Established the Securities and Exchange Commission (SEC), which was responsible for enforcing the requirement of the Securities Act, including that all new issues had to be registered with the SEC and regulating broker-dealers

[a] Securities regulation falls within provincial jurisdiction. All of the provinces have securities commissions with similar powers. A passport system allows corporations to issue securities in various provinces.
[b] In 1935 the *Finance Act* of 1914 and the *Dominion Notes Act* of 1868 were repealed.

1923 to August 1924, and October to November 1929, the exchange rate remained very close to parity until September 1931 when the U.K. pound began depreciating. The Canadian dollar depreciated by about 17 percent until December 1931 before recovering and fluctuating between 10 percent

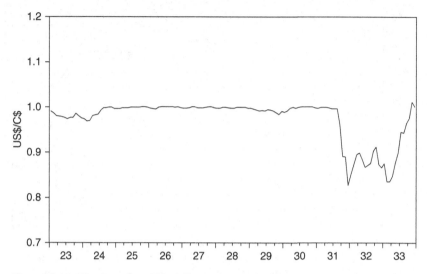

Figure 12.13. The Canadian–U.S. dollar exchange rate.

and 16 percent of parity until March 1933 when the United States also left the gold standard. The depreciation of the U.K. pound was much larger during the same period.[31] The smaller Canadian dollar depreciation can be attributed to Canadian interest policy. The advance rate was maintained at a high level of 4.5 percent until 1931 while the U.S. discount rate declined to 1.5 percent.[32] This policy also raised the Canadian real interest rate relative to the U.S. rate at a time when large deflation was bringing about a huge increase in real interest rates. Although there is controversy about how to measure the real rates in this period, our simple measure (nominal rate minus four-quarter inflation) indicates that the Canadian real policy rate stayed above the U.S. rate from 1930 Q3 to 1931 Q4 and this differential rose to 4 percent in 1931 Q3 (see Figure 12.14). The behavior of the real interest may have offset the effect of the modest depreciation and could provide an explanation of Canadian poor performance during the Great Depression.

---

[31] The U.K. pound depreciated by about 31 percent by December 1931, and then fluctuated between 24 percent and 33 percent of its initial value.

[32] Some relief was provided by a lower special advance rate from September 1928 to October 1931, but this relief was not available from October 1931 to October 1932. Moreover, because the special rate was available only for limited advances, it is not clear if it was effective in lowering money market rates.

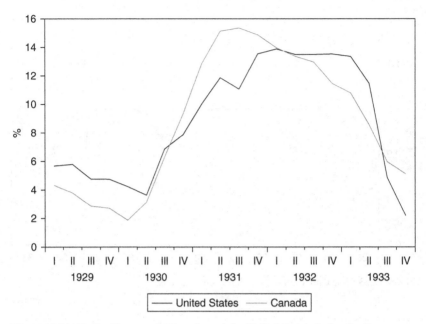

Figure 12.14. Real policy rates in Canada and the United States during the Great Depression.

CONCLUDING REMARKS

There are interesting parallels between monetary policies in the booms of the 1920s and 2000s for both United States and Canada. In both periods, the U.S. monetary policy was unusually easy before the boom and became very tight at the end of the boom. Canadian monetary policy followed a similar course, but it was more moderate in the easy as well as the tight phase. The similar behavior of Canadian monetary policy in the twin booms is remarkable because Canada did not even have a central bank in the early period. The monetary policy differences between the two countries affected their relative macroeconomic performance during the boom in each period: the Canadian output gap was smaller than the U.S. gap in the early and larger in the late phase of the boom. However, these monetary policy differences between Canada and the United States in different stages of the booms do not explain their experience in the crashes that followed the booms.

In the recent financial crisis, Canadian economic activity did not decline as much as in the United States. Surprisingly, house prices in Canada kept on rising, after a temporary decline, while they fell sharply in the United States. Although a more moderate stance of Canadian monetary policy may have also helped, a likely explanation of why Canada fared better in the crises is that different financial stability policies prevented a decline in Canadian house prices.

Canada did not fare better than the United States during the Great Depression. Some spillover of the U.S. depression into Canada was inevitable because of Canada's proximity and economic ties with the United States. Interestingly, however, two factors could have helped Canada escape the severity of the depression. First, the branch banking system in Canada made Canada less prone to banking crises. Second, and more important, Canada left the gold standard before the depression started and thus could have followed an independent monetary policy. However, Canada did not utilize these advantages by following an inflexible interest rate and exchange rate policy.

Interestingly, the key policy lessons from the Great Depression seemed to have been learned by central banks and other public authorities in the advanced economies because in the immediate aftermath of the recent financial crisis they responded quickly with sharp declines in policy rates, massive injections of liquidity, and substantial exchange rate depreciations in some cases, such as Canada. In contrast, the monetary policy and financial stability policy lessons from the boom of the 1920s were not fully absorbed during the most recent boom. Some of the regulation that was put in place in the 1930s in response to the crisis of the 1920s (most notably the Glass–Steagall Act) was removed. Micro- and macroprudential regulatory policies were not used effectively to counter the credit expansion and monetary policy generally leaned with the expansion rather than against it. Indeed, the U.S. banking system almost collapsed because of its close ties to the unregulated shadow banking and over-the-counter derivatives markets.

Fortunately, these lessons are now being taken into account, given the efforts of the G20 and Financial Stability Board, as well as central banks and other regulatory bodies, to put in pacing sweeping financial regulatory and supervisory reform and macroprudential policy to address systemic risks in the financial system, especially related to procyclicality. Basel III and Dodd–Frank are important examples. Central banks are also paying greater attention to financial stability and the nexus between financial stability and monetary policies.

APPENDIX: DESCRIPTION AND SOURCES OF DATA

U.S. Data

For the recent period, quarterly data for actual and potential real GDP, and monthly data for core CPI index, U.S. Federal Funds Rate, and house prices were obtained from Federal Reserve Bank of St. Louis Database (FRED). Potential real GDP data are based on CBO estimates; core CPI (all items less food and energy) is seasonally adjusted; and house prices represent S&P Case–Shiller 20 city (seasonally adjusted) home price index. This index was converted to a three-month moving average to make it comparable with the Canadian index discussed in the section that follows. Output gap was calculated as the log difference between actual and potential real GDP (multiplied by 100). After converting monthly data to quarterly frequency, four-quarter core CPI inflation was calculated as the log difference between CPI in the current and current minus four quarters (multiplied by 100).

For the early period, monthly data for New York Fed Discount Rate, three-month T-bill rate, CPI index, and stock prices are from the National Bureau for Economic Research (NBER) Macrohistory Database, and for industrial production (seasonally adjusted) are from FRED. The three-month T-bill rate represents average of daily figures for U.S. Treasury three- to six- month notes and certificates. The CPI in the early period was called the cost of living index. To calculate an output gap measure based on industrial production data, these data were converted to quarterly frequency, a linear trend was fitted to quarterly data from 1919 Q1 to 1933 Q4, and the gap was calculated as the log difference between actual and trend levels (multiplied by 100). Four-quarter CPI inflation was calculated the same way as in the recent period.

Canadian Data

For the recent period, monthly data for the core CPI and the Canadian Target Rate, and the quarterly data for the output gap are from Bank of Canada. Data for Canadian house prices represent Teranet bank eleven-city house price index (three-month moving average). The four-quarter inflation rate index is calculated the same way as the U.S. index.

For the early period, monthly data for CPI are from Dominion Bureau of Statistics, *Cost of Living Index Numbers for Canada, 1913–46*; monthly data for industrial production and stock prices are from Dominion Bureau of Statistics, Economic Tendencies in Canada from 1919 to 1930, and Monthly Review of Business Statistics (various issues); monthly data (average of daily rates) for exchange rates (Canada–U.S. and U.K.–U.S. rates) are from *Banking and Monetary Statistics, 1914–1941*; *International Financial Statistics*; and Canadian Advance Rate data are from Shearer and Clark (1984). Industrial production based output gap and the four-quarter inflation indexes are calculated the same way as the U.S. indexes.

REFERENCES

Amaral, P., and J. MacGee. (2002). "The Great Depression in Canada and the United States: A Neoclassical Perspective." *Review of Economic Dynamics* 5:45–72.

Angelides Commission. (2011). *Final Report of the National Commission on the Causes of the Financial and Economic Crisis in the United States.* Washington, DC: U.S. Government Printing Office.

Bernanke, B. (1983). "Nonmonetary Effects of the Financial Crisis in the Propagation of the Great Depression." *American Economic Review* 73:257–276.

(1995). "The Macroeconomics of the Great Depression: A Comparative Approach." *Journal of Money, Credit and Banking* 27:1–28.

(2002). "Asset-price 'Bubbles' and Monetary Policy." Remarks before the New York Chapter of the National Association for Business Economics, New York, NY, October 15.

(2010). "Causes of the Recent Financial and Economic Crisis." Statement before the Financial Crisis Inquiry Commission, Washington, DC, September 2. Retrieved from http://www.federalreserve.gov/newsevents/testimony/bernanke 20100902a.htm

(2010). "Monetary Policy and the Housing Bubble." Presentation at the American Economic Association Annual Meeting, Atlanta, January 3. Retrieved from http://www.federalreserve.gov/newsevents/speech/bernanke20100103a.htm

Bernanke, B., M. Gertler, and S. Gilchrist. (1999). "The Financial Accelerator in a Quantitative Business Cycle Framework." In J. B. Taylor and M. Woodford (eds), *Handbook of Macroeconomic*, Vol. IC, pp. 1341–1393. Amsterdam: Elsevier Science, North-Holland.

Bertaut, C., L. Pounder DeMarco, S. Kamin, and R. Tryon. (2012). "ABS Inflows to the United States and the Global Financial Crisis." *Journal of International Economics* 88:219–234.

Betts, C., M. Bordo, and A. Redish. (1996). "A Small Open Economy in Depression: Lessons from Canada in the 1930s." *Canadian Journal of Economics* 39:1–36.

Bini Smaghi, L. (2008). "The Financial Crisis and Global Imbalances – Two Sides of the Same Coin." Speech at the Asia Europe Economic Forum conference *The Global Financial Crisis: Policy Choices in Asia and Europe*, Beijing, December 9. Retrieved from http://www.bis.org/review/r081212d.pdf

Bordo, M., and R. MacDonald. (2005). "Interest Rate Interactions in the Classical Gold Standard, 1880–1914: Was There Any Monetary Independence?" *Journal of Monetary Economics* 52:307–327.

Bordo, M., and A. Redish. (1990). "Credible Commitment and Exchange Rate Stability: Canada's Interwar Experience." *Canadian Journal of Economics* 23:357–380.

Borio, C., and P. Lowe. (2002). "Asset Prices, Financial and Monetary Stability – Exploring the Nexus." BIS Working Paper 114. Basel, Switzerland: Bank for International Settlements.

Canzoneri, M., R. Cumby, B. Diba, and D. Lopez-Salido. (2008). "Monetary Aggregates and Liquidity in a Neo-Wicksellian Framework." *Journal of Money, Credit and Banking* 40:1667–1698.

Choudhri, E., and L. Kochin. (1980). "The Exchange Rate and the Transmission of Monetary Disturbances." *Journal of Money Banking and Credit* 12:565–574.

Clarida, R., J. Gali, and M. Gertler. (1999). "The Science of Monetary Policy: A New Keynesian Perspective." *Journal of Economic Literature* 37:1661–1707.

Dokko, J., B. Doyle, M. Kiley, J. Kim, S. Sherlund, J. Sim, and S. Van den Heuvel. (2009). "Monetary Policy and the Housing Bubble." Finance and Economics Discussion Paper No. 2009-49. Washington, DC: Board of Governors of the Federal System.

Drummond, D. (1991). "Why Canadian Banks Did Not Collapse in the 1930s." In H. James, H. Lindgren, and A. Teichova (eds), *The Role of Banks in the Interwar Economy*. Cambridge: Cambridge University Press.

Eichengreen, B. (1992). *Golden Fetters: The Gold Standard and the Great Depression, 1919-1939*. Oxford: Oxford University Press.

Eichengreen, B., and K. Michener. (2003). "The Great Depression as a Credit Boom Gone Wrong." BIS Working Paper 137. Basel, Switzerland: Bank for International Settlements.

Estey Commission. (1986). *The Report of the Inquiry into the Collapse of the CCB and Northland Bank*. Ottawa: Supply and Services Canada.

Fatás, A., P. Kannan, P. Rabanal, and A. Scott. (2009). "Lessons for Monetary Policy from Asset Price Fluctuations." In *World Economic Outlook* (Fall), chapter 3. Washington, DC: International Monetary Fund.

Financial Stability Board. (2012). *Peer Review Report of Canada*. Retrieved from www.financialstabilityboard.org.

Firestone, O. J. (1951). *Residential Real Estate in Canada*. Toronto: University of Toronto Press.

Fleming, M. (2012). "Federal Reserve Liquidity Provision during the Financial Crisis of 2007-2009." Federal Reserve Bank of New York Staff Report No. 563.

Friedman, M., and A. Schwartz. (1963). *A Monetary History of the United States, 1867 to 1960*. Princeton, NJ: Princeton University Press.

Galbraith, J. K. (1955). *The Great Crash 1929*. Boston: Houghton Mifflin.

Goodfriend, M., and B. McCallum. (2007). "Banking and Interest Rates in Monetary Policy Analysis: A Quantitative Exploration." *Journal of Monetary Economics* 54:1480-1507.

Gower, D. (1992). "A Note on Canadian Unemployment since 1921." *Statistics Canada: Perspectives on Labour and Income* 4:8-30.

Kiff, J. (2009). "Canadian Residential Mortgage Markets: Boring but Effective? *IMF Working Paper* 09/130. Washington, DC: International Monetary Fund.

Kindleberger, C. (1978). *Manias, Panics and Crashes*. New York: Basic Books.

Kryzanowski, L., and G. Roberts. (1993). "Canadian Banking Solvency, 1922-40." *Journal of Money, Credit and Banking* 25(3):361-376.

Laidler, D. (2003). "The Price Level, Relative Prices and Economic Stability: Aspects of the Interwar Debate." BIS Working Paper 136. Basel, Switzerland: Bank for International Settlements.

Lubik, T., and F. Schorfheide. (2007). "Do Central Banks Respond to Exchange Rate Movements? A Structural Investigation." *Journal of Monetary Economics* 54:1069-1087.

Macmillan Commission. (1933). *The Report of the Royal Commission on Banking and Currency in Canada*. Ottawa: J. F. Patenaude.

Meltzer, A. (2003). *A History of the Federal Reserve, Vol. 1: 1913-51*. Chicago: University of Chicago Press.

Minsky, H. (1986). *Stabilizing an Unstable Economy*. New Haven, CT: Yale University Press.

Obstfeld, M., and K. Rogoff. (2009). "Global Imbalances and the Financial Crisis: Products of Common Causes." In *Asia and the Global Financial Crisis*: 131–72. Proceedings of a conference held by the Federal Reserve Bank of San Francisco, October 19–20.

Organisation for Economic Co-operation and Development (OECD). (2010). *Annual Review of the Canadian Economy*. Paris: Organisation for Economic Co-operation and Development.

Partnoy, F. (2003). *Infectious Greed*. New York: Times Books.

Pecora, F. (1939). *Wall Street Under Oath: The Story of Our Modern Money Changers*. New York: A. M. Kelley.

Rajan, R. (2010). *Fault Lines*. Princeton, NJ: Princeton University Press.

Rajan, R., and R. Ramcharan. (2012). "The Anatomy of a Credit Crisis: The Boom and Busts in Farm Land Prices in the United States in the 1920s." NBER Working Paper 18027. Cambridge, MA: National Bureau of Economic Research.

Ratnovski, L., and R. Huang. (2009). "Why Are Canadian Banks More Resilient? IMF Working Paper 09/152. Washington, DC: International Monetary Fund.

Safarian, E. (1959). *The Canadian Economy in the Great Depression*. Toronto: University of Toronto Press.

Shearer, R., and C. Clark. (1984). "Canada and the Interwar Gold Standard, 1920–35: Monetary Policy without a Central Bank." In M. Bordo and A. Schwartz (eds), *A Retrospective on the Classical Gold Standard, 1821–1931*. Chicago: University of Chicago Press.

Taylor, J. (1993). "Discretion versus Policy Rules in Practice." *Carnegie-Rochester Conference Series on Public Policy* 39:195–214.

(2008). "The Financial Crisis and the Policy Responses: An Empirical Analysis of What Went Wrong." In *A Festschrift in Honour of David Dodge's Contributions to Canadian Public Policy*. Ottawa: Bank of Canada.

(2012). "Monetary Policy Rules Work and Discretion Doesn't: A Tale of Two Eras." *Journal of Money Banking and Credit* 44:1017–1034.

Wheelock, D. (1992). "Monetary Policy in the Great Depression: What the Fed Did and Why." *The Federal Reserve Bank of St. Louis Review* 74:3–28.

White, E. (1990a). "When the Ticker Ran Late: The Stock Market Boom and Crash of 1929." In E. White (ed), *Crashes and Panics: The Lessons from History*. Homewood, IL: Dow-Jones Irwin.

(1990b). "The Stock Market Boom and Crash of 1929 Revisited." *Journal of Economic Perspectives* 4:67–83.

(2009). "Lessons from the Great American Real Estate Boom and Bust of the 1920s." *NBER Working* Paper 15573. Cambridge, MA: National Bureau of Economic Research.

Woodford, M. (2003). *Interest and Prices: Foundations of a Theory of Monetary Policy*. Princeton, NJ: Princeton University Press.

13

It Is History but It's No Accident

*Differences in Residential Mortgage Markets in
Canada and the United States*

Angela Redish

Residential mortgages are typically the largest debts that a household takes on and are also a significant share of the credit in an economy. This latter makes the structure of the mortgage market important for both financial stability and for the transmission of monetary policy. The financial crisis of 2008 is frequently attributed to innovation in U.S. mortgage markets that fed a housing bubble which when it burst inflicted deep damage to the U.S. financial system. This sequence has led many economists to a renewed focus on the close connection between mortgage markets and financial stability.

A recent paper (Bordo et al. 2014) contrasted the stability of the Canadian financial system in 2008 with the financial fragility in the United States and noted that a similar contrast could have been drawn about crises in 1933, 1907, or 1896. The paper argued that the roots of Canadian (relative) financial stability lie in the very different histories of the U.S. and Canadian banking systems and that the oligopolistic Canadian system was embedded in a political economy that emphasized stability.

The goal of this chapter is to connect these two stories – to examine channels by which the historical evolution of the banking system had an impact on the structure of mortgage markets. The chapter begins by characterizing mortgage markets in Canada at the beginning of the twentieth century and then analyzes the changes in mortgage finance that resulted from (1) the Great Depression and the postwar housing boom and (2) the inflationary era of the 1970s, and the financial innovations of the 1990s. In each case the market for residential mortgages changed in different ways in the United States and Canada, and in each case the underlying banking system structure was crucial in the nature of that evolution.

Many thanks to Jim MacGee for his insightful discussion, to Eric Bond and Siavash Tahan for research assistance, and the Social Science and Humanities Research Council of Canada (SSHRCC) for financial support. As always, many thanks to Mike Bordo for his comments and suggestions.

˙ The analysis in this chapter contains a response to the question posed by John Campbell (2012, p. 1), who, having characterized the wide variation in mortgage market structure across countries, asked "whether this variation has deep fundamental causes or is the result of historical accident." The answer is both, at least in the case of the comparison between Canada and the United States: it is history, but it is no accident.

By the year 2005, residential mortgage lending in the United States and Canada looked very different. In the United States, most residential mortgages were long-term (thirty-year) loans to households that were originated by banks and then were sold ("distributed") to a government-sponsored entity such as Fannie Mae, which securitized the loans and sold them in carefully constructed tranches to investors in the United States and internationally – MacGee (2011) reports that in Canada in 2007 roughly 25 percent of mortgages were securitized, compared to 60 percent in the United States. In Canada mortgages were (typically) five-year loans made by a bank that then kept the loan on its own balance sheet. The extent of "subprime" lending was far higher in the United States (in Canada subprime lenders had a market share of roughly 5 percent compared to 22 percent in the United States). Furthermore, in Canada subprime mortgages were primarily loans to individuals amortizing over a longer period rather than interest-only mortgage, for example (MacGee 2009). In both countries governments provide some insurance – implicit or explicit – either of the loan itself or of the securitized instruments.

Without being excessively monocausal, this chapter argues that the different structure of financial institutions in the nineteenth century – in particular, the fragmented system of unit banking in the United States in contrast to the nationwide branch banking system in Canada – had an important impact on the differences in the structure of mortgage markets at the end of the twentieth century. Some specifics suggest the line of argument. The collapse of U.S. financial institutions in the Great Depression led to (1) regulation Q that limited interest rates on deposits in U.S. banks, (2) the establishment of Fannie Mae, and (c) the widespread use of long-term mortgages. In the 1970s, the maturity mismatch on the balance sheets of financial institutions, combined with the inability of banks to pay market (high) interest rates on deposits, led to failures of savings and loan corporations and difficulties for banks to fund mortgages. The need to tap into national funding markets and to access funds in money market mutual funds (MMMFs) created incentives to securitize mortgages.[1] In Canada, the banks did not face a maturity mismatch because the mortgages typically had a five-year term, and they did not need to securitize

---

[1] There were also important differences in how Canada and the United States regulated off-balance sheet related financial institutions. See later and MacGee (2009).

to access nationwide markets because the banks had branches across the country.

The lessons from this viewpoint are twofold: first, the stability that emerged from the Canadian institutions came at a price. In Canada, households have to refinance their mortgages roughly every five years, and so have to absorb interest rate risk that in the United States is borne (for a price) by the financial sector (Courchane and Giles 2002). Second, the early 2000s is not the end of the story. Although Canadian banks can readily tap national funding sources, they may wish to tap global funding sources, in which case securitization will increase.

RESIDENTIAL MORTGAGE LENDING IN CANADA FROM 1900 TO THE 1930S

The Canadian residential mortgage industry in 1900 looked very different from its structure today, and although there were important differences between Canada and the United States, they were less stark than today. The "terms and conditions" in both countries were similar. A typical residential mortgage was a loan for five years on which interest was paid semiannually. Some repayment of principal might accompany the interest payments but it would be a small portion of the loan and the borrower would be obliged to repay the majority of the principle at the end of five years. Typically, that repayment was made through a rollover of the outstanding balance. The loan-to-value ratio was usually less than 50 percent.[2]

Figure 13.1 shows the available (and incomplete) data on the type and amount of mortgage lending as a proportion of gross national product (GNP).[3] We have normalized the data by showing the stock of mortgages outstanding relative to gross domestic product (GDP). In general, this is useful as it shows the changes in the economy's use of mortgage debt; however, it does not differentiate between increasing use of mortgages and declines in GDP. Thus, although the ratio rose in the 1920s, reflecting a building boom, it also rose in the early 1930s, reflecting the collapse of nominal GDP.

Significant gaps in the data include the lack of any aggregate data on personal mortgage lending before 1926 and the absence of data on mortgages by Trust and Mortgage Loan Companies between 1913 and 1926.[4]

---

[2] This picture of a "typical" Canadian residential mortgage is drawn from Poapst (1962, pp. 66–67). Life insurance companies were legally prohibited from making loans with more than 60 percent loan to value. (Woodard 1959, p. 9).

[3] Although the objective is to report only lending on residential mortgages, farm mortgages may be included in the early data.

[4] Trust and Mortgage Loan companies could have a federal or provincial charter, with the latter restricting the firm's activity to the province in which it was chartered. Prior to 1913 the federal government assembled data on all financial institutions but after 1913 the data

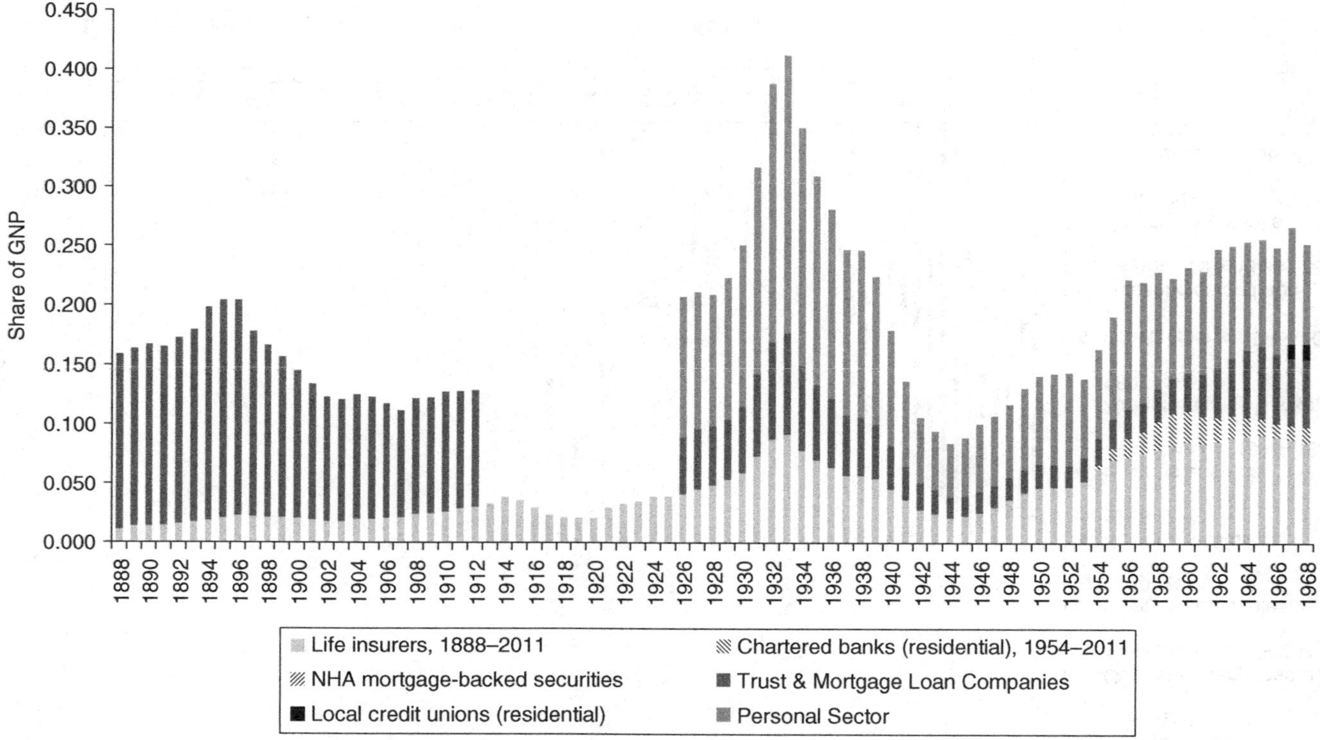

Figure 13.1. Outstanding mortgage debt as a proportion of GNP by institution type in Canada.

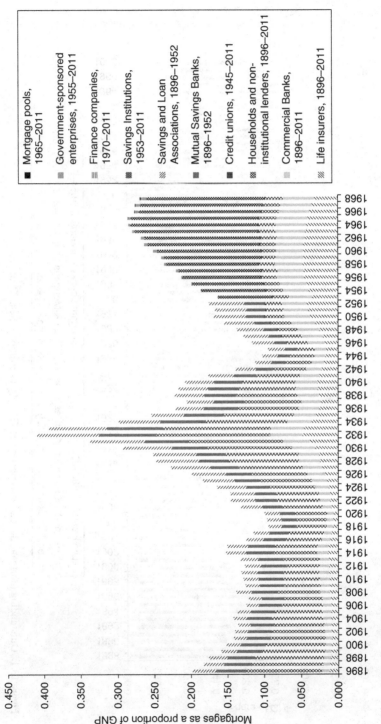

Figure 13.2. U.S. residential mortgages as a proportion of GNP by institution type.

Nonbank financial institutions were important lenders for residential mortgage loans, but the noninstitutional sector was also extremely important. Naturally, data on the size of that part of the market are difficult to come by. There are estimates of the extent of "personal" loans after 1926 and they suggest that just over half of stock of residential mortgage loans were held in the "personal" sector. The personal sector included both loans between individuals and by unregistered pension funds, and the Canada Mortgage and Housing Corporation (CMHC) emphasizes that the data are sketchy.[5] This last caution advises against relying on details of the data, but it does not preclude the conclusion that the noninstitutional sector provided a major share of the funding of mortgages prior to the Depression.

Some further details on the role of the personal sector are provided by an analysis of a (5 percent) longitudinal sample of first mortgages from Hamilton, Ontario. This sample shows the proportion of mortgages held by individuals (i.e., as creditors) to have been roughly 90 percent from 1901 to 1921 and then to have declined gradually to 60 percent in 1951 (Harris and Ragonetti 1998, p. 231).[6] Analysis of the housing market more broadly shows that the up until the mid-1950s, "a quarter of all families acquired their homes without going into debt" (Harris and Ragonetti 1998, p. 233), often because they had built their own home.

The key financial institutions making mortgage loans were life insurance companies, trust companies, and mortgage and loan companies.[7] As Figure 13.1 shows, the life insurance companies held a relatively small share of the market in the late nineteenth century, but reflecting the dramatic growth of the life insurance industry in the early twentieth century, they held a larger share than the combined trust and mortgage and loan companies by the 1920s.

At the turn of the century mortgage loan companies were the largest institutional lender for mortgage loans. The companies had grown out of building societies, which had begun as cooperative terminating building societies but by 1900 were mostly for-profit incorporated institutions. They raised their funds by selling debentures in Canada (an average of 20 percent of funds) and the United Kingdom (43 percent of funds), and

---

for provincially regulated mortgage and loan companies was not collected. In 1926 collection resumed.

[5] The data come from a report commissioned by CMHC in 1970 (CMHC Economic Research Bulletin Number 77, Appendix D) and subsequently lost – only the table remains. See Smith and Sparks (1973, p. 12) and Harris and Ragonetti (1998, p. 224).

[6] The authors argue that the share of the number of mortgages exceeds the share of the value, which might have been closer to 85 percent in the early years.

[7] Only consolidated data for trust companies and mortgage loan companies are available for the period before 1914.

to a lesser extent from deposit-taking (20 percent). They were regulated as to minimum capital and leverage ratios as well as having restrictions on the types of assets (mortgages, cash, and government securities) they could hold.[8]

Trust companies held a smaller share of the market than the other two types of financial institutions but most of the data sources combine mortgage loan and trust company balance sheets so that we report the amalgamated totals. An important difference between the two is that for trust companies, mortgages represented a "use" of funds to support their core business – trust services. For mortgage loan companies, mortgages were their core business and they sold debentures to support the mortgage lending.

Finally, we discuss the institutions that we don't see. The Canadian banks were prohibited from lending on mortgages until 1954. This is in contrast with the United States, where banks were important mortgage lenders, and where deposits were an important source of mortgage funds at both banks and savings and loan companies. From Confederation to the Great Depression the Canadian banks were the largest financial institution in Canada, measured both in terms of the size of the sector and in terms of the size of individual institutions.[9] At Confederation the decision was made to continue the colonial system of chartered banks. In 1900 there were thirty-five banks, but primarily through mergers and acquisitions this had been reduced to eleven by the Great Depression. All were branching banks, and the five largest banks held 90 percent of industry assets and had branches across the country as well as internationally.

There was no central bank and very little monitoring of banks. Indeed, until a major bank failure in 1923, there was no government inspection of banks. There were strict minimum capital requirements, double liability of shareholders, restrictions on note issues, and capital adequacy requirements. There were also tight rules on the assets that banks could hold. These rules were based on the "real bills doctrine" that underlay the pre-colonial banking system, and essentially required banks to lend by "discounting" real bills – IOUs drawn against stock in trade. Banks could also hold government securities.

It is always harder to explain an omission than a commission. The consequences of the banks' absence from mortgage lending were the size of the mortgage loan companies and the amount of personal lending. The

---

[8] See Neufeld (1972, chapter 7) for a detailed description of the legislation affecting building societies and mortgage loan companies.

[9] In 1900 the assets of the chartered banks were 50 percent more than the sum of the assets of all other financial institutions. The discussion in this paragraph draws on Bordo et al. (2014).

banks themselves seem to have never expressed the desire to get into the mortgage business, and as we see in the text that follows were hesitant to enter when it was first proposed.

THE IMPACT OF THE DEPRESSION AND POSTWAR HOUSING BOOM

The Canadian mortgage market changed significantly during the Great Depression as the federal government intervened in the market, and the nature of mortgage instruments changed in response. This is in parallel with events in the United States, but the similarities are limited. In the United States, the government intervention was driven largely by difficulties in the credit market; in Canada the objectives were increasing employment and improving housing (Woodard 1959, p. 32). Further, although the interventions are significant because of their persistence, the scale of intervention in Canada was much smaller than that in the United States.

The extent of mortgage difficulties in Canada during the 1930s is not well established. Reports from mortgage loan and trust companies (which combine residential, farm, and nonfarm mortgages) show a spike in mortgages in distress, but at a peak of 2 percent of all mortgages (see Figure 13.3). These apparently low rates of compulsory proceedings are at odds with the extensive legislation passed by provincial and federal governments to reduce the difficulties of agricultural borrowers.[10]

The Dominion Housing Act in 1935 was the government's vehicle for intervening in the housing market.[11] The act aimed to increase the supply of new housing and increase employment in the construction sector by having the government supply some of the funds for mortgage loans. The innovations – other than the government supplying some of the funding and taking part of any losses – included the introduction of high ratio loans (up to 70 to 80 percent loan-to-value [LTV] ratio), terms up to twenty years, and blended monthly payments. That is, the payments would amortize the mortgage over its term. Loans were to be made by "approved lenders," that is, life insurance companies, trust companies, and mortgage loan companies that were federally or provincially incorporated. Loans were strictly for newly constructed housing.

---

[10] Prairie provincial governments typically introduced moratoria, and the Federal Government Farmers' Creditors Arrangement Act of 1934 deferred payments and reduced them. In the first sixteen months of operation the Board settled 11,000 cases reducing the debt by an average of 30 percent (Easterbrook and W. B. H. 1936). Haubrich (1990) argues that the extent of financial distress in the Canadian Prairie provinces was of the same order as in the United States but differences in data sources make comparisons difficult.

[11] In 1918, the federal government had lent $25 million to provincial governments that they were to lend to municipalities for housing construction. Firestone (1951, p. 480) reports that 6,000 units were built.

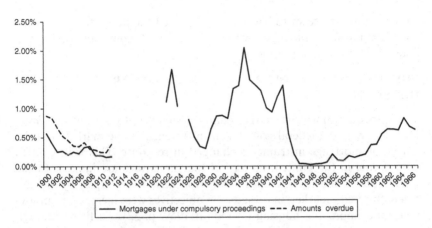

Figure 13.3. Trust and loan companies: mortgages in distress as a proportion of total real estate under mortgage.

The act cannot be said to have had a large direct impact. It remained in place for only three years and fewer than 5,000 units were built. Conventional mortgages (i.e., for existing rather than new residential housing) continued to have semiannual interest and minor principal payments, although the term more frequently extended to ten years. Institutional lenders still imposed a maximum of 60 percent LTV ratio.

In 1938 the Dominion Housing Act was replaced by the National Housing Act (NHA), which added incentives for housing construction in remote communities and for low-income households. The act continued (1) to authorize blended payment amortizing loans, (2) to permit amortization over long periods, (3) to permit high-LTV ratio loans, and (4) to require the government to share in any credit losses. The act was amended numerous times, most notably in 1944 when the CMHC was established to implement sections of the NHA.[12]

In the United States, as in Canada, the Depression led the federal government to intervene in the residential mortgage market, but in the United States the intervention was earlier and more aggressive. Furthermore, the intervention was a direct response to the financial institution failures of the early 1930s, rather than aimed specifically at employment. Green and Wachter (2005, p. 95) estimate that in the worst year of the Depression approximately 10 percent of homes were in foreclosure. In the United States – as in Canada – LTV ratios were low, but

---

[12] The CMHC – structured as a Crown Corporation – continues to be the housing agency for the Canadian government today although the title has changed from Central Mortgage and Housing Corporation to Canada Mortgage and Housing Corporation.

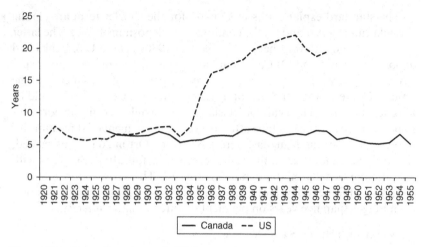

Figure 13.4. Term of mortgages by life insurance companies.

when mortgages came due the entire principal was owed, and in the face
of bank failures, the loans were not renewed. When borrowers could not
refinance they defaulted. The government responded by creating financial institutions to increase the availability of mortgage funds. The Home
Owner's Loan Corporation (HOLC) was created in 1933 to raise funds
by selling government bonds and then use the proceeds to purchase
defaulted mortgages that were then reinstated with long (twenty-year)
terms and amortized payments.

The Federal Housing Administration (FHA) was created in 1934 to
provide mortgage insurance and thereby make the mortgages held by
the HOLC marketable. Finally, in 1938, the Federal National Mortgage
Association (FNMA, or Fannie Mae) was established to build a secondary
market for FHA mortgages.

As shown in Figure 13.4, after the Great Depression, mortgage terms
in Canada and the United States were starkly different. The U.S. mortgage
market was characterized by long-term loans that had eliminated interest rate and liquidity risk for borrowers. In Canada, although loans were
amortized over long periods, the terms were still typically less than five
years and the borrowers were liable to the need to roll over their loans at a
variable interest rate. On the other hand, because mortgages were funded
primarily with short-term deposits, the Canadian lenders faced less maturity mismatch than U.S. lenders, the consequences of which we turn to
next. The lengthening of the term of U.S. mortgages has important effects
and by implication the non-lengthening in Canada is also significant, but
it is not clear why Canada retained shorter terms.

The standard explanations in Canada for the shorter term are (1) the Canada Interest Act and (2) the conditions of deposit insurance. The latter is obviously not relevant here, as in the late 1930s (1) the U.S. banks had deposit insurance and (2) Canadian banks neither lent on mortgage security nor had deposit insurance. The former is perhaps more salient. At the time of Confederation the lack of a right of prepayment for what could be long-term loans led to a call for legislation that would permit the borrower to pay out the loan at any time after five years on payment of three months' interest. In 1880 the Canada Interest Act (the "Orton Act") was passed, which in Section 10 gives the right to repay in full after five years with a maximum penalty of three months' interest. The act with amendments continues in force today, and Canadians have the right to repay loans of a term longer than five years on payment of three months' interest.[13]

CANADA IN THE POSTWAR ERA

NHA mortgages continued to be restricted to new housing but in the housing boom immediately after World War II they played a significant role. Smith (1974, p. 8) estimated that in 1948, about half of mortgage initiations (by value) by financial institutions were for new residential units and about half of those were financed with NHA mortgages.[14] That said, it is important to recall that estimates of the "personal sector" suggest that (very) approximately a third of mortgage debt was held outside the financial sector.

The postwar baby boom created an increase in housing demand that led the government to amend the NHA in 1954 to permit banks to be among the authorized lenders for NHA mortgages. The high demand for mortgage loans and the fact that the federal government had to put up roughly 25 percent of the funds for the NHA mortgages was creating a fiscal problem for the government. The banks were the largest financial institutions in the country and they had access to depositor funds as a source of loanable funds. The banks had not asked for this amendment and were reported to be unenthusiastic but, as Figure 13.1 shows, they did get into the business line almost immediately. The amendment provided that the government would no longer be a source of funds, and it also replaced the "share of

---

[13] How the act relates to renewals of mortgages was articulated in a Supreme Court case in 1985 (see Waldron 1987/1988). See also the 2008 report of the Working Group of the Uniform Law Conference of Canada.

[14] There were limits to the value that the NHA would loan so that "luxury homes" were not financed by NHA loans. The other half of initiations were for either existing residential or nonresidential property. (Harris [1999] points out that the restriction of NHA mortgages to new construction had the regressive effect of subsidizing construction in the new suburbs to the cost of inner city homes.)

the losses" provision with loan insurance paid for by the borrower. The act further made provision for the sale of mortgages, with the hope that as in the United States, this would enable nonapproved lenders to be a source of mortgage funds (Poapst 1962, p. 177).

Two provisions continued to be important. NHA mortgages were only for new construction and the interest rate on loans was prescribed – specifically to be 2.25 percent higher than the twenty-year government bond rate (Poapst 1962, p. 175). This latter prescription had implications for the amount of lending by banks as the Bank Act limited bank lending to 6 percent, and in December 1959 when the NHA mortgage interest rate rose to 6.75 percent the banks effectively got out of mortgage lending.[15]

In summary, between 1954 and 1967 the Canadian banks were permitted to make mortgage loans where the mortgages carried government insurance and were for new construction. The banks were active in making such mortgage loans between 1954 and 1959. The increase in the share of NHA mortgages through the 1950s led to a spread of the terms on NHA mortgages to conventional mortgages. In 1950, it was still the case that conventional mortgages had LTV ratios of 50 percent, and a term of five years. By 1961 when the Royal Commission of Banking and Finance studied mortgage markets, the life insurance companies were lending up to 66.6 percent LTV ratio, and term and amortization rates were twenty or twenty-five years (Poapst 1962, p. 72).[16]

Figures 13.1 and 13.2 show that in both countries the stock of mortgages relative to GDP rose from about 10 percent in the late 1940s to around 25 percent in the late 1960s. In Canada the life insurance companies had provided the funding for much of that growth, and in the United States, savings and loan companies had filled the demand for housing finance.

The 1967 Bank Act revision in Canada removed the 6 percent cap on interest rates on bank lending and the banks fairly quickly resumed mortgage lending. Simultaneously, the banks were permitted to lend on conventional mortgages as well as NHA-insured mortgages. However, lending on conventional mortgages was restricted to those with LTV ratio less than 75 percent unless the mortgagor bought insurance from CMHC.[17] The other major change in 1967 was the introduction of deposit insurance. The banks were required to become members of the Canadian

---

[15] Because the banks were lending at 6 percent on commercial loans, and the NHA rate was a maximum rate not required rate, it is not completely clear why lending on an asset with no default risk was not preferred to lending to commercial clients. However, the banks instead purchased mortgage loan companies that were free to make the higher interest loans.

[16] In 1965 the ratio was increased to 75 percent. Mortgage and loan companies faced similar requirements (Neufeld 1972, p. 216).

[17] Canadian mortgage insurance is structured slightly differently from that offered by FNMA. The NHA insurance is paid for at the origination of the mortgage and covers the entire amount of the loan for the entire period of the loan.

Deposit Insurance Corporation (CDIC), and all deposits up to $20,000 were insured (a cap currently at $100,000). The financial institutions were required to pay an insurance fee, which was initially not risk adjusted, which the large banks resented.[18] Only deposits with a term of five years or less were insured.

The introduction of deposit insurance reflected the impact of the same forces that drove U.S. banking history – federal/provincial jurisdictional debates and bank/near bank competition. Specifically, Canadian banks were all federally incorporated, regulated, and monitored. Trust companies, life insurance companies, and mortgage and loan companies could be federally or provincially incorporated. In the mid-1960s a major trust company (British Mortgage and Loan) required emergency funding from the Ontario government when a subsidiary (Atlantic Acceptance Corporation) failed. This led some trust companies to support a call for deposit insurance. The federal enquiry (Porter Commission) into banking in the mid-1960s argued for the inclusion of trust companies under the Bank Act because their activities overlapped significantly with banking activities. When the changes recommended by the Commission were implemented in 1967, the broad inclusion of the trust companies was omitted, but the creation of a Crown Corporation to provide mandatory deposit insurance to federally incorporated financial institutions was included.

As noted earlier, there is some debate over whether the limit of five-year term for deposits to be insurable explains the absence of long-term mortgage. That is, because most deposits are for five years or less, the banks prefer to make mortgage loans with similar terms to avoid any maturity mismatch (Freedman 1998). However, Canadian mortgages had that characteristic since the Depression and it seems more likely that it reflects the interest act, which allows homeowners to pay off mortgages after five years with a maximum penalty of ninety days' interest (Lessard 1975).

THE IMPACT OF THE GREAT INFLATION

From the mid-1960s a series of exogenous forces drove change in the financial sector in both Canada and the United States: inflation rates rose, the clear distinctions between financial institutions eroded, and innovations in information technology changed the set of feasible financial instruments. But how these forces changed the sector differed between the two countries, reflecting their different starting points.

Figures 13.5 and 13.6 show the consequences of these changes on the suppliers of mortgage funds. In Canada, the ratio of mortgages outstanding to GDP rose from 30 percent in the late 1970s to 45 percent in 2005;

---

[18] The fee was 1/30th of 1 percent of insured deposits. Coverage included twenty-eight federally regulated financial institutions that were required to join and forty-one provincially regulated institutions that chose to join (Wagster 2007, p. 1657).

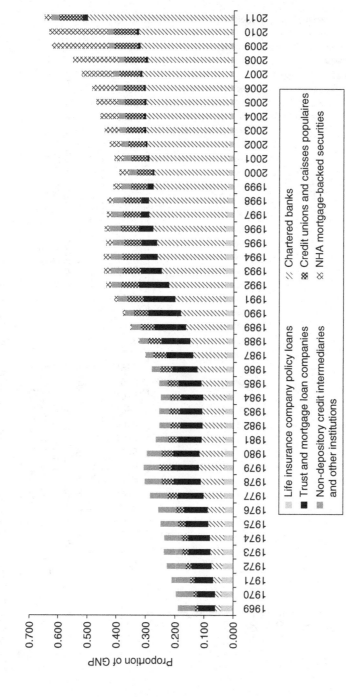

Figure 13.5. Residential mortgage debt as a proportion of GNP by institution type in Canada.

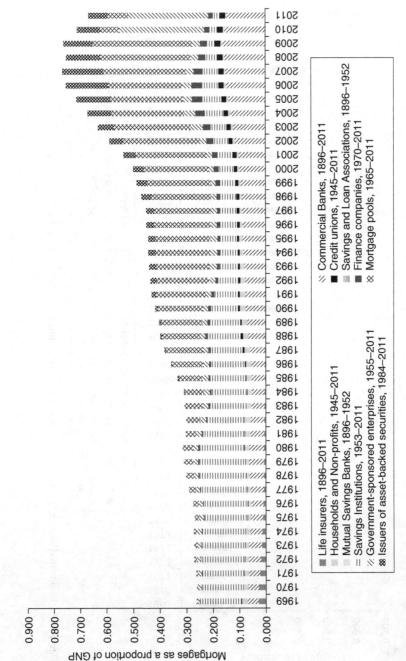

Figure 13.6. U.S. residential mortgages as proportion of GNP by institution type.

Table 13.1. Chartered Bank Absorptions of Financial Institutions

Chartered Bank Owned	Mortgage and Loan	Trust Company	Securities Dealers
Canadian Imperial Bank of Commerce (CIBC)	Kinross Mortgage (1963)	National Trust	Wood Gundy
Toronto-Dominion Bank (TD)	Canada Permanent		
Bank of Nova Scotia (BNS)	Holborough Investments		McLeod Weir Young
Royal Bank	Roymor (1968)	Montreal Trust	Dominion Securities
Bank of Montreal (BMO)		Royal Trust	Nesbitt Thomson

Sources: Bordo et al. (2014); Neufeld (1972).

in the United States the ratio started at a similar point but rose to 70 percent in 2005. In Canada, the picture is one of minimal securitization, a decline of trust and mortgage loan companies, and a dramatic increase in the share of mortgage lending by chartered banks. In the United States, the share of lending by savings and loan companies decreased, but the share of mortgages that were financed through mortgage pools and securitization increased.

The increase in inflation rates caused challenges in both Canada and the United States. In both cases, the banks faced regulations on the interest rate on deposits. In Canada, mortgages were still relatively short-term instruments so that the maturity mismatch for financial institutions was much less severe than for the U.S. savings and loan companies. The switch in Canada between lending by mortgage and loan companies and banks overstates the changes in the flow of funds in Canada since each of the large banks acquired a mortgage and loan company. Indeed, this is the recent history of the Canadian financial sector: over time the banks also acquired trust companies and – once permitted by 1987 changes to the Bank Act – securities dealers (see Table 13.1).

One consequence of the concentration of financial assets in one part of the financial system is that the supervision of the financial system is similarly concentrated. The Office of the Superintendent of Financial Institutions (OSFI) regulates and supervises all federally incorporated financial institutions.[19] There are many differences in regulation between

---

[19] That said, OSFI was established in 1987 in response to the 1985 failure of two small Canadian banks, the Canadian Commercial Bank and the Northland Bank of Canada.

the United States and Canada but a critical distinction lies in the extent to which banks are regulated as consolidated entities. Thus, the banks are required to report consolidated balance sheets that include their trust and mortgage company subsidiaries.

INFLATION AND DEREGULATION IN THE UNITED STATES

Regulation Q, a clause of the Banking Act of 1933, prohibited the payment of interest on demand deposits and imposed ceilings on interest rates on other deposits.[20] In 1966, deposits in mutual savings banks and savings and loans associations were brought under the policy. From 1933 to 1966, the ceilings exceeded the yields on Treasury bills and were typically not binding. This changed in the late 1970s when inflation, and interest rates, rose dramatically. Regulation Q constrained the ability of the savings and loan companies to attract deposits, but their assets were long-term low-interest mortgages. Simultaneously, Money Market Mutual Funds (MMMFs) were created, which being outside Regulation Q could offer a savings instrument that was as liquid for investors as a savings account with far higher returns: between 1978 and 1983, the ratio of MMMFs to bank deposits rose from 1 percent to 11 percent. In contrast, in Canada the ratio rose from 0.1 percent to 0.2 percent.[21]

The shift of funds out of depository institutions (shrinking of the liability side of depository institutions) was accompanied by a shift of mortgage lending out of depository institutions (shrinking of the asset side). Depositories shifted from an "originate and hold" model to "originate to distribute" and securitized mortgage loans that were then sold and resold. Securitization addressed three problems for U.S. depository institutions – capital regulation, maturity mismatch, and access to national and international capital markets.

Capital regulation required that banks hold capital against risky assets and by getting mortgages off their books banks could reduce their capital charges. Ideally, by pooling mortgages and tranching them by risk,

---

These two banks, which had started business in 1975 and which held most of their assets in Western Canada, had expanded aggressively in the late 1970s and were hard hit by the recession of the early 1980s. The banks held only approximately 0.75 of 1 percent of Canadian banking assets, however, the government, shocked by the first bank failure since 1923, revisited bank oversight and integrated the regulation of all federally incorporated financial institutions – banks, insurance companies, and pension plans.

[20] Commercial banks that were members of the Federal Reserve System were covered by the clause in the Banking Act of 1933, which was extended to nonmember commercial banks by the Banking Act of 1935. Gilbert (1986, p. 22). The goals of the legislation included encouraging lending by local banks, rather than sending funds out of the locality on deposit to city banks and limiting risk taking by reducing the competition for deposits.

[21] And when MMMFs did become more popular in Canada they were created by the banks (and on the banks' balance sheets; Bordo et al., 2014 table 2).

risk sharing would reduce idiosyncratic risks. The Canadian banks were sufficiently large that within the bank mortgage risk could be reduced. Furthermore, Canadian regulators regulated the consolidated institution so that moving risk to an off-balance sheet subsidiary was much less likely to reduce capital requirements.

U.S. mortgage lenders face significantly greater prepayment risk than Canadian lenders. Again, for an individual lender this risk can get pooled through the securitization process. In Canada, loans are for shorter terms and prepayment penalties are high, so that pooling of prepayment risk did not provide an incentive for Canadian banks to securitize mortgages.

Finally, the branching structure of Canadian banks meant that funds could be transferred interregionally within a single bank. In the United States, this was much more challenging. In addition, the decades of unit banking had created a financial system in which markets were used to move funds interregionally rather than internal transfers within institutions. U.S. financial markets were far deeper and more developed than Canadian financial markets, creating a path dependency that encouraged mortgage securitization.

In 2007, 60 percent of mortgages in the United States were securitized while only 25 percent of Canadian mortgages were securitized. MacGee (2009) cites data stating that 22 percent of U.S. mortgages were by subprime lenders compared to 5 percent in Canada – and the subprime mortgages in the United States were likely to be interest-only loans to subprime borrowers, while in Canada they would be long amortization loans to near-prime borrowers.

CONCLUSION

Post-crisis analysis (e.g., Mian and Sufi 2009) has shown the importance of the securitization of mortgages, especially subprime mortgages, in the mortgage default crisis. Levitin and Wachter (2012), among many others, argue that the channel for this importance was the asymmetric information created by the "complexity, opacity, and heterogeneity" of the market for these private-label mortgage-backed securities. In Canada the extent of subprime mortgage lending was very small relative to that in the United States and the degree of securitization was similarly low. The majority of mortgages were kept on the books of the banks so that the asymmetric information problems were far less present.

MacGee (2009) argues that Canada had the advantage of being a "late adopter of innovations" and of having an approach to regulation and supervision that was more consistent with good corporate governance, but that leads to the question of why this was so. This chapter has argued that the differences have deep roots in the historical structure of the financial systems of the two countries.

At the beginning of the twentieth century, the United States had a fragmented banking system and, in part as a consequence, relatively deep markets for fixed income securities. Canada had a concentrated, and politically powerful, banking system comprising nationwide branching banks and, again in part as a consequence, relatively thin markets for fixed income securities. From this background perhaps it is unsurprising that across the twentieth century, mortgage lending in Canada came to be dominated by banks and funded by deposits, while in the United States, mortgage funding turned to securities markets. The interesting part of the story relates how this transition occurred, and weaves in the changing role of governments in providing the institutional framework for the mortgage markets.

DATA APPENDIX

Figure 13.1

GNP: 1888–1926: Urquhart. Table 1.6 – Gross national product in current and constant dollars and real gross national product per capita, 1870–1925; **1926–1960**: *Historical Statistics of Canada* Ed. 1, Series E1-12 – National income and gross national product, 1926–1960; **1961–1968**: *Statistics Canada*. Table 380-0030 – Gross domestic product (GDP) and gross national product (GNP) at market prices and net national income at basic prices, annual, 1960–2011 (accessed August 8, 2012).

Life insurers (nonfarm mortgages): **1888–1959**: *Historical Statistics of Canada* Ed. 1. Series H373-408 – Total assets of Canadian life insurance companies under federal registration and assets in Canada of British and foreign companies under federal registration, 1888–1959; **1960–1976**: *Historical Statistics of Canada* Ed. 2. Series J428-444 – Life insurance companies and fraternal benefit societies, 1959 to 1976; **1977–2011**: *Statistics Canada*. Table 176-0024 – Life insurers, including accident, sickness branches, and segregated funds, annual, 1977–2011 (accessed August 8, 2012).

Trust and Mortgage Loan Companies: **1888–1912** (nonfarm mortgages): Department of Finance. Table of Assets – Assets of building societies, loan, and trust companies. Report on the Affairs of Building Societies, Loan, and Trust Companies, 1912. **1926–1932** (residential mortgages): Canada Mortgage and Housing Corporation. Appendix D – Mortgage loans outstanding in Canada. *Economic Research Bulletin* 77, 1971. **1933–1964** (residential mortgages): Canada Mortgage and Housing Corporation. Table 77 – Mortgage loans outstanding, holdings by lending institutions, governments, corporate lenders, and part of personal sector, Canada. Canadian Housing Statistics, 1974. **1965–1968** (residential mortgages): *Historical Statistics of Canada* Ed. 2. Series J273-309 – Trust companies, 1963–1976 and Series J310-350 – Mortgage companies, 1963–1976.

Chartered Banks (residential mortgages): **1954–1968**: *Statistics Canada.* Table 176-0015 – Chartered banks, assets, and liabilities, at month-end, annual, 1954–2011 (accessed August 7, 2012).

Local credit unions (residential mortgages): **1967–1968**: *Statistics Canada.* Table 176-0026 – Local credit unions and caisses populaires: quarterly statement of assets and liabilities, end of period, annual, 1967–2011 (accessed August 8, 2012).

Personal Sector (residential mortgages): **1926–1968**: Canada Mortgage and Housing Corporation. Appendix D – Mortgage loans outstanding in Canada. *Economic Research Bulletin* 77, 1971.

Figure 13.2
Residential Mortgages

1896–1952: Life insurers, commercial banks, mutual savings banks, savings and loan associations, households, and noninstitutional lenders: *Historical Statistics of the United States* Millennial Ed. Table Dc907-911 – Mortgage debt on residential structures by type of lender, 1896–1952.

1945–1968: Credit unions: Federal Reserve Bank of the United States. Table L.218 – Home mortgage levels by type of lender. Flow of Funds (Z), 1945–2011.

1953–1968: Life insurers, commercial banks, savings institutions, government-sponsored enterprises, mortgage pools, households, and noninstitutional lenders: Federal Reserve Bank of the United States. Table L.218 – Home mortgage levels by type of lender. Flow of Funds (Z), 1945–2011.

GNP: **1896–1928**: *Historical Statistics of the United States* Millennial Ed. Table Ca188 – Kendrik gross national product in current dollars, 1889–1929; **1929–2011**: Bureau of Economic Analysis. Table 1.7.5. Relation of gross domestic product, gross national product, net national product, national income, and personal income, 1929–2011.

Figure 13.3

Canada average term: *Historical Statistics of Canada* Ed. 1. Series H419
US average term: *Historical Statistics of the United States* Millennial Ed. Table Dc1198.

Figure 13.4

Residential mortgage data: *Statistics Canada*. Table 176-0069 – Residential mortgage credit, outstanding balances of major private institutional lenders, annual (December month-end) (accessed August 6, 2012).

GNP: *Statistics Canada*. Table 380-0030 – Gross domestic product (GDP) and gross national product (GNP) at market prices and net national income at basic prices, annual (accessed August 8, 2012).

REFERENCES

Bordo, M., A. Redish, and H. Rockoff. (2014). "Why Didn't Canada Have a Banking Crisis in 2008 (or in 1930, or 1907, or ...)?" *Economic History Review* DOI: 10.1111/1468-0289.665; also at NBER Working Paper w17312. Cambridge, MA: National Bureau of Economic Research.

Campbell, J. (2012). "Mortgage Market Design." NBER Working Paper w18339. Cambridge, MA: National Bureau of Economic Research.

Courchane, M., and J. Giles. (2002). "A Comparison of US and Canadian Residential Mortgage Markets." *Property Management* (Suppl. IRES special issue Part 1), 20(5): 326–368.

Easterbrook, W. and W. B. H. (1936). "Agricultural Debt Adjustment." *Canadian Journal of Economics and Political Science* (August):390–403.

Firestone, O. (1951). *Residential Real Estate in Canada*. Toronto: University of Toronto Press.

Freedman, C. (1998). "The Canadian Banking System." Bank of Canada Technical Report 81.

Gilbert, R. A. (1986). "Requiem for Regulation Q: What It Did and Why It Passed Away." *Federal Reserve Bank of St. Louis Review* (February):22–37.

Green, R. K., and S. Wachter. (2005). "The American Mortgage in Historical and International Context." *Journal of Economic Perspectives* 19(4):93–114.

Green, R. K., and Susan M. Wachter. (2007). "The Housing Finance Revolution." Housing, Housing Finance and Monetary Policy, A Symposium Sponsored the Federal Reserve Bank of Kansas City, August 30–September 1, pp. 21–67.

Harris, R. (1999). "Housing and Social Policy: A Historical Perspective on Canadian-American Differences." *Urban Studies* 36:1169–1175.

Harris, R., and D. Ragonetti. (1998). "Where Credit Is Due: Residential Mortgage Finance in Canada, 1901 to 1954." *Journal of Real Estate Finance and Economics* 16(2):223–238.

Hatch, J. (1975). *The Canadian Mortgage Market*. Toronto: Queens Printer.

Haubrich, J. (1990). "Nonmonetary Effects of Financial Crises: Lessons from the Great Depression in Canada." *Journal of Monetary Economics* (March): 223–252.

Kiff, J. (2010). "Canadian Residential Mortgage Markets: Boring but Effective?" Washington, DC: International Monetary Fund.

Lessard, D. (1975). "Roll-over Mortgages in Canada." in Federal Reserve Bank of Boston, New Mortgage Designs for an Inflationary Environment, Conference Series 14 (January):131–141.

Levitin, A., and S. Wachtel. (2012). "Explaining the Housing Bubble." *Georgetown Law Journal* 100,(4):1177–1258.

MacGee, J. (2009). "Why Didn't Canada's Housing Market Go Bust?" Economic Commentary. Federal Reserve Bank of Cleveland, September.

Mian, A., and S. Sufi. (2009). "The Consequences of Mortgage Credit Expansion: Evidence from the US Mortgage Default Crisis." *Quarterly Journal of Economics* 124:1449–1496.

Neufeld, E. (1972). *The Financial System of Canada: Its Growth and Development.* Toronto: Macmillan.

Poapst, J. (1962). "The Residential Mortgage Market." Working paper prepared for the Royal Commission on Banking and Finance.

(1975). *Developing the Residential Mortgage Market*, Vol. II. Mortgage Investment Companies, Toronto: Canada Housing and Mortgage Corporation.

Slater, D. (1968). "The 1967 Revision of the Canadian Banking Acts Part I: An Economist's View." *Canadian Journal of Economics* (February):79–91.

Smith, L. (1974). *The Postwar Canadian Housing and Residential Mortgage Markets and the Role of Government.* Toronto: University of Toronto Press.

Smith, L., and G. Sparks. (1973). "Institutional Mortgage Lending in Canada, 1954–68: An Econometric Analysis." *Bank of Canada Staff Research Studies*, 9.

Traclet V. (2005). "Structure of the Canadian Housing Market and Finance System." Paper prepared for the CGFS.

Wagster, John D. (2007). "Wealth and Risk Effects of Adopting Deposit Insurance in Canada: Evidence of Risk Shifting by Banks and Trust Companies." *Journal of Money Credit and Banking* 39(7):1651–1681.

Waldron, M. (1987–1988). "Section 10 of the Interest Act: All the King's Men." *Canadian Business Law Journal* 13:468–489.

Woodard, H. (1959). *Canadian Mortgages.* Toronto: Collins.

14

Monetary Regimes and Policy on a Global Scale
The Oeuvre of Michael D. Bordo

Hugh Rockoff and Eugene N. White

> If I have seen further, it is by standing on the shoulders of giants.
>
> – Sir Isaac Newton

In the field of economics, Michael David Bordo (MDB) stands out as one of the leading financial and monetary historians of the late twentieth and early twenty-first centuries. He is known around the globe for giving us a clearer vision of the central issues of monetary policy and choice of exchange rate regimes through the lens of economic history. His energy and enthusiasm make him a favorite collaborator with graduate students and senior scholars alike. One imagines there is scarcely a central bank he has not visited to present his work, advise policymakers, and consult with the research staff.

In this chapter, we attempt to survey Bordo's immense oeuvre, of 244 published articles, chapters, surveys, and reviews and 12 books and edited volumes at last count. Given his vast range of interests there is no easy summary of the topics to which he has contributed. We think his work is best understood in terms of the role that it has played in the development of macroeconomics. In a 1994 article in the *Journal of Monetary Economics*, Jeffrey Miron lamented the yawning gap between Milton Friedman and Anna J. Schwartz's 1963 *A Monetary History of the United States, 1867–1960* and contemporary macroeconomics. He wrote:

> The difference between the kind of empirical work presented by Friedman and Schwartz in *A Monetary History* and the kind of empirical work taught in graduate schools and practiced as 'state-of-the-art' is just as striking now as in the early 1980s. [when he was in graduate school] Even more striking is the dramatic difference between the lasting impact of *A Monetary History* and the ephemeral impact achieved by the bulk of more technically endowed research. (p. 18)

Praising the narrative approach employed by Friedman and Schwartz, Miron identified its four main components: a method of identification (by way of natural experiments), the treatment of economic theory, the style of presenting empirical results, and the construction of new data. Miron saw little way to reconcile this enormously fruitful approach with cutting-edge macroeconomics.

Bordo's accomplishment has been precisely to bridge this gap and show how the narrative of *A Monetary History* can be married to state-of-the art theory and econometrics. His work embodies all of its four components and a fifth, modern econometrics. Not only has this assured him a place of honor on the reading lists of graduate macroeconomics courses, but more importantly his achievement has yielded a growing dialogue between macroeconomists, historians, and policymakers. He has been the right man in the right place. When the certainties of the post–World War II Bretton Woods world of low inflation, fixed exchange rates, and minimal crises began to evaporate, he was there to provide evidence that the distant past of the nineteenth century had more to teach policymakers than recent decades. In all of these respects, he has been faithful to his great predecessors.

We begin our survey with Bordo's contributions to the study of the Great Depression, the very heart of *A Monetary History*. The question he has impressed on so many of us, "What about Canada?" is answered in the second section where we discuss his insightful comparisons of the United States and Canada. Respectful of earlier generations of monetary theorists, empiricists, and historians, he has also made notable contributions to the history of thought, which are covered in the third section. His work on the gold standard and exchange rates are examined in the fourth and fifth sections. Bordo's careful comparative analyses of financial market integration and financial crises in the two eras of globalization are discussed in the sixth and seventh sections. The always important but oh-so current questions of monetary policy that Bordo has tackled are presented in the eighth section, leading us to an attempted conclusion.

THE GREAT DEPRESSION

Michael Bordo was not born during the Great Depression of 1929–1933, but as a student of Milton Friedman and Anna Schwartz, he was certainly born to the Great Depression. His formative text was naturally the 1963 *Monetary History*. According to *A Monetary History*, a mild recession in 1929 was turned into a catastrophe by the Federal Reserve's failure to respond to a series of banking panics that collapsed the money stock, driving down the economy. In later twentieth century terminology (Romer 1993), the banking panics working through several transmission channels caused aggregate demand to quickly shrink against a relatively static aggregate supply. In addition, the falling price level, if it was expected, produced high real ex ante interest rates (Cecchetti 1992), slashing consumption and investment; or if it was unexpected, yielded high real ex post interest rates (Hamilton 1992), adding to debt-deflation. In this evolving analysis, a non-monetary channel of propagation via the disruption of financial interme-diation was added by Bernanke (1983).[1]

Could the Great Depression have been avoided by preventing a col-lapse of the monetary system–keeping money "stable," by following a simple monetary rule? While this classic question had been addressed by McCallum (1990) and others, Bordo, Choudhri, and Schwartz (1995) developed a more general model in the spirit of the *Monetary History*. Employing a parsimonious model for money demand, output, prices, and the money stock, where money may have a short-term effect on output, they examined the consequences of both a strong and a weak form of Friedman's constant money growth rule. For the first, the Fed should have kept the money stock at its long-term growth rate by offsetting changes in the money multiplier; and for the second, the Fed could have observed the money multiplier only with a quarter lag and adjusted accordingly to keep money growth at its expected rate. Following these rules, they forecast that the decline in real output for 1929–1933 between 11 and 22 percent. Compared to an actual decline of 36 percent, a Friedman rule would thus have limited the damage; and within this range, it would have been within the bounds of other recessions.

One of the biggest challenges to the Friedman and Schwartz's classic tale of the Fed's failure of intellect or nerve to prevent the collapse of the money stock concerns the gold standard constraint. Both Eichengreen (1992) and Temin (1989) contend that the monetary authorities could not have engaged in expansionary monetary policy because they had to maintain an adequate gold cover to remain on the gold standard. The central threat to any overexpansion by the Fed would have been a specu-lative attack on the dollar. Bordo, Choudhri, and Schwartz (2002) argue that although "golden fetters" may have constrained small economies, the United States, as a large economy, with a vast gold stock, had plenty of latitude to respond to initiating shocks between late 1930 and early 1932. They conduct simulations that show $1 billion interventions at these critical junctures would not have led to a gold outflow sufficient to put U.S. convertibility at risk. Critical to this finding is their estimate of the offset coefficient, the proportion of the increase in U.S. domestic credit that would have been offset by gold outflows. At less than one, a credit expansion would have been only partially offset by gold outflows. Over a wide range of specifications, the United States would have been able to maintain its 40 percent gold cover for Federal Reserve notes, thus affirming

---

[1] Bordo provided global policymakers in the IMF's *World Economic Outlook* (2002) with a quick summary of the Great Depression literature and its policy relevance.

that Fed officials were not constrained by the gold standard and could have halted the slide into depression.

Although no one would disagree with the importance of the Great Depression for the 1930s, its lasting effect on the course of the American and world economy by the end of the twentieth century is less certain. Exploring the effects of the depression on the international monetary system, Bordo and Barry Eichengreen (1998) simulate the evolution of the post–World War II world without the 1930s collapse, assuming the Federal Reserve would have followed a stable money policy. Their simulation is based on the gold standard model of Bordo and Ellson (1985), which in turn was inspired by Barro's (1979) theoretical model of a world gold standard. A center country holds only gold and the rest of the world holds a mix of gold and foreign exchange. In this long-run model, differential growth rates allocate the distribution of the world gold supply among countries, which, allowing for sterilization permitted by the gold exchange standard, would determine price levels. They contend that without the depression, the interwar gold exchange standard would have lasted until the outbreak of World War II. In the absence of a depression, the gold exchange standard would have been seen as a success; and thus there would have been no postwar impetus for a Bretton Woods Conference and its resulting system. After World War II, a gold exchange standard with free capital mobility would have been restored, with the United States accepting a deflation to move back to gold at its prewar parity. However, this regime would have been even less suited to manage the post-1945 imbalances. Bordo and Eichengreen calculate that the United States would have had to double the size of the Marshall Plan from $13 to $26 billion to restart the monetary system. Without capital controls, postwar adjustment would have been far more difficult. The "Triffin Crisis" would have emerged in the late 1950s, well ahead of the actual event. Consequently, this regime would have collapsed more quickly to a system of floating exchange rates than did the Bretton Woods System.

By the late 1990s, the *Monetary History*'s analytical framework was no longer cutting edge. A new challenge to Friedman and Schwartz's interpretation of the depression arose from the real business cycle theorists whose dynamic general equilibrium models found weak, if little, support for a demand-generated economic cataclysm. A central factor in these models is the relationship between output and labor productivity. In a paper with Charles Evans (1995), Bordo found that the relationship to be countercyclical for manufacturing as a whole, assuming that there were no technological shocks. Although there was procyclicality in some sectors, due perhaps to labor hoarding, the finding of countercyclicality is consistent with the basic Friedman–Schwartz story of demand shocks inducing the depression, as falling output caused firms to lay off marginal workers, thereby raising productivity.

Combining forces with Christopher Erceg and Charles Evans (2001), Bordo sought to place the Friedman and Schwartz story into a modern general equilibrium model. In this framework, recovery had little chance because the Federal Reserve's continued failure to offset the banking panic-induced decline in the money stock yielded deflation. In the presence of sticky nominal wages, real wages jumped, contributing to a further decline. They estimated that monetary shocks can account for 70 percent of the drop in output from 1929 to 1932. For the remainder of the 1930s, they found that National Industrial Recovery Act wage schedules that raised real wages limited economy recovery. At the same time as Erceg, Evans, and Bordo were working on their model, Harold Cole and Lee Ohanian (2001) created an alternative model that conflicted with Friedman and Schwartz's monetary-deflation explanation and Bernanke's (1983) banking crisis-financial intermediation explanation. Their two-sector model – manufacturing and agriculture – had a fixed wage above the market clearing rate in the first sector and a market wage in the second sector with an intermediate and a final good. When simulated, neither a monetary nor an intermediation shock could explain the fall in output in their model. Cole and Ohanian concluded that the only credible factor remaining to explain the depression was a very large negative productivity shock. Money and finance played no role in initiating the depression? Bordo, Erceg, and Evans (2001) then probed the Cole and Ohanian paper and discovered that the surprising result was driven by the fact that the whole of the nonmanufacturing sector covering 72 percent of the economy was treated as a flexible wage sector. Although farming, accounting for 11 percent of the economy, could be treated as having flexible wages, this was not true for services or especially government, which accounted for the remainder of the nonmanufacturing sector. Real wages did not fall as a result of declining productivity, as implied by Cole and Ohanian, but rather remained high and rose, as observed during the depression and replicated by Bordo, Erceg, and Evans (2001).

While papers on the Great Depression written before 2008 might have been considered just as part of an academic debate, the specter of the 1930s looms much larger now and policy makers and the public rightfully ask what are the lessons from the 1930s? A central question is whether panics are driven by illiquidity or insolvency. Bernanke and other members of the Federal Reserve Board, who were well versed in the *Monetary History* responded to the panic of 2008 by flooding the market with liquidity. However, what was missed at the outset was that this scramble for liquidity was driven by the widespread insolvency of major financial institutions. Consequently, simple neutral open market operations and lending via the discount window did not relieve the pressure on the financial system, leading to a bailout of what were believed to be systemically important institutions.[2] Was this also true in the Great Depression? In two papers, one with John Landon-Lane (2010a) and one with Harold James (2010), Bordo addressed this question. The cumulative evidence of many researchers indicates that the banking sector was very weak on the eve of the depression, with their balance sheets continuing to deteriorate. Yet, liquidity problems peaked during the panics. Thus, a combination of these two factors dragged down the financial sector, and the Friedman and Schwartz story survives as part of a more complex picture (Richardson and Troost 2009). Estimates of the relative number of illiquid and insolvent banks depend on the design of the vector autoregression (VAR) model. Whereas Richardson (2007) concluded that 60 percent of suspensions were attributable to insolvency and 40 percent to liquidity, Bordo and Landon-Lane (2010) offered an alternative where the identifying assumption is that an illiquidity shock caused some insolvent banks to fail contemporaneously but an insolvency shock led failures as a result of illiquidity only with a lag. Based on this specification, their results showed that 1930 and 1931 are liquidity events primarily and 1933 is mainly a solvency event.

Summing up, Bordo and James (2010) identified key lessons from the 1930s. They found that although the Fed has the tools and the understanding of how to halt financial crises once they begin, they were less certain that the Fed will be able to reduce its balance sheet, as it may face a high political and economic cost of tightening. They also warn that bailouts – as occurred in the United States and Germany in the 1930s – may cause distortions and lead to economic nationalism and a retreat from the global economy.

CANADIAN EXCEPTIONALISM AND A LESSON FROM ARGENTINA

For those of us who know MDB as a member of a seminar audience, the question: "What about Canada?" is a familiar one. The history of money and banking in Canada provide important insights into why some banking systems seem prone to repeated crises while others seem resilient to even the largest of shocks. Given the greatly varied regulations, supervision, and customs, cross-country comparisons of financial systems are difficult and not easily summarized by a series of dummy variables. But, given the great similarity of Canada and the United States in these dimensions, a comparison of their banking systems is highly informative. The American banking

---

[2] Bordo and Landon-Lane (2010a) pointed out Bernanke's concern for financial intermediation based on the channel he identified for the Great Depression and the threat of widespread insolvencies let to the creation of an array of targeted lending programs and an expansion of the Fed's balance sheet. As these were not a neutral injection of liquidity, these actions have placed the Fed in an awkward position of politicizing credit and making it difficult to reduce its massive holdings of securities without repercussions.

system has been characterized by easy entry and competition, partly a product of the long prohibition on branching, whereas the Canadian system of a few branching banks tends toward cartelization. In terms of stability, only one bank failed in Canada between 1920 and 1980, in contrast to the vast number of insolvencies in the United States. One would expect that there would be a large trade-off between efficiency and stability, but in three papers with Angela Redish and Hugh Rockoff, Bordo (1994, 1996a, 1996b) identified at most a modest trade-off. From the Great Depression to 1980, there seems little evidence of the potential cartel in extracting rents, as yields on loans appear to be roughly equal in both countries and Canadian depositors were paid higher rates of interest than their American peers. The big difference between the two systems is that Canadian banks were more leveraged so that given borrowing and lending rates, they had a significantly higher rate of return on equity than American banks. The ability of Canadian institutions to survive with a smaller equity cushion is a reflection of their greater regional diversification and size that gained them economies of scale.[3]

What is the appropriate mandate for a central bank? The varied history of central banks in all major countries makes answering these questions tortuously difficult, as the contentious literature on the subject makes clear. What is MDB's contribution? Canada, of course; Canada is a very interesting case because it is the last major Western economy to establish a central bank (1935), raising the question of whether or not central banks are truly necessary. Bordo and Redish (1987) examined three hypotheses about central bank origins: (1) central banks naturally evolved out of fractional reserve banking systems, (2) central banks are needed when there is no nominal anchor like the gold standard for a largely unregulated banking system, and (3) creation of central banks is determined primarily by other political factors. In Canada, at the beginning of the twentieth century, most of the traditional central banking functions were managed by private institutions or directly by the government. Stability appears to have been largely the result of nationwide branching, in contrast to the crisis-prone, unit-banked United States; and clearing and collection of checks was handled by the Montreal Clearing House. Liquidity was usually found in the call money market in New York, where most Canadian banks parked their excess funds. However, twice when this market was unable to succor Canada's liquidity needs in 1907 and 1914, the Government of Canada stepped into the breach. Additional liquidity was provided by the Finance Act of 1914, which permitted the issue of Dominion notes to provide discounts by the Treasury Board to banks with appropriate collateral.

---

[3] For some but not all years, higher reserve requirements and interest rate controls in the United States contributed to this result.

Hypothesis 2 might be appealing, as Canada returned to the gold standard in 1926, and then abandoned it provisionally in 1928 and permanently in 1931. Departure from the gold standard did not lead to over expansion by the banks – there was instead deflation and the expectation after 1931 that there would be a return to gold. The Commission responsible for the creation of the Bank of Canada believed that a return to gold would be within a managed system of cooperation between central banks and thus it was imperative that Canada have one. To support this narrative Bordo and Redish searched for regime shifts but found little "policy" effect for the Bank of Canada, as there is an absence of any structural breaks in macroeconomic variables at the time of its creation. What they do see behind the system was the demand for inflation to counter the economic decline and attacks on the cartel of banks, which were often conflated, with the banks blamed for deflation as they closed branches in the declining economy. The calls from the political right and left for government intervention and rising nationalism made the creation of a central bank an advantageous and internationally acceptable act of emphasizing Canada's independence from London and New York, even if there was no regime change.

Although most scholars have focused on the big countries – the United States, the United Kingdom, France, and Germany – for understanding the Great Depression, Bordo's ever insightful question – What about Canada?–has been most instructive. In the standard story, a monetary shock emanated from the United States to the rest of the world because of the Federal Reserve's failure to counter the effects of banking panics on the money stock. If any country should have been dragged into a recession by this mistake, it was the United States's smaller open economy neighbor to the north. Caroline Betts, Angela Redish and, Bordo (1996) investigated this possible source of the depression for Canada. They provided a small open economy model of the Canadian economy in the Mundell–Fleming tradition, where long-run domestic output is exogenously determined but can deviate from trend in the short run because of nominal rigidities. They found that the onset, depth, and duration of the depression in Canada and the United States are almost all entirely attributable to a common output shock, although there is a short-run response of the Canadian money stock to shocks from the American monetary shocks.

Although in late 2008 the United States was engulfed in the worst financial crisis since the Great Depression, Canadians sat snugly and safely north of the border. Was this simply a random result? Hardly. As Bordo and his collaborators (Bordo, Redish, and Rockoff 2014) showed, Canadian exceptionalism has some very important lessons for the United States. Systemic risk was managed in Canada because the regulations set down in the nineteenth century created a banking system that evolved into a concentrated oligopoly, which entered into a compact with the regulatory authorities, ensuring limited competition in exchange for limited risk-taking. In contrast, the United States opted for a unit banking system of thousands of highly competitive and undiversified banks in the nineteenth century that pushed long-term corporate finance into the securities markets, which had the flexibility and latitude to provide adequate capital for America's growing industrial sector. Whereas clearing and collection of checks was highly centralized by 1900 in Canada and reserves were based within well-diversified banks, the management of these essential functions in the United States was executed within the framework of a delicately structured network of interbank relationships far more vulnerable to shocks. Bordo, Redish, and Rockoff identified the concentration of authority over banks in the Canadian federal government as a key element, comparing this arrangement to the uneasily shared authority between the federal government and the states that produced competition among regulators with many opportunities for regulatory arbitrage. Critically, in the mortgage market, the U.S. federal government encouraged the use of thirty-year fixed rate amortized mortgages with the borrower prepayment option. In Canada, mortgages were amortizable over twenty-five years but had only a five-year term, yielding a smaller maturity mismatch. To manage the regulation-induced mortgage problems, U.S. banks securitized their mortgages and moved them off-balance sheet, evading capital requirements, something Canadian banks could not do. The Canadian chartered banks also absorbed the Canadian broker-dealers in the late 1980s, establishing universal banking. This prevented the "shadow banking" problem the United States had. Along with a consolidated banking system Canada had a consolidated regulator, the Office of the Superintendent of Financial Institutions. Together, consolidated banking and consolidated regulation made effective regulation easier. Bordo, Redish, and Rockoff viewed this as a path-dependent outcome, for which there is depressingly little chance of reform, as they underline with a salient quote in 1893 from George Walker, President of the Canadian Bank of Commerce: "For over half a century, banking in the United States has been following lines of development opposed in many respects to the Canadian system, and it may well be that no matter how desirable, it is too late to adopt our practices."

A key point of MDB's oeuvre is that comparisons, especially comparisons with embedded counterfactual questions, can provide profound insights into some of the essential issues of monetary economics. Perhaps, one of his most interesting contributions in this genre is his paper (2002) with Carlos Vegh, "What if Alexander Hamilton had been Argentinean? Not a comparison that many would have dreamed up, as the republic in the Northern hemisphere, after a bout of violent revolutionary war inflation, enjoyed relative price stability that encouraged economic growth while the one in the Southern Hemisphere had persistent high inflation detrimental to economic growth and political stability. Yet, both were New World republics in resource-rich, land-intensive, temperate zones. As the title implies, perhaps if Hamilton had appeared in Buenos Aires and not New York, Argentina might have established the fiscal and monetary institutions that were so successful. Drawing on the theory of optimal taxation, Bordo and Vegh offer some novel insights. First, in the United States, although the states and Continental Congress found access to bond issue and taxation difficult and resorted to money finance, the conditions that led to a hyperinflation did not continue into the Constitutional period. In contrast, the continuing wars in Argentina kept tax collection costs high and further reduced access to foreign capital, making the Southern Republic dependent on money creation. Both early histories of government finance may be viewed as optimal choices, given the constraints, though the institutions engineered by Hamilton, in the lull between wars, produced a credible regime that enabled the United States to switch to more efficient bond-finance subsequently. Thus, it was the external constraints, not the lack of brilliant men that burdened Argentina.

MONEY AND THE ECONOMY IN HISTORICAL PERSPECTIVE

Much of Bordo's early work in monetary economics was based in the quantity-theory tradition developed by his mentors Milton Friedman and Anna Schwartz. The quantity theory has lost traction in modern macroeconomic research. But much of Bordo's work in this area, we believe, is still relevant because it provides empirical insights that transcend the original theoretical framework that gave rise to them. And, as Bordo likes to point out, the reputation of the quantity theory tends to rise and fall with the rate of inflation. If the rate of inflation accelerates once again – not an impossible prospect given our current fiscal difficulties – we can expect the quantity theory to make a comeback.

The debate over the quantity theory was hot and heavy in the 1970s, as the rate of inflation accelerated. The monetarists, led by Milton Friedman, Karl Bruner, and Alan Meltzer, maintained that inflation was "always and everywhere a monetary phenomenon," in Friedman's famous statement. But opponents of monetary explanations pointed to a number of alternative factors that could explain the inflation. Perhaps inflation was the result of powerful corporations pushing up prices (administered inflation) or of unions pushing up wages (cost push inflation). Sometimes advocates of nonmonetary explanations pointed to (and continue to point to) shortages of fuel and food as factors that were pushing up prices in one sector, creating pressures that would produce a general increase in prices. At one point, for example, it was suggested that the disappearance of anchovies off the coast of South America had contributed to a worldwide shortage of protein, an increase in food prices, and general inflation (Blinder and Rudd 2013).[4]

Bordo made a number of contributions to this debate. In two papers based on his dissertation Bordo (1975a, 1977) showed that the effects of monetary changes on income were much the same, even when the sources of monetary change were very different. This evidence supported the claim that a causal relationship ran from money to income. If Bordo had found, on the other hand, that there was a strong correlation between money and income when the Federal Reserve was the source of new money, but no correlation when the United States was on the gold standard, the inference would be that there was no causal relationship between money and income. The correlation under the Federal Reserve regime would have been a byproduct of the way the Federal Reserve anticipated changes in income.[5]

With Anna Schwartz, Bordo wrote two papers (1980, 1981) that were critical of the "it is not money that is causing the inflation" view by going back to arguments and data from the nineteenth century. After all, the argument that inflation in the sense of an economy-wide increase in prices could be produced by an increase in prices in one sector was an old argument, one that often surfaced when inflation accelerated. In the nineteenth century Thomas Tooke had argued that inflation was the result of increases in the prices of agricultural produced by events in agricultural markets, and not the product of monetary forces. But despite the attractiveness of this argument to later generations of economic historians, Bordo and Schwartz were able to show that the elasticities of substitution between sectors were not high enough to enable Tooke's explanation to work.

MDB's 1980 *Journal of Political Economy* paper is a good illustration of how work growing out of the quantity-theory tradition, and perhaps for that reason, likely to be overlooked by the younger generation of monetary economists and historians, still has much to teach us. In that paper he returned to the work of John Elliot Cairnes, which he had previously studied (1975a). Cairnes, often described as the last of the classical economists, had made a shrewd observation about the effects of the monetary expansion that followed the discovery of gold in California in the 1850s. Prices in highly competitive markets, such as markets for agricultural products, had responded more quickly to the monetary expansion, than had other prices. Cairnes had explained this in terms of differing supply elasticities. Bordo

---

[4] Neoclassical economists argued, of course, that shocks in individual markets would produce increases in relative prices rather than a general increase in prices.

[5] This was the claim made in James Tobin's (1970) famous paper "post hoc ergo propter hoc." In addition, Tobin's (1965) review of *A Monetary History* in the *American Economic Review* had argued that changes in the composition of the stock of money could have important effects on the economy.

revisited this prediction and found, remarkably, that it held a century later. To explain the relationship, MDB used a modern characteristic of some industries having long-term contracts.

In his first paper with Schwartz (1977), Bordo provided a survey of monetary issues and their impact on economic history at the critical moment when the cliometric revolution had begun to influence macroeconomic history. Revealing very catholic tastes, his periodic surveys of the state of the art of monetary and financial history have been of immense value to beginning students and seasoned researchers alike. His most recent contribution to this genre appeared in *The New Palgrave Dictionary of Economics* (2008), where he focused on the evolution of monetary theory and central banking.

The Chicago tradition interprets the monetary economy as the result of a money supply equation (based on the quantity of high-powered money and the behavior of banks and the public) and a money demand equation (based on income, interest rates, and other variables). In this tradition the equation of exchange is interpreted as the money demand equation. Bordo explored this interpretation in his work with Lars Jonung. Much of this was summarized in Bordo and Jonung (1987), in which the authors identified the key variables determining long-term trends in velocity. Economists interested in the role of finance in economic development are likely to find these results of interest, even if they reject the quantity theory as a tool for short-term macroeconomic management. Bordo and Jonung have continued to update this work (Bordo and Jonung 1999; Bordo, Jonung, and Siklos 1997).

Interest among economists in the field of history of thought has declined in the last few decades. And courses in the history of economic thought have disappeared from most of the leading graduate programs, a development that has troubled Bordo, a contributor to the field. This decline may reflect the sometimes correct perception that historians of thought are interested mainly in resuscitating the reputations of minor figures or previously rejected ideas, or acting as scolds to economists that mislabel ideas. However, in Bordo's hands history of thought becomes a fruitful source of ideas and empirical observations, as was true for his mentors Friedman and Schwartz.[6] One notable contribution was his 1979 paper with Anna Schwartz on the pioneer monetarist Clark Warburton. Friedman and Schwartz had been criticized for not giving sufficient credit to Warburton, although Warburton was acknowledged at various points in *A Monetary History*. In this paper Bordo and Schwartz addressed that

---

[6] MDB has suggested to us that Friedman's revival of Irving Fisher's distinction between real and nominal interest may be one of the most important examples of history of thought contributing to contemporary economic practice.

issue by acknowledging the many contributions of Warburton to the analysis of monetary history and how Warburton's work based on different data strengthens the case that money matters.

By the end of the twentieth century inflation had moderated to the point that deflation became a major worry. This concern was rooted in the belief that inflation provided a needed "lubricant" for labor markets. Sometimes it was necessary to lower wages, but attempts to lower nominal wages in a regime of stable prices or falling prices would meet stiff resistance. In a regime of moderate inflation, however, nominal wages could be kept constant and real wages would still fall. But deflation also had a bad name because deflation is associated with the Great Depression. In *A Monetary History* Friedman and Schwartz had noted that during the second half of the nineteenth century long periods of mild and anticipated deflation had been associated with rapid growth of industrial production and real per capita income. In two papers with John Landon-Lane and Angela Redish (2009, 2010) and Andrew Filardo (2005) Bordo and his co-authors used new data and recent time series econometric techniques to confirm that indeed mild and anticipated deflation had not damaged the economy. One way of looking at the policy conclusions from this exercise is to say that policymakers need not avoid a policy of price stability for fear of a short-term mild deflation as economic expansion could continue.

THE GOLD STANDARD

In this section we consider Bordo's studies of the gold standard and the gold exchange standards of the interwar period. Although this is separate from the next section on Bretton Woods and subsequent exchange rate regimes, we view both sections as an integrated body of work. MDB's examination of the Bretton Woods System and his work on Canada's fluctuating exchange rates, for example, shed additional light, by way of contrast, on the gold standard. These clever comparisons reveal why Bordo is widely regarded as one of the world's leading experts, if not the leading expert, on the history of exchange rate regimes.

Although metallic standards have been used for thousands of years, and although Britain remained on the gold standard from the end of the Napoleonic wars until World War I, the era of the classical gold standard is usually taken to be 1879–1914. It began when the United States returned to the gold standard after the Civil War and ended when the European nations were driven off by World War I. During this period the currencies of all of the leading industrial nations were convertible into gold. Exchange rates were fixed; increases in the money supply were constrained by the need to import or mine gold, and ordinary citizens carried gold coins in their pockets. To many people at the time, and to many subsequent observers, these characteristics defined an ideal monetary system.

But, as becomes clear when we explore Bordo's work, the issue is far more complicated. Most industrial nations, with the important exception of the United States, abandoned gold during World War I. The attempts to revive the gold standard in the 1920s met with mixed success, and most nations including the United States abandoned gold during the Great Depression.

The Bretton Woods system attempted a new exchange rate system that would return to the fixed exchange rates of the gold standard, but would allow individual nations a degree of control over their own money supplies. During the 1950s and 1960s, when Bordo was learning his economics, there was little interest in the gold standard, a monetary and exchange rate system that seemed to be a mysterious obsession of past generations. In the late 1970s and early 1980s, public interest in how the gold standard worked increased, and some enthusiasts began calling for a return to the gold standard. The reason was simply that the existing monetary regime was not working. The rate of inflation around the world was rising. In the United States inflation (the consumer price index) rose from an already high annual rate of 5.6 percent in 1976 to 12.7 percent in 1980. U.S. short-term interest rates rose from 5.0 percent in 1976 to a peak of 14.0 percent in 1981.[7] Inflation had become a key political and economic issue. It was natural then, for Bordo to turn his scholarly searchlight on the gold standard that seemed to hold a promise of price stability.

In 1981 he wrote a paper for the *Federal Reserve Bank of St. Louis Review* "The Classical Gold Standard: Some Lessons for Today" that drew a remarkable amount of attention from both scholars and the general public. The paper looked at the history of thought concerning the gold standard and the empirical evidence how it had worked in practice. Some of the numbers Bordo presented are reproduced in Table 14.1. We have also updated the table to show more recent periods.[8]

Inflation, in the first column, was lower under the classical gold standard. Indeed, for practical purposes the price level was essentially stable over the life of the gold standard although there were subperiods of mild deflation and mild inflation. Advocates of a return to the gold standard typically stress this measure of performance above all else. Bordo argued that there were both costs and benefits to the classical gold standard. Some of the other measures are not so favorable. Surprisingly, the rate of price change and the rate of growth of per capita income in columns 2 and 3 were more variable under the classical gold standard than under

---

[7] Data from www.measuringworth.com

[8] Bordo (1993) presented an updated table for the United States, United Kingdom, Germany, France, Japan, and Italy. It included data on interest rates, but not unemployment. We have included the total Bretton Woods regime from that table, and more recent data.

Table 14.1. Descriptive Statistics of Selected Macro Variables 1870–2011

	Average Percentage Change in the Price Level (%) (1)	Coefficient of Variation of Annual Percentage Changes in the Price Level (2)	Coefficient of Variation of Annual Percentage Changes in Real Per Capita Income (3)	Average Level of the Unemployment Rate (%) (4)
U.S. gold standard (1879–1913)	0.1	17.0	3.5	6.8[a]
U.K. gold standard (1870–1913)	–0.7	–14.9	2.5	5.8
U.S. interwar (1919–1940)	–2.5	–6.2	6.6	11.3
U.K. interwar (1919–1938)	–4.6	–3.8	4.9	10.4
Bretton Woods U.S. (1946–1970)	2.8	0.8	1.4	4.7
Bretton Woods U.K. (1946–1970)	4.3	0.6	0.8	1.9
Great Inflation U.S. (1971–1982)	6.9	0.3	1.7	6.8
Great Inflation U.K. (1971–1982)	12.4	0.4	1.6	5.6
Great Moderation U.S. (1983–2007)	2.7	0.3	0.7	5.8
Great Moderation U.K. (1983–2007)	3.6	0.5	0.6	7.7
Great Recession U.S. (2008–2011)	1.8	0.3	–5.0	8.4
Great Recession U.K. (2008–2010)	2.5	0.4	–1.6	6.6

Sources: All data except U.K. unemployment, 1879–1940, Bordo (1981), p. 14;
Unemployment, U.S., 1946–1982, in *Historical Statistics of the United States: Earliest
Times to the Present, Millennial Ed.*, Carter et al. (2006), series Ba475; 1982–2011,
Economic Report of the President 2012, table B-42. Unemployment U.K., 1870–1999,
Boyer and Hatton (2002, table 6, p. 667); 2000–2010: Global Financial Data. Prices (GDP
deflator) and real GDP per capita, 1946–2011, U.S. and U.K., Louis Johnston and Samuel
H. Williamson (2012).
[a] 1890–1913.

subsequent regimes. There is also evidence, although mixed, that the rate of unemployment was higher under the gold standard.

The 1980 Republican platform included veiled language suggesting that it might be wise to return to the gold standard. Shortly after the election, Congress established the Gold Commission to examine and report on the appropriate role for gold in the monetary system. Anna J. Schwartz was the research director and MDB, as he tells the story, was the "research staff." The Commission reported on March 31, 1982. Its findings and recommendations did not bring much joy to the two Congressional sponsors of the bill establishing the Commission, Senator Jesse Helms and Congressman Ron Paul.[9] The Commission did not recommend a return to the classical gold standard or any version of it. Instead its main substantive recommendation was that the U.S. Mint be authorized to mint gold coins from the U.S. stock of monetary gold at Fort Knox. The coins would be of specified weight, but not denominated in dollars, and would not be legal tender. The recommendation offered something to numismatists without altering the monetary system. This conclusion was satisfactory to Schwartz and Bordo, both of whom maintained that the classical gold standard, although it accomplished many good things in its time, was not an appropriate system for the modern world.

In 1982 Bordo and Schwartz organized a National Bureau of Economic Research (NBER) conference at Hilton Head, South Carolina on the classical gold standard. The resulting conference volume (1984) has become a basic resource for anyone studying the history of the gold standard. The paper that Bordo wrote for the conference, "The Gold Standard: The Traditional Approach" (1984), defined the classical understanding of how the gold standard worked. Bordo carefully parsed the work of its main developers – Cantillon, Hume, Ricardo, Thornton, Mill, Cairnes, Goschen, Bagehot, among others – and organized their ideas on a number of themes. He then showed how the traditional understanding of the gold standard had been refined and challenged by later writers, such as Fisher, Keynes, Hawtrey, and Sayers. MDB had already published an important essay on Cairnes (1975), and would soon publish one on Cantillon (1983).[10] Another paper with Richard Ellson (1985) developed a model that showed how the physical properties of gold – a durable but depletable natural resource – would shape the behavior of the price level when gold became the base of the money supply.

---

[9] Schwartz (1987) analyzes the history of the Gold Commission.

[10] Some writers would consider Smith as part of the classical school, but as Bordo noted there is controversy because Smith was the developer of the real bills doctrine. More recent research has tended to reassert Smith's claim to be part of the classical tradition.

Interest in the gold standard as a mechanism for maintaining price stability faded when inflation moderated after 1982. From 1982 to 2007, the rate of inflation in the United States averaged 3.06 percent per year; and in the United Kingdom, 3.77 percent. However, even as the world moved to flexible exchanges rates as advocated by Bordo's mentor, Friedman (1953), another feature of the gold standard, the long-term fixing of exchange rates, continued to attract admirers. They maintained that the flexible exchange rates were doing more harm than good, and hankered for a return to the Bretton Woods System or even the gold standard.

In a long series of papers Bordo explored natural experiments in monetary history that illuminated the way that various institutional arrangements influenced the credibility and ultimately the success of these regimes. MDB would often turn to Canada for natural experiments and contrasts with the United States. It was an obvious and insightful choice for a man born and reared in Montreal. With his frequent coauthor Redish, Bordo investigated the strange behavior of Canada's exchange rate after Canada left the gold standard in 1929. One might have expected that by eliminating the gold anchor, the Canadian dollar would depreciate, but Bordo and Redish (1987, 1990) showed that a firm commitment to a stable rate by the Canadian government stabilized the exchange rate. To permit depreciation would have been viewed as reneging on debt payments and would have damaged Canada's reputation as a debtor, hindering its capacity to borrow.

In two papers with Eugene White (1991, 1993) attention was drawn to the informative contrast between British and French finance during the Napoleonic Wars. After 1800, France remained on its traditional bimetallic standard and experienced relatively little inflation; Britain left the gold standard in 1797 and experienced considerable inflation. On the surface it might seem that France was showing greater financial conservatism. But Bordo and White argue persuasively that the reality was very different. Britain had a long tradition of meeting its financial obligations. For that reason it was able to borrow at relatively low cost during the wars despite relying to some extent on the printing press. France, on the other hand, had suffered from a long series of financial disasters including the assignat inflation. Its ability to borrow was limited and it had to rely more heavily on taxes and maintaining a noninflationary monetary regime. In an often cited paper with Finn Kydland (1995) Bordo showed that Britain's behavior during the Napoleonic war was well understood by contemporaries. The gold standard was, in the Bordo-Kydland terminology, a "contingent rule." Markets understood that countries could leave the gold standard during emergencies, war being the most important, and countries would not be punished with higher interest rates, if they convincingly committed to return after the emergency had passed.

In papers with Anna Schwartz (1996) and Hugh Rockoff (1996), Bordo offered more evidence that adherence to the gold standard rule – subject in many cases, especially in peripheral countries, to a degree of uncertainty – influenced investment decisions. The paper with Rockoff, which analyzed sovereign bond yields for evidence that adherence (or attempted adherence) to the gold standard lowered interest rates, stirred up a storm of comments and extensions, some highly critical and some supportive. In a subsequent paper with Michael Edelstein and Rockoff (2002), Bordo looked at the impact of the return to the gold standard after World War I on sovereign bond yields.[11]

Bordo's work demonstrating that the gold standard was sufficiently flexible to accommodate the special circumstances of war finance, and his papers showing how the spread of the gold standard contributed to the internationalization of the capital market, served to bolster the reputation of the gold standard. Yet, the gold standard's achievements were constrained. With his Ph.D. student Bernhard Eschweiler, Bordo (1994) wrote a study of German monetary history covering the period 1880–1989. They concluded that, in Germany, a regime that combined a fiduciary monetary system controlled by an independent central bank dedicated to price stability had produced better outcomes than alternative monetary regimes, including the classical gold standard.

Bordo's paper with Kydland (1995) and his related work showed that the economic consequences of joining and then leaving the gold standard must be considered part of any full evaluation of the gold standard. Joined by several coauthors, Bordo explored crucial episodes in German, French, Swiss, and British as well as American history to provide a more comprehensive vision of the gold standard. In a paper with Tamin Bayoumi (1998) Bordo compared the United Status's return to gold after the Civil War, which has been treated as a success, with Britain's return to gold after World War I, which has typically been regarded as a failure.[12] They concluded that although policies varied somewhat in the two cases, the main difference in the two outcomes was the result of factors that policymakers could not control. The United States was aided by rapid growth that made it the world's leading industrial country, whereas Britain was hindered by an anemic postwar performance.

Barry Eichengreen and Bordo (1993) looked at the use of gold as a central bank reserve, even after the world monetary system became

---

[11] A number of MDB's key papers on the gold standard were collected in a volume published by Cambridge University Press (1999).

[12] Before the Civil War the United States was on a de facto gold standard: silver was still legal tender. So, as the advocates of bimetallism liked to point out, technically the United States was establishing a new standard after the Civil War, rather than returning to an old one.

increasingly detached from gold. One of their important conclusions was that the development of a world monetary system that combined an inelastically supplied base currency, gold, with elastically supplied foreign exchange to meet central bank liquidity needs was inherently fragile. Ronald MacDonald and Bordo (2002) showed that the interwar gold exchange system was credible, even though it allowed central banks some scope for independent monetary policies. In a subsequent paper, they (2005) returned to the classical gold standard and uncovered evidence that even in that era central banks had some independent control over short-term interest rate movements.[13]

With Pierre-Cyrille Hautcoeur (2007), Bordo explored the French stabilization of its currency in 1926 at a substantial devaluation of its prewar parity and compared it with the policy followed by Britain in 1924. Bordo and Hautcoeur concluded that it would have been difficult or impossible for the French to have followed the British lead because of the debt and monetary overhang in France that resulted from World War I. But they also suggested that if there had been an agency similar to the International Monetary Fund in place that could have coordinated the return of the major European belligerents to the gold standard, the extreme French devaluation that produced a rapid accumulation of gold in France and undermined the international monetary system in the late 1920s might have been avoided.

Joining with Harold James and Thomas Helbing (2007), Bordo investigated Switzerland's decision to adhere to the gold standard until 1936. They demonstrated that Switzerland would have been better off devaluing earlier, but a number of factors, including Switzerland's financial conservatism and the difficulties inherent in making economic policy changes in a democracy, explain Switzerland's decision to stick to an overvalued currency. In a paper with Robert D. Dittmar and William T. Gavin (2007), MDB addressed the problem of price stability under alternative exchange rate regimes in a theoretical framework. They determined that a pure inflation target provides more short-term price level stability than the gold standard and that for horizons shorter than twenty years as much long-term price stability as the gold standard. In addition, they saw that the Taylor rule produced a high degree of long-term uncertainty about the price level, though it can be modified to eliminate this problem.

As one can see from these investigations, MDB has examined the gold standard from every possible angle: history of thought, case studies for a number of countries, and the performance of the gold standard in a

---

[13] A number of papers on the origin and functioning of the Federal Reserve originally presented at a conference to mark the 100th anniversary of the founding of the Federal Reserve has been published in Bordo and Roberds (2013).

variety of statistical and theoretical models. To put it somewhat differently, Bordo is not married to one methodology; he believes in and practices a "full court press." His conclusions therefore have enormous weight. For the gold standard, when Bordo says that the gold standard made a good deal of sense in its day but is no longer appropriate, policymakers should pay close attention.

BRETTON WOODS, THE EUROPEAN MONETARY UNION, AND OTHER REGIMES

In the late 1980s exchange rates moved to the forefront of the political agenda. The famous Plaza Agreement in 1985 called for a coordinated effort to depreciate the U.S. dollar against a number of key currencies, especially the Japanese yen, because the weakness of U.S. exports. The Plaza accord is sometimes held out as a successful case of direct intervention in foreign exchange markets because a significant depreciation of the dollar followed. Yet, Bordo and Schwartz (1991) were skeptical that sterilized exchange operations on the scale that were actually taken in the years following the agreement could have had much effect. They pointed out that unsterilized operations were simply another way of conducting monetary policy and might have unintended effects on interest rates and foreign exchange markets.

It was also a propitious moment for Bordo and Eichengreen to organize an NBER conference on the Bretton Woods system. Held at Bretton Woods, New Hampshire in September 1991 it preceded the fiftieth anniversary of the international conference that had established the system. Like the earlier conference that Bordo and Schwartz had organized on the gold standard, the Bretton Woods conference produced a landmark scholarly conference volume (1993). The "Overview" that Bordo (1993) wrote for the conference remains the best account of the history of the Bretton Woods system.

In subsequent work, MDB continued to explore the functioning of the Bretton Woods system and subsequent exchange rate regimes. Bordo, Oliver, and MacDonald (2009) used daily data to analyze the sterling crisis of 1964 to 1969. They showed that prior to the devaluation in 1967, the British exchange rate was not credible, and that it was maintained only by various rescue operations. Even after the devaluation, doubts remained about the new value of the pound until the Basel agreements in 1968 provided sufficient central bank support to maintain the pound at its new value. The sterling crisis illustrated one of the problems inherent in the Bretton Woods system: the tendency of surplus countries to sterilize inflows and thus shift the burden of adjustment to deficit countries.

Although the sterling crisis illustrated the weaknesses of the Bretton Woods system, it did not fundamentally undermine it. The central problem was the behavior of the United States, whose currency was supposed to be a gold-equivalent reserve for other currencies. Pressure on the United States from France was one of the key factors leading to the demise of the system. It has often been attributed to the perverse political ambitions of Charles de Gaulle. However, in a paper with Dominique Simard and Eugene White (1995), Bordo argued that France's actions were actually part of a well-intentioned plan to achieve a more balanced international financial system.[14]

What the French failed to realize, and what ultimately brought down the system, was the unwillingness of the United States to subordinate its domestic concerns about unemployment to its international monetary role and foreign nations were no longer willing to passively import American inflation. Even with rapid economic growth, the Bretton Woods system ended after being in full operation for only twelve years. In contrast, the classical gold standard, although it passed through some major trials, lasted forty years. This comparison was spelled out in a paper Bordo presented at the 1995 meeting of American Economic Association in 1995, where he concluded that "the best prescription for world economic stability is for each country independently to pursue stable monetary and fiscal policies" (p. 322).

The idea of a fixed exchange rate regime did not die with Bretton Woods. The European Monetary Union (EMU) was a conscious attempt to gain the advantages of the fixed exchange rates on a more limited European scale. Bordo and Lars Jonung (2003) and more recently Bordo and James (2008, 2010, 2012) have drawn on the history of monetary regimes and monetary unions to consider the future of the EMU. These papers agree with most observers that the EMU began life with a number of weaknesses: there was no central authority for supervising financial institutions, no central fiscal authority, and a set of economically diverse regions that did not constitute an optimal currency area among others. They conclude that only a strong political will can overcome these obstacles in order to achieve a united Europe – and on whether that will is strong enough, the jury is still out.

Finally, we should mention that Bordo, Owen Humpage, and Schwartz have been working for some years on an in-depth study of Federal Reserve exchange market intervention. In their first paper (2007), they trace the history U.S. government exchange market interventions beginning from the Second Bank of the United States to the present. Their forthcoming

---

[14] Bordo and Fernando Santos (1995) explored the delayed decision of a smaller nation, Portugal, to join the Bretton Woods system. The trade-off was between economic nationalism and a dislike of institutions dominated by the United States, on one hand, and the desire to become eligible for World Bank loans on the other.

University of Chicago Press volume will prove to be the defining text for scholars and policymakers studying exchange market intervention.

GLOBALIZATION

By the 1990s, international flows of capital, goods, and labor grew so fast that comparisons with the seemingly ancient pre-1914 era began to be conjured. The trade barriers, immigration restrictions and capital controls, erected during two world wars and the Great Depression and sustained through the first two decades of post–World War II recovery, had crumbled, producing a new globalization of markets.

One of Bordo's important gifts to the professions – economics, history, political science – are his broad panoramic, usually exhaustive, surveys. MDB (2003) provided a summary of the empirical evidence on the international integration of financial markets from 1880 to the end of the twentieth century. The striking finding is that globalization of financial markets followed a strong U-shaped pattern over this 120-year period for ratios of net flows and stocks of foreign investment to gross domestic product (GDP). This pattern emerges no matter the measure, including Feldstein–Horioka correlations of savings and investment, covered interest parity or real interest parity. In this literature Bordo contributed several papers with Jongwoo Kim (1998) and with Barry Eichengreen and Douglas Irwin (2000a, 2000b); and with Alan Taylor and Jeffrey Williamson (2003) he organized an important conference. Although there is a pronounced U-shape in foreign investment, the more important change may have been in the composition of foreign investment. Before 1914, it was concentrated in bonds of governments, railways, and mines that were relatively easy to monitor at a long distance. In the newer period of globalization, direct foreign investment is more important, with equities equaling debt finance. Although by some measures the pre-1914 era showed greater integration, today's markets are broader and deeper thanks to reductions in information asymmetries because of technological innovation in the collection, transmission, and analysis of financial data.

While the open capital markets before World War I served to transfer resources to fast-growing emerging economies, it also made them open to financial crises, with today's more open emergers even more prone to crises. Bordo and Murshid (2006) tackled the difficult problem of comparing the strength of shocks and the patterns of their transmission, focusing on currency crises for the periods 1880–1914 and 1975–2001. They found that the co-movement of interest rate spreads were greater in the earlier period. Given Bordo's earlier findings of larger relative capital imports and greater persistence in the earlier period, it is not surprising that financial market shocks were more globalized before 1914, a fact that they attributed to the strong links fostered by the gold standard. Using a measure of exchange market pressure, they identified the strongest co-movement for the pre-1914 period. Before 1914, the gold standard and tight trade and investment links between the European core countries (United Kingdom, France, and Germany) and the emerging markets (United States, Canada, Australia, and Latin America) meant that financial shocks were disseminated quickly through the globalized economy, generated by the core – primarily the United Kingdom. Similarly, the likelihood of a financial crisis was greater in the past, though it is as high among advanced countries today as it was in the past. In the more recent era of globalization, while the core countries in Europe and the United States are affected by each other's shocks, the emerging economies of the late twentieth century do not have the same synchronicity of crises. The growth of new financial centers and the ability of policy authorities to better offset shocks with tools means more insulation.

How much did financial crises cost countries in the two eras of globalization? Bordo and Schwartz (1999) estimated that growth declined by 2 percent relative to trend for single banking or currency crises before 1914 and 3 percent in the post-1973 era. Double crises were more punishing with shortfalls of approximately 5 percent in both periods. These periods also saw rescue packages that reflected different institutional structures. In the pre–World War I era, private bankers arranged loans between central banks to cover short-term current account shortfalls, whereas in the post-1973 period international institutions brokered larger rescues, though these are believed to have induced moral hazard and contributed to the apparently larger recent crises. Bordo (2003) concluded that although the benefits of integration were long term, the short-term costs delivered with the punch of financial crises contributed to political backlash in the pre-1914 era, a warning to the present.

The question, "To float or not to float," in a globalized economy where large capital flows are sensitive to policy failures is addressed by Bordo and Flandreau (2003), who find that emerging nations are often pushed to extreme choices in exchange rate regimes. In the nineteenth century, the gold standard imposed monetary and fiscal discipline on those nations that joined the regime, enabling the development of deep and liquid money and capital markets. These benefits were garnered by the core countries, most importantly, the United Kingdom, France, and Germany, with the implied currency bands giving policymakers relatively little leeway to smooth the adjustment for GDP to shocks. By the 1970s, increased financial maturity – deeper markets and new means of signaling commitment to monetary and fiscal sobriety – permitted core countries, including now the United States and Japan, to float and gain more policy independence needed to manage the income-smoothing demands of democracy. In both periods, the situation in both periods for countries on the periphery was quite different, owing to their lack of financial maturity. Measuring financial development by M2 to GDP, Bordo and Flandreau provided econometric evidence that countries that joined the gold standard were more financially developed in the decades before 1914, but the ability to float was more closely associated with financial development post-1973. Many emergers lacked the ability to adhere to the rigid strictures of the gold standard; and at the same time, floating endangered their ability to borrow. The upshot was that in both periods, peripheral countries adopted super-hard fixed exchange rates (100 percent gold reserves or currency boards) to limit policymakers' options.

FINANCIAL CRISES

Bordo came of age as an economist just as the Bretton Woods system was breaking down. The certainties about fixed exchange rates, and low inflation were ebbing. For a financial and monetary historian, this was a prime opportunity. The past, the pre-1939 period and even more importantly the pre-1914, when the first era of globalization was in full swing, offered the best analogies for understanding the emerging problems. None of these was more important than the reappearance of international financial crises, as capital controls fell into abeyance and global financial markets reintegrated.

For many observers, the last few decades seem to be more crisis-ridden, including the severe combination of twin banking and currency crises that had vanished in the calm times of the mid-twentieth century. To provide a rigorously historical perspective on this question, Bordo, Eichengreen, Daniela Klingebiel, and Maria Soledad Martinez-Peria (2001) examined the global record for the last 120 years and found that crises have grown more frequent, notably twin crises, doubling the rate of the Bretton Woods and the classical gold standard eras and matching the turbulent 1920s and 1930s. However, more common, crises were not longer, nor were output losses larger. They attributed the increased frequency to a combination of high capital mobility, which had prevailed under the classical gold standard, and something new, the development of financial safety nets for financial institutions that encouraged them to accumulate foreign currency debt in pegged exchange regimes.

Unfortunately, some countries, chiefly the emerging economics, are particularly prone to crises. In the world of globalized capital markets, they find it difficult to borrow in their own currency and borrow at long maturities. As these are long-standing problems, the phenomenon has been christened the problem of "original sin." It is typically measured as the ratio of gold-back or foreign currency debt to total public debt. This problem existed in the first era of globalization and, naturally, comparisons are instructive for how nations might be able to escape this severe capital market limitation. Bordo, Meissner, and Redish (2005) found that sound fiscal institutions, high monetary credibility, and broad financial development are not sufficient to escape from original sin. Salvation also required some combination of scale, becoming a key currency or membership in the British Empire. These nations issued long-term domestic from their earliest years, though their external debt was in foreign currencies or carried gold clauses. The handful of escapees are the United States, Canada, Australia, New Zealand, and South Africa. The United States' checkered history in the nineteenth century, with state defaults and the Greenback suspension, led to most debt requiring some form of a gold clause. Breaking completely free was possible only in 1933 when the United States abandoned the gold standard and the gold clause was excusably eliminated. For Canada, the opportunity came when World War I limited the sterling market for the Dominions, with the escape completed with the demise of the Bretton Woods system, which saw the creation of derivatives that enabled the issue of foreign bonds in relatively thin markets. In contrast with today's emergers, the burden of original sin was smaller given the escapees' superior fiscal and monetary institutions that left them with fewer, more manageable imbalances.

In the short run, emerging countries in the present and the past that became dependent on large foreign capital inflows have dreaded "sudden stops." These precipitous breaks or reversals of capital flows have brought economies to an unexpected standstill, as painfully illustrated by the Mexican crisis (1994), the Russian crisis (1998), and the East Asian crisis of the late 1990s. To gain more insight into these phenomena, Bordo, Cavallo, and Meissner (2010) studied sudden stops under the classical gold standard, 1880–1913. Their results showed that these were very similar to the late twentieth century sudden stops. Probit regressions with a variety of definitions of a sudden stop revealed that high levels of foreign currency denominated debt and large current account deficits made nations more prone to experience a sudden stop. The threat was somewhat mitigated by greater trade openness and large international reserves – emphasizing the importance of balance sheet effects. Sudden stops accompanied by financial crises were the most grievous threat to a country and caused output per capita to fall 3 to 4 percent below trend growth. Although these momentous events had grave consequences they were temporary, in contrast to unconnected sudden stops that appear to have been associated with a drop in trend growth, reflecting changed fundamentals.

Following this work, Bordo and Meissner (2006) and Bordo, Meissner, and Stuckler (2010) investigated whether foreign currency debt has a similar propensity to cause a financial crisis and diminish economic growth for countries in both the gold standard era and the post-Bretton Woods years, 1973–2003. Higher foreign debt to total debt after large foreign capital inflows increased the likelihood of a crisis, though higher reserves and greater policy credibility reduced the probability of a crisis. Worse yet, financial crises driven by foreign debt resulted in permanently lower output, with a one-year crisis being associated with the loss of one full year's growth of output. Again, although capital inflows seemed to raise output in the short term there was a difference between the post-Bretton Woods era where permanent changes to capital flows raised long-term output whereas in the earlier era they slightly lowered levels of output. In both periods, crises had a permanent negative effect on output, 4 percent in the first period of globalization and 1.5 percent for the second. Noting the precarious borrowing practices of contemporary Eastern European countries, Bordo, Meissner, and Stuckler (2010) offered out-of-sample forecasts for them reporting small probabilities of financial crises and expected growth losses, chiefly because the ratio of foreign to total debt is well below 100 percent.

Skill in managing a crisis can limit the penalty from original sin. Bordo and Meissner (2006) found this to be the case for the United States, British Dominions, and Scandinavia before 1913. This result is striking because some of these nations, especially the British "offshoots," had the highest level of "original sin" but compensated for it with credible institutions and policies – an important historical lesson that does not jump out of the twentieth-century data. For emerging markets vulnerable to sudden stops, Bordo, Eichengreen, Klingebiel, and Martinez-Peria (2001) recommend monetary, fiscal, and exchange rate policies to limit current account deficits, curbing maturity mismatches when borrowing and strengthening market discipline for financial institutions to compensate for the moral hazard created by the safety nets.

A key policy question arising from a currency crisis is, Should the afflicted country receive aid from other countries or international agencies? That is, should the country get a bailout? Although there has been international assistance during the last two centuries, the size of assistance has grown very rapidly in the past two decades. Bordo (1999) and Bordo and Schwartz (1999) identified the 1990s as a watershed. Previously, rescue packages that headed off a devaluation or abandonment of the gold standard were modest and required remedial policies. In most cases they were successful and the loans were repaid. They were also arranged by private institutions, the Rothschilds, the Barings, or J. P. Morgan, in contrast to the international agencies such as the International Monetary Fund (IMF), the Bank for International Settlements (BIS), and the World Bank that have dominated the scene since World War II. The latter bailouts delivered substantial funds to limit wealth losses of foreign lenders and domestic investors after devaluations of a pegged exchange rates.

The characteristics of successful and unsuccessful earlier international assistance offer key policy insights, and Bordo and Schwartz (2000) provided a connoisseur's guide to vast and diverse international crisis experience. Because fundamentals were sound, the temporary assistance granted in 1825, 1866, and 1890 to the Bank of England by the Bank of France, through the intermediation of the Rothschilds, and the rescue of the U.S. Treasury in 1895 by the Belmont–Morgan syndicate were successful. On the other hand, the interwar rescue efforts in 1931 for Austria, Germany, and the United Kingdom all failed, as the countries were unable to change the underlying fundamentals of deepening national and international deflations and recessions. Initially, after World War II, rescue efforts by the IMF for Britain in 1956, Canada in 1962, and Italy in 1964 replenished central banks' lost reserves on the central bank and staved off collapse. But beginning in the late 1960s, as its fundamentals deteriorated, Britain received assistance on several occasions that only delayed devaluation that came in 1967.

The trend worsened after the collapse of Bretton Woods and the Mexican, Asian, and Russian crises. Notably these occurred after capital account reversals – reflecting unsustainable fundamentals, rather than current account reversals that were typical of the previous century. This dismal record, Bordo and Schwartz attributed to the belief that domestic lenders are protected by the safety net from failure. The moral hazard arising from this protection induced banks to take greater risks abroad as well as domestically; and it is worsened by the belief of some countries that they would receive assistance from the IMF if they get into trouble. Intervention after devaluation was justified to avoid the spread of contagion. In an environment of high capital mobility, the underlying problem is that in an environment of high capital mobility countries become invested in a pegged exchange rate and, if subjected to large unexpected shocks, cannot adjust. Instead, they should be on a floating exchange rate. To avoid large losses, Bordo and Schwartz concluded that contemporary international lenders should lend subject to strict eligibility, with short-term loans at a high rate – following Bagehot's recommendation and the successful lending experience of the nineteenth century.

Finally, there is the very basic question: does IMF assistance help a country? Bordo and Eichengreen (1999) gave us the essential facts. Two features immediately jump out of their summary of IMF assistance to Asia and Latin America. First, some countries are frequent borrowers and poor economic performers, and second there has been the spectacular increase in the size of loans, especially since the Mexican bailout of 1995. To assess the effects of IMF assistance more carefully, Bordo and Schwartz (2000) used a "with-without" approach to compare countries that experienced similar external shocks but did and did not receive

IMF assistance, using ten macro variables to measure the results. The overall picture is not encouraging for those who believe that the IMF has eased the effects of crises. Most importantly, recovery was faster for non-IMF–aided countries, though there was eventual growth convergence. Within a medium-term window, there is the disturbing result that real GDP per capita and consumption are lower for IMF aid recipients. The tough question is, of course, What would have happened in the absence of IMF intervention? Bordo and Schwartz examined a counterfactual that adjusts for the self-selection bias that countries that run large fiscal deficits and have rapid monetary expansions with fragile financial systems tend to be IMF customers and takes into account via a reaction function for policy target variables what actions countries would have taken in the absence of IMF assistance. They concluded that although turning to the IMF may be not be harmful to a country's economic performance, it certainly did not enhance it.

Some contrast is found in Bordo, Mody, and Oomes (2004), where the IMF's rescue packages are viewed as having significant benefits in spite of some scholars' misgivings about the agency's role in international capital markets. This trio posed a key question: When an emerging market country experiences a crisis because of a "sudden stop" in capital flows, can IMF programs improve capital flows and macroeconomic performance? To answer this question, they identify a realistic counterfactual for a country in the absence of the IMF program, which must be conditioned on the initial conditions for the country receiving assistance. For the years 1980 to 2002, they provide a simple four-bin framework for categorizing initial conditions from very bad to very good, depending on ratios of current account to GDP, reserves to imports, short-term debt to reserves, and external debt to GDP. The positive influence of the IMF is hypothesized to arise from (1) the provision of "good housekeeping" seal of approval, (2) the IMF's use of superior information and assessment capabilities as delegated monitor and lender, and (3) the IMF's role as "catalytic lender" that halts otherwise irreversible decline. Bordo and his coauthors uncovered evidence to support (2) and (3) with the greatest success for interventions in countries where the fundamentals are bad but not "too bad."

HISTORICAL GUIDANCE FOR MONETARY POLICY

As we all know, the proper role of a central bank was well understood and agreed on until 2008. Targeting inflation in ordinary times had secured the Great Moderation, and if there were a financial crisis, the central bank would follow Bagehot's prescription and flood the market with liquidity. But, of course, we all would have been wiser had we been carefully reading Bordo's oeuvre on the subject of central banking and monetary policy. In his 1990 papers, he provided an overview of four schools of thought that have disputed the proper role for a lender of last resort (LOLR) for over a century: (1) The classical Thornton-Bagehot school: the LOLR should discount freely to anyone having good collateral at a high rate with the objective of channeling funds to illiquid but not insolvent banks in order to halt a panic. (2) The Goodfriend and King position: open market operations is the only instrument required to halt a liquidity crisis because discount window lending to selected banks is distortionary and better handled by the private sector. (3) The Goodhart view: the LOLR should provide funds to illiquid and insolvent banks because it is impossible to distinguish between them in a crisis and failure of banks severs valuable customer relationships, impeding recovery. (4) Free Banking School: there is no role for a LOLR when there is no monopoly of note issue because the public and markets can distinguish between insolvent and solvent banks and runs will not degenerate into panics.

To examine these alternatives, Bordo (1990) drew upon his work (1986) that classified crises for the United States, the United Kingdom, France, Germany, Sweden, and Canada for 1870–1933 into financial, banking, and stock market crises. In general, Bordo found that banking panics are rare events, associated typically with serious recessions, with falls in the money stock and price level, exacerbated by bad banking structure.[15] Drawing on this history of crises, he set out the external factors (abrupt relative price changes and changes in the price level) that can lead to a banking run or panic, and the internal factors that can mitigate it (a diversified branch banking system and cooperative clearing houses). But Bordo emphasized that only a central bank can stem a nationwide panic because of its ability to create high-powered money, noting that although deposit insurance can remove the public's reason for panicking, it needs an LOLR to back the insurance system, as a system of private clearing houses will not provide sufficient liquidity.

Here and elsewhere, Bordo took seriously the challenge of free banking proponents that a central bank is unnecessary and the claim that a system of competitive banks of issue would be provide more stability. Reviewing the historical evidence, Bordo and Schwartz (1995) rejected the three variants of this school. The classical version is expressed in the "real bills doctrine." Although it informed banking practice in the nineteenth century, it is a destabilizing pro-cyclical policy as banks lend only short term on what is perceived to be good collateral. Another variant gives clearing houses a central role in the monitoring and control of member banks. Looking at the Scottish, Canadian, and American clearing houses, Bordo and Schwartz did not see them as bulwarks against instability in the monetary

---

[15] Although MDB regards deposit insurance as not a necessary institution to prevent panics, it "solved the problem of banking panics in the U.S."

system as there was no guard against all banks expanding simultaneously; and in Canada and Scotland there were other factors including branching and unlimited liability that contributed to the success of their banking systems. The third group of free banking proponents identifies competitive note issue by banks as the guarantor of stability. Given that there is no historical episode that conforms to the ideal, it is hard to evaluate.

Unlike the free banking view, the more interventionist approach to central banking embodied in the Goodhart view of the proper conduct for an LOLR holds considerable sway among central bankers and other policymakers. Yet, Bordo's historical survey found no evidence of Goodhart's necessity for lending to insolvent banks, as it was not practiced before the 1970s. Goodhart's modification of the Bagehot–Thornton approach treats discounting as an essential function of a central bank. However, the discount window might be considered a historical artifact of a time when there was no deep market in government securities or other important assets where a central bank could conduct open market operations. Consequently, LOLR functions had to be made through collateralized lending directly to banks, which raises the issue of the quality of collateral, which as Goodhart argued may be impossible to evaluate in a crisis.

Nevertheless, banking policy has important consequences for financial stability; and Bordo (1991) views the particular instability of the U.S. financial system as a product of constraints on the ability of banks to be flexible and diversify in the face of a host of New Deal regulations plus morally hazardous deposit insurance that increases risk-taking. In addition to eliminating these types of regulation, Bordo and Schwartz (1995) argue that only minimal regulation and supervision would be needed to promote financial stability if owners and managers would have greater liability in the event of the failure of their institution, rather than depositors and taxpayers. The key responsibility of a regulatory agency should be to promptly close insolvent institutions; the agency need not be tied to the central bank and a private agency delegated the task by the legislature.

There are additional issues that have important bearing on the ability to a central bank to conduct monetary policy in ordinary and extraordinary times. Empirically, for monetary policy and LOLR policy to be effective, it is necessary for them to operate via the money channel and not engender large feedback effects from the credit channel. In addition, the pursuit of price stability should not undermine financial stability.

A substantial fraction of Bordo's work on monetary policy studies these complex relationships. After the 2008 crisis, a renewed belief emerged that financial cycles are driven by credit, not money – the evolution of the asset side of banks' balance sheets not their liability side. Bordo argued that it is vital to examine the issue in other periods and environments to ensure that there are no special contemporary circumstances that color empirical findings. Looking at the money versus credit question during gold standard–National Banking Era 1880–1914 is particularly useful as the U.S. macroeconomy seems to have been highly unstable (Bordo, Rappoport, and Schwartz, 1992). From a monetarist point of view, changes in the balance of payments and banking panics affected deposits and spending via aggregate demand and interest rates, whereas the credit view sees changes in bank loans and other forms of credit as critical to driving cycles. The latter class of models posits that credit rationing by banks limits the effects of interest rates on spending, so that when faced with restrictive monetary policy banks may cut back further than expected inducing a greater contraction. Bordo, Rappoport, and Schwartz found that in structural VAR models it was difficult to disentangle the effects of money and credit as causality seemed to flow both ways – that is, until the effects of the stock market were taken into account. Because a large fraction of bank loans in this period were invested in the stock market, volatility of the stock market can be shown to have affected real activity, as only loans collateralized with securities affected real activity, not other loans. In contrast, the effect of money remained robust. They pointed out that this result would have pleased contemporaries who established the Federal Reserve to cope with the "inelasticity" of currency.

In addition, the monetary authorities' targeting of price stability should not undermine financial stability. Based on his studies of recent and historical episodes, Bordo sees considerable evidence that a focus on price stability will not unsettle but instead will steady the financial system. In a 1998 article with David Wheelock, Bordo investigated the "Schwartz hypothesis" that instability in the price level creates financial instability and that a central bank should focus on maintaining price stability because this will lessen the incidence and severity of financial instability. From the vantage point of the 1990s, the sustained and varying inflation of the 1970s and 1980s followed by sharp disinflation was a spur to speculation in the boom and bankruptcies and bank failures in the bust. Exploring the history of the United States, the United Kingdom, and Canada, Bordo and Wheelock found that these countries experience is broadly consistent with the Schwartz hypothesis. U.S. data from 1789 through the 1990s shows that banking crises and financial distress were associated with sharp deflations. However, banking regulation is an important complement to stable monetary policy. Whereas the United States suffered from banking panics and failures, the United Kingdom did not experience banking panics from 1866 until 2008 because of the appropriate LOLR interventions of the Bank of England and the more stable structure of the U.K. banking system. Although not experiencing panics like the United States, the United Kingdom and Canada had more subtle symptoms of financial distress when there was a lack of price stability, providing further support for the Schwartz hypothesis.

Furthering this work, Bordo, Michael Dueker, and Wheelock (2002, 2003) studied how inflation and inflation variability have affected countries over a long horizon. Constructing a new index of financial conditions, by building on and extending the compilation of economic and financial conditions of Willard Thorp, Hildegarde Thorp, and Wesley Clair Mitchell (1926), they investigated the effects of price/inflation shocks on financial stability in the United States over two centuries, using a dynamic probit model to measure the contribution of these shocks to financial instability. Reflecting the monetary regimes of the gold standard and fiat money, price level shocks were important for 1820–1931 and inflation shocks for 1931–1999. In general they find that "price stability and financial stability are complementary" (p. 164). The danger of a financial crisis or heightened financial distress is that it will exacerbate the business cycle. Bordo and Haubrich (2010) showed that financial distress events – measured by risk spreads – exacerbated business cycle downturns in both the nineteenth and twentieth centuries. Covering the twenty-nine business cycles from 1875 to the present, they followed the Friedman–Schwartz approach by first graphing the data and narrating the developments of each key episode of financial crisis then provide an econometric assessment using the Harding–Pagan algorithm to identify turning points. They saw that financial shocks exacerbated contractions. In addition, they pointed out that, although quantity of money is not synchronized with business cycles, when cycles do coincide, monetary tightness significantly contributes to major recessions. The 2007–2009 recession thus represented the perfect storm, combining a monetary policy errors, a credit crunch, an asset price bust, and a banking crisis. The frustratingly slow recovery from the recession then became a major focus of attention by economists and policymakers. The conventional wisdom was that recoveries from financial crises are usually slow, and so the current pace of recovery was to be expected. But Bordo and Joseph Haubrich (2012) showed that the historical record for the United States proved the opposite: typically recessions caused by financial crises were severe, but the recoveries were rapid. Although all the evidence is not yet in, the current recovery may be attributed to a failure to adopt appropriate policies to mitigate the fallout from the real estate bust.

The quest for price stability appears to be often frustrated by constraints on the Federal Reserve. To study how the Fed sought to counter rising inflation, Bordo and Landon-Lane (2010a), looked at the Fed's use of several instruments of monetary policy to respond to macroeconomic developments over fourteen business cycles from 1920 to 2007. Employing descriptive statistics and narrative in the Friedman and Schwartz tradition plus econometric analysis, they discovered that there is a distinct difference in the Fed's behavior between the first and second halves of the twentieth century. In the 1920s and 1950s, the Fed would tighten up when prices started to rise; but after 1960, it did not tighten immediately when inflation started to climb. Instead, the Fed reacted when employment peaked, implying that the Fed missed opportunities to restrain inflation. They pointed out that this difference maps into very different regimes. In the interwar period, gold standard orthodoxy prevailed and the Fed focused on price stability, whereas in the post–World War II era, there was increased political pressure to focus on employment and Keynesian–Phillips Curve ideas influenced policymakers.

Questions about the relationship of policies for price and financial stability have, of course, taken on a new life in the twenty-first century following the dot.com bubble and the real estate boom and bust. The central issues are whether monetary policy substantially contributes to the formation and collapse of asset bubbles and whether monetary policy should target asset bubbles with the intention to prick them before they grow so big that their collapse will inflict major costs on the economy.

A key question that has divided economists is whether stock market booms have been associated with low inflation and stable prices or whether they flourish in inflationary periods. To approach this question, Bordo and Wheelock (2007) used a simple metric to identify stock market booms in the United States. Providing a grand tabular display of booms, busts and "normal" periods with a narrative of each big swing in the tradition of *A Monetary History*, they showed that booms arose in periods of rapid growth of industrial production, real GDP, and productivity, implying that they were driven primarily by fundamentals. They see no relationship between booms and inflation. Although booms in the nineteenth century tended to occur during a monetary expansion, there is little evidence that they were driven by excessive growth of money and credit. Typically booms ended shortly after monetary policy tightened in response to inflation. Bordo and Wheelock's (2009) next paper looked beyond the United States to include Australia, Canada, France, Germany, Italy, Japan, the Netherlands, Sweden, and the United Kingdom and found very similar results. Following on this work, Bordo, Dueker, and Wheelock (2008), examined the relationship between the stock market and inflation using a latent variable VAR and discovered that inflation and interest shocks were most strongly felt by the stock market in the post–World War II era. Their evidence indicated that disinflation shocks contributed to booms while inflation shocks led to busts, leaving them – like Bordo and Wheelock (1998) – to conclude that the best means for central banks to contribute to the stability of financial markets is to minimize the unanticipated changes in inflation. As with his many other contributions, Bordo has presented influential summaries of his research in a variety of policy venues. His work on monetary policy and asset booms was featured in the IMF's *World Economic Outlook* (2003).

Should a central bank stick strictly to targeting prices or inflation? For a student of *A Monetary History*, this is a center stage issue, partly because Friedman and Schwartz blame the Great Depression on the Federal Reserve's failure to concentrate on price stability. Instead the Federal Reserve became obsessed with arresting the stock market boom of 1928–1929 and between 1930 and 1933 with protecting its gold reserve rather than counteracting the banking panic induced declines in the money stock.

For most of his academic writing, Bordo has endorsed the strict central bank focus on price/inflation stability, he has considered an alternative policy. Bordo and Jeanne (2002) developed an argument for preemptive monetary policy in the face of an asset boom in equities or real estate. Such intervention, they saw as an insurance policy, and argued that interventions should be rare and dependent on exceptional developments. They contend that a policy of benign neglect of asset market booms, with the central bank only entering on the scene when there is a bust and a collateral-induced credit crunch, implies that the authorities are willing to sacrifice their price stability goals ex post. Hence, some precautionary intervention ex ante might be preferable. Bernanke and Gertler (2001) claimed that asset prices should be taken into consideration only if they convey information about future inflation, whereas Cecchetti et.al. (2000) emphasized that central banks should identify bubbles and prick them. Bordo and Jeanne stake a middle ground with a policy that is closely approximated to an augmented Taylor rule for asset prices with the risk of asset price reversal summarized by several macroeconomic variables. The tricky feat is to detect a boom or a bust, which they identify as occurring when an asset price growth in a three-year moving-average moves outside of a confidence interval determined by historical first and second moments of the prices.

I WANT TO BE LIKE MIKE

Space does not permit us to mention all of Bordo's papers. Undoubtedly, we will hear from colleagues who were disappointed because we failed to mention one of their favorites. This is inevitable given his productivity. Our recent count found that he had published approximately 244 papers including many in leading economic journals such as the *American Economic Review*, the *Journal of Political Economy*, and the *Review of Economics and Statistics*; and he had written or edited twelve books published by prestigious university presses. But this count does not tell the whole story because he continues to remain highly productive. Indeed, many of his unpublished National Bureau of Economic Research Working Papers have already been widely cited. Ultimately, Bordo's reputation rests on more than mere numbers of publications. Since the financial crisis of 2008, and recent events in Europe, there has been a surge of interest in precisely the issues – exchange rates, monetary policy, and financial crises – that have long engaged him. Too often, however, policies are advocated on the basis of a single current or historical case study, or at the other extreme, on the basis of masses of data gleaned from countries around the globe with little attention to their history or provenance. Bordo's central point has always been that history must be studied in all of its rich variety and in detail to provide effective guidance for policy. Inevitably, history teaches us, as Bordo has thoroughly demonstrated, that changes in monetary policies and reforms of monetary institutions produce a wide range of effects that must be carefully measured and weighed to assay the trade-offs before final choices are made. History provides useful lessons, but you need a grand-master of monetary history to draw the right lessons.

REFERENCES

Barro, Robert J. (1979). "Money and the Price Level under the Gold Standard." *Economic Journal* 89(353):13–33.

Bayoumi, Tamim, and Michael D. Bordo. (1998). "Getting Pegged: Comparing the 1879 and 1925 Gold Resumptions." *Oxford Economic Papers* 50(1):122–149.

Bernanke, Ben S. (1983). "Nonmonetary Effects of the Financial Crisis in Propagation of the Great Depression." *American Economic Review* 73(3):257–276.

Bernanke, Ben S., and Mark Gertler. (2001). "Should Central Banks Respond to Movements in Asset Prices?" *American Economic Review* 91(2):253–257.

Betts, Caroline M., Michael D. Bordo, and Angela Redish. (1996). "A Small Open Economy in Depression: Lessons from Canada in the 1930s." *The Canadian Journal of Economics/Revue Canadienne d'Economique* 29(1):1–36.

Blinder, Alan S., and Jeremy B. Rudd. (2013). "The Supply-Shock Explanation of the Great Stagflation Revisited." In Michael D. Bordo and Athanasios Orphanides (eds), *The Great Inflation: The Rebirth of Modern Central Banking.* Chicago: University of Chicago Press.

Bordo, Michael D. (1975a). "The Income Effects of the Sources of Monetary Change: An Historical Approach." *Economic Inquiry* 13(4):505–525.

(1975b). "John E. Cairnes on the Effects of the Australian Gold Discoveries, 1851–73: An Early Application of the Methodology of Positive Economics." *History of Political Economy* 7(3):337–359.

(1977). "The Income Effects of the Sources of New Money: A Comparison of the United States and the United Kingdom, 1870–1913." *Explorations in Economic History* 14(1):20–43.

(1980). "The Effects of Monetary Change on Relative Commodity Prices and the Role of Long-term Contracts." *Journal of Political Economy* 88(6):1088–1109.

(1981). "The Classical Gold Standard: Some Lessons for Today." *Federal Reserve Bank of St. Louis Review* 63(5):2–17.

(1982). "Monetary Innovation in America: Discussion." *The Journal of Economic History* 42 (1, The Tasks of Economic History) (March):31–32.

(1983). "Some Aspects of the Monetary Economics of Richard Cantillon." *Journal of Monetary Economics* 12(2):235–258.

(1986). "Financial Crises, Banking Crises, Stock Market Crashes and the Money Supply: Some International Evidence, 1870–1933." In Forrest Capie and Geoffrey E. Wood (eds), *Financial Crises and the World Banking System*, pp. 190–248. New York: St. Martin's Press.

(1990). "The Lender of Last Resort: Alternative Views and Historical Experience." *Federal Reserve Bank of Richmond Economic Review* 76(1):18–29.

(1991). "Does Bank Regulation Produce Stability? Lessons from the United States: Comment." In Forrest H. Capie and Geoffrey E. Wood (eds), *Unregulated Banking: Chaos or Order*, pp. 233–235. New York: St. Martin's Press.

(1992). *Financial Crises, 2 vols.* The International Library of Macroeconomic and Financial History, 5. Aldershot, U.K. and Brookfield, VT: Elgar.

(1995). "Is There a Good Case for a New Bretton Woods International Monetary System?" *The American Economic Review* 85 (2, Papers and Proceedings of the Hundredth and Seventh Annual Meeting of the American Economic Association Washington, DC, January 6–8, 1995) (May):317–322.

(1999). *The Gold Standard and Related Regimes.* Cambridge: Cambridge University Press.

(1999). "International Rescues versus Bailouts: A Historical Perspective." *Cato Journal* 18(3):363–375.

(2000). "Sound Money and Sound Financial Policy." *Journal of Financial Services Research* 18(2–3):129–155.

(2002). "The Great Depression." *IMF World Economic Outlook* (April):110–111.

(2003a). Comment on "The Great Depression and the Friedman-Schwartz Hypothesis" by Lawrence Christiano, Roberto Motto, and Massimo Rostagno. *Journal of Money, Credit and Banking* 35 (6, Part 2: Recent Developments in Monetary Economics) (December):1199–1203.

(2003b). "The Globalization of International Financial Markets: What Can History Teach Us?" In Leonardo Auernheimer (ed), *International Financial Markets*, pp. 29–78. Chicago: University of Chicago Press.

(2003c). "A Historical Perspective on Booms, Busts, and Recessions." *IMF World Economic Outlook* (April):64–66.

(2003d). "Market Discipline and Financial Crisis Policy: A Historical Perspective." In George G. Kaufman (ed), *Market Discipline in Banking: Theory and Evidence*, pp. 157–182. *Research in Financial Services: Private and Public Policy*, Vol. 15. Amsterdam, London, and New York: Elsevier, JAI.

(2004). "The United States as a Monetary Union and the Euro: A Historical Perspective." *Cato Journal* 24(1–2):163–170.

(2008). "History of Monetary Policy." In Steven N. Durlauf and Lawrence E. Blume (eds), *The New Palgrave Dictionary of Economics*, 2nd ed. New York: Palgrave Macmillan. Retrieved from www.dictionaryofeconomics .com

(2009). "The Crisis of 2007: The Same Old Story, Only the Players Have Changed." In Douglas D. Evanoff, David S. Hoelscher, and George G. Kaufman (eds), *Globalization and Systemic Risk*, pp. 39–50. World Scientific Studies in International Economics, Vol. 6. Hackensack, NJ and Singapore: World Scientific.

Bordo, Michael D., and Forrest Capie. (2006). *Monetary Regimes in Transition*. Cambridge and New York: Cambridge University Press.

Bordo, Michael D., Alberto F. Cavallo, and Christopher M. Meissner. (2010). "Sudden Stops: Determinants and Output Effects in the First Era of Globalization, 1880–1913." *Journal of Development Economics* 91(2):227–241.

Bordo, Michael D., and Ehsan U. Choudhri. (1982). "Currency Substitution and the Demand for Money: Some Evidence for Canada." *Journal of Money, Credit and Banking* 14(1):48–57.

Bordo, Michael D., Ehsan U. Choudhri, and Anna J. Schwartz. (1987). "The Behavior of Money Stock under Interest Rate Control: Some Evidence for Canada." *Journal of Money, Credit and Banking* 19(2):181–197.

(1995). "Could Stable Money Have Averted the Great Contraction?" *Economic Inquiry* 33(3):484–505.

(2002). "Was Expansionary Monetary Policy Feasible during the Great Contraction? An Examination of the Gold Standard Constraint." *Explorations in Economic History* 39(1):1–28.

Bordo, Michael D., and Roberto Cortés Conde. (2001). *Transferring Wealth and Power from the Old to the New World: Monetary and Fiscal Institutions in the 17th through the 19th Century*. Studies in Macroeconomic History. Cambridge and New York: Cambridge University Press.

Bordo, Michael D., Robert D. Dittmar, and William Gavin. (2007). "Gold, Fiat Money and Price Stability." *B.E. Journals, Topics in Macroeconomics* 7(1), Article 26.

Bordo, Michael D., Michael J. Dueker and David C. Wheelock. (2002). "Aggregate Price Shocks and Financial Instability: A Historical Analysis." *Economic Inquiry* 40(4):521–538.

(2003). "Aggregate Price Shocks and Financial Stability: The United Kingdom 1796–1999." *Explorations in Economic History* 40(2):143–169.

(2008). "Inflation, Monetary Policy and Stock Market Conditions." Federal Reserve Bank of St. Louis Working Paper 2008–012.

Bordo, Michael D., Michael Edelstein, and Hugh Rockoff. (2003). "Was Adherence to the Gold Standard a 'Good Housekeeping Seal of Approval' during the Interwar Period?" In Stanley L. Engerman, Philip T. Hoffman, Jean-Laurent Rosenthal, and Kenneth L. Sokoloff (eds), *Finance, Intermediaries, and Economic Development*, pp. 288–318. New York: Cambridge University Press.

Bordo, Michael D., and Barry Eichengreen. (1998). "Implications of the Great Depression for the Development of the International Monetary System." In Michael D. Bordo, Claudia Goldin, and Eugene N. White (eds), *The Defining Moment: The Great Depression and the American Economy in the Twentieth Century*, pp. 403–453. NBER Project Report Series. Chicago and London: University of Chicago Press.

Bordo, Michael D., Barry Eichengreen, and Douglas A. Irwin. (2000a). "Is Globalization Today Really Different than Globalization a Hundred years Ago? Part II: Financial Integration." *Wirtschaftspolitische Blatter* 47(2):121–129.

(2000b). "Is Globalization Today Really Different from Globalization a Hundred Years Ago? Part 1: Commercial Integration." *Wirtschaftspolitische Blatter* 47(1):3–12.

Bordo, Michael D., Barry Eichengreen and Jongwoo Kim. (1998). "Was There Really an Earlier Period of International Financial Integration Comparable to Today?" NBER Working Papers 6738. Cambridge, MA: National Bureau of Economic Research. Retrieved from http://search.ebscohost.com/login.asp x?direct=true&db=ecn&AN=0717395&site=ehost-live; http://www.nber.org /papers/w6738.pdf

Bordo, Michael D., Barry Eichengreen, Daniela Klingebiel, and Maria Martinez-Peria. (2001). "Financial Crises: Lessons from the Last 120 Years." *Economic Policy* 16 (April):51–82.

(2008). "Is the Crisis Problem Growing More Severe?" In Franklin Allen and Douglas Gale (eds), *Financial Crises*, pp. 3–32. Elgar Reference Collection. International Library of Critical Writings in Economics, Vol. 218. Cheltenham, U.K. and Northampton, MA: Elgar.

Bordo, Michael D., Barry J. Eichengreen, and National Bureau of Economic Research. (1993). *A Retrospective on the Bretton Woods System: Lessons for International Monetary Reform*. A National Bureau of Economic Research Project Report. Chicago: University of Chicago Press.

Bordo, Michael D., and Richard Wayne Ellson. (1985). "A Model of the Classical Gold Standard with Depletion." *Journal of Monetary Economics* 16(1):109–120.

Bordo, Michael D., Christopher J. Erceg, and Charles L. Evans. (2000). "Money, Sticky Wages, and the Great Depression." *American Economic Review* 90(5):1447–1463.

(2001). "Re-examining the Contributions of Money and Banking Shocks to the U.S. Great Depression: Comment." In Ben S. Bernanke and Kenneth Rogoff (eds), *NBER Macroeconomics Annual 2000*, Vol. 15, pp. 227–237. Cambridge and London: MIT Press.

(2005). "Money, Sticky Wages, and the Great Depression." In Pierre L. Siklos (ed), *Economics of Deflation*, Vol. 2, pp. 157–173. International Library of Critical Writings in Economics series, Vol. 189. An Elgar Reference Collection, Cheltenham, U.K. and Northampton, MA: Elgar.

Bordo, Michael D., and Charles L. Evans. (1995). "Labor Productivity during the Great Depression." *Economics Letters* 47(1):41–45.

Bordo, Michael D., and Andrew Filardo. (2005). "Deflation and Monetary Policy in a Historical Perspective: Remembering the Past or Being Condemned to Repeat It?" *Economic Policy* 44(October): 840–844.

(2007). "Money Still Makes the World Go Round: The Zonal View." *Journal of the European Economic Association* 5(2–3):509–523.

Bordo, Michael D., and Marc Flandreau. (2003). "Core, Periphery, Exchange Rate Regimes, and Globalization." In Michael D. Bordo, Alan M. Taylor, and Jeffrey G. Williamson (eds), *Globalization in Historical Perspective*, pp. 417–468. NBER Conference Report Series. Chicago and London: University of Chicago Press.

Bordo, Michael D., Claudia Dale Goldin, and Eugene Nelson White. (1998). *The Defining Moment: The Great Depression and the American Economy in the Twentieth Century*. A National Bureau of Economic Research Project Report. Chicago: University of Chicago Press.

Bordo, Michael D., Tamara Gomes, and Lawrence L. Schembri. (2010). "Canada and the IMF: Trailblazer or Prodigal Son?" *Open Economies Review* 21(2):309–333.

Bordo, Michael D., and Joseph G. Haubrich. (2008a). "Forecasting with the Yield Curve: Level, Slope, and Output 1875–1997." *Economics Letters* 99(1):48–50.

(2008b). "The Yield Curve as a Predictor of Growth: Long-run Evidence, 1875–1997." *The Review of Economics and Statistics* 90(1):182–185.

(2010). "Credit Crises, Money and Contractions: An Historical View." *Journal of Monetary Economics* 57(1):1–18.

(2012). "Deep Recessions, Fast Recoveries, and Financial Crises: Evidence from the American Record." NBER Working Paper 18194. Cambridge, MA: National Bureau of Economic Research.

Bordo, Michael D., and Pierre-Cyrille Hautcoeur. (2007). "Why Didn't France Follow the British Stabilisation after World War I?" *European Review of Economic History* 11(1):3–37.

Bordo, Michael D., Thomas Helbling, and Harold James. (2007). "Swiss Exchange Rate Policy in the 1930s: Was the Delay in Devaluation Too High a Price to Pay for Conservatism?" *Open Economies Review* 18(1):1–25.

Bordo, Michael D., Owen Humpage, and Anna J. Schwartz. (2007). "The Historical Origins of US Exchange Market Intervention Policy." *International Journal of Finance and Economics* 12(2):109–132.

Bordo, Michael D., Owen F. Humpage, and Anna J. Schwartz. (2007). "The Historical Origins of US Exchange Market Intervention Policy." *International Journal of Finance and Economics* 12(2):109–132.

(2011a). "On the Evolution of U.S. Foreign-Exchange-Market Intervention: Thesis, Theory, and Institutions." Working Paper/Federal Reserve Bank of Cleveland, Vol. 1113. Cleveland: Federal Reserve Bank of Cleveland.

(2011b). "US Intervention during the Bretton Woods Era, 1962–1973." NBER Working Paper 16946. Cambridge, MA: National Bureau of Economic Research.

(2015). *Strained Relations: U.S. Foreign-Exchange Operations and Monetary Policy in the Twentieth Century.* Chicago: University of Chicago Press.

Bordo, Michael D., and Harold James. (2008). "A Long Term Perspective on the Euro." NBER Working Paper 13815. Cambridge, MA: National Bureau of Economic Research.

(2010). "The Past Mirror: Notes, Surveys, Debates: The Great Depression Analogy." *Financial History Review* 17(2):127–140.

(2012). "Reserves and Baskets." *Open Economies Review* 23(1):113–127.

Bordo, Michael D., and Olivier Jeanne. (2002). "Monetary Policy and Asset Prices: Does 'Benign Neglect' Make Sense?" *International Finance* 5(2):139–164.

(2004). "Boom-Busts in Asset Prices, Economic Instability, and Monetary Policy." In Richard C. K. Burdekin and Pierre L. Siklos (eds), *Deflation: Current and Historical Perspectives*, pp. 131–165. Studies in Macroeconomic History. Cambridge and New York: Cambridge University Press.

Bordo, Michael D., and Lars Jonung. (1987). *The Long-run Behavior of the Velocity of Circulation: The International Evidence.* Cambridge and New York: Cambridge University Press.

(1997). "The History of Monetary Regimes – Some Lessons for Sweden and the EMU." *Swedish Economic Policy Review* 4(2):285–358.

(1999). "The Long-run Behavior of Velocity: The Institutional Approach Revisited." In David Laidler (ed), *The Foundations of Monetary Economics*, pp. 517–549. 3 vols. Elgar Reference Collection. Cheltenham, U.K. and Northampton, MA: Elgar.

(2003). "The Future of EMU: What Does the History of Monetary Unions Tell Us?" In Forrest H. Capie and Geoffrey E. Wood (eds), *Monetary Unions: Theory, History, Public Choice*, pp. 42–69. International Studies in Money and Banking, Vol. 18. London and New York: Routledge.

Bordo, Michael D., Lars Jonung, and Pierre L. Siklos. (1997). "Institutional Change and the Velocity of Money: A Century of Evidence." *Economic Inquiry* 35(4):710–724.

Bordo, Michael D., and Finn E. Kydland. (1995). "The Gold Standard as a Rule: An Essay in Exploration." *Explorations in Economic History* 32(4):423–464.

Bordo, Michael D., and John Landon-Lane. (2010a). "The Banking Panics in the United States in the 1930s: Some Lessons for Today." *Oxford Review of Economic Policy* 26(3):486–509.

(2010b). "Exits from Recessions: The U.S. Experience 1920–2007." NBER Working Paper 15731. Cambridge, MA: National Bureau of Economic Research. Retrieved from http://search.ebscohost.com/login.aspx?direct =true&db=ecn&AN=1089388&site=ehost-live; http://www.nber.org/papers /w15731.pdf

Bordo, Michael D., John Landon-Lane, and Angela Redish. (2009). "Good versus Bad Deflation: Lessons from the Gold Standard Era." In David E. Altig and Ed Nosal (ed), *Monetary Policy in Low-Inflation Economies*, pp. 127–174. Cambridge and New York: Cambridge University Press.

(2010). "Deflation, Productivity Shocks and Gold: Evidence from the 1880–1914 Period." *Open Economies Review* 21(4):515–546.

Bordo, Michael D., and Ronald MacDonald. (2003). "The Inter-war Gold Exchange Standard: Credibility and Monetary Independence." *Journal of International Money and Finance* 22(1):1–32.

(2005). "Interest Rate Interactions in the Classical Gold Standard, 1880–1914: Was There Any Monetary Independence?" *Journal of Monetary Economics* 52(2):307–327.

(2012). *Credibility and the International Monetary Regime: A Historical Perspective*. Studies in Macroeconomic History. Cambridge and New York: Cambridge University Press.

Bordo, Michael D., Ronald MacDonald, and Michael J. Oliver. (2009). "Sterling in Crisis, 1964–1967." *European Review of Economic History* 13(3):437–459.

Bordo, Michael D., and Christopher M. Meissner. (2006). "The Role of Foreign Currency Debt in Financial Crises: 1880–1913 versus 1972–1997." *Journal of Banking and Finance* 30(12):3299–3329.

(2011). "Foreign Capital, Financial Crises and Incomes in the First Era of Globalization." *European Review of Economic History* 15(1):61–91.

Bordo, Michael D., Christopher M. Meissner, and Angela Redish. (2005). "How Original Sin Was Overcome: The Evolution of External Debt Denominated in Domestic Currencies in the United States and the British Dominions, 1800–2000. In Barry Eichengreen and Ricardo Hausmann (eds), *Other People's Money: Debt Denomination and Financial Instability in Emerging Market Economies*, pp. 122–153. Chicago and London: University of Chicago Press.

Bordo, Michael D., Christopher M. Meissner, and David Stuckler. (2010). "Foreign Currency Debt, Financial Crises and Economic Growth: A Long-run View." *Journal of International Money and Finance* 29(4):642–665.

Bordo, Michael D., Christopher M. Meissner, and Marc D. Weidenmier. (2009). "Identifying the Effects of an Exchange Rate Depreciation on Country Risk: Evidence from a Natural Experiment." *Journal of International Money and Finance* 28(6):1022–1044.

Bordo, Michael D., Ashoka Mody, and Nienke Oomes. (2006). "Keeping Capital Flowing: The Role of the IMF." In Ashoka Mody and Alessandro Rebucci (eds), *IMF-Supported Programs: Recent Staff Research*, pp. 228–244. Washington, DC: International Monetary Fund.

(2004). "Keeping Capital Flowing: The Role of the IMF." *International Finance* 7(3):421–450.

Bordo, Michael D., and Antu Panini Murshid (2003). "Globalization and Changing Patterns in Crisis Transmission." In William C. Hunter, George G. Kaufman, and Michael Pomerleano (eds), *Asset Price Bubbles: The Implications for Monetary, Regulatory, and International Policies*, pp. 309–322. Cambridge and London: MIT Press.

Bordo, Michael D., and Antu Panini Murshid. (2006). "Globalization and Changing Patterns in the International Transmission of Shocks in Financial Markets." *Journal of International Money and Finance* 25(4):655–674.

Bordo, Michael D., and Athanasios Orphanides. (2013). *The Great Inflation: The Rebirth of Modern Central Banking*. National Bureau of Economic Research Conference Report. Chicago: University of Chicago Press.

Bordo, Michael D., Peter Rappoport, and Anna J. Schwartz. (1992). "Money versus Credit Rationing: Evidence for the National Banking Era, 1880–1914." In Claudia Goldin and Hugh Rockoff (eds), *Strategic Factors in Nineteenth Century American Economic History: A Volume to Honor Robert W. Fogel*, pp. 189–223. A National Bureau of Economic Research Conference Report. Chicago and London: University of Chicago Press.

Bordo, Michael D., and Angela Redish. (1987). "Why Did the Bank of Canada Emerge in 1935?" *Journal of Economic History* 47(2):405–417.

(1990). "Credible Commitment and Exchange Rate Stability: Canada's Interwar Experience." *The Canadian Journal of Economics/Revue Canadienne d'Economique* 23(2):357–380.

(2004). "Is Deflation Depressing? Evidence from the Classical Gold Standard." In Richard C. K. Burdekin and Pierre L. Siklos (eds), *Deflation: Current and Historical Perspectives*, pp. 191–217. Studies in Macroeconomic History. Cambridge and New York: Cambridge University Press.

Bordo, Michael D., Angela Redish, and Hugh Rockoff. (1994). "The U.S. Banking System from a Northern Exposure: Stability versus efficiency." *The Journal of Economic History* 54 (2, Papers Presented at the Fifty-Third Annual Meeting of the Economic History Association) (June):325–341.

(1996a). "A Comparison of the Stability and Efficiency of the Canadian and American Banking Systems, 1870–1925." *Financial History Review* 3(April):29–48.

(1996b). "A Comparison of the United States and Canadian Banking Systems in the Twentieth Century." In Michael D. Bordo and Richard Sylla (eds), *Anglo-American Financial Systems*, pp. 11–40. Burr Ridge, NJ: Irwin.

(2014). "Why Didn't Canada Have a Banking Crisis in 2008 (or in 1930, or 1907, or ...)?" *Economic History Review, DOI: 10.1111/1468-0289.665; also at NBER Working Paper w17312*.

Bordo, Michael D., and William Roberds, eds. (2013). *The Origins, History, and Future of the Federal Reserve: A Return to Jekyll Island*. New York: Cambridge University Press.

Bordo, Michael D., and Hugh Rockoff. (1996). "The Gold Standard as a 'Good Housekeeping Seal of Approval'." *The Journal of Economic History* 56(2, Papers Presented at the Fifty-Fifth Annual Meeting of the Economic History Association) (June):389–428.

Bordo, Michael D., and Peter L. Rousseau. (2006). "Legal-Political Factors and the Historical Evolution of the Finance-Growth Link." *European Review of Economic History* 10(3):421–444.

(2011). "Historical Evidence on the Finance-Trade-Growth Nexus." NBER Working Paper 17024. Cambridge, MA:. National Bureau of Economic Research.

Bordo, Michael D., and Anna J. Schwartz. (1977). "Issues in Monetary Economics and Their Impact on Research in Economic History." In R. Gallman (ed),

Research in Economic History: Recent Developments in the Study of Business and Economic History: Essays in Memory of Herman E. Kroos. Supplement 1, pp. 81–130.Greenwich, CT: JAI Press.

(1979). "Clark Warburton: Pioneer Monetarist." *Journal of Monetary Economics* 5(1):43–65.

(1980). "Money and Prices in the Nineteenth Century: An Old debate Rejoined." *The Journal of Economic History* 40(10, The Tasks of Economic History) (March):61–67.

(1981). "Money and Prices in the 19th Century: Was Thomas Tooke Right?" *Explorations in Economic History* 18(2):97–127.

Bordo, Michael D., and Anna J. Schwartz. (1991). "What Has Foreign Exchange Market Intervention since the Plaza Agreement Accomplished?" *Open Economies Review* 2(1):39–64.

Bordo, Michael D., and Anna J. Schwartz. (1995). "The Performance and Stability of Banking Systems under 'Self-regulation': Theory and Evidence." *Cato Journal* 14(3):453–479.

(1996). "Why Clashes between Internal and External Stability Goals End in Currency Crises, 1797–1994." *Open Economies Review* 7(1):437–468.

(1999). "Under What Circumstances, Past and Present, Have International Rescues of Countries in Financial Distress Been Successful?" *Journal of International Money and Finance* 18(4):683–708.

(2000). "Measuring Real Economic Effects of Bailouts: Historical Perspectives on How Countries in Financial Distress Have Fared with and without Bailouts." *Carnegie-Rochester Conference Series on Public Policy* 53(12):81–167.

(2003). "Charles Goodhart's Contributions to the History of Monetary Institutions." In Paul Mizen (ed), *Essays in Honour of Charles Goodhart. Vol. 2: Monetary History, Exchange Rates and Financial Markets*, pp. 34–35. Cheltenham, U.K. and Northampton, MA: Elgar.

(2004). "IS-LM and Monetarism." *History of Political Economy* 36:217–239.

(2010). "David Laidler on Monetarism." In Robert Leeson (ed), *David Laidler's Contributions to Economics*, pp. 44–56, 57–59. New York: St. Martin's Press, Palgrave Macmillan.

Bordo, Michael D., Anna J. Schwartz, and National Bureau of Economic Research. (1984). *A Retrospective on the Classical Gold Standard, 1821–1931*. National Bureau of Economic Research Conference Report. Chicago: University of Chicago Press.

Bordo, Michael D., Dominique Simard, and Eugene N. White. (1995). "France and the Bretton Woods International Monetary System 1960 to 1968." In Jaime Reis (ed), *International Monetary Systems in Historical Perspective*, pp. 153–180. New York: St. Martin's Press; London: Macmillan Press.

Bordo, Michael D., Richard Eugene Sylla, and New York University. Salomon Center. (1995). *Anglo-American Financial Systems: Institutions and Markets in the Twentieth Century*. Burr Ridge, IL: Irwin.

Bordo, Michael D., Alan M. Taylor, Jeffrey G. Williamson, and National Bureau of Economic Research. (2003). *Globalization in Historical Perspective*. National

Bureau of Economic Research Conference Report. Chicago: University of Chicago Press.

Bordo, Michael D., and Carlos A. Vegh. (2002). "What if Alexander Hamilton Had Been Argentinean? A Comparison of the Early Monetary Experiences of Argentina and the United States." *Journal of Monetary Economics* 49(3):459–494.

Bordo, Michael D., and David C. Wheelock. (1998). "Price Stability and Financial Stability: The Historical Record." *Federal Reserve Bank of St. Louis Review* 80(5):41–62.

(2004). "Monetary Policy and Asset Prices: A Look Back at Past U.S. Stock Market Booms." *Federal Reserve Bank of St. Louis Review* 86(6):19–44.

(2007). "Stock Market Booms and Monetary Policy in the Twentieth Century." *Federal Reserve Bank of St. Louis Review* 89(2):91–122.

(2009). "When Do Stock Market Booms Occur? The Macroeconomic and Policy Environments of Twentieth Century Booms." In Jeremy Atack and Larry Neal (eds), *The Origins and Development of Financial Markets and Institutions: From the Seventeenth Century to the Present*, pp. 416–449. Cambridge and New York: Cambridge University Press.

Bordo, Michael D., and Eugene N. White. (1991). "A Tale of Two Currencies: British and French Finance during the Napoleonic Wars." *The Journal of Economic History* 51(2):303–316.

(1993). British and French Finance during the Napoleonic Wars. In Michael D. Bordo and Forrest Capie (eds), *Monetary Regimes in Transition*, pp. 241–274. Cambridge: Cambridge University Press.

Boyer, George R., and Timothy J. Hatton. (2002). "New Estimates of British Unemployment, 1870–1913." *Journal of Economic History* 62(3):643–675.

Carter, Susan B., Scott Sigmund Gartner, Michael R. Haines, Alan L. Olmstead, Richard Sutch, and Gavin Wright. (2006). *Historical Statistics of the United States: Earliest Times to the Present*. Millennial Ed. New York: Cambridge University Press.

Cecchetti, Stephen G. (1992). "Prices during the Great Depression: Was the Deflation of 1930–1932 Really Unanticipated?" *American Economic Review* 82(1):141–156.

Cecchetti, Stephen G., Pok-sang Lam, and Nelson C. Mark. (2000). "Asset Pricing with Distorted Beliefs: Are Equity Returns Too Good to Be True?" *American Economic Review* 90(4):787–805.

Cole, Harold L., and Lee E. Ohanian. (2001). "Re-examining the Contributions of Money and Banking Shocks to the U.S. Great Depression." In Ben S. Bernanke and Kenneth Rogoff (eds), *NBER Macroeconomics Annual 2000*, Vol. 15, pp. 183–227. Cambridge and London: MIT Press.

Economic Report of the President. (2012). Washington, DC: U.S. Government Printing Office.

Eichengreen, Barry. (1992). *Golden Fetters: The Gold Standard and the Great Depression, 1919–1939*. NBER Series on Long-Term Factors in Economic Development. New York and Oxford: Oxford University Press.

Eichengreen, Barry, and Michael D. Bordo. (2003). "Crises Now and Then: What Lessons from the Last Era of Financial Globalization?" In Paul Mizen (ed), *Essays in Honour of Charles Goodhart, Vol. 2: Monetary History, Exchange Rates and Financial Markets*, pp. 52–91. Cheltenham, U.K. and Northampton, MA: Elgar.

Eschweiler, Bernhard, and Michael D. Bordo. (1994). "Rules, Discretion, and Central Bank Independence: The German Experience, 1880–1989." In Pierre L. Siklos (ed), *Varieties of Monetary Reforms: Lessons and Experiences on the Road to Monetary Union*, pp. 279–321. Dordrecht and Boston: Kluwer Academic.

Friedman, Milton. (1953). "The Case for Flexible Exchange Rates." In Milton Friedman (ed), *Essays in Positive Economics*, pp. 157–203. Chicago: University of Chicago Press.

Friedman, Milton, and Anna Schwartz. (1963). *A Monetary History of the United States, 1867–1960. National Bureau of Economic Research. Studies in Business Cycles.* Vol. 12. Princeton, NJ: Princeton University Press.

Global Financial Data. [cited December 2012]. Retrieved from www.global financialdata.com.

Hamilton, James D. (1992). "Was the Deflation during the Great Depression Anticipated? Evidence from the Commodity Futures Market." *American Economic Review* 82(1):157–178.

Johnston, Louis, and Williamson, Samuel H. (2011). "What was the U.S. GDP Then? 2011 [cited June/1 2011]. Retrieved from http://www.measuringworth .org/usgdp/

McCallum, Bennett T. (1990). "Could a Monetary Base Rule Have Prevented the Great Depression?" *Journal of Monetary Economics* 26(1):3–26.

Miron, Jeffrey A. (1994). "Empirical Methodology in Macroeconomics: Explaining the Success of Friedman and Schwartz's 'A Monetary History of the United States, 1867–1960'." *Journal of Monetary Economics* 34(1):17–25.

Richardson, Gary. (2007). "Categories and Causes of Bank Distress during the Great Depression, 1929–1933: The Illiquidity versus Insolvency Debate Revisited." *Explorations in Economic History* 44(4):588–607.

Richardson, Gary, and William Troost. (2009). "Monetary Intervention Mitigated Banking Panics during the Great Depression: Quasi-experimental Evidence from a Federal Reserve District Border, 1929–1933." *Journal of Political Economy* 117(6):1031–1073.

Romer, Christina D. (1993). "The Nation in Depression." *Journal of Economic Perspectives* 7(2):19–39.

Schwartz, Anna J., and Michael D. Bordo. (1989). *Money, History, and International Finance: Essays in Honor of Anna J. Schwartz*. A National Bureau of Economic Research Conference Report. Chicago: University of Chicago Press.

Temin, Peter. (1989). *Lessons from the Great Depression: The Lionel Robbins Lectures for 1989.* Lionel Robbins Lectures. Cambridge, MA: MIT Press.

Thorp, Willard Long, Hildegarde E. Thorp, and Wesley C. Mitchell. (1926). *Business Annals: United states, England, France, Germany, Austria, Russia, Sweden, Netherlands, Italy, Argentina, Brazil, Canada, South Africa, Australia,*

India, Japan, China. Publications of the National Bureau of Economic Research, Vol. 8. New York: National Bureau of Economic Research.

Tobin, James. (1965). "The Monetary Interpretation of History." *The American Economic Review* 55(3, June):464–485.

(1970). "Money and Income: Post Hoc Ergo Propter Hoc?" *Quarterly Journal of Economics* 84(2):301–317.

15

Reflections on the History and Future of Central Banking

Michael D. Bordo

The recent global financial crisis and the Great Recession has led many to wish to remake the model of central banking to focus more on financial stability. Others have argued that central banks should stick to the successful model that led to the Great Moderation and should continue to attach ultimate importance to maintaining credibility for low inflation. In remarks I made at a Norges Bank conference in November 2010 I argued the case for sticking to the tried and true – that financial stability concerns should be treated by a Financial Stability Authority, or if based within the central bank by statute, should be managed by tools other than the policy rate. My views haven't changed but I would like to amplify them somewhat.

I argued that central banking evolved into a golden age during the Classical gold standard era from 1880–1914 of following credible rules based on adherence to gold convertibility to maintain price stability and to serve as a lender of last resort. The Great Depression threw central banks into the dark ages, a fate created by their own adherence to flawed doctrine (real bills) and the gold exchange standard. As a consequence central banks lost their independence in the 1930s and became adjuncts of the fiscal authorities. They regained their independence starting in the 1950s (in the United States after the Federal Reserve Treasury Accord in 1951) but lost it again with the Great Inflation in the 1960s and 1970s. The Great Inflation, like the Great Depression, had much to do with following faulty doctrines (The Phillips Curve trade-off). The renaissance of central banking following the Volcker/Thatcher Shocks of 1979 to 1918, which broke the back of inflationary expectations but at the expense of a deep recession, led to a new regime of a credible nominal anchor in fiat money regime based on rules similar to the gold standard convertibility rule. This led to the Great Moderation from the mid-1980s to 2006.

The recent global crisis stemmed from policy failures in the United States The subprime mortgage crisis of 2007–2008 originated in the United States and spread to the rest of the world. It was precipitated by the collapse of a major housing boom in 2006 that severely impacted the financial system. Its causes include U.S. government policies since the 1930s to extend home ownership, major changes in regulation, lax regulatory oversight, a relaxation of normal standards of prudent lending, and a period of abnormally low interest rates. The Federal Reserve and other central banks were criticized for not preventing the crisis. The indictment included the following; the Fed fueled the housing boom with low interest rates in 2002 to 2005; the Fed kept rates too high in 2008 to prevent recession; the Fed created panic by first rescuing Bear Stearns in March 2008 and then letting Lehman brothers fail in September; the Fed's credit policy picked favorites; the bailouts that occurred were based on "too interconnected to fail"; the central banks did not follow Bagehot's strictures; the Fed and other central banks lost their independence; and the threat of fiscal dominance has reemerged.

These criticisms and more led to calls for changes in the basic central bank model based on rules prescribing credibility for low inflation and central bank independence. Reforms suggested included greatly increasing the central bank's role in financial stability; using monetary policy tools to lean against the wind of asset price booms; central banks administering macro prudential rules for commercial and investment banks (capital and leverage ratios); and central banks working closely with the fiscal authorities.

The financial crisis and the Great Recession led many policymakers to decide that financial stability should be an important goal of central banks along with inflation (and overall macro stability). The new view argued that central banks should be closely monitoring asset price developments and the state of the financial system (including banks and nonbanks) and be willing to use policy to defuse threatening imbalances. This became known as the case for macro prudential regulation, which promoted the use of policy tools such as countercyclical capital requirements and liquidity ratios. This case, fostered by the Bank for International Settlements (BIS) and many others, has led to important changes in the financial regulatory landscape including the 2010 Dodd–Frank Act in the United States, which has given the Federal Reserve greatly expanded powers over the financial system as a whole.

The question arises of whether the new financial stability powers of central banks will work to prevent another crisis. There is also the question of whether the new impetus has gone too far in encroaching on the traditional role of central banks to maintain price stability and act as lenders of last resort to the banking system and protectors of the integrity of the payments system.

The history of financial regulation after big financial crises such as the Great Depression suggests that often the government overreacts and in the name of safety suppresses financial development and the price discovery mechanism of financial markets. The regime of the 1930s to 1970s gave us financial stability at the expense of unworkable firewalls between complementary functions (Glass–Steagall) and price controls and ceilings such as regulation Q and the prohibition of the payment of interest on demand deposits. These regulations broke down in the face of the Great Inflation and financial market arbitrage and innovation. In addition in the immediate post–World War II period central banks lost their independence to the fiscal authorities, who had other, politically driven, objectives in mind. It would not be surprising if that happened again.

More fundamentally, many of the recent institutional changes pose threats to the independence of central banks and their ability to perform their core mission, which is to maintain the value of money. Central banks were also supposed to act as lenders of last resort to the banking system. They were not responsible for the solvency of banks or any other entities or the financing of government deficits (except in wartime).

The bottom line is that asset price booms, which were blamed for the recent crisis, are important, potentially dangerous to the real economy, and should be closely monitored and possibly defused. However, the policy tools to do this should not be the traditional tools of monetary policy. Other tools such as margin requirements for stock prices, minimum down payments for housing and risk weighted, bank size weighted, capital requirements for banks could be used. Authorities other than central banks should preferably perform these tasks to prevent central banks from being diverted from their main functions.

The history of central banking teaches us that the first responsibility of a central bank is to maintain price stability. If the central bank is successful in maintaining a stable and credible nominal anchor then real economic stability should obtain, although in the event of adverse shocks central banks should follow short-run stabilization policies consistent with their objective of price stability.

History also suggests that central banks should serve as lenders of last resort to the money market in the face of liquidity shocks. Lender of last resort policy involves temporarily expanding liquidity and then returning to the path consistent with price stability. The central bank should preferably do this by open market operations rather than by discount window lending to individual banks, to let market forces choose the recipients of funds rather than relying on discretion. But if the discount window is to be used, loans should be made only to solvent institutions. Bailouts should be avoided.

History also suggests that the central bank should protect the payments mechanism and be ready to provide liquidity assistance only to institutions that provide means of payment. The role of a central bank is not to protect nonbank institutions that do not provide means of payment. The supervision and regulation of these institutions should be handled by other regulatory authorities.

The events of the recent crisis in light of the history of central banking leads to the conclusion that central banks should stick to following transparent, credible, and well understood rules. They should restrict their mandates to the traditional ones of price (and overall macro) stability, lenders of last resort, and protecting the payments system.

Index